THE
COLUMBIA DICTIONARY

OF

MODERN **LITERARY**

AND

CULTURAL CRITICISM

This book is presented as a gift to

~~The J.R. Masterman School~~

in honor of

Isabelle Rastain
name

for

her 16th Birthday

on

June 2000

Printed and Donated by Eldon Press 215.836.4400

THE
COLUMBIA DICTIONARY

OF
MODERN **LITERARY**

AND
CULTURAL CRITICISM

Joseph Childers and Gary Hentzi

GENERAL EDITORS

COLUMBIA UNIVERSITY PRESS NEW YORK

Columbia University Press
New York   Chichester, West Sussex
Copyright © 1995 Columbia University Press
All rights reserved

Library of Congress Cataloging-in-Publication Data
The Columbia dictionary of modern literary and cultural criticism /
   Joseph Childers and Gary Hentzi, general editors.
       p.   cm.
   Includes bibliographical references and index.
   ISBN 0–231–07242–2   PA ISBN 0–231–07243–0
   1. Criticism—Dictionaries.   2. Humanities—Philosophy—
Dictionaries.   3. Social sciences—Philosophy—Dictionaries.
I. Childers, Joseph.   II. Hentzi, Gary.
BH39.C62   1995
001.3'03—dc 20   94–42535
                                                      CIP

Casebound editions of Columbia University Press books are printed on
permanent and durable acid-free paper.

Printed in the United States of America
c 10 9 8 7 6 5 4
p 10 9 8 7

CONTENTS

PREFACE

In recent years, the fastest growing, most provocative, and potentially farthest-reaching specialty in the humanities and social sciences has been literary and cultural criticism and theory. One indication of the extent of this growth is the amount of specialized terminology from these and affiliated disciplines that has made its way into our everyday writing and speech. But whether nonspecialists are interested in Marxism, psychoanalysis, the various types of postmodernism, or feminism, they almost universally complain that cultural and literary studies have become too arcane and thus inaccessible to the generalist. This, unfortunately, is a very real problem. These disciplines, just as any special branch of study, must have their own language, or rather—given the numerous types of theory and criticism—their own languages; however, too many in theoretical and critical studies have used these languages carelessly, without regard for their readers. In place of a precise, descriptive set of terms that can be the basis of a lingua franca for studies in literature, cultural analysis, film, history, art, as well as the various social sciences, theory has produced a patois that is all but unintelligible to the uninitiated.

If literary and cultural studies were isolated intellectual enterprises that attracted only a few adherents, such obfuscation would be a relatively minor problem; but increasing numbers both outside and within the academy are interested in what is happening in these disciplines and are anxious to know how developments in theory and criticism affect the way people perceive and order the world around them. It has therefore become necessary to devise a means by which those who are not, properly speaking, "theorists" or specially trained as literary or cultural critics can gain access to the language of theory.

In compiling *The Columbia Dictionary of Modern Literary and Cultural Criticism*, we have undertaken to provide a lexicon that can go a good distance toward meeting that need. This book is designed precisely for those who are not formally trained in theory and criticism, but who nonetheless desire a fundamental facility with its terminology. One of our guiding principles for including terms in this book was to choose those that are most commonly encountered by specialist and nonspecialist readers alike. Also, because in contemporary American intellectual culture, theory and criticism is a hybrid field that draws on a variety of disciplines, both traditional and recently inaugurated, we cast as wide a net as possible, while simultaneously excluding such concepts and terms as seemed too specifically confined to one discipline and too readily available in other, more narrowly focused reference texts. Thus, some terms that may seem to belong more properly to other disciplines such as *psychoanalysis, philosophy*, or even *film theory* have been included in this book because of their appropriation by, and the important roles they play in, current literary, cultural, or media studies. Overall, our goal has been to offer succinct but useful definitions of terms and concepts that have a wide currency but often do not make their way into books of this kind.

Because *The Columbia Dictionary of Modern Literary and Cultural Criticism* is intended as a reader's companion and not an exhaustive guide to contemporary theory, we have kept the definitions as concise as possible. In some instances, we have provided longer essays on major concepts and schools of thought, but in all cases the needs of the nonacademic reader or beginning student who encounters an unfamiliar term and requires a summary of its most important meanings, usages, and associations have been our foremost concern.

Although this book has been written with the nonspecialist in mind, we anticipate, nevertheless, that readers with some background in the field of theory and criticism will find the book useful as a reference tool. For this reason, and to help the beginning student who wishes to become better informed about specific ideas, the majority of the terms is supplemented by individual bibliographies; further, a full-length, comprehensive bibliography appears at the conclusion of the book, along with an index of the names of the theoreticians and critics who are cited or discussed in the book's entries. Also, while this book was composed in a truly collaborative effort with a number of contributors, we have sought to indicate important threads in the textual weave by connecting individual entries through a system of cross-references (signaled by the use of small capitals).

It is our hope that the definitions of important critical terms and the supplementary bibliographic material offered in this book will help readers to a greater proficiency with theory and criticism, but we cannot stress strongly enough that these entries are no substitute for encountering these concepts in their original contexts. Our definitions are not intended to exhaust the avenues of thought that a given concept opens up, nor are they meant to satisfy all the demands of a specialist. Neither do we envision this book as a "primer" or "grammar" of the complex languages of theory. Just as it would be nearly impossible to attain fluency in any language solely through the use of a dictionary, attaining proficiency in theory through the use of this text would be an equally difficult task. Ultimately, we are providing a guide to further studies in literary and cultural criticism, a place to begin inquiry, not to end it.

Joseph Childers
Gary Hentzi

ACKNOWLEDGMENTS

In the years since the inception of this project a number of people have furnished valuable assistance in bringing it to fruition. Jonathan Arac and Michael Seidel provided support and advice during the formative phases of the project. Jon Anderson and Richard Moye were instrumental in conceiving of the possibility of creating such a text and in setting its composition in motion. Sue de Bord and Erik Kruger gave us indispensable copyediting and clerical assistance in the early stages. Katherine Kinney and Parama Roy offered helpful suggestions and insights about several important terms. Of course, we are grateful to our contributors and contributing editors who provided us with so many excellent entries. We are especially indebted to Deborah Hatheway and Carlton Smith, whose contributions were both timely and invaluable. Kate Watt's innumerable hours in libraries and in front of computer screens have been essential in the compilation of the bibliographies and the name index. Karen Smith helped us overcome some eleventh-hour computer snafus. The University of California at Riverside Committee on Research helped underwrite this project with several generous research grants. Columbia University Press's Keith Frome's suggestions after reading an early draft of the entire manuscript helped us to smooth over many rough edges that might otherwise have gone unnoticed.

Finally, special thanks goes to James Raimes, Assistant Director of the Press for Reference Publishing at Columbia University Press. He first proposed *The Columbia Dictionary of Modern Literary and Cultural Criticism,* and despite our best efforts to test their limits, his openmindedness and patience never failed.

Contributing Editors:
  Martha Buskirk
  James M. Buzard
  Reinhold Dooley
  Susan Fraiman
  Eric Lott
  Carole-Anne Tyler

Contributors:
  Susan Barstow
  Michael Bennett
  Matthew Brown
  Elizabeth Crocker
  John Cunat
  Laurie Davie
  Mark Dolan
  Michael Furlough
  Laurie Greer
  Deborah Hatheway
  Peter Hitchcock
  Karen Hornick
  Rebecca Human
  Nancy Loevinger
  Paul Outka
  Anthony Rizzuto
  Corinna Rohse
  Steven Rubenstein
  Carlton Smith
  Harry Stecopoulos
  Mason Stokes
  Michael Uebel
  Doris Witt

THE

COLUMBIA DICTIONARY

OF

MODERN **LITERARY**

AND

CULTURAL CRITICISM

A

ABJECTION. According to Julia Kristeva's book-length "essay on abjection," *Powers of Horror* (1980), the abject is that which "disturbs identity, system, order. What does not respect borders, positions, rules." Filth, waste, pus, bodily fluids, the dead body itself are all abject, as are "the traitor, the liar, the lawbreaker with a good conscience, the shameless rapist, the killer who claims he is a savior"—any criminal who underlines the fragility of the law through an extra measure of premeditation, cunning, cowardice, or hypocrisy. The concept of abjection belongs to an important tradition in French literature, which includes writers like Baudelaire, Lautréamont, Antonin Artaud, Georges Bataille, and, above all, Louis-Ferdinand Céline. It is, however, Kristeva who, along with the revival of Bataille and the dissident Surrealists among a host of French and American critics (see SURREALISM), is largely responsible for the growth of contemporary interest in the topic. Closely related to the concepts of the DECENTERED SUBJECT and the TRANSITIONAL OBJECT, the abject represents what human life and culture exclude in order to sustain themselves. At the same time, it possesses an uncanniness that is as tempting and fascinating as it is revolting.

Kristeva, Julia. *Powers of Horror: An Essay on Abjection*. Trans. Leon S. Roudiez. New York: Columbia University Press, 1982.

ABREACTION. Abreaction (**ABreeAKshun**) is a Freudian term used to describe a moment of affective discharge in which the emotions attached to a traumatic event are purged, either through the repetition of that event or in therapy. The production of an abreaction, which usually takes the form of tears or expressions of violence, is thus a crucial means of treating neurosis. When it occurs in the therapeutic context, the analyst will try to help the analysand make the connection between his or her experience of emotion and memory of the original trauma, which has been repressed (see REPRESSION, TRANSFERENCE).

Freud, Sigmund. *Beyond the Pleasure Principle*. Trans. and ed. James Strachey. New York: Liveright, 1961.

—. "On the Psychical Mechanism of Hysterical Phenomena." In *The Standard Edition of the Complete Psychological Works of Sigmund Freud*, vol 2. Trans. James Strachey. London: Hogarth and Institute of Psycho-Analysis, 1974.

ABSENCE/PRESENCE. The terms *absence* and *presence* refer to two major concepts that the philospher Jacques Derrida has emphasized in his writings. According to Derrida, Western intellectual traditions depend upon some conception of presence—be it an originary moment, a transcendental being, or the univocal meaning of an utterance or text—as the unifying ground from which all thought can proceed. For Derrida this presence is an illusion, and all the apparatuses and traditions of Western philosophy, from the reliance on authority to the privileging of systems as explanatory, contribute to its power and dominance as a way of thinking. DECONSTRUCTION, especially in Derrida's hands, seeks to decenter, or undercut, Western philosophy's insistence on closure and foundations. In its stead Derrida asserts the importance of "absence" in which meaning, closure, foundation are always and forever deferred. For Derrida the important connection between a thing or a concept and the language (word) or SIGN that describes it is not based on some metaphysical linkage between word and object and the adequacy of language to allow one to know a "thing in itself." Rather, Derrida values DIF-FÉRANCE, the unbridgeable gap between word and thing and the continual deferral of stable and univocal meaning. The concept of différance is at the heart of Derrida's formulation of absence, since difference (between word and thing, signifier and signified) exists only in terms of absence. That is, when two (or more) things differ they are described according to the attributes that they do *not* have in common, the attributes that are *absent* in one (or more) of the entities being examined. For Derrida, différance, absence, is the place to begin philosophical and literary investigations for it is there that critics and thinkers can begin to repudiate the constraining presumptions of Western metaphysics and to recognize the neverending PLAY of meaning that is not so much *in* a text as the condition of its existence. See also APORIA, DECENTERING, SUPPLEMENT, UNDECIDABLITY.

Derrida, Jacques. *Speech and Phenomena and Other Essays on Husserl's Theory of Signs*. Trans. David Allison. Evanston, Ill.: Northwestern University Press, 1973.

—. *Of Grammatology.* Trans. G. C. Spivak. Baltimore: Johns Hopkins University Press, 1976.

—. *Positions.* Trans. Alan Bass. Chicago: University of Chicago Press, 1981.

ABSURDISM. Absurdism is a literary and philosophical movement that flourished after the Second World War and bears a close relationship to EXISTENTIALISM. Although it dates back to Kierkegaard's notion of the absurd in *Fear and Trembling,* twentieth-century philosophical works like Albert Camus's *The Myth of Sysiphus* offer the most familiar presentation of the movement's central ideas: in a world without God, human life and human suffering have no intrinsic meaning. This sense of a fundamental incongruity between human beings and the conditions of their existence is a recognition of the absurd and calls for a response that mixes humor and despair. The signature attitude of absurdism is therefore black humor, an ambiguous mixture of tragic pathos and preposterous comedy, which finds its most compelling literary expression in the work of writers like Samuel Beckett, Harold Pinter, and Eugène Ionesco. For example, in the latter's most famous play, *Rhinoceros,* the characters exist in a world where people are transformed, one by one, into rhinoceroses for no apparent reason.

Camus, Albert. *The Myth of Sisyphus.* Trans. Justin O'Brien. London: H. Hamilton, 1955.

Esslin, Martin. *The Theatre of the Absurd.* Garden City, N.Y.: Anchor Books, 1969.

Ionesco, Eugène. *Rhinoceros.* Trans. Derek Prouse. London: Calder and Boyars, 1960.

Kierkegaard, Søren. *Fear and Trembling: Repetition.* Trans. and ed. Howard V. Hong and Edna H. Hong. Princeton: Princeton University Press, 1983.

ACTANTIAL MODEL. The actantial model (AKTANshul) is a means of analyzing narrative associated with the work of the French narratologist A. J. Greimas, whose theories represent an important contribution to structuralist thought (see STRUCTURALISM). Building on the ideas of the Russian folklorist Vladimir Propp, Greimas identifies six fundamental actions and functions, or "actants," which take the form of binary oppositions and are accorded precedence over more traditional narrative categories like character or theme: Subject and Object (the fundamental pair), Sender and Receiver, and Helper and Opponent. The relationships of the actants comprise the actantial model, which constitutes the DEEP STRUCTURE or "grammar of plot" underlying the surface structure of any specific narrative. Greimas draws a key distinction between actants and actors; the latter are the concrete manifestations of actantial roles and can be understood as analogous to characters in the traditional literary sense of that term, although there is no one-to-one relationship between actants and actors. Certain actions and functions may be duplicated, or a single character may combine aspects of more than one actant. Indeed, an actant need not be represented by an anthropomorphic figure at all, but may take the form of a thing or even an abstract idea.

Greimas, A. J. "Narrative Grammar: Units and Levels." *Modern Language Notes* 86, 1971.
—. "Elements of a Narrative Grammar." *Diacritics* 7, 1977.
—. *Structural Semantics: An Attempt at a Method.* Trans. Daniele McDowell et al. Lincoln: University of Nebraska Press, 1983.

AESTHETICISM.   Aestheticism is best defined as an attitude or sensibility that promotes beauty as an end in itself and views the creation of beauty as the only proper function of the artist, rejecting all utilitarian or moralistic ends for art. The familiar slogan "art for art's sake," which came into prominence with the work of the English critic Walter Pater, develops a certain strain of romanticism and was anticipated by such earlier formulations as the German philosopher Immanuel Kant's definition of art as "purposiveness without a purpose" and the French writer Théophile Gautier's argument for the independence of art in the preface to his novel *Mademoiselle de Maupin* (1835). But it was Pater and his most notorious follower, Oscar Wilde, who did the most to popularize the aesthetic attitude in the final decade of the nineteenth century. Reacting implicitly against Victorian moralism as well as the objectivist understanding of DISINTERESTEDNESS promoted by Matthew Arnold, Pater argued—most famously in the "Conclusion" to *The Renaissance* (1873)—for an impressionistic criticism that aims to free itself from habit and theoretical abstraction and begin with a passionate apprehension of one's own responses to experience. The influence of this position can be felt in more than one strain of twentieth-century criticism, from the separation of art and society in American NEW CRITICISM to the antitheoretical bias of major critics like William Empson.

Chai, Leon. *Aestheticism: The Religion of Art in Post-Romantic Literature.* New York: Columbia University Press, 1990.

Pater, Walter. *The Renaissance.* Ed. Donald L. Hill. Berkeley: University of California Press, 1980.

Wilde, Oscar. *The Decay of Lying.* New York: Sunflower Co., 1902.

AESTHETIC IDEOLOGY. The phrase *aesthetic ideology* describes the set of beliefs and practices under which the production of both literature and literary criticism operates, including the valuation of the literary text and the centering of aesthetic considerations. The relation between IDEOLOGY and aesthetics has long been a contested area in Marxist criticism. The theory of aesthetic ideology has been most thoroughly formulated by Terry Eagleton, who, following Louis Althusser, has insisted that an aesthetic ideology inhabits that region of "general ideology" that pertains to art. For Eagleton, the power of aesthetic response is that it associates itself with individual experience, which is understood as spontaneous and nonideological. Thus, the types of knowledge aesthetic ideology gives rise to seem "natural," when in fact they have been historically constructed. One of the tasks of Marxist criticism is to analyze the ideological underpinnings of this knowledge and its function in relation to general ideology (of which it is a part). Recently, Jerome J. McGann has influentially argued the Romantic derivation of the currently dominant aesthetic ideology.

Althusser, Louis. *Lenin and Philosophy and Other Essays.* Trans. Ben Brewster. New York: Monthly Review Press, 1971.

Eagleton, Terry. *Criticism and Ideology: A Study in Marxist Literary Theory.* London: Verso, 1976.

—. *The Ideology of the Aesthetic.* Cambridge, Mass.: Blackwell, 1990.

McGann, Jerome J. *The Romantic Ideology: A Critical Investigation.* Chicago: University of Chicago Press, 1983.

AFFECTIVE FALLACY. The affective fallacy is the error of judging a text in terms of its effects, particularly its emotional effects upon the reader. The term was coined by W. K. Wimsatt and Monroe C. Beardsley to indicate the failure to make a theoretical distinction between the text and the reader. It is the "confusion between the poem and its result" (what it *is* and what it *does*). Along with its counterpart, the INTENTIONAL FALLACY, the affective fallacy derives from and promotes the New Critics' view of meaning as independent of factors outside the text itself (see NEW CRITICISM). It was employed to ensure the objectivity of the formalist enterprise, which assumed that focusing upon the reader's psychological response would preclude reliable, unbiased evaluation of the work. Beardsley later amended his view, admitting that critical evaluation must take into account the effect of the aesthetic object upon the perceiver. However, he maintained that objectivity need not be sacrificed if analysis concentrated upon the elements that precede and create the reader's response.

Beardsley, Monroe C. *Aesthetics: Problems in the Philosophy of Criticism*. New York: Harcourt Brace Jovanovich, 1958.
Wimsatt, W. K. *The Verbal Icon*. Lexington: University Press of Kentucky, 1954.

AGENCY. See AGENT.

AGENT. In its most elementary sense, *agent* refers to one who acts or has the capacity to act, often as a representative of someone or something else. In theoretical and political discussions, the term is often used interchangeably with the similar yet distinct concept of the SUBJECT. In humanist and some Marxist theories, the one implies the other; the subject is capable of thought and critique, and thus is also capable of choice and action. This identity of agent and subject has been roundly criticized by most varieties of poststructuralism. For proponents of these theories, agency is never free or a choice, and the agent is not a self-creating individual. Rather, all subjects are constructed through DISCOURSE or IDEOLOGY and are incapable of acting or thinking outside the limits of that construction. Thus, for poststructuralist thinkers, the concept of the agent is seen in its sense of the person (or persons) acting for or in place of someone or something else, namely the discourse(s) or ideology(ies) that position, motivate, and constrain individuals and are beyond their comprehension and control.

The difficulty with this concept of the agent and agency has to do with theorizing change, especially political and social change. If the individual is always subjected to ideological and/or discursive constraints, and all his or her actions—even the ones that seem oppositional—are always accountable in terms of those ideologies and discourses, how then is it that anything can change? Some new historicists, like Louis Montrose, have argued that agents and their concomitant agency are both constrained and *enabled* by the interaction of these power structures, and that it is then possible to think of individual agency as at once informed by and separate from these power structures (see NEW HISTORICISM). For Montrose, the formation of the subject is an equivocal process, one that both limits and engenders the possibility of poltical or social activity that can produce change. See also POWER, SUBJECT-OBJECT.

Dews, Peter. "Power and Subjectivity in Foucault." *New Left Review* 4, 1984.

Foucault, Michel. "The Subject and Power." *Critical Inquiry* 8, 1982.

Giddens, Anthony. *Central Problems in Social Theory.* Berkeley: University of California Press, 1979.

Montrose, Louis. "Professing the Renaissance: The Poetics and Politics of Culture." In H. Aram Veeser, ed., *The New Historicism.* New York: Routledge, 1989.

AGON. A Greek word meaning "contest," *agon* is most familiar to contemporary critics from Harold Bloom's theory of poetic influence (see ANXIETY OF INFLUENCE), where it refers to the contest between the belated poet and his strong precursor. For Bloom, the writing of original poetry is always a struggle for imaginative space with earlier poets, whose work appears to usurp all the available possibilities of creation. As a result, the new poet, or *ephebe*, must develop a strategy of revisionism by which his imaginative debts are disguised and his work comes to add something to poetic tradition. See also MISPRISION.

Bloom, Harold. *Agon: Toward a Theory of Revisionism.* Oxford: Oxford University Press, 1982.

ALIENATION. The recognition of the self as a distinct and separate entity within a larger and frequently antagonistic society is the basis of alienation. Hegel suggested this when he maintained that alienation was a "discordant relation" between the individual and society, as well as a harmful distinction between an individual's actual condition and his or her "essential nature." For the early Marx, who borrowed the concept from Hegel, alienation had a very specific meaning, relevant to his larger economic argument. Marxist alienation refers to the worker's literal and psychic distance from the product of his or her labor and, ultimately, to the destruction of human and familial bonds through the power of capitalism. This isolation, produced through economic slavery, leads to social dysfunction and finally to social rebellion within bourgeois capitalistic culture.

In European EXISTENTIALISM, the word *alienation* found further resonance. Jean-Paul Sartre maintained that death and what he perceived as the essential meaninglessness of our lives result in a painfully ruptured consciousness and in an increased division between selfhood and the institutions of society. It is in a modification of this sense that alienation functions as a theme throughout twentieth-century literature: not only might one be isolated from society but even from one's own self. Some theorists have argued that alienation is a fundamental condition of existence in postindustrial Western societies that are based upon FRAGMENTATION and the devaluation of the "real" by SIMULATION. See also DECENTERED SUBJECT.

Fromm, Erich. *Marx's Concept of Man*. New York: F. Unger, 1961.

Ollmann, Bertell. *Alienation: Marx's Conception of Man in Capitalist Society*. Cambridge: Cambridge University Press, 1971.

Sartre, Jean-Paul. *Being and Nothingness*. Trans. Hazel E. Barnes. New York: Washington Square Press, 1956.

ALIENATION EFFECT. See EPIC THEATER.

ALLEGORY. In its most common usage, *allegory* refers to a narrative or an image that has at least two distinct meanings, one of which is partially concealed by the visible or literal meaning. Often allegory portrays abstractions as humans, or as entities with human characteristics. It is in this sense that one can speak of the Statue of Liberty or statues of Justice or Victory as allegorical. In other instances, allegories incorporate the abstractions present in doctrines or systems of thought into narratives, presenting these abstractions as places, people, or events. One of the most famous allegories in English literature is John Bunyan's *The Pilgrim's Progress*, in which such figures as Mr. Wordly Wiseman, Faithful, and Hopeful accompany the hero Christian in his travels from the City of Destruction to the Celestial City. The places and people of the story represent particular concepts of Puritan doctrine. And while the story of Christian's pilgrimage is coherent in its own right, it also is the more general account of *every* Christian's journey through life toward salvation. Nor is allegory limited only to religious writing; authors like Jonathan Swift and George Orwell have used allegory effectively in their works on political issues.

Allegory was important for certain kinds of Christian biblical EXEGE-SIS in the Middle Ages as a means of identifying correspondences between the spiritual and physical worlds or between the Old and New Testaments (see TYPOLOGY). During the Romantic era, critics began to distinguish between symbol and allegory, though until that time the terms had been used almost interchangeably. The Romantic poet, critic, and clergyman Samuel Taylor Coleridge argued that the symbol was "an actual or essential part of . . . the whole which it represents." Allegory, on the other hand, is arbitrary, and thus less "natural." This distinction has not survived without repudiation by a number of formidable critics. Walter Benjamin, for one, argues that allegory is in fact more important than symbol, for it situates a text or painting against a mythical, histori-cized background. In contrast, the symbol for Benjamin is only momen-tary and transient. Paul de Man has also argued for the primacy of alle-gory. For him, symbols attempt to combine image and substance in such a way as to imply some kind of transcendent knowledge or truth, which de Man sees as unattainable. By contrast, allegory is more useful and "honest." It calls attention to its distance from its own origin. By so doing it does not pretend that unchanging, transcendental truths can be estab-lished beyond the contingencies of human knowledge and existence. See also DECONSTRUCTION.

Adams, Hazard. *Philosophy of the Literary Symbolic.* Tallahassee: Florida State Univer-sity Press, 1983.

Benjamin, Walter. *The Origin of German Tragic Drama.* Trans. John Osborne. London: New Left Books, 1977.

Coleridge, Samuel Taylor. *The Statesman's Manual.* In *Lay Sermons*, ed. R. J. White, in *Collected Works*, vol. 6, ed. K. Coburn. London: Routledge Kegan Paul, 1969–1984.

De Man, Paul. "The Rhetoric of Temporality." In *Blindness and Insight: Essays in the Rhetoric of Contemporary Criticism*, 2d, rev. ed. Minneapolis: University of Min-nesota Press, 1983.

AMBIGUITY. A forerunner of such New Critical concepts as IRONY and PARADOX (see NEW CRITICISM), ambiguity is the capacity of certain texts to allow more than one interpretation. In William Empson's words, it is "any verbal nuance, however slight, which gives room for alternative reac-tions to the same piece of language." Anticipating contemporary propo-nents of the indeterminacy of meaning, Empson argued that so much of the richness and subtlety of literary works results from ambiguity that it may be considered the defining characteristic of poetic language; and his influential book *Seven Types of Ambiguity* (1930) offered a typology and analysis of such effects across the historical spectrum of English poetry.

Empson, William. *Seven Types of Ambiguity*. London: Chatto and Windus, 1930.

ANACHRONY. A term from NARRATOLOGY used to describe a discrepancy between the order of events in a story and the order in which they are presented, anachrony (anAKruhNEE) takes two basic forms: flashback, or ANALEPSIS, and flashforward, or PROLEPSIS.

ANALEPSIS. The opposite of PROLEPSIS, analepsis (**AN**uhLEPsis) is a type of ANACHRONY that refers to the practice of relating certain events in a story after later events in the story have been recounted (see NARRATOLOGY). Most narratives that begin *in medias res* or "in the middle of things," will use analepsis to account for how the story moved to its current point. Sometimes called "flashback," "retrospective," or, in film and drama, "exposition," analepsis allows the narrative to fill in background information about characters or events.

ANALYSIS. Analysis is a method of investigation in which the object of study is described or evaluated by being broken down into its constituent elements. Analyses vary in the kinds of relationships they seek to establish between part and whole and in whether a "whole" is understood to exist before the analysis begins. The textual analysis of the New Critics, for example, assumes that an individual text has its own unique wholeness (sometimes called "organic unity") whose constituent elements (image, theme, etc.) are said to convey meaning according to what they contribute to this whole (see NEW CRITICISM). In some theories of psychoanalysis, by contrast, the objective is the eventual therapeutic construction of a "whole" human being. Analysis is an ancient Western technique that has been particularly favored since the late eighteenth century, when practitioners of the human sciences began to assume the wholeness of such concepts as "society" and "culture." Contemporary theorists, however, have cast suspicion on the intrinsic idealism of this approach: the "whole," they have argued, is an abstraction, and its parts are always constructed ideologically. Nevertheless, analysis remains a highly privileged, frequently used, and virtually unavoidable method.

ANDROCENTRIC. From *andros,* the Greek word for "man," and "center," *androcentric* refers to literary concepts and models based on an exclusively male tradition, yet taken to be normative for literary and critical texts generally. As the dominant frame of reference in a patriarchal culture, androcentrism subordinates female experiences, concerns, and values, and suppresses women's texts or labels them inferior in terms of specifically male standards of literary worth. Charlotte Perkins Gilman first applied this equation of patriarchal attitudes with universal truths in her 1911 treatise, *The Man-made World; or, Our Androcentric Culture,* in which she analyzed how "one sex . . . monopolized all human activities." In 1981 Elaine Showalter suggested that even criticizing writing by men from a feminist perspective (what she called "FEMINIST CRITIQUE") may remain androcentric insofar as it continues to focus on male texts and to work within frameworks derived from these. See also MASCULINIST, PATRIARCHY.

Gilman, Charlotte Perkins. *The Man-made World; or, Our Androcentric Culture.* New York: Source Book Press, 1970.
Showalter, Elaine. "Feminist Criticism in the Wilderness." In Elaine Showalter, ed., *The New Feminist Criticism.* New York: Pantheon,1985.

ANDROGYNY. *Androgyny,* a term derived from the Greek words for "male" (*andro*) and "female" (*gyn*), suggests an identity based on the union not of male and female biological characteristics (hermaphroditism), but of those traits conventionally defined as masculine and feminine, thus challenging the view of the two genders as antithetical. For some feminists, the concept of androgyny has offered the possibility of access to a full range of experience, encompassing both "masculinity" and "femininity." Virginia Woolf, in a much-discussed passage from *A Room of One's Own* (1929), celebrated the notion of androgyny and Coleridge's association of the androgynous mind with creative genius. Carolyn Heilbrun's *Toward a Recognition of Androgyny* (1973) claimed Woolf's aesthetic ideal as a social and political one, arguing that androgyny can move us "away from sexual polarization and the prison of gender." Elaine Showalter, on the other hand, criticized Woolf's vision as a wishful "flight" from the material conditions that oppress women *as* women, and from the need to struggle against these. Others have worried that androgyny, like "humanity," may only seem to transcend sexism and actually disguise a bias in favor of the masculine. More recently, Toril Moi has returned to androgyny, linking it to the poststructuralist feminist project of dismantling what has been seen as the essential opposition between female and male. Though the meaning of both terms has been much debated, the implications of *androgyny* for Anglo-American feminists have been in some ways analogous to those of *bisexuality* for the French. See also BISEXUALITY.

Heilbrun, Carolyn G. *Toward a Recognition of Androgyny.* New York: Norton, 1982.
Moi, Toril. *Sexual/Textual Politics.* New York: Routledge, 1985.
Showalter, Elaine. *A Literature of Their Own: British Women Novelists from Brontë to Lessing.* Princeton: Princeton University Press, 1977.
Woolf, Virginia. *A Room of One's Own.* New York: Harcourt, Brace, Jovanovich, 1957.

ANGLE/CAMERA ANGLE. Having to do with the framing of the film image, *angle* refers to the perspective afforded by the camera position on what has been filmed, whether high (looking down), low (looking up), oblique (looking at a slant), or straight on. It is a different matter from camera height: the camera may be placed low without being angled up for a low-angle perspective (for example, it may be low but straight on). It is also not the same as camera level or "cant" (a canted or "off kilter" framing is achieved by rolling the camera a few degrees on its longitudinal axis, which runs from its lens to the subject filmed). Finally, it differs from angle of view, which may be broad or narrow, depending on whether a wide-angle or telephoto lens is used. See also FRAME/FRAMING, SCALE/SHOT SCALE.

ANTANACLASIS. Antanaclasis (anTANuhCLAYsis) is the repetition of a word with a different meaning each time. In Benjamin Franklin's quip, "Your argument is sound, nothing but sound," while the first use of "sound" means "well-constructed" or "sensible," the second use signifies "empty" or "nonsensical." Although the second meaning revises or overturns the first, the humor of the phrase relies on the presence of both (in this case, incompatible) meanings. Michael Riffaterre uses this rhetorical device to understand the generation of narratives from syllepsis, in which two meanings are activated in a single use of a word. See also SYLLEPSIS.

Riffaterre, Michael. *Fictional Truth.* Baltimore: Johns Hopkins University Press, 1990.

ANTHROPOCENTRISM. Anthropocentrism is the belief that human beings are at the center of the universe of other beings and things. It is not the dogma of any one school of thought, but a description of tendencies toward the denial of priority to the nonhuman—animals and plants, the physical universe, God. Originally, the term was used most often as the opposite of theocentric (god-centered), and in this sense its meaning is close to that of HUMANISM. John Ruskin's discussion of the PATHETIC FALLACY, the attribution of human qualities and emotions to nature and the inanimate world, also invokes an idea parallel to that expressed by anthropocentrism.

ANTI-ESSENTIALISM. See ESSENTIALISM, PRAGMATISM.

ANTI-FOUNDATIONALISM. See PRAGMATISM.

ANTIPOSITIVISM. Generally speaking, *antipositivism* refers to any view that is opposed to POSITIVISM, a mid-nineteenth-century philosophy associated with Auguste Comte. Acccording to Comte, philosophers and scientists should abandon the search for the metaphysical origins of things and concern themselves only with facts that can be empirically observed and scientifically organized. The critique of this method is based on a critique of empiricism itself. Observable facts depend for their objectivity on the assumption that the observer is capable of complete DISINTERESTEDNESS—an assumption that is highly debatable. Further, positivism limits itself to entities that are subject to physical, repeatable, or verifiable measurement. This discounts a number of experiences and phenomena that do not lend themselves to such cataloging. It is important to note that while positivism is often confused with empiricism and hard science, Comte himself was primarily concerned with sociological and historical analysis. It is in these disciplines that the antipositivist movement has been centered; moreover, the general shift since the nineteenth century in literary studies from philology to interpretation is often seen as an antipositivist development.

ANXIETY OF AUTHORSHIP. The phrase *anxiety of authorship* refers to a feminist theory of the relations between women writers, which was

developed by Sandra Gilbert and Susan Gubar in a revision of Harold
Bloom's theory of poetic influence. Drawing on Freud, Bloom contends
that a young poet suffers from an anxiety that he will not successfully
rival his literary father: in Bloom's phrase, the ANXIETY OF INFLUENCE.
In their study of nineteenth-century women writers, Gilbert and Gubar
revised Bloom's male-centered model to take into account the experience
of literary daughters. Women such as Jane Austen and Emily Dickinson
were not, they argued, daunted by the examples of maternal precursors
so much as discouraged from writing altogether by the virtual absence of
such precursors. The paucity of female models and the pervasive view of
writing as a male activity—of the pen as a "metaphorical penis"—were
responsible for what Gilbert and Gubar called the anxiety of authorship.
Three notions follow. First, the relation of female novelists and poets to
their foremothers may therefore be characterized (at least until the twentieth century) less by competition than by grateful connection. Second,
these women's deep insecurity about writing may "infect" their works
with signs of uneasiness, alienation, and rage. And third, since nineteenth-century women writers were already on the verge of impropriety
by taking up the pen at all, they may hide their most radical material
beneath apparently conventional cover stories. See also PALIMPSEST.

Bloom, Harold. *The Anxiety of Influence: A Theory of Poetry.* New York: Oxford University Press, 1973.
Gilbert, Sandra, and Susan Gubar. *The Madwoman in the Attic: The Woman Writer
and the Nineteenth-Century Literary Imagination.* New Haven: Yale University
Press, 1979.

ANXIETY OF INFLUENCE. Coined by the American literary critic
Harold Bloom, the term *anxiety of influence* describes the experience in
which poets feel the work of their precursors as threats to the scope of
their own imaginative achievement. Bloom understands the relationship
between the "strong" precursor and the "belated" poet as a version of the
Freudian OEDIPUS COMPLEX, with the precursor occupying the position
of the father and the young writer or "ephebe" that of the son who desires
the mother (the muse). This is a struggle that the ephebe must lose, for
the precursor's work cannot simply be replicated, however enabling it
may be as an example; for this reason, the latecomer is forced to resort to
various strategies in order to establish his or her own space as an imaginative being. Thus, in Bloom's conception of literary history, the entire

course of English poetry since Milton is understood as a series of creative (and defensive) misreadings (or MISPRISIONS) of the work of earlier poets, a process that is both an inevitable diminishment and an exemplary, larger-than-life drama of familial love-hate relations. See also ANXIETY OF AUTHORSHIP, INTERTEXTUALITY, TRADITION.

Bloom, Harold. *The Anxiety of Influence: A Theory of Poetry.* New York: Oxford University Press, 1973.
—. *Kabbalah and Criticism.* New York: Seabury Press, 1975.
—. *A Map of Misreading.* New York: Oxford University Press, 1975.
—. *Poetry and Repression: Revisionism from Blake to Stevens..* New Haven: Yale University Press, 1976.

APHANISIS. A Greek word used by Ernest Jones in his discussion of female sexuality, *aphanisis* (AfaNEEsis) refers to the disappearance of sexual desire. Jones's study of female sexuality led him to conclude that the fear of aphanisis is, in both sexes, even more fundamental and powerful than the fear of castration. In contrast to Freud's emphasis on the castration complex, Jones stressed those aspects of female sexuality that cannot be described as resulting from an awareness of the absence of the penis and pointed out that some men actually *desire* castration, suggesting that the fear of castration is actually a form of the more basic fear of the loss of desire. See also CASTRATION COMPLEX.

Jones, Ernest. "Early Development of Female Sexuality." In *Papers on Psychoanalysis,* 5th ed. Boston: Beacon Press, 1961.

APODEIXIS. The term *apodeixis* (APODAICKSuhs) is Greek for demonstration or proof. Aristotle, in his *Topics,* identifies apodeixis as one of three types of reasoning, distinguishing it from the dialectical and the contentious. For Aristotle, apodiectic (or demonstrative) reasoning begins from premises that are "true and primary or of such a kind that we have derived our original knowledge of them from premises that are primary and true." This is in direct contrast to dialectical reasoning, which begins from generally accepted opinions, and contentious reasoning, which begins from premises that only appear to be generally accepted but in fact are not. Because apodeictic statements point to something that is assumed to be preexisting and true (as in the phrase, "She was one of those women who . . . " where it is assumed that there exists a group of women who conform to the subsequent characterization), scholars like Michael Riffaterre have argued that apodeictic statements seem true by depriving "the reader of any ground to question the statement." Apodeictic statements are true in that they are perfectly tautological, perfectly circular: What kind of woman was she? She was one of *those* women. What kind of woman is that? Exactly like the character described. Riffaterre uses the presence of such apodeictic statements in novels to show that the "truth value" of fictional texts does not rest in any sort of "accuracy" in the representation, but in the narrative strategies designed to give the impression of truth. See also DEIXIS.

Aristotle. *Topics.* Trans. E. S. Forster. Cambridge, Mass.: Harvard University Press, 1926.
Riffaterre, Michael. *Fictional Truth.* Baltimore: Johns Hopkins University Press, 1990.

APORIA. *Aporia* (aporEEuh) may simply refer to the inherent contradictions that are found in any text, which causes the text to resist interpretation. Most commonly used by deconstructionists, *aporia* more often describes the gap between the linguistic and philosophical coherence of a text and the subversive contradictions and paradoxes that shadow that coherence. Such subversions serve not just to reverse interpretation but to open the text to a free play of possibilities, making the text "undecidable" and disrupting systemization. Aporetic texts, however, are distinguished from texts that seem to *mark* and to *organize* a structure of resistance to, as Jacques Derrida puts it, "the philosophical conceptuality that allegedly dominated or comprehended them." Derrida includes among these texts the works of Freud, Nietzsche, Saussure, and Heidegger in philosophy, and in literature the works of Mallarmé and Artaud. See also DECONSTRUCTION, LOGOCENTRISM, UNDECIDABILITY.

APPARATUS. The term *apparatus* is often used to describe the ensemble of theories, concepts, and methods brought to bear in the analysis of a work of art or literature, as in the phrase "critical apparatus." It also refers to the trappings of academic writing, such as footnotes, bibliography, index, and appendices. The word has a somewhat different meaning in FILM THEORY, however, where it designates the entire complex of elements and operations that go into the experience of viewing a film: the various mechanisms used in making and showing a film (camera, film, projector, screen, and the beam of light in a darkened theater); the text of the film itself; and the psychological mechanism of the spectator, understood in psychoanalytic terms.

Cha, Theresa Hak Kyung, ed. *Apparatus.* New York: Tanam Press, 1980.
Rosen, Phil, ed. *Narrative, Apparatus, Ideology: A Film Theory Reader.* New York: Columbia University Press, 1986.

APPROPRIATION.   In common parlance, appropriation refers to the taking of something, often without permission, for use exclusively by one's self. The use of the term in CULTURAL STUDIES is quite similar. In that context, appropriation designates an act whereby a form of CULTURAL CAPITAL is taken over and turned against its original possessor. Thus, for example, the English language itself has often been appropriated by writers hailing from former English colonies for the purpose of criticizing their ex-colonizers and the culture of COLONIALISM that has shaped their lives. Appropriation need not be subversive, however. Some music critics have suggested that rap and hip-hop have been appropriated by the music industry for commercial purposes and have thus been expropriated of their subversive, countercultural impulse as they have been turned into commodities.

A related term, *reappropriation,* has become important in cultural studies, where it is used as a synonym for resignification and BRICOLAGE, which involve making a sign signify, or mean, differently by recontextualizing it. Proponents of cultural studies have pointed out that in a world colonized by capitalism, all objects may already have a COMMODITY function to which they are destined by their place in the production process. To signal resistance to bourgeois domination, a subgroup member may have to consume such commodities (since they are all that are available) but in a way different from that for which they have been marketed, as when punk rockers wear safety pins as earrings. In a similar vein, some feminists have argued for the reappropriation of femininity, because it comprises values and behavior at odds with masculinity and so can operate to critique patriarchal values, even though it has been constituted inside patriarchy. Such feminists, like many proponents of cultural studies, accept that there can be no such thing as "authentic resistance," that which is enacted in the name of some mode of being untainted by oppressive culture, such as "genuine femininity" (versus that which we currently have). This recognition of the impossibility of accessing the authentically subversive and totally escaping the constraints of our culture and language has also animated DECONSTRUCTION, which reappropriates metaphysical concepts and puts them "under ERASURE" to signify they no longer mean what they once did, but that it is impossible to perform a critique of METAPHYSICS without using its terms, albeit differently. There is no outside to metaphysical systems; they have to be critiqued from within.

Finally, some gay and lesbian critics have also argued against a politics based on a belief in authentic identities and authentic (versus compromised) resistance, suggesting instead the CAMP or parodic reappropriation of straight gender roles for subversive purposes, including the subversion of the heterosexist assumption that gender is the expression of a biological essence that is by definition "straight."

Chambers, Iain. *Popular Culture: The Metropolitan Experience*. London: Methuen, 1986.

ARCHAEOLOGY. The term *archaeology* is closely associated in contemporary theory with the work of Michel Foucault, who uses it to describe the method of historical investigation that he favored during the earlier part of his career. Renouncing all truth claims, the archaeologist instead aims to present a history of systems of meaning, or DISCOURSES, such as clinical medicine, which are treated as autonomous and rule-governed. Foucaultian archaeology is not restricted by conventional disciplinary boundaries and the assumptions that they imply about what constitutes a worthwhile intellectual project. Rather, it aims to describe the system of rules that consciously or unconsciously govern the production of knowledge, of social and institutional practices, and of the very objects of study, in the various disciplines, as well as the distinctions between the disciplines themselves. Thus, in *Madness and Civilization*, his first book, Foucault produces an archaeology of madness, analyzing how madness emerged as distinct from reason in the seventeenth century, in tandem with the development of the sciences of madness, psychiatry, and psychology. See also GENEALOGY, IDEOLOGY.

Foucault, Michel. *Madness and Civilization*. Trans. Richard Howard. New York: Pantheon, 1965.
—. *The Archaeology of Knowledge*. Trans. A. M. Sheridan Smith. New York: Pantheon, 1972.

ARCHAISM. An archaism (ARkayIZuhm), an old word or expression, is used intentionally to give a special rhetorical effect to a text. When Charles Lamb, for instance, writes "What a careless even deportment hath your borrower!" the use of the archaic "hath" (in addition to the older syntax) gives the line a comical flavor. Michael Riffaterre comments that an archaism "runs the risk of blending into its context, since the other words of that context all seem dated to the modern reader," and anyone who might think that people in nineteenth-century England ordinarily expressed themselves as Lamb did would miss the humor of the archaism. However, archaisms have an important deictic or "pointing" function (see DEIXIS). The archaism points readers to a different context or intertext—in this case, to lofty Biblical language—for ironic or straight comparison. With Lamb, the comparison is ironic: he highlights the difference between his subject matter (people who habitually borrow money from others) and the lofty language used in the description. In other cases, "hath" might be used to liken the text or the speech of a character to an elevated intertext.

Riffaterre, Michael. *Text Production*. Trans. Terese Lyons. New York: Columbia University Press, 1983.

ARCHE. *Arche* is the Greek word for "origin." Much POSTMODERN thought is critical of the search for origins, which it views as a form of METAPHYSICS. In this view, the function of origins, which must be constructed after the fact, is to permit one to dictate the meaning of events according to their relation to this source of AUTHORITY. Perhaps paradoxically, *arche* is also the root of the word ARCHAEOLOGY, which in the work of Michel Foucault and others refers to a form of historical investigation that specifically rejects the search for origins. See also TELOS.

ARCHETYPE. According to the proponents of "archetypal" or MYTH CRITICISM, archetypes are the basic narrative motifs that provide the models for all culturally significant stories. The concept is influenced both by the psychologist Carl Gustav Jung, who posited the existence of a "collective unconscious" composed of inherited ideas and predispositions like the animus (male side of the female psyche) and anima (female side of the male psyche), and by the anthropologist James G. Frazer's *The Golden Bough* (1890–1915), which argued that the circle of life and death found in many fertility cults was the common basis for a number of mythologies (see MYTH). The identification of archetypes in works of literature thus serves to emphasize the continuities of human life from the earliest times to the present and to minimize cultural and historical differences, a tendency that has brought the concept into disfavor in recent years.

Frazer, James G. *The Golden Bough.* New York: Macmillan, 1922.

Jung, Carl Gustav. "On the Relation of Analytical Psychology to Poetic Art." In *Contributions to Analytical Psychology.* Trans. H. G. and Cary F. Baynes. Harcourt Brace, 1928.

—. *The Archetypes and the Collective Unconscious.* Vol. 9 of *Collected Works.* Trans. R. F. C. Hull. New York: Pantheon, 1959.

ARCHETYPAL CRITICISM. See MYTH CRITICISM.

ARISTOTELIAN CRITICISM. Aristotelian criticism refers to the systematic, formal, judicial criticism of the Greek philosopher Aristotle (384–322 B.C.) and the methodologies that stem from Aristotle's *Poetics.* Eschewing the idealism of his teacher Plato, Aristotle adopted a scientific, materialist view of the world as process and change, which directly influenced his view of poetry (literature). Aristotelian criticism defines poetry as the imitation of human action. However, poetic art is not merely the copying of degraded forms, as Plato would have it. Rather, through the translation of reality into another medium by the artful application of six literary elements (PLOT, CHARACTER, thought, diction, sound, spectacle), the poet creates a work purged of the random and incoherent dross of the material world, and thus illuminates the universal essence of reality. A work that simply mirrors the world would not qualify as art. Thus, plot, because it discovers the order and unity in human action by removing the incidental and accidental, is valued over all other literary elements.

Aristotelian criticism focuses on the complex interrelationship of the six literary elements as they pertain to genres such as comedy, epic, lyric, and particularly tragedy. Evaluation of a literary work is therefore not extrinsic; it is not a function of external moral or political factors, as it is for Plato. While Aristotle does believe that tragedy provides a purgative effect (rather than the corruptive effect Plato feared) and is thus conducive to maintaining political order, his main criteria for literary evaluation stem from an intrinsic approach. A work is judged by the standards of its particular genre; the grounds of judgment grow out of the very nature of the work judged. Aristotelian criticism has thus been very influential with the New Critics (see NEW CRITICISM) and the CHICAGO SCHOOL (also known as the NEO-ARISTOTELIANS). See also DIANOIA, MIMESIS.

Aristotle. *Poetics.* Trans. Leon Golden, with a commentary by O. B. Hardison. Englewood Cliffs, N.J.: Prentice-Hall, 1968.

AUDIENCE. The question of the audience for a work of literature or art has taken on greater importance as an increasing number of theories have emphasized that the interpretation of a work will be determined at least in part by the context in which it is received. This emphasis on the role of the audience stems from the recognition that a work's meaning is not limited to those meanings intended by the author, nor is it inherent in the text itself. Rather, a variety of contemporary theories stress the role of the audience in producing meaning. Thus, in his influential book *S/Z,* the French critic Roland Barthes introduced the concept of the "writerly" text as an ideal that would allow a creative participation on the part of the reader comparable to that of the writer him or herself. Another important critical school that stresses the text's reception is that of READER-RESPONSE CRITICISM, represented in Germany by such figures as Hans Robert Jauss and Wolfgang Iser, and in the United States by, among others, Stanley Fish, whose concept of "interpretive communities" makes explicit the link between this school and the more general problem of the audience. Finally, the various forms of CULTURAL STUDIES, CULTURAL MATERIALISM, and NEW HISTORICISM represent the most visible evidence of the significance attributed in contemporary criticism to the ways a text is received by its audience.

Barthes, Roland. *S/Z.* Trans. Richard Miller. New York: Hill and Wang, 1974.
Fish, Stanley. *Is There a Text in This Class?* Cambridge, Mass.: Harvard University Press, 1980.

AUTHENTIC RESISTANCE/SUBVERSION. See APPROPRIATION.

AUTEUR THEORY. The phrase *auteur theory* (oTUR) refers to an approach to the study of film which holds that the director is the principal creative consciousness behind the film. It is derived from the French *la politique des auteurs* (politics or "policy" of the author) and was coined by the director François Truffaut in an article that appeared in 1954 in *Cahiers du Cinéma*, the French film journal with which auteur theory became associated. Critics whose work takes this approach, like André Bazin and, in the United States, Andrew Sarris, assume that films are the product of a single AUTHOR or auteur, whose ideas, values, and world-view the film expresses. Such critics credit the director as the originating source, despite crucial creative contributions to the film made by the scriptwriter, cinematographer, editor(s), actors, set, costume and light-ing designers, etc., all of whom might be regarded as collaborators or co-authors. They also draw a distinction between the "true auteur," who has a personal vision, and the mere *"metteur en scène,"* who knows the lan-guage of cinema but has neither a coherent worldview nor a unique style.

Auteur theory enabled film critics to talk about films as literary crit-ics talked about literature. Assuming that the director is a creative and original genius who expresses his ideas and values in his films, these crit-ics conclude that there must be significant links between his works, and between his life and his works, which it is their task to recover: the recur-rent themes or motifs and visual obsessions that comprise a style. Thus, an author-centered approach to film was sanctioned by auteur theory, and it soon became as important as other approaches, such as those that were genre-centered or those that concentrated on a film's REALISM, both of which tended to minimize the importance of any one contributor.

Since its inception many critics have taken issue with auteur theory. As they have noted, it tends toward romantic INDIVIDUALISM, often sup-posing that great geniuses transcend history, ideology, and the con-straints of cinema itself (including not only those associated with the genre in which the auteur has chosen to work, but also those that derive from tensions between the visions and activities of the various contribu-tors to a film, and between them and the studio or producers, who value commercial success above all). Like literary author-centered approaches, auteur theory also tends to privilege authorial intention as the ground of interpretation, ignoring the significance of the spectator's reception of the film and of INTERTEXTUALITY.

Auteur theory does, however, have several strengths. It provided an impetus for the analysis of (and in some cases rediscovery of) popular commercial films, including Hollywood cinema, some of whose direc-tors were argued to be auteurs and so deserving of the same kind of attention given to "cinema of quality" (adaptations of literary works) and European "art film." It also shifted attention somewhat away from literary values (how well the ideas or themes of a novel were expressed in the film adaptation) to cinematic values (the film's style, its mise-en-scène, camera movements, lighting, editing, etc., all of which might be said to be characteristic of a particular auteur). Finally, it represented another alternative to sociologically oriented, audience research approaches to film, which were (and still are) popular in America and which generally repress the aesthetic dimension of cinema altogether.

Bazin, André. *What is Cinema? Essays.* 2 vols. Trans. Hugh Gray. Berkeley: University of California Press, 1967–1972.
Kael, Pauline. *I Lost it at the Movies.* Boston: Little, Brown, 1965.

AUTHOR. At first glance, the concept of the author hardly seems a difficult one to grasp. After all, every schoolchild knows that an author is someone who writes books, essays, poems, or other texts. Yet within a broad historical context, it becomes obvious that notions of authority change drastically with the conditions of production of texts. For instance, it is only in the nineteenth century that authors emerge as a distinct professional group who have certain rights to their intellectual property—their texts. Other issues, such as whether the author's intention is the basis of meaning in a text, whether, indeed, all writers should be considered authors, or whether an author is merely a conduit for divine (or perhaps demonic) inspiration have vexed theorists at least since Plato and Longinus.

Recent theoretical discussions of authorship have espoused the "death of the author," after an essay of the same name by Roland Barthes. Barthes argues that it is impossible to answer the questions we usually reserve for authorship, whether they concern intention or the multifarious historical conditions that surround the composition (and reception) of a text. For Barthes, the concept of the "author" is an ideological construct that allows us to codify a text as univocal and originating or emanating from a singular, unified source. Barthes offers in place of this singular AUTHORITY as a source of meaning and origination, the concept that all texts are plural, equivocal, and indeterminate. They arise from a number of contestatory voices or DISCOURSES and cannot be traced back to an originary meaning or unified source. The effect of Barthes' position is to redefine the process of reading as one that is not in search of a singular, uncontested meaning for a text, but as an activity that confronts and works with (or against) the various CODES that comprise a text. A further effect of his theory is to rest the control of textual meaning from the author and extend it to the reader. For Barthes, the reader is "the space on which all the quotations that make up a writing are inscribed without any of them being lost; a text's unity lies not in its origin but in its destination." Meaning thus is volatile and contingent upon the reading of a text and is ultimately without reference to the author as the entity that fixes all meaning.

The French philosopher Michel Foucault has also contributed notably to the debate over the status of the author. In his essay "What is an Author?," he historicizes the concept, arguing that it is more interesting and useful to consider an author more as a function of a text's reception and a creation of a text's readers than as the creative genius of a work of art. For Foucault, we may still speak of authors, but in ways that identify them as historical, constructed entities. Except for figures such as Nietzsche, Freud, and Marx, whose names and authority signal specific epistemological shifts in Western thought, Foucault envisages the possibility of anonymous texts considered in light of the discourses in which they participate and to which they contribute. See also AUTHOR FUNCTION.

Barthes, Roland. "The Death of the Author." In *Image, Music, Text.* Trans. Stephen Heath. New York: Hill and Wang, 1977.

Foucault, Michel. "What is an Author?" In *Language, Counter-Memory, Practice: Selected Essays and Interviews.* Trans. Donald F. Bouchard and Sherry Simon. Ithaca, N.Y.: Cornell University Press, 1977.

AUTHOR FUNCTION. With contemporary criticism's problematization of the concept of the AUTHOR (inaugurated by Roland Barthes' essay "The Death of the Author"), it has become commonplace for critics to speak and write of authors as text-specific. Thus, rather than discussing "Dickens" or "Cather," for example, in a general sense, critics now often refer to "the Dickens of *Bleak House*" or "the Cather of *Death Comes for the Archbishop*." Or when critics do speak of an author in general terms, it is usually with the understanding that they are not referring to the person who put pen to paper; they are instead using the author's name as a means of indicating the various voices and opinions within a text that cannot be reduced to a simple question of biography or intent. In much contemporary criticism, the author no longer retains a reverenced place as the source of creative genius or of textual meaning but becomes another product of the text and of reading. For those who follow a Marxist or NEW HISTORICIST theoretical agenda, the function of the author within a work is also a product of the cultural circumstances that converged to produce the text at a given point in history. See also AUTHORITY, AUTHOR.

Barthes, Roland. *S/Z.* Trans. Richard Miller. New York: Hill and Wang, 1974.
—. "The Death of the Author." In *Image, Music, Text.* Trans. Stephen Heath. New York: Hill and Wang, 1977.
Foucault, Michel, "What is an Author?" *Language, Counter-Memory, Practice: Selected Essays and Interviews.* Trans. Donald F. Bouchard and Sherry Simon. Ithaca, N.Y.: Cornell University Press, 1977.

AUTHORITY. For many critics, discussions of authority often begin with theorizations of the AUTHOR or a text's AUTHOR FUNCTION, but almost invariably such theorizing leads to deliberations on authority in its broader social and political connotations. At issue in the textual realm of these discussions is the amount of power over meaning and interpretation that should be granted to the originator (author) of a given text. In recent critical debates, it has become customary to deny the author any special place in relation to his or her text and thus to relegate the author to a function of the work. Such a critical move "opens" the text to a seemingly infinite number of interpretations and shifts the authority over a text from its author to its reader.

Political and social issues come into play when the concept of the TEXT is extended beyond printed material to any combination of SIGNS that can be interpreted. When the world itself is considered a text to be read and construed, then the question of authority, and thus POWER, over that text naturally arises. For many leftist critics, authority of any sort is perceived as an illegitimate function of power that relies on IDEOLOGY or HEGEMONY to coerce individuals into certain actions or mind sets. Others, such as Michel Foucault, make careful distinctions between authority and power, and point out that while authority may indeed always be coercive, power is not necessarily synonymous with authority, nor is power or its exercise always negative.

Adorno, T. W., et al. *The Authoritarian Personality.* New York: Harper, 1950.
Foucault, Michel. *The History of Sexuality.* Trans. Robert Hurley. New York: Pantheon, 1978.

—. *Discipline and Punish.* Trans. Alan Sheridan. New York: Vintage, 1979.

Marcuse, Herbert. *One-Dimensional Man.* Boston: Beacon Press, 1964.

Mill, John Stuart. *On Liberty.* Ed. John Gray. Oxford: Oxford University Press, 1991.

AVANT-GARDE. Originally a military term referring to the most forwardly placed troops, *avant-garde* (avAHNT GARD) first began to be applied to artistic movements in nineteenth-century France, where its usage reflects a new emphasis on innovation and experiment. Perhaps its most common association, however, is with the MODERNISM of the late nineteenth and early twentieth centuries. It is in this sense that Clement Greenberg used the term in his influential 1939 essay "Avant-Garde and Kitsch," which draws a distinction between the deliberately difficult and sometimes off-putting innovations of the modernist era and the much more accessible but degraded products of mass culture. Greenberg's essay was a product of the leftist atmosphere of the thirties, and one unifying thread running through the many different forms taken by the avant-garde is an anti-bourgeois stance. In this view, the formal experimentation of much modernist art is linked to a rejection of the values of a business society. More recently, however, such theorists as Peter Bürger and Andreas Huyssen have insisted on a distinction between avant-garde and modernism, which is viewed as being primarily characterized by a self-referential AESTHETICISM, whereas the avant-garde is seen as aiming to eliminate the distinction between art and life, often by incorporating elements of mass culture into the work of art or by promoting specific political programs. In fact, this overtly political emphasis did result in occasional liaisons between avant-garde and working-class movements, as was the case with French SURREALISM and Russian CONSTRUCTIVISM. In a rather different vein, other critics have argued that the avant-garde proper ceased to exist with the decline of modernism and the rise of an all-embracing media culture in the era of POSTMODERNISM.

Bürger, Peter. *Theory of the Avant-Garde.* Trans. Michael Shaw. Minneapolis: University of Minnesota Press, 1984.

Greenberg, Clement. "Avant-Garde and Kitsch." In *Art and Culture.* Boston: Beacon Press, 1961.

Poggioli, Renato. *The Theory of the Avant-Garde.* Trans. Gerald Fitzgerald. Cambridge, Mass.: Harvard University Press, 1968.

Timms, Edward, and Peter Collier, eds. *Visions and Blueprints: Avant-Garde Culture and Radical Politics in Early Twentieth-Century Europe.* Manchester: Manchester University Press, 1988.

B

BASE AND SUPERSTRUCTURE. *Base* and *superstructure* are Marxist terms referring to the interdependent and reflexive relationship
between the economic foundations of society (base) and the forms of
state and social consciousness which inevitably follow that structure.
First propounded by Marx and Engels in such texts as *The German Ideology* (1859) and *A Contribution to the Critique of Political Economy*, the
metaphor of base and superstructure is meant to underscore the critical
Marxist notion that the specific form(s) of the state and the social consciousness of a particular society are not autonomous, but rather are
always conditioned by the economic foundations of the society.

Significantly, within the ideological development of Marxist and
post-Marxist thought, the base/superstructure formulation has undergone considerable debate and revision. For example, Engels, resisting the
overly reductive structural implications of the metaphor, settled upon a
conceptualization of a superstructure as not simply a static result of the
economic base but a concrete result of "an endless host of accidents." In
other words, the relationship between the base and the superstructure is
vastly more complex than the mere mechanical correlation that so-called
VULGAR MARXISM might suggest.

In the context of literary criticism, the concepts of base and superstructure inevitably pervade the criticism of such theorists as Fredric
Jameson and Raymond Williams. For such critics, these concepts underwrite their attempts at investigating the subtle ways that the economic
exigencies of capitalism prefigure the material world.

Hall, Stuart. "Rethinking the 'Base and Superstructure' Metaphor." In Jan Bloomfield,
ed., *Papers on Class, Hegemony and Party: The Communist University of London*.
London: Lawrence and Wishart, 1977.

Jameson, Fredric. *Marxism and Form: Twentieth Century Dialectical Theories of Literature*. Princeton: Princeton University Press, 1971.

Williams, Raymond. *Marxism and Literature*. Oxford: Oxford University Press, 1977.

BIRMINGHAM CENTER FOR CONTEMPORARY CULTURAL STUDIES (BCCCS). Founded in 1964 at Birmingham University in England, the BCCCS was initially under the directorship of Richard Hoggart, who emphasized the theoretical work he had begun in his study *The Uses of Literacy* (1957). Modeled after F. R. Leavis' and *Scrutiny's* work on the cultural contexts of literary works, Hoggart's—and consequently the BCCCS's—approach to CULTURAL STUDIES stressed the principal role that literary analysis played in evaluations and even definitions of culture. In his lecture, "Schools of English and Contemporary Society," inaugurating the center and its agenda, Hoggart stated that "work in Contemporary Cultural Studies can be divided into three parts: one is, roughly, historical and philosophical; another is, again roughly, sociological; the third—which will be the most important—is the literary critical."

In 1968 Stuart Hall replaced Hoggart as director of the center, and for a time under Hall, center work concentrated on " 'neglected' materials drawn from popular culture and the mass media," which were to help provide "important evidence of the new stresses and directions of contemporary culture," and did not "widely pursue" literary studies "as such," though since the late 1970s it has "once again been able to find a serious basis for this work." During that decade between 1968 and 1978, the general interests of the center shifted from emphasizing analyses of "texts and cultural forms" to studies of "practices and institutions." It was in this decade that the center, which had originally been a part of the English department at the University of Birmingham, was made independent, though it remains in the Faculty of the Arts at the university. It was also during this period that the center began to admit students with social sciences backgrounds as well as those with literary training.

Although the influx of social scientists into the school helped to alter the direction of the center as it became increasingly involved in topics that had traditionally been considered within the realm of sociology, members of the center did not wholeheartedly accept conventional sociological methods of investigations, which they felt to be too constraining. Increasingly, center members found themselves drawn to the then "neglected" Germanic tradition of classical sociology—especially the works of Max Weber and Georg Simmel. A short time later, when translations of the literary-historical works of Georg Lukács, Walter Benjamin, and the FRANKFURT SCHOOL began to appear in conjunction with works such as Lucien Goldmann's *The Hidden God* and Jean-Paul Sartre's

Question of Method, the BCCCS moved away from what might be termed "empirical social science" and decidedly toward the intricate legacy of Western Marxism.

In the years since Hall's departure as director (1979), the center has continued to affiliate itself with certain strains of Marxist thinking, especially the works of Louis Althusser. Under recent directors Richard Johnson and Jorge Lorrain, emphasis has moved from textual analysis to historical studies. The center has been especially notable for its theoretical and analytical work on SUBCULTURES, COLONIALISM, and POSTCOLONIALISM, and feminism. A number of important scholars, including Dick Hebdige, Dorothy Hobson, David Morely, Phil Cohen, Charlotte Brundson, Angela McRobbie, Paul Willis, Iain Chambers, Janice Winship, and to an extent even Raymond Williams, have in some way been affiliated with the BCCCS and its work. See also CULTURAL MATERIALISM.

Brantlinger, Patrick. *Crusoe's Footprints: Cultural Studies in Britain and America.* New York: Routledge, 1990.

Hall, Stuart. *Culture, Media, Language; Working Papers in Cultural Studies, 1972–79.* London: Hutchinson, 1980.

Hoggart, Richard. *Uses of Literacy.* London: Chatto and Windus, 1957.

Turner, Graeme. *British Cultural Studies: An Introduction.* Boston: Unwin Hyman, 1990.

BISEXUALITY. Bisexuality is commonly used to designate the state of having both heterosexual and homosexual desires. In psychoanalytic theory it often refers to the undifferentiated nature of infantile sexuality and to the condition of hysteria in (female) adults. Traditional psychoanalysts tend to see "normal" development proceeding away from bisexuality. This is not the case for a number of feminists. Hélène Cixous, for example, sees bisexuality as not only origin but goal, which the heroic among us may regain. Cixous opposes it less to homosexuality in the usual sense than to the "monosexuality" of men, for whom sex—whether with women or men—is focused primarily on the phallus, to the exclusion of female desires. Bisexuality, by contrast, is a state of inclusion, complexity, openness, variety. Calling the usual definition of bisexuality "asexual" (two halves making a neutral whole), Cixous introduces a definition of an "other bisexuality" as the presence of both sexes, the multiplication of pleasures. At this point in history, she argues, women are closer to such bisexuality than men, though it is latent in boys as well as girls. More recently, Judith Butler has questioned the idea that bisexuality is "natural," prelinguistic and original; she identifies it instead as a linguistic construct that works negatively to limit our sense of sexual possibilities, defining some as normal, others as deviant. See also ÉCRITURE FEMININE, JOUISSANCE.

Butler, Judith. *Gender Trouble: Feminism and the Subversion of Identity*. New York: Routledge, 1990.
Cixous, Hélène. "The Laugh of the Medusa." In Elaine Marks and Isabelle de Courtivron, eds., *New French Feminisms*. Trans. Keith Cohen and Paula Cohen. Amherst: University of Massachusetts Press, 1980.
—, and Catherine Clément. *The Newly Born Woman*. Trans. Betsy Wing. Minneapolis: University of Minnesota Press, 1986.

BLACK AESTHETIC. First articulated by Amiri Baraka (LeRoi Jones) in "The Myth of Negro Literature" (1962), the concept of a black aesthetic signals the reversal of previous understandings of African-American artistic production. Whereas earlier critics called for the integration of black art into mainstream America, black aestheticians demanded that African-American artists look not to the white middle class for their artistic criteria, but to their own unique and vibrant culture. As formulated by the critic and poet Larry Neal, the black aesthetic "proposes a separate symbolism, mythology, critique, and iconology." Privileging the vernacular, and relying on the example set by black jazz musicians, the black aesthetic is a profoundly nonassimilationist concept—insisting that black culture alone is enough to produce and legitimate works of African-American art. See also BLACK ARTS MOVEMENT, VERNACULAR.

Baker, Houston A., Jr. *The Journey Back: Issues in Black Literature and Criticism*. Chicago: University of Chicago Press, 1980.
—. *Blues, Ideology, and Afro-American Literature: A Vernacular Theory*. Chicago: University of Chicago Press, 1984.
Baraka, Amiri. "The Myth of Negro Literature." In *Home, Social Essays*. New York: William Morrow, 1966.
Gayle, Addison, Jr., ed. *The Black Aesthetic*. New York: Doubleday, 1971.

BLACK ARTS MOVEMENT. Exemplified by Amiri Baraka's founding of the Harlem Black Arts Repertory Theatre/School in 1965, and based upon an adherence to the BLACK AESTHETIC, the Black Arts Movement was designed to produce and legitimate black art according to purely black standards and ideals. Led by Amiri Baraka (LeRoi Jones) and Larry Neal in the early and mid-sixties, it was, according to Neal, "the aesthetic and spiritual sister of the Black Power concept." Hostile to white middle-class notions of artistic production, the writers and critics of this movement hoped to create an autonomous and highly political group of black artists, who would work through their art to combat racism and societal inequity. Directly addressing black audiences, this movement marked a profound shift in the ongoing debate between integrationist and separatist ideology, and was a major force in creating the populist atmosphere of the late sixties and early seventies. See also BLACK CULTURAL NATION-ALISM.

Baker, Houston A., Jr. *Blues, Ideology, and Afro-American Literature: A Vernacular Theory.* Chicago: University of Chicago Press, 1984.
Neal, Larry. "The Black Arts Movement." In Addison Gayle, Jr., ed., *The Black Aesthetic.* New York: Doubleday, 1971.
Smith, David Lionel. "The Black Arts Movement and Its Critics." *American Literary History* 3, 1991.

BLACK CULTURAL NATIONALISM. In contrast to those black artists of the 1950s who believed that America would one day fulfill its promises of freedom and equality, black artists and critics of the 1960s and early 1970s proclaimed that it was "Nation time," thus inaugurating the black cultural nationalist agenda. First articulated in Amiri Baraka's "Black is a Country," the nationalist ideology asserted that black Americans must declare for themselves a separate and sovereign state, based on the premise that "blackness" constitutes grounds for nationhood. This new nation would be founded upon cultural and political values antithetical to those of white America, thus realizing the goal of complete freedom from Western racism. Informed by Marxism, black nationalism was a major force in both the black arts movement and the black power movement until its gradual decline in the mid-1970s. See also BLACK AESTHETIC, BLACK ARTS MOVEMENT.

Baker, Houston A., Jr. *The Journey Back: Issues in Black Literature and Criticism.* Chicago: University of Chicago Press, 1980.
—. *Blues, Ideology, and Afro-American Literature: A Vernacular Theory.* Chicago: University of Chicago Press, 1984.
Baraka, Amiri. "Black is a Country." In *Home, Social Essays.* New York: William Morrow, 1966.

BLACK FEMINIST CRITICISM. *Black feminist criticism* generally refers to literary, social, and cultural analysis written from a feminist (or womanist) perspective that takes the writings, history, and lives of black women as its primary subject. Though black feminism has roots that extend back at least into the nineteenth century, the current resurgence of black feminist criticism stems in part from the failure of the civil rights movement of the 1960s and the feminist movement of the 1970s to address the concerns of black women. Early anthologies such as *This Bridge Called My Back* (1981), *All the Women Are White, All the Blacks Are Men, but Some of Us Are Brave* (1982), and *Home Girls* (1983) helped formulate the agenda of grassroots black feminism while also stimulating interest in black feminist scholarship in the academy.

One of the first problems faced by practitioners of academic black feminist criticism was, as Deborah McDowell wrote in her influential 1980 essay, the need "to formulate some clear definitions of what Black feminist criticism is"—for example, whether or not persons other than black women could write black feminist criticism. McDowell's own proposed definition (which answered "yes" to this question) was later praised by Hazel Carby for its call to study works in their historical context, but criticized for its suggestion that work by black women not written from a feminist perspective might be considered black feminist criticism. McDowell's essay was itself a response to Barbara Smith's "Toward a Black Feminist Criticism" (1977), and both were important catalysts for the subsequent outpouring of black feminist criticism in the academy. In conjunction with contemporary black women fiction writers and poets, Smith, McDowell, and Carby (along with Barbara Christian, Claudia Tate, Mary Helen Washington, Trudier Harris, Hortense Spillers, Valerie Smith, Susan Willis, Mae Henderson, Henry Louis Gates, and many others) have worked to recover and reprint "lost" writings by black women, to establish a black women's literary tradition (while simultaneously questioning the concept of "tradition"), and to encourage scholarship about this literature.

In recent years many other critics have joined them in discussing the difficulty of formulating a black feminist aesthetic, in exploring the relationship between aesthetic and social/political criticism, in debating the distinction often made between literary "criticism" and literary "theory," and in examining the ways that black feminist criticism/theory intersects with white feminist, African-American, and lesbian criticism and theory. Their work has both enabled and been enabled by a more widespread shift of attention toward black women in the humanities and social sciences. Historians Gerda Lerner, Paula Giddings, Jacqueline Jones, Elizabeth Fox-Genovese, Deborah Gray White, Rosalyn Terborg-Penn, social critics Angela Davis and bell hooks, and sociologist Patricia Hill Collins, to name only a few, have laid the groundwork for black feminist scholarship in other disciplines. The degree varies to which the work of these scholars is responsive to the social exigencies of black women outside the academy; by and large, however, the intellectuals engaged in black feminist criticism are motivated by a desire not only to remedy the omission of black women from the academy (both as scholars and as subjects of scholarship), but also to combat the multiple forms of oppression that black women still confront. See also CONJURING.

Carby, Hazel. *Reconstructing Womanhood: The Emergence of the Afro-American Woman Novelist.* New York: Oxford University Press, 1987.

Giddings, Paula. *When and Where I Enter: The Impact of Black Women on Race and Sex in America.* New York: William Morrow, 1984.

hooks, bell. *Ain't I a Woman.* Boston: South End Press, 1981.

Hull, Gloria, Patricia Bell Scott, and Barbara Smith, eds. *All the Women Are White, All the Blacks Are Men, But Some of Us Are Brave.* Old Westbury, N.Y.: Feminist Press, 1982.

McDowell, Deborah. "New Directions for Black Feminist Criticism." In Elaine Showalter, ed., *The New Feminist Criticism.* New York: Pantheon, 1985.

Smith, Barbara. "Toward a Black Feminist Criticism." In Elaine Showalter, ed., *The New Feminist Criticism.* New York: Pantheon, 1985.

BLUES AESTHETIC. A term introduced to literary study by Houston A. Baker, Jr. in his book, *Blues, Ideology, and Afro-American Literature, blues aesthetic* refers to the ways that the structures and traditions of blues music have provided African Americans with strategies for creative resistance in the face of slavery, racism, and poverty. The blues aesthetic denotes a vibrant cultural network, which mediates oppositions such as poverty and abundance, creativity and commerce. Polymorphous, neverending, rich with possibilities, the blues speak of absence, but their rhythms always suggest change. Claiming the blues as an aesthetic capable of "liberating rhythms," Baker turns to literature to analyze those moments in African-American texts when black characters perform the tragedies of their lives even as they simultaneously "sing" their revolutionary hope for dignity and a better existence. See also THE CHANGING SAME, SIGNIFYIN(G).

Baker, Houston A., Jr. *Blues, Ideology, and Afro-American Literature: A Vernacular Theory*. Chicago: University of Chicago Press, 1984.

BRICOLAGE. In his book *The Savage Mind* (*La Pensée Sauvage*), the French anthropologist Claude Lévi-Strauss uses the term *bricolage* (breeKOLAHZH) to describe the kind of intellectual activity represented by the myths and rites of tribal societies. Though adept at performing a wide variety of tasks, the bricoleur must work with a limited stock of materials and tools. Thus, he or she learns to make do with the leftover products of earlier efforts, so that ends now come to play the role of means. Lévi-Strauss distinguishes the activity of the bricoleur from those of the modern scientist, the engineer, and the artist; however, it is this description of an improvisatory activity performed by a kind of intellectual jack-of-all-trades with whatever happens to be available that has caught the imagination of many contemporary theorists, who view the practice of theory as itself a form of bricolage performed with concepts and ideas retrieved from the grand theories of the past. While recognizing that the claims of these systems to universality have been discredited, the contemporary bricoleur prefers to work with bits and pieces of the intellectual materials that they supply, since the very possibility of creating new universal systems has become doubtful in the POSTMODERN era.

Lévi-Strauss, Claude. *The Savage Mind*. Trans. George Weidenfeld and Nicolson Ltd., eds. Julian Pitt-Rivers and Ernest Gellner. Chicago: University of Chicago Press, 1966.

BUTCH/FEMME. The term *butch/femme* is used to describe lesbian couples in which the roles correspond roughly to those in traditional heterosexual relationships. Butches may adopt habits commonly designated masculine, cross-dress, and/or assume the dominant position in relation to their partners. Femmes may exaggerate their femininity, as opposed to the stereotype of the "mannish lesbian." Butch/femme relationships have been most famously portrayed in Radclyffe Hall's novel *The Well of Loneliness* (1928), and numerous discussions of the lesbian in literature have centered on Hall's controversial classic. Because the butch-femme paradigm has been used to caricature and stigmatize lesbians, and because it appears to reproduce patriarchal and heterosexist gender roles, many lesbian feminists of the 1970s condemned it, insisting that women-loving-women create new, more equitable models for their relationships, in defiance of heterosexual norms. In the early 1980s, however, lesbians identifying themselves as butch or femme as well as feminist argued that the model continues to reflect the experience of many lesbians, that it represents a range of valid and various sexual identities, and that it does not simply impersonate men's power over women. The effect of this less restrictive view of lesbian sexuality has been to open up the feminist discussion of sexuality generally, and pave the way for richer, more complex readings of lesbian texts. See also CAMP, LESBIAN CRITICISM.

Case, Sue Ellen. "Toward a Butch-Femme Aesthetic." *Discourse* 11:1, 1989.

Hall, Radclyffe. *The Well of Loneliness*. London: Virago, 1982.

Hollibaugh, Amber, and Cherrie Moraga. "What We're Rollin' Around in Bed With: Sexual Silences in Feminism." In Ann Snitow, Christine Stansell, and Sharon Thompson, eds., *Powers of Desire: The Politics of Sexuality*. New York: Monthly Review Press, 1983.

Nestle, Joan. "The Fem Question." In Carol S. Vance, ed., *Pleasure and Danger:Exploring Female Sexuality*. Boston: Routledge, 1984.

Newton, Esther. "The Mythic Mannish Lesbian: Radclyffe Hall and the New Woman." In Martin Bauml Duberman, Martha Vicinus, and George Chauncey, Jr., eds., *Hidden from History: Reclaiming the Gay and Lesbian Past*. New York: New American Library, 1989.

C

CALL AND RESPONSE. *Call and response* is an African-American vernacular form brought to the attention of literary scholars by Robert Stepto in his book, *From Behind the Veil*. Originating in the rhythmic lead-and-chorus relationship of a spiritual leader and his or her congregation, call and response serves as a dialogue in and of community—the cry of one voice eliciting the legitimating reply of others, the collective response underwriting the power of the speaker. Call and response names a conversation of opposed yet complimentary cultural voices, which promotes the authorization and empowerment of African-American subjectivity in an oppressive racist environment. Robert Stepto and Henry Louis Gates, Jr. have shown the importance of the call-and-response paradigm as a model for understanding the intertextual connections between texts such as *The Souls of Black Folk* and *Invisible Man*; and in a recent essay on Jean Toomer's *Cane*, Barbara Bowen has demonstrated the way that call and response operates as a rhetorical figure within individual African-American literary works. See also THE CHANGING SAME, SIGNIFYIN(G).

Bowen, Barbara. "Untroubled Voice: Call and Response in *Cane*." In Henry Louis Gates, Jr., ed., *Black Literature and Literary Theory*. New York: Methuen, 1984.

Gates, Henry Louis, Jr. *The Signifyin(g) Monkey: A Theory of African-American Literary Criticism*. New York: Oxford University Press, 1988.

Stepto, Robert. *From Behind the Veil: A Study of Afro-American Narrative*. Urbana: University of Illinois Press, 1979.

CAMERA ANGLE. See ANGLE.

CAMP. To esteem a cultural object for its camp value is to relish that which is exaggerated, artificial, or even crass in modern culture. The camp attitude combines appreciation and condescension, celebrating the most overblown works of high culture and the most shameless products of mass culture alike. Cultural objects that are valued for their campiness were generally not intended to be percieved in this way; rather, in their original setting, most such objects were intended to be read "straight," whether as art or as embodiments of their owner's status. Although, like some versions of MODERNISM, the origins of the camp attitude are in late nineteenth-century AESTHETICISM, it represents an alternative to high modernist seriousness and has affinities with certain versions of POSTMODERNISM in its openness to mass culture, even though that openness often involves an element of arrogance toward the objects that it adopts. Moreover, since the time of Oscar Wilde, camp has been a familiar part of many urban gay cultures; and gay critics have promoted it as a corrective to what they view as the excessively deterministic view of the subject in some postmodernist theories. Thus, Sue Ellen Case has argued that the exaggerated play of gendered identities among working-class lesbians offers a more active and creative model of gay subjectivity than do theories that describe the subject as constituted entirely by cultural forces that are entirely beyond the control of the individual. See also APPROPRIATION, GAY CRITICISM.

Case, Sue Ellen. "Toward a Butch-Femme Aesthetic." *Discourse* 11:1, 1989.

Ross, Andrew. "Uses of Camp." In *No Respect: Intellectuals and Popular Culture.* New York: Routledge, 1989.

Sontag, Susan. "Notes on 'Camp.' " *Against Interpretation.* New York: Dell, 1966.

CANON/*CANON* FORMATION. The term *canon,* from the Greek word for ruler or measuring stick, originally referred to the books of the Old and New Testaments of the Christian Bible that were approved by church authorities as the revealed word of God, the Holy Scriptures. Several books that were related to the scriptures but not included in approved versions of the Bible became known as the apocrypha, a term often specifically applied to the eleven books of the Roman Catholic Bible that are not included in the biblical canon of Protestants.

Canon has been adapted to literary criticism to designate those works and authors whom the literary establishment, through a loose consensus, considers "major." Although many literary critics seem to regard the canon as rather hidebound and resistive to change, in fact it has always been very mutable. Certainly such authors as Milton, Shakespeare, Chaucer, and Wordsworth occupy a central place in the canon of English literature, and it is unlikely they will lose their standing. Yet other authors, such as John Donne, Aphra Behn, or George Meredith have been more or less recognized as central according to the reception of their work by critics at specific times.

The process by which an author or work is established as "canonical" is called "canon formation." This is by no means a formal procedure but rather an accumulation of a number of factors, including repeated reference to an author or a work by critics and writers, the currency of an author or work within the general community, and the inclusion of the author or a work in school and college curricula. In recent years, as literary and theoretical studies have become increasingly interested in the institutional and ideological implications of distinguishing between "major" and "minor" works and authors, the process of canon formation has come under considerable attack. The most common charge has been that the canon of "great books" in literary study has been formed primarily by a privileged, elite group of white male critics and teachers. The result is that the canon reproduces the shared interests of the members of that group and excludes the works and voices of other significant but marginalized groups such as women, homosexuals, or people of color. Also at issue are such concepts as TRADITION and literary merit. For many who oppose the standard canon of humanist works, roughly from Plato to Freud, tradition and merit are merely ways of putting IDEOLOGY to work and of reproducing the very intellectual conditions that marginalized excluded works in the first place.

Because of the influence of institutional practices in canon formation, much of the battle between defenders and detractors of the traditional canon has been fought in educational journals and in curriculum committee meetings on college and university campuses. One of the many approaches to broadening the canon has been to expand the "core" humanities curricula of many undergraduate institutions to include a greater variety of works by those who had customarily been considered minor and excluded from study. Another approach has been to establish parallel, oppositional canons, say, of work by women, African Americans, or gays and lesbians. A more radical position has been to repudiate the concept of canon entirely and to undertake humanistic studies in a nonelitist, more eclectic way that refuses arbitrary distinctions of high and low culture. Defenders of the standard canon often agree to its expansion, while insisting that however many formerly excluded texts make it onto syllabi, the traditional canonical texts are those upon which most attention must be directed, for it is those texts that have been fundamental in the shaping of Western culture. See also CLASSIC, COUNTER-MEMORY, CULTURAL LITERACY, MULTICULTURALISM.

Altieri, Charles. "An Idea and Ideal of a Literary Canon." *Critical Inquiry* 10, 1983.
Arnold, Matthew. "The Study of Poetry." In *The Complete Works of Matthew Arnold*, vol. 9. Ed. R. H. Super. Ann Arbor: University of Michigan Press, 1960–77.
Bloom, Allan. *The Closing of the American Mind*. New York: Simon and Schuster, 1987.
Bloom, Harold, *The Western Canon*. New York: Harcourt Brace, 1994.
Fish, Stanley. *Is there a Text in This Class?* Cambridge, Mass.: Harvard University Press, 1980.
Hirsch, E. D. *Cultural Literacy*. Boston: Houghton Mifflin, 1987.
Kermode, Frank. "Institutional Control of Interpretation." *Salmagundi* 43, 1979.
Lauter, Paul. "Race and Gender in the Shaping of the American Literary Canon." *Feminist Studies* 9, 1983.
Leavis, F.R. *Revaluation: Tradition and Development in English Poetry*. London: Chatto and Windus, 1963.
Smith, Barbara Herrnstein. *Contingencies of Value*. Cambridge, Mass.: Harvard University Press, 1988.

CARNIVALESQUE. A term coined by the Russian critic Mikhail Bakhtin, *carnivalesque* (CARnivuhlESK) refers to a literary mode that subverts and liberates the assumptions of the traditional literary CANON through humor and chaos. In his *Rabelais and His World*, Bakhtin likens the carnivalesque in literature to the type of activity that often takes place in the carnivals of popular culture, particularly the lampooning and overturning of traditional hierarchies and values by mingling "high culture" with the profane. Forms like the novel provide a space for such carnivalization, and as a result allow for alternative voices within the text. This, for Bakhtin, is the site of resistance to the authority of literary culture and the place where cultural, and potentially political, change can take place. See also DIALOGISM.

Bakhtin, Mikhail. *Rabelais and His World*. Trans. Helene Iswolsky. Cambridge, Mass.: MIT Press, 1968.

CASTRATION COMPLEX. In Freudian psychoanalysis, the term *castration complex* refers to an UNCONSCIOUS group of ideas that appears in response to the child's confrontation with the fact of anatomical difference between the sexes, which he or she explains with the hypothesis that the woman's penis has been cut off. The castration complex has a different structure and sequel in the two sexes. The male child responds with fear of castration, viewing it as the father's response to his sexual activity; this "castration anxiety" becomes a permanent feature of his mental life and can be symbolized by any threat to the wholeness of the body, such as the blinding of Oedipus (see OEDIPUS COMPLEX). By contrast, the female child views the absence of the penis as an affliction that produces the emotion of "penis envy." This absence must be denied or remedied by acquiring a penis "within oneself"—that is, by having a child. Nevertheless, according to Freud, women experience the castration complex in a less focused and more attenuated way, and their oedipal concerns are less powerful. In consequence, he maintained, their sense of justice and ethics is also less developed.

The French psychoanalyst Jacques Lacan built upon the Freudian model, but understood it to be also a problem of language. For Lacan, the PHALLUS is the chief signifier, and man's fear of castration is an intellectual construction that expresses his anxiety about the rupture between the state of nature and its representation, that is, between language—the SIGNIFIER—and everything else—the SIGNIFIED. According to Lacan, it is with the child's entry into language that the unconscious itself comes into being (see NAME-OF-THE-FATHER, SYMBOLIC).

The Freudian account of the female child's reaction to the castration complex has proven highly controversial; and many feminist theorists have rejected it as symptomatic of Freud's own patriarchal assumptions. Rather than being defined by their lack of a penis, Hélène Cixous has argued, women are differentiated by their "affirmation," identified, like Joyce's Molly Bloom, by the word "yes," instead of by a "negative void." Other writers, like Gilles Deleuze and Félix Guattari, reject the entire theory of the Oedipus complex as a reinforcement of capitalism in the realm of personal relations (see DETERRITORIALIZATION, RHIZOME, SCHIZO-ANALYSIS).

Cixous, Hélène. "The Laugh of the Medusa." In Elaine Marks and Isabelle de Courtivron, eds., New French Feminisms. Trans. Keith Cohen and Paula Cohen. Amherst: University of Massachusetts Press, 1980.

Deleuze, Gilles, and Guattari, Félix. Anti-Oedipus: Capitalism and Szhizophrenia. Trans. Robert Hurley, Mark Seem, and Helen R. Lane. New York: Viking, 1977.

Freud, Sigmund. "The Passing of the Oedipus Complex." In Standard Edition of the Complete Psychological Works of Sigmund Freud, vol. 19. Trans. James Strachey. London: Hogarth Press and Institute of Psycho-Analysis, 1974.

Lacan, Jacques. "The Agency of the Letter in the Unconscious or Reason Since Freud." In Ecrits. Trans. Alan Sheridan. New York: Norton, 1977.

CATACHRESIS. Catachresis (KATuh**KREE**sis) is the misapplication of a word, often in a strained or mixed METAPHOR or in an implied metaphor. For example, in a line from the famous "To be or not to be" soliloquy, Hamlet wonders whether it is advisable "to take arms against a sea of troubles." Obviously, one cannot take arms against the sea, but the effectiveness of the line lies, in part, in precisely that impossibility and the futility of its attempt. Thus, catachresis may be simply sloppy diction (e.g., "He boiled down the argument to a string of assertions"), or may be employed to underscore the surprising aspect of a particular metaphor.

CATHEXIS. *Cathexis* (kaTHEKsis)—a translation of the German *Besetzung*, or "occupation"—is a Freudian term designating the attachment of psychic energy to an idea. It is a feature of psychic life that certain ideas, groups of ideas, objects, or images become charged through association with pleasant or unpleasant experiences. When an experience is traumatic, it may be repressed, and all that remains available to consciousness is an emotional or sometimes even physical reaction to something that has become associated with the experience through a psychic mechanism such as DISPLACEMENT (see also ABREACTION). In such cases, a cathexis of the associated idea is said to have taken place.

Freud, Sigmund. *The Interpretation of Dreams.* Trans. and ed. James Strachey. London: Hogarth Press, 1953.

—. *Beyond the Pleasure Principle.* Rev. ed. Trans. and ed. James Strachey. New York: Liveright, 1961.

—, and Joseph Breuer. *Studies in Hysteria.* Trans. A. A. Brill. Boston: Beacon Press, 1961.

THE CHANGING SAME. The changing same is a theory of "generational connections" in African-American culture first articulated by Amiri Baraka and later developed by Deborah E. McDowell. Emphasizing the importance of maintaining positive, nonantagonistic cultural genealogies, the changing same conceptualizes ways of preserving African-American traditions in a harsh, ever-changing world. In his essay "The Changing Same," an examination of the state of rhythm-and-blues in the 1960s, Baraka argues for the continuity of the black musical tradition through history, contending that contemporary African-American music repeats and reasserts (albeit with some variation) structures and patterns of African religious culture—CALL AND RESPONSE, for example. Similarly, in her article on *The Color Purple* and *Iola Leroy*, Deborah E. McDowell stresses the ways that Alice Walker inherited and carried on the rhetorical language and narrative concerns expressed in Frances Harper's late nineteenth-century text. See also SIGNIFYIN(G).

Baraka, Imamu Amiri. *Black Music.* New York: William Morrow, 1968.

McDowell, Deborah E. "The Changing Same: Generational Connections and Black Women Novelists." *New Literary History* 18, 1987.

CHARACTER. The term *character* describes a figure or personality who appears in a literary work. Although characters need not always be representations of human beings, they are almost invariably anthropomorphic in some respect. The study of literary characters is related to the more general question of the SUBJECT and the politics of INDIVIDUALISM, with which the history of the novel of REALISM is bound up, since it is so often about the building of character. For example, the subgenre of the bildungsroman (or novel of education), popular in the nineteenth century, is concerned with the development and stabilization of the right values and understanding of the protagonist, or main character, as in *David Copperfield* or *Great Expectations* by Charles Dickens.

Some POSTSTRUCTURALIST critics and POSTMODERNIST novelists have announced the death of character. This is consistent with the calling into question of man, who is no longer credited with the kind of AGENCY or fixity and unity HUMANISM attributed to him, just as the "character," or values and worldview to which he was to aspire have also been critiqued. Thus, the French theorist Roland Barthes has declared in *S/Z* that what is "obsolescent" in the contemporary novel "is the character; what can no longer be written is the Proper Name." This poststructuralist understanding of character has underscored the problems with discussing a character as if it were a real person, rather than a construct of the text.

Barthes, Roland. *S/Z*. Trans. Richard Miller. New York: Hill and Wang, 1974.

CHIASMUS. Chiasmus is named for the Greek letter *chi* (x), and it refers to a rhetorical criss-crossing in which the syntax or sense of the first of two parallel phrases is reversed in the second. A common eighteenth-century poetic device, chiasmus is illustrated by Alexander Pope's line, "Works without show, and without pomp presides," in which the placement of the verb is reversed. Chiasmus often uses the repetition of words in the phrases, but does not depend upon it.

CHICAGO CRITICS. The Chicago Critics or Chicago School was a group of critics associated with the University of Chicago from the 1930s to the 1950s whose best-known members included R. S. Crane, Elder Olson, Richard McKeon, Norman MacLean, and Wayne Booth. Because they were influence by Aristotle's *Poetics* in their concern with the principles of literary construction and literary esthetics, they were also known as the NEO-ARISTOTELIANS. The manifesto of the school is *Critics and Criticism: Ancient and Modern* (1952), edited by R. S. Crane, which includes twenty articles by six different critics and focuses on the limitations of the then-current NEW CRITICISM, the pluralist nature of the criticism of the past, and the reading strategies appropriate for a good contemporary literary criticism. Some of their methodology was similar to that of the New Criticism, which developed at about the same time and which was also founded on the assumption that an interpretation of a text must be grounded in a close analysis of its formal qualities rather than in the investigation of its place in literary history. However, the Chicago Critics believed that New Criticism was too restrictive because in its readings it bracketed (or claimed to bracket) as external, and therefore incidental, certain considerations that the Chicago Critics found important—principally, those relating to literary theory itself but also those relating to the intentions or life and times of a text's author. The Chicago Critics were pluralists who believed that different texts demanded different critical approaches, which they thought the history of literary theory and practice clearly demonstrated—and that meant nothing could be bracketed in advance as extraneous or irrelevant.

In its day, the school did not have much impact beyond the University of Chicago and witnessed the ascendancy of the New Criticism it critiqued. However, the pluralism it advocated has continued to be championed by Wayne Booth, although he is also associated with READER RESPONSE CRITICISM, having shifted from a text-centered to a reader-centered approach. Booth has been very influential as a spokesman for pluralism, participating in a number of lively debates on the topic in the 1970s and 1980s, some of which have appeared in *Critical Inquiry*, the journal of literary theory founded in 1974 by a second generation of pluralist Chicago Critics. See also PLURALISM.

Crane, Ronald Salmon, ed. *Critics and Criticism, Ancient and Modern.* Chicago: University of Chicago Press, 1952.

CINEMA VERITÉ. The signature style of French NEW WAVE filmmakers, cinema verité (**SAN**ayMuh VAree**TAY**) aimed to create a sense of immediacy that would stand in contrast to the artifice characteristic of mainstream studio techniques of shooting and editing. Typical of cinema verité are such devices as the handheld camera, characters who speak directly to the camera, and scenes filmed on location that incorporate the nonactors who normally occupy such venues. These techniques were used both in documentary, such as the work of Frederick Wiseman, and in nondocumentary work, such as the early films of Jean-Luc Godard and François Truffaut.

CIRCULATION. A term that has been popularized by Stephen Greenblatt, *circulation* designates the kind of activity that he intends his "poetics of culture" to study. According to Greenblatt, what circulates in English Renaissance culture, between the theater of Shakespeare and the rest of society, is "social energy." Such energy originates nowhere but has effects everywhere, and Greenblatt describes its movement as "a subtle, elusive set of exchanges, a network of trades and trade-offs, a jostling of competing representations, a negotiation between joint-stock companies." To study such an amorphous object, Greenblatt recommends a highly detailed act of reconstruction, which rejects the notion of an autonomous aesthetic sphere and takes account of the larger social dimension of literature. See also NEW HISTORICISM.

Greenblatt, Stephen. *Shakespearean Negotiations: The Circulation of Social Energy in Renaissance England*. Berkeley: University of California Press, 1988.

CLASS CONSCIOUSNESS. In Marxist theory, *class consciousness* refers to the awareness on the part of a social class of their situation and collective interests, an awareness that, according to Marx, was achieved with much struggle by the bourgeoisie at the time of the French Revolution and played an important role in the empowerment of that class. The question of proletarian class consciousness is therefore crucial to the Marxist theory of revolution and has been a subject of debate among later Marxists. The most influential position has been that of Lenin, who held that the necessary degree of consciousness can only be brought to the proletariat by the intellectuals of a revolutionary party. By contrast, other thinkers, such as Rosa Luxemburg, stressed the role of experience, and especially the experience of class struggle, in the formation of class consciousness. Perhaps the most interestingly nuanced position, however, belongs to Georg Lukács, whose ideas were rejected by Lenin as metaphysical, although they are in fact a philosophical elaboration of the Leninist position. Lukács argued that class consciousness must be conceived in the context of the social TOTALITY. From this standpoint, it becomes possible to view the proletariat as a COLLECTIVE SUBJECT and to "impute" thoughts and feelings to that subject appropriate to its situation within the whole. The historical actions of the class can be understood only in terms of this consciousness, even though it is neither the consciousness of any one typical individual nor the sum of all the thoughts and feelings experienced by members of the class. By becoming aware of this consciousness, the proletariat becomes capable of politically significant action.

Lukács, Georg. *History and Class Consciousness.* Trans. Rodney Livingstone. Cambridge, Mass.: MIT Press, 1971.

CLASSIC. The term *classic* traditionally refers to a work of the highest class, one recognized by a consensus of readers to be superior and permanently capable of enriching the human spirit, like the original "classics" of ancient Greece and Rome. According to this absolutist definition, those works that survive the test of time (one hundred years, according to Samuel Johnson) do so because they possess inherent value, which transcends time and place. The more recent and opposing viewpoint is that of the relativists, who critique traditional notions of canon formation on political grounds. Far from being a neutral process, the selection of classics is, in this view, a function of ideology and institutional factors. A work becomes a classic not because of its absolute intrinsic value, but rather because it reflects the political interests and meets the cultural needs of a dominant class. Finally, some critics have attempted to stake out compromise positions, like Frank Kermode, who argues that a classic is defined by its richness. For him, such works offer a surplus of interpretive possibilities, which exceed the efforts of any generation of interpreters.

Kermode, Frank. *The Classic: Literary Images of Permanence and Change.* New York: Viking, 1975.
Smith, Barbara Herrnstein. *Contingencies of Value.* Cambridge, Mass.: Harvard University Press, 1988.

CLASSIC HOLLYWOOD CINEMA. *Classic Hollywood cinema* is the term used to describe films produced by Hollywood motion picture companies that pioneered the use of linear narrative and related techniques in editing. Although many of these techniques were introduced during the era of silent films, they still form the basis for a large proportion of the movies produced by Hollywood studios up to this day.

One of the first films to employ linear narrative was Edwin S. Porter's *The Great Train Robbery* (1903). Narrative techniques were expanded and refined in the silent films of such directors as D. W. Griffith and Cecil B. DeMille. These techniques included fades, the combiboth long shots and close-ups within a single scene, parallel cutting to combine spacially disparate parts of a single action, and strong contrasts between light and dark. Also important was the development of the basic continuity principles (e.g., the use of shots/reverse shots, or establishing point of view from both axes of action), which became the standard style for Hollywood film by the 1920s. See also CUT, SHOT.

CODE. The term *code* refers to the shared set of rules, conventions, restraints, and norms that permit the communication of a message between a receiver and a sender. Primarily used in semiotic and structural analyses, a code may be as large a shared set of rules as a language, or as exclusive as hand signals between a sender and receiver that only they can understand. For the theorist Roman Jakobson, the code is one of the six essential components to his important theory of communication. Later theorists like Umberto Eco have argued that together with its signals, a code must contain rules for a semantic system, a set of the receiver's possible behavioral responses to the message, and rules that link these systems. The act of sending a message, putting it into a particular code used by the sender but also utilized by the receiver, is called *encoding*. The reverse process, in which the receiver extracts the message, partly through a recognition of the sender's codes and partly by using his own codes, is called *decoding*. In such an analysis, pure intersubjective communication is rare. The norm is that a message is only partially communicated, since neither sender nor receiver can be fully aware of the other's entire complement of codes or their functions. Other important work, such as Roland Barthes' influential *S/Z*, draws upon the assumption held by many structuralists and semioticians that texts, including literary texts, rely upon already encoded meanings for their expression. Thus Barthes delineates five major codes in a short story by Balzac, such as the "hermeneutic" code, which establishes the suspense of the story and helps drive the narrative, and the "cultural" code, which invokes accepted social norms, values, and prejudices. See also DECODE.

Barthes, Roland. *S/Z*. Trans. Richard Miller. New York: Hill and Wang, 1974.
Eco, Umberto. *A Theory of Semiotics*. Bloomington: Indiana University Press, 1979.
Jakobson, Roman. "Closing Statement: Linguistics and Poetics." 1960.

COGITO. Cogito (**KOjeeTO**) is short for the Latin phrase "Cogito ergo sum," or, "I think, therefore I am." In the skeptical philosophy of René Descartes (1596–1650), the truth of this statement is the one thing that cannot be doubted, and the existence of the individual thinker becomes the basic proposition from which the whole of the Cartesian system is deduced. Although not Descartes' manifest intent, the effect of this procedure for those following him was to privilege the conscious and rational human mind and to place it at the top of the philosophical hierarchy, at the expense of both God and the human body. Many contemporary critics have rejected this position because it supports a belief in the individual as a sovereign SUBJECT, that is, one able to act freely and rationally, as if CONSCIOUSNESS were not conditioned by social being and fractured by UNCONSCIOUS desires. See also AGENCY, HUMANISM.

Descartes, René. *A Discourse on Method.* Trans. John Veitch. New York: E. P. Dutton, 1949.
—. *Meditations on First Philosophy.* Ed. and trans. George Heffernan. Notre Dame, Ind.: University of Notre Dame Press, 1990.
Smith, Paul. *Discerning the Subject.* Minneapolis: University of Minnesota Press, 1988.

COGNITIVE COMPETENCE/PERFORMANCE. Coined by the linguist/philosopher Noam Chomsky, cognitive competence refers to speakers' unconscious linguistic knowledge, which allows them to speak and comprehend their native language automatically, without having to consider every word or phrase. Roughly correspondent with LANGUE or the entire system and possibilities of utterance within a language, competence allows speakers to understand words and phrases they may never have heard before. Performance, similar to PAROLE, or actually produced words or phrases that have meaning, is what speakers do with their knowledge of the language; that is, the execution of an individual utterance. See also LITERARY COMPETENCE.

Chomsky, Noam. *Syntactic Structures.* New York: Mouton, 1957.
—. *Aspects of the Theory of Syntax.* Cambridge, Mass.: MIT Press, 1965.

COLLAGE. A technique that involves attaching various materials to the surface of the artwork, collage was developed in 1912 by Pablo Picasso and Georges Braque in the context of their exploration of cubism and is also characteristic of such other early twentieth-century AVANT-GARDE movements as DADA and CONSTRUCTIVISM. More recently, the concept of collage has been used by critics like Peter Bürger and Andreas Huyssen to distinguish between avant-garde and modernist tendencies in the first half of the twentieth century. Unlike works of modernism proper, collage is an assault on the integrity of the work of art in that it brings foreign materials into the space previously reserved for paint on the canvas. Since these materials include such things as newspaper clippings, collage thus forges a link between "high" art and mass culture. Closely related to the technique of collage is that of photomontage, in which disparate fragments of graphic material (photographs, printed text, etc.) are assembled and rephotographed; the result is then presented as a photographic print.

Ades, Dawn. *Photomontage*. London: Thames and Hudson, 1976.
Bürger, Peter. *Theory of the Avant-Garde*. Trans. Michael Shaw. Minneapolis: University of Minnesota Press, 1984.
Weschler, Herta. *Collage*. Trans. Robert E. Wolf. New York: Abrams, 1971.

COLLECTIVE SUBJECT. The concept of the collective subject derives from Hegelian philosophy and plays a significant role in some versions of Marxism, particularly that of Georg Lukács. If a class of people like the proletariat can be conceived of collectively as a SUBJECT, it then becomes possible to speak of CLASS CONSCIOUSNESS and to conceive of the development of that class as involving a relationship between its consciousness and the material conditions of its existence. In this usage, the collective subject is an abstraction; it does not refer to the consciousness of any specific person, nor should it be assumed that the consciousness imputed to a particular class is possessed by every member of that class; neither does this use of the term refer to the sum of individual consciousnesses within a class. See also AGENCY, IDEOLOGY.

Lukács, Georg. *History and Class Consciousness*. Trans. Rodney Livingstone. Cambridge, Mass.: MIT Press, 1971.

COLONIALISM. Colonialism is the direct political control of one country or society by another and refers first of all to historical episodes, like the long history of British rule in India. The concept of colonialism has also been of great interest to political theorists, who have sought to understand it both as a social and political phenomenon in itself and as the product of a necessary "imperialist" stage in the development of advanced capitalist countries. These latter theorists, usually Marxists, have tried with limited success to demonstrate that at a certain point in the development of capitalism it becomes necessary to export capital and seek new markets outside of the mother country among less-developed societies, which are consequently more vulnerable to occupation and exploitation. More recently, with the overthrow of many colonial regimes, a substantial body of writing has appeared that analyzes the colonial experience from the point of view of indigenous peoples. These works, which include such notable books as Frantz Fanon's *The Wretched of the Earth*, have become central to progressive political thought about the third world. See also POSTCOLONIALISM.

Barratt-Brown, Michael. *The Economics of Imperialism.* Harmondsworth, U.K.: Penguin, 1974.

Fanon, Frantz. *The Wretched of the Earth.* Trans. Constance Farrington. New York: Grove Press, 1968.

Lenin, Vladimir. *Imperialism: The Highest Stage of Capitalism.* Rev. trans. London: Lawrence and Wishart, 1948.

Marx, Karl. *Capital.* Vol. III. Moscow: Progress Publishers, 1965.

—. *Grundrisse.* Trans. Martin Nicolaus. New York: Vintage, 1973.

Warren, B. *Imperialism: Pioneer of Capitalism.* Ed. John Sender. 1980.

COMBAHEE RIVER COLLECTIVE. The Combahee River Collective is a group of feminists of color who began meeting together in Boston in 1974. The collective took its name from a military campaign conceived and led by Harriet Tubman in 1863, which freed more than 750 slaves. Initially the group focused primarily on consciousness-raising rather than political activism, though individual members were involved in a variety of causes ranging from lesbian politics to sterilization abuse. Members also formed a study group and established Kitchen Table: Women of Color Press. The Kitchen Table Press has provided a means of publication for creative writing and social criticism that might not otherwise have made it into print via a mainstream press. In April 1977 the collective issued "A Black Feminist Statement," which explains the group's history and outlines an agenda for feminists of color; the statement had a significant influence on subsequent feminist criticism, particularly in its stress on the interconnections among oppressions based upon gender, race, class, and sexual orientation. See also BLACK FEMINIST CRITICISM.

Combahee River Collective. "A Black Feminist Statement." In Cherrie Moraga and Gloria Anzaldúa, eds., *This Bridge Called My Back: Writings by Radical Women of Color.* Watertown, Mass.: Kitchen Table Press, 1981.

COMMODITY. In its most general sense, a commodity is anything that may be bought, sold, or bartered. In Marxist analyses of culture, the concept of the commodity takes on particular importance, for it is the form that products assume when the production and reproduction of the material conditions of a society are organized through exchange. As a product within a system of exchange, any commodity has two distinct properties. The first, identified by the eighteenth-century political economist Adam Smith, is use value. This refers to the commodity's ability to satisfy some human want or desire. The second of these properties is discussed by Marx and is labeled simply value, though it is sometimes referred to as EXCHANGE VALUE, to distinguish it from USE VALUE. This property is a commodity's capacity to command other commodities in exchange.

From these two properties of the commodity Marx is able to move toward a labor theory of value. All commodities may be discussed in terms of value: as use values, each commodity is unique and thus qualitatively different. Whereas a loaf of bread and a pair of socks might require the same amount of labor to be produced, they do not meet the same human needs, and so cannot be compared. On the other hand, because they both require labor to produce, they can be compared in terms of exchange value. According to Marx, when commodities confront each other in exchange, their value (the amount of labor required to produce each) becomes apparent as exchange value.

Marx refers to the labor that is expended in commodity production as "social labor." The entity produced is not consumed by the laborer, but by another who obtains it through exchange. In a society based upon commodity production, subsistence and the means of production are provided by others. Nevertheless, in such a society production *appears* private: the producer perceives the product of his labor to exist independent of society as a whole. Thus the cabinet maker perceives his cabinets as his own products, even though he depended on a number of other producers to provide him with wood and tools, and will exchange his cabinets for the means to acquire both subsistence and more materials for producing more cabinets. In such a commodity-based society, says

Marx, the complex interrelations that humans have to one another are reduced to a relation between commodities and their exchangeability. This relationship Marx calls FETISHISM, and while it is not false—the cabinetmaker's shelves do have a relation to the woodcutter's lumber—it conceals the human relation between producers.

By utilizing this concept in an analysis of cultural commodities such as literary texts, paintings, music, etc., Marxist critics have pointed out that such products can also appear to float free of human determination and take on value primarily in relation to one another. As a result, they mask the social forces that inform their representations. One goal of much Marxist criticism has been to expose the formal devices that a text employs to effect this masking.

Feltes, N. N. *Modes of Production of Victorian Novels.* Chicago: University of Chicago Press, 1986.

Marx, Karl. *Capital.* Vol. 1. Moscow: Progress Publishers, 1965.

Rubin, Isaak. *Essays on Marx's Theory of Value.* Trans. Milos Samardzija and Fredy Perlman. Detroit: Black and Red, 1972.

COMPETENCE, LITERARY. Whenever readers encounter a poem, novel, play, or any other work of literature, they bring to it certain expectations and a familiarity with the conventions that define a work as "literary." This implicit understanding of the way literature works allows a reader to make sense of a text, or as Jonathan Culler has argued, it allows the reader to read the text "*as* literature." Without this literary competence, a reader might be able to read the words of a text, and even to understand phrases and sentences within the text, but the text as a whole would be undecipherable. See also COGNITIVE COMPETENCE/PERFORMANCE, LANGUE, PAROLE, STRUCTURALISM.

Culler, Jonathan. *Structuralist Poetics: Structuralism, Linguistics, and the Study of Literature.* London: Routledge, 1975.

COMPULSION TO REPEAT, OR REPETITION COMPULSION. Freud and later psychoanalysts use this term to designate an uncontrollable need to repeat a previous experience, which the patient does not recall (see ABREACTION). Because these experiences are often neither pleasurable nor rationally motivated, the existence of the repetition compulsion posed a problem for Freud, who had earlier attempted to explain all human actions as products of either a desire for pleasure or a recognition of the demands of reality (see PLEASURE PRINCIPLE, REALITY PRINCIPLE). The repetition compulsion originates in the unconscious and expresses what Freud came to see as the fundamentally conservative nature of the instincts. Carrying this insight one step further, Freud argued that the repetition compulsion reveals a deeply seated desire to return to an earlier state of existence; moreover, since the earliest conceivable state is that of inorganic matter, he postulated a new psychic opposition between the LIFE INSTINCTS, which now include both the pleasure and reality principles, and the DEATH INSTINCTS, which seek to remove all tension and return to this inanimate state. Thus, repetition compulsions are effects of the death instincts.

Freud, Sigmund. *Beyond the Pleasure Principle*. Rev. ed. Trans. and ed. James Strachey. New York: Liveright, 1961.

—. "The Uncanny." In *Standard Edition of the Complete Psychological Works of Sigmund Freud*, vol. 17. Trans. James Strachey. London: Hogarth Press and Institute of Psycho-Analysis, 1974.

COMPULSORY HETEROSEXUALITY. In her 1980 essay of the same title, feminist poet, essayist, and activist Adrienne Rich uses this term to suggest that heterosexuality, though commonly understood as a natural and personal "preference," is actually shaped and imposed upon women by society. A social and cultural "institution" that Rich sees as fundamental to the subordination of women by men, it is upheld by means ranging from physical violence and economic coercion to the idealization of heterosexual romance and erasure of lesbian sexuality from history and literature. Specific techniques mentioned by Rich include rape and wife-beating, clitoridectomy and the psychoanalytic denial of the clitoris, unpaid maternal and domestic labor, sexual harassment of and discrimination against women in the workplace, persecution of lesbians, and the destruction of documents relating to lesbian experience, among many others. As this list implies, Rich takes heterosexuality in its broadest sense to mean the general viewing of women and measuring of female value in terms of male needs and desires. Against "compulsory heterosexuality," Rich poses the LESBIAN CONTINUUM, by which she means the broad spectrum of ways in which women, despite compulsory heterosexuality, have historically been primary to each other.

Rich, Adrienne. "Compulsory Heterosexuality and Lesbian Existence." In *Blood, Bread, and Poetry: Selected Prose 1979–1985*. New York: Norton, 1986.

CONCRETIZATION. In phenomenological criticism, *concretization* (KONkritiZAYshun) refers to the process by which a reader actualizes, "fills out," or brings to life a literary work. The phenomenological approach to literature is fundamentally concerned with how individual readers engage with texts, how the convergence of the reader and text brings the literary work into being. According to Roman Ingarden, a text consists of schematized aspects; that is, texts present aspects of reality not in their entirety but rather schematically, in a skeletal form. The reader then concretizes, or fleshes out the text based on the potentialities of its schematic outline. A character in a novel, for example, can never be completely depicted within the pages of a given text; the character must instead be "realized" (Wolfgang Iser's term for concretization) or brought to life by the active involvement of the reader's imagination. Reading a text therefore involves a continual repetition of such concretizations.

The text as a site of potentiality is always richer than any of its individual concretizations. Because it occurs at the individual level, there are numerous possible concretizations of a given text. However, Ingarden does regard some concretizations as preferable to others, and he checks rampant subjectivity by suggesting that the text exerts control over the reader's actualization of it. Iser, a follower of Ingarden, is more ambiguous about this controversial question regarding the primacy of the reader or text in formulating a concretization. See also GAPS, PHENOMENOLOGY, READER-RESPONSE CRITICISM.

Ingarden, Roman. *The Cognition of the Literary Work of Art*. Trans. Ruth Ann Crowley and Kenneth R. Olson. Evanston, Ill.: Northwestern University Press, 1973.
Iser, Wolfgang. *The Act of Reading: A Theory of Aesthetic Response*. Baltimore: Johns Hopkins University Press, 1978.

CONDENSATION. In Freudian psychoanalysis, *condensation* is a term used to describe one of the fundamental unconscious processes; it expresses the way that a single idea or mental impression may come to represent more than one chain of associations, which touch upon one another at this point of intersection. The latter thus receives the sum of the energies associated with those chains (see OVERDETERMINATION). Condensation can be observed in manifestations of the unconscious, such as symptoms and above all in dreams. In fact, it was in *The Interpretation of Dreams* that Freud first described the process of condensation and used it to explain the compressed quality that many dreams possess. According to this account, it is only through the condensed, often enigmatic dream content that the unconscious is able both to submit to and to escape from the censorship that separates it from the other parts of the psyche. See also DISPLACEMENT, LATENT CONTENT, MANIFEST CONTENT, UNCONSCIOUS.

CONJURING. Broadly speaking, *conjuring* refers to a black folk tradition (sometimes known as "hoodoo" or "voodoo") in which a person possessing magical powers works spells, often using roots and herbs. Two of the best-known depictions of conjuring are to be found in Charles Chesnutt's *The Conjure Woman* (1901) and Zora Neale Hurston's *Mules and Men* (1935). But since the publication in 1985 of *Conjuring: Black Women, Fiction, and Literary Tradition,* a collection of black feminist literary criticism, the term has also become associated with the current resurgence among black women writers. In her introduction to the volume, Marjorie Pryse argues that in recent decades "black women novelists have become metaphorical conjure women, 'mediums,' like Alice Walker, who make it possible for their readers and for each other to recognize their common literary ancestors (gardeners, quilt makers, grandmothers, rootworkers, and women who wrote autobiographies)." Conjuring thus signifies the way that contemporary authors have translated their nonliterary cultural and artistic heritage into written form. Hortense Spillers's afterword to the volume elaborates on the notion that black women are conjuring into existence a literary tradition. "Traditions are not born. They are made," she explains. Spillers also cautions against merely substituting a "counter-tradition" for the one from which black women have been excluded. This tension in *Conjuring* between the need to construct alternative literary canons while also criticizing the idea of the canonical is central to the work of many scholars of women's and minority literature. See also BLACK FEMINIST CRITICISM.

Chesnutt, Charles. *The Conjure Woman.* Ann Arbor: University of Michigan Press, 1969.

Hurston, Zora Neale. *Mules and Men.* Bloomington: Indiana University Press, 1935.

Pryse, Marjorie, and Hortense J. Spillers, eds. *Conjuring: Black Women, Fiction, and Literary Tradition*. Bloomington: Indiana University Press, 1985.

CONNOTATION/DENOTATION. Connotation is the range of secondary associations that a word or phrase may suggest. Unlike the literal meaning of the word, its denotation, connotations may invoke emotional or intellectual responses, contexts, or qualities connected to the word's referent (the "actual" entity to which the word refers). These associations are culturally as well as personally bound, and their invocation often depends upon context. For instance, the word *snake* denotes a legless reptile. Connotatively, however, we can speak of someone snaking through a crowd, and the metaphor insinuates a smooth, back-and-forth motion. Similarly, when we speak of someone as a "snake," we usually are describing that person as untrustworthy and sneakily aggressive—a connotation that may not exist for a herpetologist or in a culture that reveres snakes.

CONSCIOUSNESS. The term *consciousness* applies generally to the mental realm. It is a key concept in such fields as psychoanalysis (where it is opposed to the UNCONSCIOUS) and PHENOMENOLOGY (where it refers to the center of objects and so is always "consciousness of" something—see the writings of Roman Ingarden, Gaston Bachelard, Edmund Husserl and Maurice Merleau-Ponty). It is also crucial to the work of the so-called critics of consciousness or "Geneva school" of literary criticism (Georges Poulet, Albert Béguin, Marcel Raymond, Jean Rousset, Jean-Pierre Richard, Jean Starobinski) and the existential phenomenologists (like Jean-Paul Sartre and Albert Camus). Contemporary theory has been concerned with the nature of consciousness and conscious agency, as well as with the interaction of consciousness and textuality. See also PHENOMENOLOGY.

Freud, Sigmund. *The Interpretation of Dreams*. Trans. and ed. James Strachey. London: Hogarth Press, 1953.

Lawall, Sarah. *Critics of Consciousness*. Cambridge, Mass.: Harvard University Press, 1968.

Sartre, Jean-Paul. *What is Literature?* Trans. Bernard Frechtman. London: Methuen, 1950.

CONSTATIVE UTTERANCE. In J. L. Austin's SPEECH ACT THEORY, constative utterances are those with which speakers make true or false statements. This, argues Austin, is one of the primary functions of all speech. By contrast, PERFORMATIVE UTTERANCES are those which execute some verbal act, such as to threaten or to promise. Nevertheless, Austin observes that, in a sense, constative utterances are also performative, at least implicitly, since they do perform the act of asserting something. See also ILLOCUTIONARY ACT, LOCUTIONARY ACT, PERLOCUTIONARY ACT.

Austin, J. L. *How To Do Things With Words.* Cambridge, Mass.: Harvard University Press, 1962.

Felman, Shoshona. *The Literary Speech Act.* Trans. Catherine Porter. Ithaca, N.Y.: Cornell University Press, 1983.

Pratt, Mary Louise. *Toward a Speech Act Theory of Literary Discourse.* Bloomington: Indiana University Press, 1977.

Searle, John R. *Speech Acts: An Essay in the Philosophy of Language.* London: Oxford University Press, 1969.

CONSTRUCTIVISM. Constructivism was an AVANT-GARDE movement which had its roots in the relief constructions that the Russian artist Vladimir Tatlin began producing in 1913 after visiting Paris and Berlin. As a full-fledged movement, however, constructivism originated in 1917 in response to the Russian Revolution.

Like DADA, Russian constructivism was not an artistic style; rather, it consisted of an approach to working with materials and a program (much more specifically political than that of dada) which emphasized participating in and promoting social and political transformation. Tatlin, Alexander Rodchenko, Gustav Klutsis, El Lissitzky, Varvara Stepanova, and Liubov Popova, among others, were engaged in a range of activities that included investigations (termed "laboratory work") into elements of material, form, construction, and design that could potentially be used toward utilitarian ends; architecture; graphic design; photomontage; theater sets; and designs for clothing, fabric, and furniture. Among their more well-known works were Tatlin's attempt to synthesize sculpture and architecture in his 1920 design for a monument to the Third International in the form of a spiraling tower and the political posters of Klutsis and Rodchenko, which made innovative use of photomontage and new kinds of typography. The constructivists rejected the traditional work of art as an example of bourgeois individualism; their desire to break down the distinction between art and life was reflected in their political goals and in their embrace of factory production. (Two other artists who are sometimes associated with Russian constructivism, Naum Gabo and Antoine Pevsner, also engaged in related experiments in composition but did not share the utilitarian and social aspirations of the constructivists.)

Barron, Stephanie, and Maurice Tuchman, eds. *The Avant-Garde in Russia, 1910–1930: New Perspectives.* Los Angeles and Cambridge, Mass.: Los Angeles County Museum of Art and MIT Press, 1980.

Henry Art Gallery. *Art into Life: Russian Constructivism, 1914–32.* New York: Rizzoli, 1990.

Lodder, Christina. *Russian Constructivism.* New Haven: Yale University Press, 1983.

CONTENT. See FORM.

CONVENTION. The use of the term *convention* in cultural criticism is analogous to its common meaning of "custom" or "social habit." In this sense the term usually refers to the ways in which meanings are produced, underscoring the arbitrary character of SIGNS and the necessity for some consensus as to their meanings. In the study of literature or art, conventions are established practices of form or content, but are employed more out of custom and tradition than by necessity.

Aesthetic conventions may be highly stylized, such as in Kabuki theater, impressionistic painting, or movie Westerns. Beginning with Romanticism, notably in England with Wordsworth and Coleridge's *Lyrical Ballads* (1798), there have been innumerable attempts to defy or fly in the face of convention. Such endeavors, however, if successful, inevitably establish conventions of their own. Thus, the poetry of *Lyrical Ballads*, which repudiated the highly formal diction of eighteenth-century poetry, also founded new conventions that now allow us to categorize the English Romantic poets as a distinct group bound together by similar styles and interests. Similarly, the Westerns of Sergio Leone or the novels of Alain Robbe-Grillet, while originally anti- or nonconventional, are now easily identified by the very practices that defied convention. Thus, we talk about "spaghetti Westerns" or the "nouveau roman" in part because others have adopted these practices and have made them, in their turn, conventional.

COUNTER-MEMORY. Associated principally with the work of Michel Foucault, the term *counter-memory* is an attempt to characterize the kind of history writing that Foucault advocated. Much traditional historical research emphasizes continuities across the historical spectrum and presents human existence as a single, collective project. In this respect, it functions like the memory of an individual life, except that whereas individual memory works to support the impression that the individual has a stable identity throughout his or her life, history writing has often sought to establish the identity of large groups of people over time, along with their particular forms of CONSCIOUSNESS (see COLLECTIVE SUBJECT). By contrast, the Foucauldian GENEALOGY focuses on the ruptures and discontinuities in history, emphasizing historical differences and insisting on the irreducible specificity of such forms of "otherness" as madness and sexuality, which have historically proven difficult to incorporate within the concept of a unified and continuous human identity. It is in this sense that Foucault's history writing can be said to constitute a counter-memory. See also ARCHAELOGY, OTHER.

Foucault, Michel. *Language, Counter-Memory, Practice: Selected Essays and Interviews.* Trans. Donald F. Bouchard and Sherry Simon. Ithaca, N.Y.: Cornell University Press, 1977.

COUNTER-TRANSFERENCE. In psychoanalytic theory, *counter-transference* is the term given to the analyst's unconscious reactions to the patient and his or her own TRANSFERENCE. In some uses, the term is not restricted to the analyst's unconscious reactions but includes any aspect of the analyst's character or experience that may enter the analytic situation. An important part of the analyst's technique is involved in coming to recognize signs of counter-transference through personal analysis, so that they may be minimized or, occasionally, used as a guide to manifestations of the patient's unconscious.

CREOLIZATION. A term that originally referred to the process by which two or more languages converge to form a new language when different cultural groups interact over an extended period, *creolization* has been gradually extended to describe the transformations undergone in various aspects of culture when two or more groups come into prolonged contact. Beginning with Melville Herskovits's pioneering efforts to document the retention and reinterpretation of Africanisms by "New World Negroes," the term has generally been applied to the cultural adaptations made by Africans transported to the Americas. It is in this sense that Herman Gutman defined creolization as "the transformation of the African into the Afro-American." The concept of creolization has been refined by examining the ways in which "dominant" cultures are influenced by "minority" cultures (e.g., John Szwed's analysis of minstrelization) and by specifying the particular kinds of transformations observed in discrete communities (e.g., Charles Joyner's study of an antebellum South Carolina slave community's mediation between European and African forms of labor, art, food, architecture, fashion, etc.).

Gutman, Herbert G. *The Black Family in Slavery and Freedom 1750–1925.* New York: Vintage, 1976.

Herskovits, Melville J. *The Myth of the Negro Past.* Boston: Beacon Press, 1990.

Joyner, Charles. *Down by the Riverside: A South Carolina Slave Community.* Urbana: University of Illinois Press, 1984.

Szwed, John F. "Race and the Embodiment of Culture." *Ethnicity* 2, 1975.

CRITICAL CROSS-DRESSING. The term *critical cross-dressing* was originally used by Elaine Showalter in 1983 to describe the emergence at that time of feminist criticism by men, a trend she found "both gratifying and unsettling." Gratifying because it marked the recognition by established male theorists of the intellectual and political importance of feminist work. Unsettling because it was sometimes what Showalter called "phallic 'feminist' criticism": while claiming to speak for women, or even *as* a woman, critics such as Terry Eagleton in *The Rape of Clarissa* neglected the work of women in the field and implicitly touted their own masculine critical authority—showing women (as, for example, some have argued was the case in *Tootsie*) that men surpass women even at being women. Showalter suggested that male theorists sympathetic to feminism should not "cross-dress" as women, but rather explore the significance of reading *as men*, confronting the anxieties and privileges of their masculinity. See also GENDER STUDIES, MEN'S STUDIES.

Showalter, Elaine. "Critical Cross-Dressing: Male Feminists and the Woman of the Year." In Alice Jardine and Paul Smith, eds., *Men in Feminism.* New York: Methuen, 1987.

CRITICAL THEORY. Although the term *critical theory* is sometimes used as a catch-all phrase referring to any theoretical enterprise of the human or social sciences, it is more specifically and properly used to designate the ideas of the members of the Frankfurt School. This "school" of Marxist thinkers was officially titled the Institute for Social Research and was established at the University of Frankfurt in 1923. With the rise of Nazism, the institute fled Germany for the U.S. in 1933 and eventually reestablished itself in Frankfurt in the 1950s. Its members included Max Horkheimer, Theodor Adorno, Herbert Marcuse, Leo Lowenthal, and Erich Fromm. Literary critic and essayist Walter Benjamin, a close friend of Adorno's, was also associated with the institute, but never officially a member. The most prominent of the "second generation" of critical theorists is the philosopher Jürgen Habermas.

Although critical theory meant different things to the different members of the institute, some generally held principles can be identified. Perhaps most important, the institute was interested in developing a critical perspective for the analysis and discussion of all social phenomena. At root in such a perspective is a continual critique of IDEOLOGY, which the Frankfurt School characterized as distortions of reality whose purpose is to camouflage and legitimate unequal power relations. The political agenda underlying this project—which was never systematically articulated by any member of the institute—was grounded in its direct opposition to domination of any kind. For example, the Frankfurt School acknowledged that Marxism itself became a repressive, rather than liberating, ideology when it was expressed as Stalinism. The institute was also critical of the limitations of orthodox Marxism, arguing that society was much more complex than could be fathomed by analysis based only on political economy. As a result, they incorporated analytical tenets from a number of disciplines, including psychoanalysis, cultural criticism, and sociology into their work. Their objective was to demonstrate that positivist or deterministic Marxist models of historical development were unsuitable for cultural analysis (see DETERMINISM, POSITIVISM). For the Frankfurt School the movements of history did not happen behind the backs or "above the heads" of individuals and thus dispassionately create the material conditions of existence. Rather, individuals were seen as "partially knowing subjects" whose "situated conduct" makes history (see SUBJECT).

Characteristic of the thinking and writing of the Frankfurt School is their use of the DIALECTIC. Horkheimer and Adorno especially were intent on avoiding linear, syllogistic reasoning, opting instead for examining the contradictions inherent in a phenomenon or concept as the site of meanings and significance. Adorno was also specifically interested in the function of fragmentation and dissonance in aesthetics. For him a work of art, though derived from a conventional "bourgeois" order, is only successful as art when it is able to reconfigure that order, representing it in ways that allow its critical contemplation, as does the music of Schoenberg.

Despite their admiration of much bourgeois art before their time, Horkheimer and Adorno argued that most objects of aesthetic admiration in their own time had become commodities (see COMMODITY) and that culture itself had thus been transformed into an industry. The products of culture, rather than offering a site for subversion, instead reinforce the very structures of life they are ostensibly meant to provide an escape from. For these theorists, contemporary culture is how oppressive ideologies are reproduced and disseminated.

Though their work has been criticized as elitist because of their desire to maintain distinctions between high and low culture or as parochial because of their insistence that capitalism was ultimately capable of coopting opposition, Adorno, Marcuse, Horkheimer, and the other members of the Frankfurt School are often heralded as the forebears of contemporary CULTURAL STUDIES. Certainly their influence on such theorists as the BIRMINGHAM CENTER FOR CONTEMPORARY CULTURAL STUDIES has been well documented. Their continual critique of ideology in all its manifestations is often cited as an important precursor to poststructuralist thought. See also MARXIST CRITICISM, POSTMODERNISM, POSTSTRUCTURALISM.

Adorno, Theodor. *Prisms.* Trans. Samuel Weber and Shierry Weber. London: Spearman, 1967.

—. *Negative Dialectics.* Trans. E. B. Ashton. New York: Seabury Press, 1973.

— and Max Horkheimer. *Dialectic of Enlightenment.* Trans. John Cummings. New York: Seabury Press, 1972.

Dews, Peter. *Logics of Disintegration: Post-Structuralist Thought and the Claims of Critical Theory.* London: Verso, 1987.

Geuss, Raymond. *The Idea of a Critical Theory.* Cambridge: Cambridge University Press, 1981.

Held, David. *Introduction to Critical Theory: Horkheimer to Habermas.* Berkeley: University of California Press, 1980.

Horkheimer, Max. *Critical Theory.* Trans. Matthew J. O'Connell et al. New York: Herder and Herder, 1972.

Jay, Martin. *The Dialectical Imagination: A History of the Frankfurt School and the Institute of Social Research, 1923–1950.* Boston: Little, Brown, 1973.

Marcuse, Herbert. *Reason and Revolution.* Boston: Beacon Press, 1960.

CRITICS OF CONSCIOUSNESS. See PHENOMENOLOGY.

CULTURAL CAPITAL. The concept of cultural capital is based on the assertion that symbolic expression has, like money and property, an exchange value determined by the ruling class of society. The better one understands and manipulates the language most highly valued by the dominant class, the "richer" one is in cultural capital and the more one can control how cultural capital is distributed and passed on to the next generation. For Bourdieu and Passeron (who coined the term), the concept of cultural capital is useful for understanding why state education systems so often fail to distribute literacy equally among classes: although public schooling in capitalist democracies is supposed to be meritocratic, the students who most often succeed are not necessarily the most talented but those whose families enjoy a higher social, economic, and cultural status (i.e., tend to possess the greatest cultural capital). Other applications of the term have arisen in studies of working-class subcultures (especially in Britain), which have been more prone to challenge the term by asking how those low in capital of any kind nonetheless manage to originate powerful, even subversive art forms.

Passeron, Jean-Claude, and Pierre Bourdieu. *Reproduction in Education, Society and Culture.* Trans. Richard Nice. London: Sage Publications, 1977.
Willis, Paul. *Learning to Labour.* Farnborough, U.K.: Saxon House, 1977.

CULTURAL FEMINISM. Growing out of the radical feminism of the late 1960s and early 1970s, cultural feminism involves an analysis and usually a celebration of women's culture and community. The general strategy of cultural feminism is to seize upon many of those qualities traditionally ascribed to women—subjectivity, closeness to nature, compassion, reliance on others—and claim them as positive, even superior, traits. As opposed to the liberal feminist desire for access to existing male institutions, cultural feminists argue that these must be radically reimagined in terms of such "female" values. Adrienne Rich, for example, called in 1974 for a "woman-centered university" that would provide childcare, sponsor "research *for* rather than *on* human beings," and undo the usual hierarchies. Other thinkers associated with the movement include Mary Daly, Susan Griffin, Andrea Dworkin, and Carol Gilligan, to name only a few.

Though most cultural feminists emphasize that women's association with certain "female" qualities is not innate but learned, and would offer them as alternative values for men as well as women, their position has been criticized for seeming to reiterate conventional gender stereotypes—that women are nurturing, men aggressive, etc. In an attempt to stress what women have in common, cultural feminism has also often been guilty of obscuring crucial differences of race and class among women, generalizing about "women's" culture from what is actually the culture of women who are white, Western, and middle-class. Some radical feminists have further accused cultural feminists of retreating from political struggle into more private, spiritual quests, of making politics *only* personal, a matter of individual lifestyle. Notwithstanding these criticisms, it is cultural feminism that largely underlies the explosion of scholarship on women in the past two decades, and the approach has perhaps only been strengthened by having to confront its ESSENTIALISM and racial/class bias. In most areas of the humanities and social sciences, the examination of women in relation not to men but to other women—women's culture—has opened up whole new areas of inquiry. The move toward "gender studies" in the 1990s has brought a return to looking at men and women together, seeing women's cultures in relation to dominant ones. See also LIBERAL FEMINISM, RADICAL FEMINISM, SEXUAL DIFFERENCE.

Alcoff, Linda. "Cultural Feminism versus Post-Structuralism: The Identity Crisis in Feminist Theory." *Signs* 13 (3), 1988.
Daly, Mary. *Gyn/Ecology: The Metaethics of Radical Feminism.* Boston: Beacon Press, 1978.
Gilligan, Carol. *In a Different Voice: Psychological Theory and Women's Development.* Cambridge, Mass.: Harvard University Press, 1982.
Noddings, Nel. *Caring: A Feminine Approach to Ethics & Moral Education.* Berkeley: University of California Press, 1984.
Rich, Adrienne. *On Lies, Secrets, and Silence: Selected Prose 1966–1978.* New York: Norton, 1979.

CULTURAL LITERACY. A term that gained currency with the publication of E. D. Hirsch's book by the same name, *cultural literacy* refers to Hirsch's contention that a minimal, quantifiable level of knowledge about cultural phenomena—from "great" works of literature, art, music, and historical events to outstanding sports figures, popular entertainers, and movies—is requisite for optimum functioning in our society and for the maintenance of culture as we know it. Hirsch emphasizes a shared body of knowledge as the basis for effective communication among individuals in society. He has been attacked from a number of quarters for relying too heavily on the traditional Western CANON as the foundation of this knowledge and for excluding phenomena that are valued by cultures that are vital but have been marginalized in the U.S. See also CANON FORMATION, HEGEMONY, MARGINAL/MARGINALIZATION, MULTICULTURALISM.

Hirsch, E. D. *Cultural Literacy*. Boston: Houghton Mifflin, 1987.

CULTURAL MATERIALISM. The phrase *cultural materialism* originated with the English critic Raymond Williams, who sought to describe a form of critical activity in the Marxist tradition that remains a materialism but avoids the trap of attempting to understand all cultural activities as mere effects of the economic BASE. Beginning from the Marxist thesis that social being determines consciousness and insisting that culture must be understood as "a whole social process," Williams analyzed a wide variety of cultural forms, from canonical literature to television and other forms of popular culture, producing a body of work that has had considerable influence on younger generations of critics, particularly those associated with the BIRMINGHAM CENTER FOR CONTEMPORARY CULTURAL STUDIES. In recent years, cultural materialists have often chosen to investigate the contemporary reception of canonical texts and have devoted much energy to the study of Shakespeare as a cultural institution. This work is characteristic of current cultural materialism and offers a politically charged critique of the customary attitude of reverence toward the Shakespearean canon. See also CULTURAL STUDIES.

Dollimore, Jonathan, and Alan Sinfield, eds. *Political Shakespeare: New Essays in Cultural Materialism*. Manchester: Manchester University Press, 1985.
Holderness, Graham, ed. *The Shakespeare Myth*. Manchester: Manchester University Press, 1988.
Williams, Raymond. *Television: Technology and Cultural Form*. New York: Schocken, 1975.
—. *Culture and Society 1780–1950*. New York: Columbia University Press, 1983.
—. *Problems in Materialism and Culture*. London: Verso, 1980.

CULTURAL STUDIES. Cultural studies is an interdisciplinary field that encompasses a wide range of critical initiatives both in Britain and in

America. Its antecedents can be traced to work published in the 1950s and early 1960s by British leftist critics like Richard Hoggart (*The Uses of Literacy*) and Raymond Williams (*Culture and Society, The Long Revolution*), which in turn derived from F. R. Leavis and the *Scrutiny* group, although Hoggart and Williams were critical of what they considered Leavis's middle-class biases. The "official" beginning of cultural studies in Britain came, however, with the founding, by Hoggart, of the BIRMINGHAM CENTER FOR CONTEMPORARY CULTURAL STUDIES in 1964. In the early years, the center's approach to culture was more or less evenly divided between history, philosophy, sociology, and literary criticism; however, after 1968 its focus became increasingly sociological, following the replacement of Hoggart as director by Stuart Hall. It was during this period that critics affiliated with the Birmingham Center did the work for which it continues to be best known: studies of neglected aspects of contemporary culture, with an emphasis on popular materials and, above all, the defining rituals of SUBCULTURES. During this same period, members of the center adopted continental theoretical materials, especially the work of Marxist thinkers like the members of the FRANKFURT SCHOOL, Antonio Gramsci, and Louis Althusser; and in the past decade, much work done under the rubric of CULTURAL MATERIALISM has had close affinities with cultural studies.

In America, cultural studies has been influenced by the Birmingham model, although the term covers a broader and less well defined body of work. It is closely identified with the initiatives of MULTICULTURALISM, and practitioners frequently concern themselves with issues of gender, race, class, and sexual preference. Nevertheless, much work by critics like Andrew Ross on popular culture and technology cannot be adequately defined in these terms, and American practitioners of cultural studies have investigated a wide range of topics and employed an equally wide variety of critical methodologies.

Hall, Stuart, and Tony Jefferson, eds. *Resistance Through Rituals: Youth Subcultures in Postwar Britain.* London: Hutchinson, 1976.

Hebdige, Dick. *Subculture: The Meaning of Style.* London: Methuen, 1979.

Hoggart, Richard. *The Uses of Literacy.* London: Chatto and Windus, 1957.

Ross, Andrew. *No Respect: Intellectuals and Popular Culture.* New York: Routledge, 1989.

—. *Strange Weather: Culture, Science, and Technology in the Age of Limits.* London: Verso, 1991.

Williams, Raymond. *The Long Revolution.* New York: Columbia University Press, 1961.

—. *Culture and Society 1780–1950.* New York: Columbia University Press, 1983.

CULTURE. The term *culture* is one of the most often used, and rarely defined, in all of contemporary criticism. Critics and theorists tend to depend upon context to convey what they signify by their use of the term. As a result, the concepts associated with *culture* have remained both inexact and widely used—and often lead to considerable confusion.

In contemporary theoretical and critical discourse the term balances between two distinct meanings. In the social sciences, especially archaeology and anthropology, *culture* usually refers to the material production of a society. In history, literary studies, and cultural studies, however, the term refers to systems of signification and the production of meaning. The line between these two uses of the word is not always clearly drawn, since certain theoretical approaches in history, literature, and cultural studies see material production and the production of meaning as inextricably connected. For example, the works of Raymond Williams are often cited as the founding texts for an approach called CULTURAL MATE-RIALISM, which attempts to view culture as both materially informed and informing.

Williams is in many ways the descendant of a long line of British thinkers who have focused on the concept of culture, especially in its social (and moral) implications. Though in his own work Williams traces the roots of a concern with culture back at least to the pre- Romantic period, Matthew Arnold, a mid-Victorian writer, stands as the dominant figure in nineteenth- and early twentieth-century discussions of the concept. Arnold's 1867 monograph, *Culture and Anarchy*, articulated and helped to establish the assumptions that would govern the mainstream of literary studies for almost one hundred years. Some contemporary critics contend that the influence of his work is still strongly felt. Arnold argued that culture could be defined as the "best that has been thought and known." Such a formulation begs a number of questions, not least of which is by what standard might a work be judged "best." For Arnold such distinctions could be made by intellectuals who are disinterested and disassociated from class interests. These "aliens," as Arnold called them, would help, through education, to oversee the installation of "culture" at all levels of society. Once all people have appropriate access to culture, then anarchy can be averted and everyone may express his or her own opinion without fear of violently upsetting the political order of things. Thus, Arnold attempts to avert anarchy by putting in place a homogenous view of the "best that has been thought and known."

The moral and social apects of Arnold's position were taken up, amplified, and modified by a number of theorists and critics in the twentieth century, perhaps most notably by Lionel Trilling in America and F. R. Leavis and the journal *Scrutiny* in England. But the elitism and political quietism (leading, some have argued, to conservatism) in Arnold's conception of culture was criticized by later thinkers such as Richard Hoggart and Williams. While the literary was still seen as a means for understanding social phenomena, Hoggart and Williams were also concerned with uncovering and understanding those cultural artifacts and events that, by prevailing opinions, would not have been considered "the best that has been thought and known." These other cultures, they argued, have considerable impact on the ways in which people live their lives and experience (and understand) the world around them.

With the near ubiquity of mass communications, especially television, *culture* has undergone yet another transformation in its usage. We now have a seemingly limitless access to activities, attitudes, and aesthetic ideals that do not necessarily jibe with the assumptions about taste and sensibility that are promulgated by the standards of a dominant culture. The result has been to increasingly confuse what had once been rather clear distinctions between highbrow, middlebrow, and lowbrow culture. Because of this overlap, critics today often use "culture" as a shorthand for popular culture, or "the culture of the masses," a usage that is in many ways directly antithetical to the sense in which Arnold employed the term.

This rethinking of the concept of culture, both as a descriptive and theoretical term, has been instrumental in the rise of a number of new interdisciplinary approaches to the study of the social and ideological effects of culture. Broadly categorized as "cultural studies," these approaches attempt to avoid aesthetic evaluations based upon notions of high or low culture and prefer instead to focus on the ways in which aesthetic activities reinforce or resist particular social constructs such as gender, class, race, or sexuality. While much of the work that classifies itself as "cultural studies" is concerned with contemporary aesthetic and social phenomena, there has also increasingly been a move to rethink the cultural assumptions of literay-historical eras according to this revised conception of culture. See also BIRMINGHAM CENTER FOR CONTEMPORARY CULTURAL STUDIES, CULTURAL LITERACY, DISINTERESTEDNESS, IDEOLOGY, NEW HISTORICISM.

Arnold, Matthew. *Culture and Anarchy: An Essay in Political and Social Criticism.* London: Smith, Elder, 1869.

Brantlinger, Patrick. *Crusoe's Footprints: Cultural Studies in Britain and America.* New York: Routledge, 1990.

Leavis, F. R., and Denys Thompson. *Culture and Environment.* London: Chatto and Windus, 1933.

Trilling, Lionel. *Beyond Culture.* New York: Viking, 1965.

Turner, Graeme. *British Cultural Studies: An Introduction.* Boston: Unwin Hyman, 1990.

Williams, Raymond. *The Long Revolution.* New York: Columbia University Press, 1961.

—. *Culture and Society 1780–1950.* New York: Columbia University Press, 1983.

CUT. In film language, a cut is a switch from one image (or single camera shot) to another. Somewhat analogous to a scene of a play, *cut* refers more precisely to a change in the angle of the camera—many interwoven cuts (montage) can form a "scene" in a movie. The order of cuts in a film, usually determined in the editing stage, is regarded by film theorists such as Kaja Silverman as the primary means through which we grasp the information the film conveys—the cut is "the prime agency of disclosure"—and thus its role is comparable to that of a sentence in a piece of writing. Like a sentence, the information carried by a single cut is determined by the cuts preceding and following it. A "final cut" is the last arrangement of the many cuts comprising a single film. See also JUMP CUT.

Silverman, Kaja. *The Subject of Semiotics.* New York: Oxford University Press, 1983.

CYBERSPACE. Cyberspace (**SEI**bur**SPAYS**) is a virtual world being developed through the interface of the human mind and computer technology. It is an electronically defined world in which a human can experience an environment completely outside the one that he or she physically occupies. The term was coined by the science-fiction writer William Gibson in his novel *Neuromancer*, although his imaginative rendition of the concept is a good deal ahead of the technology presently available and more dystopian than most writing on the subject. "Cyberspace," says Michael Benedikt, "does not exist." But for cultural theorists, it is the sense of being that it implies which makes it so intriguing. Cyberspace represents an electronic infinitude that renders human identity fluid, digitized, spatial, and integrated (see DECENTERED SUBJECT, IDENTITY). In short, it is a dream concept for postmodernists, who see in it a model of contemporary notions of SIMULATION.

Benedikt, Michael, ed. *Cyberspace: First Steps.* Cambridge, Mass.: MIT Press, 1991.

Gibson, William. *Neuromancer.* New York: Ace Books, 1984.

CYBORG. The word *cyborg* is a contraction of "cybernetic organism" and generally refers to hybrid forms of humans and machines (either robots with humanlike qualities or humans with extensive and interactive synthetic components). Science-fiction writing and filmmaking abounds with examples of cyborgs from Fritz Lang's pioneering film *Metropolis* to Philip K. Dick's novel *Do Androids Dream of Electric Sheep?* (the source of Ridley Scott's film *Blade Runner*). Recently, the cyborg has become a controversial topic of cultural theory, primarily (though not solely) because of Donna Haraway's essay "A Manifesto for Cyborgs: Science, Technology, and Socialist Feminism in the 1980s," in which she uses the cyborg as a metaphor for postmodern concepts of IDENTITY, which are no longer conceived in humanist terms. See also DECENTERED SUBJECT, HUMANISM.

Balsamo, Anne. "Reading Cyborgs Writing Feminism." *Communication* 10 (3/4), 1988.

Haraway, Donna. "A Manifesto for Cyborgs: Science, Technology, and Socialist Feminism in the 1980s." *Socialist Review* 80, 1985.

D

DADA. Dada was an AVANT-GARDE movement that originated in Zurich around the Cabaret Voltaire, which was opened in February 1916 by the writer Hugo Ball and the cabaret actress Emmy Hennings. The name *dada* is a nonsense word that may or may not have been picked from a French-German dictionary opened at random. Regardless of how the name was chosen, the performances, poetry, and other productions associated with dada emphasized absurdity, reflected a spirit of nihilism, and celebrated the function of chance.

Among those active in Zurich dada were the poet Tristan Tzara, the artist Jean Arp, and the writer Richard Huelsenbeck. In New York, dada began in spirit, if not in name, in 1915 with the arrival of the European artists Francis Picabia and Marcel Duchamp, who quickly became associated with the American artist Man Ray. In Germany, dada took root in Berlin after Huelsenbeck's return in 1917. Artists associated with Berlin dada include Raoul Hausmann, Hannah Höch, John Heartfield, and George Grosz. During this same period, the artists Kurt Schwitters and Max Ernst were also working in Hanover and Cologne, respectively.

Dada never constituted an artistic style; instead, it can more usefully be understood as a reaction against conventional art and middle-class society. For example, Duchamp's readymades, Tzara and Huelsenbeck's simultaneous poems, and the extensive montage and collage works of Hausmann, Höch, Heartfield, and Schwitters all incorporate elements of chance, found objects, or fragments from the realm of mass culture, representing an attack on the concept of "art" as understood by bourgeois society and contributing to a blurring of the distinction between art and life. See also SURREALISM.

Ades, Dawn. *Dada and Surrealism Reviewed.* London: Arts Council of Great Britain, 1978.

Motherwell, Robert, ed. *The Dada Painters and Poets: An Anthology.* Boston: G. K. Hall, 1981.

Richter, Hans. *Dada: Art and Anti-Art.* Trans. David Britt. New York: Abrams, 1985.

Rubin, William. *Dada, Surrealism, and their Heritage.* New York: Museum of Modern Art, 1968.

Short, Robert. *Dada and Surrealism.* Secaucus, N.J.: Chartwell, 1980.

DASEIN. The philosopher Martin Heidegger uses *Dasein* (DAHzein), German for "being there," in his investigations and descriptions of human existence. For Heidegger, humanity's particular way of existing is characterized by concern with and care for surrounding objects and community members. Dasein, as the basis of human existence, is participation and involvement in the world around us. Heidegger distinguishes three important features that comprise Dasein. The first he calls factuality, meaning that any human being is "always already" in a world—a world into which one is cast or thrown (*geworfen*) and which both determines and is determined by one's existence in and perception of that world. The second characteristic of Dasein is existentiality, or the understanding of the world into which one has been "thrown." Such understanding is never complete but always a process, a becoming, an anticipation of one's possibilities. Existentiality thus refers to a neverending process of inner personal existence as well as to one's being in *and* with the world. The third feature of Dasein is "fallenness" or "forfeiture." This is the mode of existence in which most live day to day. Fallenness is a preoccupation with the mundane to the extent that we forget what Heidgegger calls "the question of the sense of Being" (*die Frage nach dem Sinn von Sein*), which as humans it is our vocation, our nature, to ask. To live without asking the question, "What does it mean 'to be?'" is to forfeit authentic existence and to alienate oneself from one's central task of "becoming" (existentiality) and thus, ultimately, to live in alienation from one's self and others. See also ESSENTIALISM, EXISTENTIALISM, PHENOMENOLOGY.

Heidegger, Martin. *Being and Time*. Trans. J. Macquarrie and E. S. Robinson. New York: Harper, 1962.

DEATH INSTINCTS. In *Beyond the Pleasure Principle*, Freud introduced the concept of the death instincts and revised his earlier thesis that psychic life is divided between the instincts of pleasure and self-preservation by grouping these previously opposed forces together under the heading of LIFE INSTINCTS (see also PLEASURE PRINCIPLE and REALITY PRINCIPLE). According to this later view, the aim of the death instincts is to reduce psychic tension to the zero degree and thus to return the organism to an inanimate state (see COMPULSION TO REPEAT). Whereas the life instincts seek to create new unities and preserve excitation at a given level (according to the principle of constancy), the death instincts seek to dissolve existing unities and ultimately to abolish excitation altogether. The problematic quality of the death instincts as a theoretical concept stems from the difficulty of isolating these supposed biological forces; and Freud specified that they often appear in combination with the life instincts, as, for example, in sexual activity, which seems a pure expression of the pleasure principle but culminates in a collapse of excitation that is characteristic of the death instincts. In spite of these qualifications, the concept of the death instincts has remained one of Freud's most controversial innovations and is discounted by many psychoanalysts.

Freud, Sigmund. *Beyond the Pleasure Principle*. Rev. ed. Trans. and ed. James Strachey. New York: Liveright, 1961.

DECENTERED SUBJECT. The concept of the decentered subject can be regarded as an instance of the larger project of DECENTERING, which has played a key role in much modern thought. As in other such cases, the intent is to show that the structure in question is not organized around a fixed center (identity, consciousness, reason, etc.) but is rather a "decentered" entity. The influence of psychoanalysis has been paramount in establishing the concept of the decentered subject, first of all with Freud's discovery of the UNCONSCIOUS, which cast doubt on whether the rational, conscious mind could be regarded as center of subjectivity, and more recently with the ideas of Jacques Lacan, particularly the concept of the MIRROR STAGE and the thesis that the subject is constituted in and by its language.

Freud, Sigmund. "The Unconscious." In *Standard Edition of the Complete Psychological Works of Sigmund Freud*, vol. 14. Trans. James Strachey. London: Hogarth Press and Institute of Psycho-Analysis, 1974.

Lacan, Jacques. *Ecrits: A Selection*. Trans. Alan Sheridan. New York: Norton, 1977.

DECENTERING. *Decentering* is a term that has come to be so widely used in contemporary thought that it is difficult to trace its influence to a single source; however, Jacques Derrida's essay "Structure, Sign, and Play in the Discourse of the Human Sciences" is certainly one important point of reference. As Derrida observes, the figure of the centered structure is as old as Western thought itself, and the concept of the center has inevitably functioned as an origin, end, or fixed point, which serves to balance and organize the structure as a whole, as well as to limit the "play" of that structure. Indeed, this figure is so much a part of our languages and habits of thought that "the notion of a structure lacking any center represents the unthinkable itself." Yet there is a contradiction in this way of conceiving the center, for in order to provide a stable point of reference that governs the constitution of the structure, the center must be at once a part of that structure and an Archimedean point standing outside of it. Whether the center takes the form of an essence, a god, or a concept of reason, its relation to the structure it governs has always involved this contradiction (see also METAPHYSICS). According to Derrida, however, modern thought has attained a new level of self-consciousness about this state of affairs and as a result has often set out to free us from the disabling or coercive qualities inherent in these systems of thought through an effort of decentering that exposes the contradictions inherent in such concepts. This project, begun by thinkers like Nietzsche, Freud, and Heidegger, has become a major effort in all kinds of contemporary criticism. See also DECONSTRUCTION.

Derrida, Jacques. "Structure, Sign, and Play in the Discourse of the Human Sciences." In *Writing and Difference*. Trans. Alan Bass. Chicago: University of Chicago Press, 1978.

DECODE. Information theory regards the process of interpretation as an act of decoding. That is, the author encodes a message (whether spoken, written, visual, or audible) that the receiver must decode by referring to the appropriate set of rules or CODE. With such a view, reading a poem or novel functions much as the understanding of Morse code or semaphore. In Morse code, for example, the reader is given a message composed of short sounds and long ones. The reader then must transcribe the sounds to writing—dots and dashes—and then consult a table of equivalencies (i.e., one dot followed by one dash equals "a") where the rules of the code are given. Eventually, the reader will translate each set of dots and dashes into letters that can be read. Decoding messages and texts, then, involves the substitution of one language for another, more comprehensible language. Some critics, however, fault this model for assuming that the message can exist independently of the processes involved.

Eco, Umberto. *Semiotics and the Philosophy of Language*. Bloomington: Indiana University Press, 1984.
Pierce, John R. *Symbols, Signals, and Noise*. New York: Harper, 1961.

DECONSTRUCTION. The term *deconstruction* was coined by the French philosopher Jacques Derrida, who has used it to characterize the kind of critical effort that he advocates. Derrida's most immediate point of reference was the notion of structure (see STRUCTURALISM), and some of his most famous essays have dealt with his structuralist predecessors (e.g., the pieces on Saussure in *Of Grammatology* and Lévi-Strauss in *Writing and Difference*). Thus, if structuralism aims to "construct" the system of logical relations governing the disposition of individual elements in a text, deconstruction is, among other things, a critique of structuralism, which is seen as simply one more episode in the history of METAPHYSICS. Informed by a philosophical tradition that includes such iconoclastic figures as Nietzsche and Heidegger, whose work constitutes a sustained critique of Western metaphysics, Derrida argues that metaphysical systems are "centered" structures that depend on a paradoxical logic according to which the center is understood as both present in, and independent of, the structure (see DECENTERING). In its simplest form, the relationship between center and structure appears as a hierarchical opposition in which one term is understood to embody truth and the other is seen as merely a pale copy: essence/appearance, spirit/matter, or—an especially important case for Derrida—speech/writing. This last opposition is the brand of metaphysics that Derrida has called LOGO-CENTRISM, and it displays the curious logic of the SUPPLEMENT, which, when teased out by a deconstructive reading, can be seen to subvert the process by which a piece of writing is said to produce meaning. Instead of appearing as a mere representation of the truth that is present in speech, writing is thus shown as what, according to Derrida, it actually is: a field of limitless play, which is characterized by the movement of DIF-FÉRANCE.

From the beginning, deconstruction has had an obvious affinity for literary texts, both because its philosophical orientation is similar to that of much modern literature and because its playfulness and self-consciousness about language give deconstructive writing a distinctly literary flavor. Since metaphysical presuppositions are actually reinforced by language itself (as Nietzsche showed in the fragment "On Truth and Lie in an Extra-Moral Sense"), one cannot simply employ language to argue against metaphysics in favor of some other way of thinking. Instead, deconstructive writing takes the form of a commentary on other texts and aims to turn the language of those texts against itself, usually by playing on the contradictory or "undecidable" (see APORIA and UNDECID-ABILITY) relationship between the literal and figurative levels of the text (although the tendency to reduce deconstruction to a method of reading or, indeed, to enclose the term within the bounds of any definition has been vigorously assailed by many of its adherents). As practiced by Derrida himself in his earlier books (*Writing and Difference* and *Of Grammatology*, both 1967), as well as by such critics of the YALE SCHOOL as Paul De Man and J. Hillis Miller, deconstruction has been one of the most influential movements in American literary criticism of the last two decades. Moreover, the anti-metaphysical or, as it is sometimes called, "anti-essentialist" thrust of deconstruction has proven highly suggestive to critics working in a variety of other fields (see ESSENTIALISM), and some now use the word *deconstruction* broadly to denote any POST-STRUCTURALIST intellectual activity (it has also been widely used by journalists, for whom it is usually little more than a synonym for ANALYSIS or "demystification"). Finally, deconstruction has come under attack from both the political right and the political left for its tendency to call all values into question, for its unwillingness to make meaningful historical or cultural distinctions between one metaphysical system and another, and for what is often taken to be its excessive emphasis on the idea of textuality.

Bloom, Harold, et al., eds. *Deconstruction & Criticism.* New York: Seabury, 1979.

De Man, Paul. *Allegories of Reading: Figural Language in Rousseau, Nietzsche, Rilke, and Proust.* New Haven: Yale University Press, 1979.

—. *Blindness and Insight: Essays in the Rhetoric of Contemporary Criticism.* Minneapolis: University of Minnesota Press, 1983.

Derrida, Jacques. *Of Grammatology.* Trans. Gayatri Chakravorty Spivak. Baltimore: Johns Hopkins University Press, 1976.

—. *Writing and Difference.* Trans. Alan Bass. Chicago: University of Chicago Press, 1978.

Heidegger, Martin. *Basic Writings.* Ed. David Farrell Krell. New York: Harper and Row, 1977.

Kamuf, Peggy, ed. *A Derrida Reader: Between the Blinds.* New York: Columbia University Press, 1991.

Miller, J. Hillis. *The Ethics of Reading.* New York: Columbia University Press, 1987.

Nietzsche, Friedrich. "On Truth and Lie in an Extra-Moral Sense." In *The Portable Nietzsche.* Trans. and ed. Walter Kauffman. New York: Viking, 1954.

DEEP STRUCTURE. A concept shared by many varieties of STRUC-TURALISM, deep structure is particularly significant in the approach to narrative developed by A. J. Greimas, the ACTANTIAL MODEL. For Greimas (as well as for such like-minded structuralist critics as Tzvetan Todorov), the surface structure of a narrative, with its various characters and actions, is merely the expression of a more basic or deep structure. As always in structuralism, the analytical procedure is to describe the basic elements of the language system (LANGUE) and the rules of the codes governing their relationships, which generate the individual utterance or speech act (PAROLE); the basic elements, together with the codes, constitute the deep structure. The model was imported into NARRATOLOGY from Noam Chomsky's transformational grammar and generative linguistics.

Chomsky, Noam. "Three Models for the Description of Language." In R. Duncan Luce, Robert R. Bush, and Eugene Galanter, eds., *Readings in Mathematical Psychology.* New York: Wiley, 1963–65.

Greimas, A. J. *Du Sens.* Paris: Editions du Seuil, 1970.

—. *Structural Semantics: An Attempt at a Method*. Trans. Daniele McDowell et al. Lincoln: University of Nebraska Press, 1983.

Todorov, Tzvetan. *Qu'est-ce que le structuralisme?* Paris: Editions du Seuil, 1968.

DEFAMILIARIZATION. A key term of RUSSIAN FORMALISM, *defamiliarization* was used by Viktor Shklovsky to describe the unique quality of artistic perception and literary discourse. *Defamiliarization* (*ostranenie*) literally means "to make strange." According to Shklovsky, literature disrupts ordinary language and habitual modes of perception; its purpose "is to make objects unfamiliar, to make forms difficult, to increase the difficulty and length of the perception process," rather than to allow conventional codes of representation to deaden perceptions. Such artistic/literary/poetic estrangement is produced by means of formal mechanisms or "artistic devices" such as rhythm, phonetics, syntax, plot. Shklovsky cites as an example Tolstoy's "Kholstomer," which employs a horse's point of view in order to "make strange" the story's content.

Not only does defamiliarization distinguish literary from ordinary language, it also refers to a dynamic within literature. When a dominant literary form has become so overused as to be taken for granted and treated like ordinary language, then a previously subordinate form is foregrounded, thus defamiliarizing the situation and effecting literary development and change.

Defamiliarization also applies to literature's ability to disrupt through its representation of reality the dominant ideas of society. This is partly attributable to the term's origins in the poetics of Russian FUTURISM, a movement that rejected traditional art in favor of more iconoclastic and radical art forms.

DEIXIS. Any term or expression that refers to the context of an utterance is considered deictic. All terms that point to time, place, speaker, and listener (such as the words "now," "I," "you," "there") are deictic. More broadly, deixis (DAYksis) also describes the sometimes subtler designation of intertexts and concepts (often it is called APODEIXIS). But although deixis seems to refer to an external context (as when a poet addresses "Winter," for instance), we know that the context is a fictional one. In fact, while a poet addressing "Winter" can be imagined looking out of a window at a blizzard, the deictic function perhaps more importantly points to a specific genre of poetry with special conventions (that include, in this instance, addressing a season as though it were a person).

Culler, Jonathan. *Structuralist Poetics: Structuralism, Linguistics and the Study of Literature.* London: Routledge, 1975.
Eco, Umberto. *A Theory of Semiotics.* Bloomington: Indiana University Press, 1979.

DEMAND. See DESIRE.

DENOTATION. See CONNOTATION.

DERIVATION. In Michael Riffaterre's theory of textual production, texts are derivations from givens or hypograms. That is, a word or a phrase may be used to generate whole texts. The given may be a cliché like "all that glitters is not gold"; any number of narratives may be produced by changing the variable features of the narrative. What will not change in each of the versions of the narrative—the "invariant"—will be the fact that something attractive turns out to be worthless. For readers to understand a narrative derivation of the cliché, they must be able to see the variables in a text in terms of the invariant rule. In a simple case, the fables of Aesop may be seen as derivations of the morals that are explicitly stated at the end of the fables.

Riffaterre, Michael. *Text Production.* Trans. Terese Lyons. New York: Columbia University Press, 1983.
—. *Fictional Truth.* Baltimore: Johns Hopkins University Press, 1990.

DESIRE. Under the influence of the French psychoanalyst Jacques Lacan and his followers, much contemporary theory, psychoanalytic and otherwise, makes use of the concept of desire, which represents an attempt to understand human motivation in a way that is free of biological reductivism. Briefly, Lacanians distinguish between *need*, which can be satisfied by the acquisition of a specific object, and *demand*, which is addressed to another and seeks reciprocity. The former is ultimately biological, whereas the latter is derived from phenomenological and Hegelian thought. Although desire involves both of these simpler concepts, it cannot be reduced to either, but is directed toward the fantasy constructions that govern the endless search for a satisfactory object in the world, a search that begins with the CASTRATION COMPLEX (see also OBJET PETIT A). Depending on the bent of the individual theorist, this "inexhaustible" quality of desire is sometimes celebrated and sometimes offered as an emblem of the restless impermanence of human existence. Moreover, it should be noted that, in the work of many writers, the concept does not retain the subtleties of the Lacanian position, but is used in a way that is roughly consistent with the romantic notion of a fundamental human energy or longing.

Lacan, Jacques. *Ecrits: A Selection.* Trans. Alan Sheridan. New York: Norton, 1977.

DETERMINISM. Determinism designates a philosophy that subordinates the importance of human choice and will to other forces that limit or even dictate human actions. There have, of course, been many different kinds of determinism in the history of Western thought, including such venerable systems as that of Spinoza. In contemporary thought, however, questions of determinism arise most frequently in connection with two major traditions of thought: Marxism—which has stressed that the economic BASE is determining of culture and consciousness in the last instance—and the various language philosophies, which emphasize the shaping power of language over human thought. See also DISCOURSE, MARXIST CRITICISM.

DETERRITORIALIZATION. Originating in the works written jointly by the French poststructuralist philosopher Gilles Deleuze and the French exponent of "anti-psychiatry" Félix Guattari, the term *deterritorialization* is related to the larger poststructuralist project of DECENTERING and refers to the process of escaping from inhibiting or coercive social and intellectual structures, which are understood geographically as territory. For Deleuze and Guattari, the schizophrenic is the deterritorialized being par excellence and serves as a model for survival under capitalism. Their books are, however, deliberately freeform and resist any attempt to reduce their proliferating theoretical concepts to the rigidity of a system, so that efforts to assign terms like *deterritorialization* too specific a definition run counter to the spirit of the project. See also RHIZOME, SCHIZOANALYSIS.

Deleuze, Gilles, and Félix Guattari. *Anti-Oedipus: Capitalism and Schizophrenia*. Trans. Robert Hurley, Mark Seem, and Helen R. Lane. New York: Viking, 1977.

—. *Kafka: Toward a Minor Literature*. Trans. Dana Polan. Minneapolis: University of Minnesota Press, 1986.

—. *A Thousand Plateaus: Capitalism and Schizophrenia*. Trans. Brian Massumi. London: Athlone Press, 1988.

Massumi, Brian. *A User's Guide to "Capitalism and Schizophrenia": Deviations from Deleuze and Guattari*. Cambridge, Mass.: MIT Press, 1992.

DEVIATION. Deviation refers to the grammatical and stylistic divergence in literary texts from some kind of established norm. Popular with the PRAGUE CIRCLE, the concept of deviation is used to distinguish literary texts (especially poetry) from ordinary language. Literariness is determined by the degree to which a text differs from some kind of everyday normal usage. Wellek and Warren describe artistic deviation in terms of "distortions from normal usage" and "organized violence committed on everyday language." Since texts establish their own sets of norms and patterns, deviation may also occur *within* a text, usually to gain special emphasis. There remain the questions of how to define the "normal" and what to do with literary texts (such as some novels) that do not seem to deviate from what most consider normal language. One solution, proposed by Michael Riffaterre, is to recast the problem of defining the norm by referring to the text's deviations from the reader's expectations. See also DEFAMILIARIZATION.

Riffaterre, Michael. *Semiotics of Poetry*. Bloomington: Indiana University Press, 1978.

Wellek, René, and Austin Warren. *Theory of Literature*. London: J. Cape, 1955.

DIACHRONY. *Diachrony* (DEIakruhnee) is one of a pair of terms (the other being SYNCHRONY) associated with SEMIOTICS, the science of signs founded by the Swiss linguist Ferdinand de Saussure. It refers to the dimension of time and history, which Saussure rejected as the primary focus of attention in the study of language. Whereas the diachronic philological studies prevalent in the nineteenth century assumed that language needed to be understood as an accumulation of gradual changes to its elements through history, Saussure believed that language is first and foremost a system of simultaneous relations. Although the terms *synchronic* and *diachronic* belong to the vocabulary of STRUCTURALISM, they have become widely familiar and are used by a variety of critics to designate relationships of simultaneity and temporality. See also LANGUE, PARADIGM, PAROLE.

Saussure, Ferdinand de. *Course in General Linguistics.* Trans. Roy Harris, eds. Charles Bally and Albert Sechehaye. London: Duckworth, 1983.

DIALECTIC. A term that has a long history in Western philosophy, in its strictest sense, *dialectic* refers simply to argumentation through conversation or discussion that focuses on contradiction as its means of arriving at the truth of an issue. This is the sense in which it is applied to Socrates' method of argumentation, which depended on question and answer for its form. After Socrates dialectic came to mean a number of things. In Plato it refers to knowledge that explains all things in terms of the Idea of Good; later in his work it is the study of the interconnection of Forms or Ideas. For Aristotle dialectic is reasoning from generally accepted (but not proven or provable) premises. Kant uses the term to designate a branch of philosophy that exposes sophistic arguments. For Hegel, to whom with the exception of Marx the term is most inextricably linked, dialectic is the logic pattern of all thought. The importance of Hegel's conception of the dialectic is his introduction of the function of contradiction and negation. For Hegel thought proceeds by contradiction and in each thought its negation can be found. Hegel's famous definition of the dialectic as thesis-antithesis-synthesis, which in turn becomes thesis, has become the classic scheme of the dialectic. It is also important to remember that since for Hegel thought and reality are one and the same, the laws that govern thought also govern reality. Thus, the development of all things—from the self to the history of the world—depends on the dialectic. Marx adopted Hegel's schema but abandoned his IDEALISM, opting instead for a MATERIALIST explanation of all phenomena. For Marx and Engels, matter is not reducible to thought (or the mind), but rather precedes, informs, and is distinct from it. Thus, both matter and thought, history and philosophy, must proceed dialectically, through negation and contradiction. As Marx points out in *Capital*, each "historically developed social form" is regarded by the dialectic "as in fluid development and is in its essence critical and revolutionary." See also CRITICAL THEORY, HEGEMONY, MARXIST CRITICISM.

Bennett, Jonathan Francis. *Kant's Dialectic.* London: Cambridge University Press, 1974.
Engels, Friedrich. *Dialectics of Nature.* Moscow: Foreign Languages Publishing House, 1954.

Evans, J. D. G. *Aristotle's Concept of Dialectic.* New York: Cambridge University Press, 1977.

Gadamer, Hans Georg. *Hegel's Dialectic : Five Hermeneutical Studies.* Trans. P. Christopher Smith. New Haven: Yale University Press, 1976.

Hegel, Georg Wilhelm Friedrich. *Encyclopedia of Philosophy.* Trans. Gustav Emil Mueller. New York: Philosophical Library, 1959.

Meszaros, Istvan. *Lukàcs' Concept of Dialectic.* London: Merlin Press, 1972.

Pinkard, Terry P. *Hegel's Dialectic: The Explanation of Possibility.* Philadelphia: Temple University Press, 1988.

Sartre, Jean-Paul. *Critique of Dialectical Reason, Theory of Practical Ensembles.* Trans. Alan Sheridan-Smith, ed. Jonathan Ree. London: New Left Books, 1976.

DIALOGIC STRUCTURE (OR DIALOGICAL). In *Problems of Dostoevsky's Poetics* (1929) Mikhail Bakhtin argued that unlike Tolstoy's novels, in which character's voices are subordinated to the single perspective of the author, Dostoevsky's novels engage in dialogism or a polyphonic interplay of various characters' voices. In a dialogic work, no voice or worldview is given superiority over others; neither is that voice which may be identified with the author's necessarily the most engaging or persuasive of all those in the text. *Dialogism* as a term is a bit misleading, since a dialogic text is not limited to only two voices. Rather, the force of the term is in its reference to the exchange between voices, much as in any dialogue. See also AUTHOR, AUTHORITY, CARNIVAL.

Bakhtin, Mikhail. *The Dialogic Imagination: Four Essays.* Trans. Caryl Emerson and Michael Holquist, ed. Michael Holquist. Austin: University of Texas Press, 1981.

—. *Problems of Dostoevsky's Poetics.* Ed. and trans. Caryl Emerson. Minneapolis: University of Minnesota Press, 1984.

DIALOGISM. See DIALOGIC STRUCTURE.

DIANOIA. A term drawn from Aristotle's *Poetics, dianoia* (DEIuhNOIuh) refers in a general sense to the theme or meaning of a literary work. The term is adopted by Northrop Frye and employed in various ways in his *Anatomy of Criticism.* Frye presents five types of meaning: 1) literal (the total pattern of a work's symbols); 2) descriptive (the work's correlation with an external body of facts or propositions); 3) formal (the work's theme); 4) archetypal (the work's significance as a literary CONVENTION or genre); and 5) anagogic (the work's relation to overall literary experience). See also MYTH CRITICISM.

Aristotle. *Poetics*. Trans. Leon Golden, commentary O. B. Hardison. Englewood Cliffs, N.J.: Prentice Hall, 1968.
Frye, Northrop. *Anatomy of Criticism*. Princeton: Princeton University Press, 1957.

DIEGESIS/DIEGETIC. *Diegesis* (DEIuhJEEsis) is a term used in narrative theory (see NARRATOLOGY) to designate the fictional world in which the narrated events (the STORY) occur. This use of the term serves to distinguish the story from the actual telling of those events. Another, older and now somewhat obscure use of the term opposes it to MIMESIS or the reproduction of a reality external to the text. In this sense, diegesis corresponds most closely to telling about a thing or event and mimesis to representing that thing or event as completely as possible. A somewhat reductive, but still useful example distinguishing between the two terms would be the difference in a play between the acting out of a particular scene (mimesis) and a character's telling of other action (taking place off stage, or before the actions represented in the play) which the audience does not get to see but only to hear reported (diegesis). The diegetic (DEIuhJETik) level of a narrative refers to the fictional world within a work in which the main events of the tale (story) take place. Since the recounting of these events typically takes place after the events and often within another, undiscussed, fictional world, the telling of the story is usually considered "extradiegetic." Some works such as Joseph Conrad's *Lord Jim* or Charles Maturin's *Melmoth the Wanderer*, for example, rely on a technique known as embedded texts. In these works, storytelling itself plays a significant role in the main narrative and characters are cast as narrators. In such instances, the stories they tell are called "hypodiegetic" or "metadiegetic" to designate their relation to the primary narrative. See also NARRATIVE INSTANT.

Aristotle. *Poetics*. Trans. Leon Golden, commentary, O. B. Hardison. Englewood Cliffs, N.J.: Prentice Hall, 1968.
Genette, Gérard. *Narrative Discourse: An Essay in Method*. Trans. Jane E. Lewin. Ithaca, N.Y.: Cornell University Press, 1980.
—. *Nouveau Discours du Récit*. Paris: Editions du Seuil, 1983.
Plato. *The Republic*. Trans. Allan Bloom. New York: Basic Books, 1968.
Rimmon, Shlomith. "A Comprehensive Theory of Narrative: Genette's *Figures III* and the Structuralist Study of Fiction." *Poetics and Theory of Literature* 1, 1976.

DIFFÉRANCE. Key in the critical lexicon of the French philosopher Jacques Derrida, *différance* (DIfay**RAHNS**)—to use Derrida's words—is "neither a word nor a concept" but a playful invention meant to refer to a number of related terms crucial to Derrida's deconstructive anti-epistemology, including *différer*, which is to differ, and the usual sense of *différance* in French, which is to postpone or delay (defer), as well as the notion of difference itself. For Derrida, the term simultaneously plays off both possible meanings of the word and is irreducible to either one or the other at any time. The subtle shift from an *e* to an *a* in *difference*, thus underscores and displays Derrida's assertion that textual meaning is not ultimately determinate or decidable, but rather always subject to the "play" of *différance* within the signifying chain of language. We can see how these two senses of the word work when we look up a definition in a dictionary. On one hand words are defined according to what they are *not*, that is, how they differ from one another, which helps to delimit the possibilities of meaning. Yet that possibility of meaning is always deferred, since words are only defined by other words, which may also need definitions consisting of words, which need definitions, ad infinitum. Even the term *différance* is itself unstable, at least in Derrida's usage, for to fix it as a determinant concept would be to remove its force and its emphasis on indeterminacy. See also DECONSTRUCTION.

Derrida, Jacques. *Of Grammatology.* Trans. Gayatri Chakravorty Spivak. Baltimore: Johns Hopkins University Press, 1976.
—. *Writing and Difference.* Trans. Alan Bass. Chicago: University of Chicago Press, 1978.
—. *Margins of Philosophy.* Trans. Alan Bass. Chicago: University of Chicago Press, 1982.
Norris, Christopher. *Deconstruction: Theory and Practice.* London: Methuen, 1982.

DIFFERENCE, NEW CULTURAL POLITICS OF. The concept of difference is one of the most frequently encountered notions in contemporary criticism and theory. An important feature of DECONSTRUCTION (see DIFFÉRANCE) and other philosophies that derive from Nietzsche, it is also at the heart of much recent work that is critical of Western cultural traditions. Studies of differences in race, gender, and sexual preference are all manifestations of this new cultural politics; and in keeping with a major emphasis of poststructuralist thought, critics working in these areas seek to assert the privileges of multiplicity and diversity over homogeneity. Moreover, an important feature of this project is its emphasis on the ways that representations are politically and culturally constructed, rather than being in any sense natural or verifiable by reference to some acknowledged truth (see REPRESENTATION). Thus, the new cultural politics of difference aims not only to criticize representations that obscure difference in the name of dominant cultural traditions but also to claim a space within the field of representation for previously excluded minorities.

DISCOURSE. In the past three decades, the term *discourse* has taken on a number of meanings other than the traditional one of a formal exposition in speech or writing. This multiplication in uses can be traced to the "linguistic turn" that theory and criticism have taken since the advent of STRUCTURALISM in the late 1960s and early 1970s. For linguists, the term refers to a complete unit of language longer than a sentence. Discourse analysis is the study of the relations of these units in written or spoken language. In NARRATOLOGY discourse indicates the narration or the language of the text (as opposed to the ordering of the events; see FAB-ULA/SUJET, PLOT).

Poststructuralist critics and theorists have also adopted the term, but use it in ways that are both connected to and distinct from its narratological and linguistic usages. For these critics, discourse refers to TEXTS, but also verbal signification in general. Often the term actually replaces "text," thus helping to emphasize (and deconstruct) what POSTSTRUC-TURALISM sees as an arbitrary and artificial distinction between literary and nonliterary works. Following Michel Foucault, the term has also been used to indicate language in use. That is, for Foucault, discourses are coherent, self-referential bodies of statements that produce an account of reality by generating "knowledge" about particular objects or concepts, and also by shaping the rules of what can be said and known about those entities. Thus, one can speak of "legal discourse," "aesthetic discourse," "medical discourse," etc. These groups of statements and rules exist historically and change as the material conditions for their possibility also change. In this sense the term is similar to one of T. S. Kuhn's concepts of PARADIGM. Foucault also argues that discourse in this sense is not defined by an exchange between individuals, but exists at a level of anonymity. Discourse is not the expression of a "thinking, knowing SUB-JECT"; rather, it is "situated at the level of the 'it is said.'" For Foucault discourse informs and shapes subjectivity, including the possible activities and knowledge of the individual (see EPISTEME).

This use of discourse has led to some confusion as to the difference between it and a post-Marxist view of IDEOLOGY. Indeed, in recent years the two have been used almost interchangeably; however, in most versions of Marxism, ideology is opposed to "science," which Foucauldian analysis considers simply another discourse. Also, a distinction is often made between ideology as a system of beliefs or the narrativized version of a subject's lived "imaginary relation to the real" and discourse as the INSTITUTIONALIZATION of such ideologies. See also HEGEMONY, POWER.

Chatman, Seymour. *Story and Discourse*. Ithaca, N.Y.: Cornell University Press, 1978.

Crusius, Timothy. *Discourse: A Critique and Synthesis of Major Theories*. New York: Modern Language Association, 1989.

Eagleton, Terry. *Ideology: An Introduction*. London: Verso, 1991.

Foucault, Michel. *The Order of Things: An Archaeology of the Human Sciences*. New York: Vintage, 1970.

—. *The Archaeology of Knowledge*. Trans. A. M. Sheridan Smith. New York: Pantheon, 1972.

Macdonell, Diane. *Theories of Discourse: An Introduction*. Oxford: Blackwell, 1986.

White, Hayden. *Tropics of Discourse: Essays in Cultural Criticism*. Baltimore: Johns Hopkins University Press, 1978.

DISINTERESTEDNESS. The term *disinterestedness* is perhaps most familiarly associated with the criticism of Matthew Arnold, although it had a long and various career among nineteenth-century English critics and continues to exert influence in some quarters today. For romantic writers like Wordsworth, Shelley, and Hazlitt, the adjective *disinterested* is distinguished from adjacent ideas like *uninterested, impartial,* and *detached*; it refers to an attitude of immersion that prepares one to render judgments free of vested interest, prejudice, or habit. This usage implies the necessity of what the romantics called *sympathy*—the ability to enter imaginatively into the condition of another. By contrast, Arnold assumed the possibility of utter selflessness and used the word *distinterestedness* to mean a state of ideal objectivity and neutrality, an impartiality that allows the critic to see an object "as in itself it really is." In his usage, the concept remains distinct from *uninterestedness*, which denotes apathy, but now involves precisely the kind of impartiality and detachment that the romantics rejected. Disinterestedness thus becomes the cornerstone of an objectivist theory of poetry, which invokes timeless standards of quality. It is this usage to which later critics, beginning with Arnold's successors, Walter Pater and Oscar Wilde, reacted (see AES-THETICISM); and anti-Arnoldian positions have become the orthodoxy in much contemporary criticism, which emphasizes the imbrication of individuals in language, history, and culture.

Arnold, Matthew. "The Function of Criticism at the Present Time." In *Poetry and Criticism of Matthew Arnold.* Ed. A. Dwight Culler. Boston: Houghton Mifflin, 1961.

Bromwich, David. "The Genealogy of Disinterestedness." In *A Choice of Inheritance: Self and Community From Edmund Burke to Robert Frost.* Cambridge, Mass.: Harvard University Press, 1989.

DISPLACEMENT. In Freudian psychoanalysis, the term *displacement* is used to describe the unconscious process by which mental energies are liable to become detached from one idea and attach themselves instead to others that are related to the first idea by association. This tendency of mental energy to displace itself along a chain of associations is one of the fundamental characteristics of UNCONSCIOUS processes, along with CONDENSATION. Following a suggestion of the linguist Roman Jakobson, the French psychoanalyst Jacques Lacan has attempted to correlate these two processes with the rhetorical figures of METAPHOR and METONYMY, which Jakobson saw as fundamental poles of linguistic invention. Thus, displacement follows the metonymic process of creating an association based on contiguity, whereas condensation corresponds to metaphor in that it creates an association based on similarity.

DOCUMENTARY HISTORY. Also sometimes called "objectivist," documentary history bases its research activities on seemingly incontrovertible facts derived from critical evaluations of disparate sources. In this view of history as a discipline, historiography—the writing of history—attempts to provide a continuous narrative based upon these sources. As Dominick LaCapra has pointed out, in such a model of history, all sources "tend to be treated . . . in terms of factual or referential propositions that may be derived from them to provide information about specific times and places."

In the wake of such theorists of history as Michel Foucault, Hayden White, and LaCapra, the documentary model of history has come under considerable attack. In such a model, they argue, the historical imagination is constrained to conceiving of history as a continuous, fluid development, and any new ways of viewing the past must be based on the discovery of new material. The "blind spot" in this method of history, argue these "new" historians, is that the very sources that inform documentary histories are themselves open to scrutiny and reinterpretation. Such reinterpretation should be based not only on the contexts of the sources but on the historical situation of their interpreters, that is, of the historians themselves. Foucault, White, LaCapra, and others claim that the objective goal of documentary history to reconstruct the past "in its own terms" is in reality a relativistic pursuit and only persists in propagating the fiction that an objective understanding of the past is possible, desirable, and necessary. See also ANTIPOSITIVISM, GENEALOGY, NEW HISTORICISM, POSITIVISM.

Foucault, Michel. *The Order of Things: An Archaeology of the Human Sciences.* New York: Vintage, 1970.

—. *Language, Counter-Memory, Practice: Selected Essays and Interviews.* Trans. Donald F. Bouchard and Sherry Simon. Ithaca, N.Y.: Cornell University Press, 1977.

LaCapra, Dominick. *Rethinking Intellectual History.* Ithaca, N.Y.: Cornell University Press, 1983.

—. *History and Criticism.* Ithaca, N.Y.: Cornell University Press, 1985.

White, Hayden. *Metahistory: The Historical Imagination in Nineteenth-Century Europe.* Baltimore: Johns Hopkins University Press, 1973.

—. *Tropics of Discourse.* Baltimore: Johns Hopkins University Press, 1978.

DOMINATION. Domination is a condition in which one individual, community, or class possesses and wields power over another individual or group. *Domination* most often describes relations of power deemed to be unfair or illegitimate—when, for instance, the interests of the dominating are not the interests of the dominated or when the dominating group's power is founded on the suppression of the rights of the dominated. An influential use of the term can be found in Antonio Gramsci's distinction between *domination* (*dominante*, which refers to the subjugation and eventual liquidation of groups opposed to the more powerful) and *leadership* (*dirigente*, which refers to the enlightened governance of "kindred and allied groups"). Cultural domination occurs when a politically or economically empowered group imposes its values (aesthetic, moral, etc.) upon those of a subordinate group. Cultural domination is a relatively modern idea. In earlier times, culture was seen as playing a role separate from the spheres of the social, political and economic. See COLONIALISM.

Gramsci, Antonio. "Notes on Italian History." In *Selections from the Prison Notebooks.* Trans. and ed. Quintin Hoare and Geoffrey Nowell Smith. New York: International Publishers, 1971.

DOUBLE CONSCIOUSNESS. Double consciousness is a term that refers to the multiple awareness of the ethnic member of a majority culture. It was first coined by the African-American scholar W. E. B. Du Bois in his discussion of "the souls of black folk": "The Negro is a sort of seventh son, born with a veil, and gifted with second-sight in this American world,—a world which yields him no true self-consciousness, but only lets him see himself through the revelation of the other world. It is a peculiar sensation, this double-consciousness." For African Americans, argues Du Bois, self-consciousness is always also informed by the majority's expectations and representations of them. Since Du Bois, the term has became one of the most important concepts of African-American criticism, and, indeed, of contemporary literary criticism in general. Henry Louis Gates, Jr., for instance, is one of the best-known contemporary critics exploring the connection between the divided African-American consciousness and the inherently double-voiced and parodic nature of the African-American text. Werner Sollors, on the other hand, sees this intense awareness of doubleness as extending to American ethnic writers in general, allowing them a playful relation to language and voice that helps lead to the discovery of new forms. He would further extend this split awareness beyond pure considerations of ethnicity to "the general situation of cultural doubleness in America."

The concept of the ethnic author as "split at the root," in Adrienne Rich's term, parallels white feminist critics' descriptions of the split consciousness of women writers, whether designated "ethnic" or not. For instance, Virginia Woolf describes women as suffering from "a sudden splitting off of consciousness" when they become aware of their gendered status, while Adrienne Rich speaks of women as "exhausted in the double life" of "the lie of compulsory heterosexuality." The exploration of the divided consciousness of this "double life" has become the primary project of ethnic and gender-related criticism today. See also COMPULSORY HETEROSEXUALITY, DOUBLE-VOICED TEXT, FREE INDIRECT DISCOURSE.

Du Bois, W. E. B. "Of Our Spiritual Strivings." In *The Souls of Black Folk.* New York: Blue Heron Press, 1953.

Gates, Henry Louis, Jr. *The Signifying Monkey: A Theory of African-American Literary Criticism.* New York: Oxford University Press, 1988.

Rich, Adrienne. "Compulsory Heterosexuality and Lesbian Existence." In *Blood, Bread, and Poetry: Selected Prose 1979–1985.* New York: Norton, 1986.

—. "Split at the Root: An Essay on Jewish Identity." *Blood, Bread, and Poetry: Selected Prose 1979–1985.* New York: Norton, 1986.

Sollors, Werner. "Ethnic Modernism and Double Audience." In *Beyond Ethnicity: Consent and Descent in American Culture.* New York: Oxford University Press, 1986.

Woolf, Virginia. *A Room of One's Own.* New York: Harcourt Brace Jovanovich, 1957.

DOUBLE FOCALIZATION. Double focalization occurs when an event or situation is presented in a narrative through two simultaneous perspectives. This is not the same as a multiple focalization, in which an event or situation may be presented a number of times from different perspectives; rather, double focalization works so as to provide the reader (or viewer, for the technique is often used in film) with two characters' or narrators' points of view at the same time. For example, in films the reading of a letter by a character is often shot in order to give the viewer's sense of the character's perspective as well as the more "objective" perspective of the camera.

DOUBLE-VOICED TEXT. A term used by Henry Louis Gates, Jr., in his book *The Signifying Monkey,* but also used by other African-American critics and white feminist critics to describe the way a work of literature reflects the double consciousness of an ethnic or woman writer. Mikhail Bakhtin also uses the term *double-voiced* to refer to words, particularly in parody, that contain opposite meanings. A text can be double-voiced in the following ways: 1) it can be addressed to a double audience; 2) it can have double literary ancestors or contain double styles; 3) it can both repeat and revise previous motifs within its tradition; or 4) it can contain a double message.

Elaine Showalter argues that women's writing, just as African-American writing, should be read as a "double-voiced discourse," following the sociological concept of women as a "muted group" within both their own and the dominant male culture. This double status produces a double text, what Sandra Gilbert and Susan Gubar call the duplicitous or "palimpsestic" nature of women's writing. The project of feminist criticism, then, is to uncover the hidden meaning or plot in women's writing related to gender, what Nancy Miller calls the "invisible intertext," just as African-American criticism uncovers the hidden meaning or plot related to race. See also DOUBLE CONSCIOUSNESS, FREE INDIRECT DISCOURSE, PALIMPSEST, PARODY, SIGNIFYING.

Bakhtin, Mikhail. "Discourse Typology in Prose." In Ladislav Matejka and Krystyna Pomorska, eds., *Readings in Russian Poetics: Formalist and Structuralist Views.* Cambridge, Mass.: MIT Press, 1971.
Gates, Henry Louis, Jr. *The Signifying Monkey: A Theory of African-American Literary Criticism.* New York: Oxford University Press, 1988.
Gilbert, Sandra M., and Susan Gubar. *The Madwoman in the Attic: The Woman Writer and the Nineteenth-Century Literary Imagination.* New Haven: Yale University Press, 1979.
Miller, Nancy K. "Emphasis Added: Plots and Plausibilities in Women's Fiction." In Elaine Showalter, ed., *The New Feminist Criticism.* New York: Pantheon, 1985.
Showalter, Elaine. "Feminist Criticism in the Wilderness." In Elaine Showalter, ed., *The New Feminist Criticism.* New York: Pantheon, 1985.

DOXA. *Doxa* is a term used by Roland Barthes to indicate common opinion or convention. As a petrified formation of a given society, the doxa threatens the vitality of the artist or critic and must constantly be countered with innovation or paradox (para-doxa). This is a neverending process, however, because the paradox eventually becomes conventional and must itself then be replaced with another paradox. Thus, for Barthes, the theoretical enterprise is also always undoing or subverting itself, challenging its own doxa.

Barthes, Roland. *Mythologies.* Trans. Annette Lavers. New York: Hill and Wang, 1972.

DRIVE. *Drive* is the now-preferred translation of the German term *trieb*, a key concept in psychoanalytic thought that has usually been translated as INSTINCT, a word that critics now agree makes sexuality seem too much a matter of biology.

DUALISM. *Dualism* designates a theory referring to the fundamental types into which individual substances may be divided. In religion dualism is expressed as the division of the universe between two independent and often equally powerful forces: good and evil. In some radical dualistic doctrines, such as ancient Zoroastrianism, all creatures are either absolutely good or absolutely evil beings. In other religions good and evil comprise beings, and salvation lies in overcoming the forces of evil.

According to philosophical theories of dualism, all things may be categorized as either mental (spiritual) or material, and neither category is reducible to the other. In Western philosophy dualistic thought can be said to occur as early as Pythagoras and Anaxagoras; and Plato's dialogues, though not dogmatic, incline toward support of the view that the soul exists independently of the body and that the intelligible world is independent of the world we perceive through our senses. After Descartes, who divides all reality into either mind or matter, modern philosophic discussions of dualism have often been expressed in terms of the SUBJECT-OBJECT division, where the subject is the perceiving, cognizant being and the object is anything external to that being. See also COGITO, MONISM.

E

ÉCRITURE.   French for "writing," the term *écriture* (AYkreeTUHR) is used in a number of ways in literary criticism. First, the term may refer to Roland Barthes's argument, from *Writing Degree Zero*, that blank or neutral writing is an illusion. For Barthes, all writing has some style that informs our perception of the world. In a later work, "Writers and Authors" ("*Écrivains et écrivants*"), Barthes uses the term to refer to writing as an intransitive activity. Barthes distinguishes between those who write about "things" in order to take the reader beyond the text (*écrivants*) and *écrivains*, or those who write "intransitively." This second type of writer "has nothing but writing itself" and intends to call the reader's attention to the very activity of writing. A third way in which *écriture* is used in literary criticism comes from Jacques Derrida's employment of the term in *Of Grammatology*. Derrida upsets the traditional, what he terms "violent," hierarchy of speech over writing as a signifying practice. For Derrida, both speech and writing are subject to the same instabilities, both lack "presence," both are indeterminate. Speech, for Derrida, is "always already" caught up in or "contaminated" by writing, which he characterizes as *différance* and which takes the place of speech as the norm for language. As a result of this move, meaning itself no longer operates as isolate and determinate—conditions that Derrida argues were always illusory. Rather, meaning becomes a series of deferrals, SUPPLEMENTS, and substitutions rather than stable and fixed. A fourth and final way *écriture* has been used is in French feminist theorist Hélène Cixous's conception of *écriture feminine*, which she defines as writing from/by the (female) body and which moves beyond the binary constraints of patriarchy.

Barthes, Roland. *Writing Degree Zero.* Trans. Annette Lavers and Colin Smith. London: Cape, 1967.

—. "Authors and Writers." In *Critical Essays.* Trans. R. Howard. Evanston, Ill.: Northwestern University Press, 1972.

Cixous, Hélène. "The Laugh of the Medusa." In Elaine Marks and Isabelle de Courtivron, eds., *New French Feminisms.* Trans. Keith Cohen and Paula Cohen. Amherst: University of Massachusetts Press, 1980.

Derrida, Jacques. *Of Grammatology.* Trans. Gayatri Chakravorty Spivak. Baltimore: Johns Hopkins University Press, 1976.

ÉCRITURE FÉMININE. Though sometimes mistakenly associated with French feminist thought generally, the concept of *écriture feminine* (AIkree**TUHR** femeeNEEN) was mainly developed in the work of the French feminist Hélène Cixous. Cixous defines it as writing from/by the (female) body. Based in part on Jacques Derrida's linguistic theories, it is a revolutionary writing that would explode the oppressive structures of conventional (male) language and thought. According to Cixous, what makes *écriture féminine* powerful is the subversive and excessive character of female sexuality; like feminine sexuality, it is multiple instead of single, diffuse instead of focused, oriented toward process instead of goal. Celebrating multiplicity and openness, *écriture féminine* breaks apart the binary oppositions that organize (masculine) writing: head/heart, active/passive, culture/nature, father/mother. Some feminists have objected to the concept of *écriture féminine* because it often seems to define femininity as a quality inherent in female biology and essentially opposed to masculinity, thereby reinforcing the very distinctions it purports to dismantle. Yet in French the adjective *féminine* is ambiguous—referring both to biological sex (the female) and to cultural/historical gender (the feminine)—and this ambiguity is also present in references to *écriture feminine* by Cixous and others. Though frequently invoking images of the female body, *écriture feminine* is sometimes defined as a product of culture and history (women learn to speak with and through their bodies more than men do), and it can therefore theoretically be applied to writing by men as well as women. In fact, Cixous names Jean Genet along with Colette and Marguerite Duras as the only writers she would actually associate with this style; the further implication here is that *écriture feminine* does not so much describe existing writing as posit a utopian ideal. See also BISEXUALITY, JOUISSANCE, SEXUAL DIFFERENCE.

Cixous, Hélène. "The Laugh of the Medusa." In Elaine Marks and Isabelle de Courtivron, eds., *New French Feminisms*. Trans. Keith Cohen and Paula Cohen. Amherst: University of Massachusetts Press, 1980.

— and Catherine Clément. *The Newly Born Woman*. Trans. Betsy Wing. Minneapolis: University of Minnesota Press, 1986.

Irigaray, Luce. *This Sex Which is Not One*. Trans. Catherine Porter. Ithaca, N.Y.: Cornell University Preess, 1985.

Kristeva, Julia. *Desire in Language: A Semiotic Approach to Literature and Art*. Trans. Alice Jardine et al., ed. Leon S. Roudiez. Oxford: Blackwell, 1980.

Moi, Toril. *Sexual/Textual Politics: Feminist Literary Theory*. New York: Routledge, 1985.

EGO. A disputed translation of the German personal pronoun *das Ich* (the "I"), this term designates one of the three agencies, along with the ID and the SUPEREGO, that make up the psychical apparatus in Freud's "second topography," which was worked out in the years after 1920 and followed his earlier distinction between the preconscious-conscious and UNCONSCIOUS systems. In this scheme, the ego is the sense of self, which exists in a mediating relation of dependency and conflict with the id and the superego. Shaped by the experience of external reality (see REALITY PRINCIPLE) and above all by IDENTIFICATION (see EGO-IDEAL), it performs a largely defensive function by calling instinctual energy into the service of preservation and the avoidance of unpleasure.

Although the concept of the ego only acquires a strict technical meaning in the second topography, it appears in Freud's work from the very beginning, plays a major role in the theory of NARCISSISM, and is in fact one of the cornerstones of psychoanalysis.

Freud, Sigmund. *The Ego and the Id.* Trans. Joan Riviere, ed. James Strachey. New York: Norton, 1960.

——. "On Narcissism: An Introduction." In *Standard Edition of the Complete Psychological Works of Sigmund Freud*, vol. 14. Trans. James Strachey. London: Hogarth Press and Institute of Psycho-Analysis, 1974.

EGO-IDEAL. *Ego-ideal* is a psychoanalytic term used to designate a model with which one identifies (see IDENTIFICATION). This model becomes an agency of the psyche, created through the combination of a narcissistic idealization of one's own EGO and an identification with one's parents or the ideals they represent. At times in Freud's later writings, the concept of the ego-ideal is interchangeable with that of the SUPEREGO. At other times, it clearly refers to a subordinate and less complex idea, and the majority of psychoanalysts have preferred to use it in this way.

Freud, Sigmund. *Group Psychology and the Analysis of the Ego.* Trans. James Strachey. London: International Psycho-Analytical Press, 1922.

——. *The Ego and the Id.* Trans. Joan Riviere, ed. James Strachey. New York: Norton, 1960.

——. *New Introductory Lectures on Psychoanalysis.* Trans. James Strachey. New York: Norton, 1965.

Freud, Sigmund. "On Narcissism: An Introduction." In *Standard Edition of the Complete Psychological Works of Sigmund Freud*, vol. 14. Trans. James Strachey. London: Hogarth Press and Institute of Psycho-Analysis, 1974.

EMPIRICISM. Empiricism is a philosophical tradition based on the assumption that knowledge is acquired through observation and experience, rather than through deductive reasoning (rationalism). In current theoretical debates, empiricism has come under attack for its presupposition that the "facts" speak for themselves and are divorced from values, beliefs, and IDEOLOGIES that structure and inform observation itself. Thus, according to POSTSTRUCTURALIST critiques, empiricism, in its selection of some events or objects as "facts" and others as "irrelevancies," fails to recognize and account for its own interpretive framework.

Operative for empiricists is the belief that facts precede theories and that one can be an impartial, objective observer of "facts." Poststructuralists, on the other hand, argue that all knowledge is partisan and cannot be divorced from the values and beliefs of the observer (ideology), and that "objectivity" is itself ideological and underwrites the major political and intellectual institutions and DISCOURSES of the Western world, including HUMANISM, INDIVIDUALISM, and capitalism.

Empiricism has been the dominant tradition in English philosophy, especially "natural philosophy," and the sciences that developed from it since John Locke (1632–1704). Other major figures in the tradition include George Berkeley (1685–1753), David Hume (1711–1776), and John Stuart Mill (1806–1873). See also ENLIGHTENMENT, POSITIVISM.

Aune, Bruce, *Rationalism, Empiricism, and Pragmatism: An Introduction.* New York: Random House, 1970.

Berkeley, George. *A Treatise Concerning the Principles of Human Knowledge.* Menston, U.K.: Scolar Press, 1971.

Cowley, Fraser. *A Critique of British Empiricism.* London: Macmillan, 1968.

Deleuze, Gilles. *Empiricism and Subjectivity: An Essay on Hume's Theory of Human Nature.* Trans. Constantin V. Boundas. New York: Columbia University Press, 1991.

Feyerabend, Paul K. *Problems of Empiricism.* Cambridge: Cambridge University Press, 1981.

Hume, David, *A Treatise of Human Nature.* Oxford: Clarendon Press, 1965.

Locke, John. *An Essay Concerning Human Understanding.* Menston: Scolar Press, 1970.

Mill, John Stuart. *A System of Logic.* 10th ed. London: Longmans, Green, and Co., 1879.

(THE) ENLIGHTENMENT. The *Enlightenment* is one of the common names given to the historical period in Europe encompassing roughly the second half of the seventeenth century and the eighteenth century. The word also refers to the major intellectual project of the era, which was described by the philosopher Immanuel Kant as "man's emergence from his self-incurred immaturity." Thinkers of the Enlightenment rejected superstition and blind faith, extolled reason, and viewed it as the crucial means of improvement in all areas of human life. The control of passion by rational thought, the mastery of nature by science and technology, and the replacement of despotism by more responsible and democratic forms of government were all understood as forms of enlightenment.

These projects of enlightenment continue to exert a significant influence on the modern world. The Marxism of Jürgen Habermas, the linguistics of Noam Chomsky, and the EXISTENTIALISM of Jean-Paul Sartre are just a few of the widely differing intellectual schools that have placed themselves within traditions of thought descended from the Enlightenment. However, a significant amount of POSTSTRUCTURALIST thought has sought to reveal the coercive or dictatorial tendencies of Enlightenment reason, firmly rejecting the existence of any such universally valid system or faculty. An important precursor of this general tendency in modern thought is Theodor Adorno and Max Horkheimer's *Dialectic of Enlightenment*, which described the historical decay of Enlightenment reason into "instrumental reason," which emphasizes the extension of technological control over nature and people in order to further capitalism. Thus, Adorno and Horkheimer argue that because of this transformation, reason has lost its liberating power and has become a force of domination and oppression.

Adorno, Theodor, and Max Horkheimer. *Dialectic of Enlightenment*. Trans. John Cummings. New York: Seabury Press, 1972.

Kant, Immanuel. "What is Enlightenment?" In *Philosophical Writings*. Trans. Lewis White Beck, ed. Ernst Behler. New York: Continuum, 1986.

EPIC THEATER. The term *epic theater* is associated with the twentieth-century German playwright Bertolt Brecht, who sought to create a theater that would further the project of Marxist revolution. It is derived from the distinction made by Goethe and Schiller, in their essay "On Epic and Dramatic Poetry," between the dramatic, which draws the audience into emotional identification, and the epic, which is received in a spirit of contemplation. According to Brecht, the sense of distance conveyed in the term *epic* is essential to the formation of an attitude that is genuinely critical of existing social forms, and he sought to create it by means of what he called *alienation effects*. These are devices that deliberately break the conventions of nineteenth-century realistic theater, which Brecht saw as encouraging passive acceptance of the status quo through absorption in the theatrical spectacle. Instead, Brecht set his plays in faraway lands and eras, introduced songs into the action, gave away plot developments by means of placards exhibited onstage, and, above all, developed a style of acting that sought to emphasize the artificial and constructed nature of the proceedings. Though influenced by the use of masks and ritualized gestures in the theaters of Asia and ancient Greece, Brecht argued that his alienation effects nevertheless represented a departure in that they did not produce "hypnotic" results. By contrast, they served to defamiliarize the familiar and thereby to encourage the kind of scientific attitude that allowed Galileo to see the strangeness of the pendulum and to inquire into the laws governing its motion. Ideally, the Brechtian spectator would come to regard society with that same attitude and to view it as the product of the historical processes defined by Marxism, rather than as a timeless and unchangeable state of affairs. Like other forms of modernist art, epic theater is thus an art of DEFAMILIARIZATION, although the Marxist inclination of Brecht's thought sets it apart from the AESTHETICISM exhibited by many varieties of modernism.

Benjamin, Walter. "What is Epic Theater?" In *Illuminations*. Trans. Harry Zohn, ed. Hannah Arendt. New York: Harcourt Brace and World, 1968.

Brecht, Bertolt. *Brecht on Theater*. Trans. and ed. John Willett. New York: Hill and Wang, 1964.

EPISTEME. In the strictest sense, taken from the Greek, *episteme* (epiS-TEEM or ePIStuhMAY) denotes scientific or philosophical knowledge—wisdom. Epistemology is literally the theory or science of the method or grounds of knowledge. In the context of contemporary structuralist and poststructuralist theory, however, *episteme* has acquired a broader and more complex resonance, particularly in the work of Michel Foucault.

In his *The Order of Things* (*Les Mots et Les Choses*), Foucault uses the term to signify the ways in which knowledge is acquired, ordered, and disseminated in a specific historical period. In his later book, *The Archaeology of Knowledge*, he extends his definition, writing that by episteme he is referring to "the total set of relations that unite, at a given period, the discursive practices that give rise to epistemological figures, sciences, and possibly formalized systems." Rather than defining the term as a particular form of knowledge or "worldview" that authorizes or confirms the unity of a period or a cognizant SUBJECT, he emphasizes that it is the "set of total relations between the sciences." The relations, or underlying assumptions about the nature of knowledge within any period, are discussed at length in *The Order of Things*. For example, he argues that in the Renaissance, knowledge was based on a system of the decoding of resemblances; in the neoclassical period this was replaced by an episteme grounded in difference and distinctions, which in turn was replaced by one based on historical development in the nineteenth century. Although the term gained considerable currency in the 1960s and early 1970s, it was often attacked as a form of STRUCTURALISM. Foucault in his later work ultimately stopped using the term in the usage he had originally formulated. See also AUTHOR, DISCOURSE, PARADIGM.

Foucault, Michel. *The Order of Things: An Archaeology of the Human Sciences*. New York: Vintage, 1970.

—. *The Archaeology of Knowledge.* Trans. A. M. Sheridan Smith. New York: Pantheon, 1972.

EPISTEMOLOGY. The branch of philosophy that is concerned with theories of knowledge, epistemology has traditionally focused on the central
issues of the nature and source of knowledge and of the ability of the
SUBJECT to possess reliable knowledge. Philosophers have been radically
divided on these topics for centuries. Plato, for example, argued that the
ideas of reason that are intrinsic to the human mind are the foundations
of all knowledge. Similarly, René Descartes' formulation "I think, therefore I am," while a statement of ONTOLOGY or being, is also fundamentally epistemological—positing the ability to know as requisite to existence. In contrast to this rationalism is the EMPIRICISM of thinkers like
John Locke and David Hume who argue that our ideas (knowledge)
spring from sense experience: thus, Locke's famous formulation of the
human mind as a *tabula rasa* or "clean slate" upon which the record of
experiences is written as thought.

The eighteenth-century German philosopher Immanuel Kant, in
contradistinction to Locke and Hume, argued that some categories of
understanding, such as time and space, exist independently of our experience of them. They are inherent to the human mind and help to order
our experiences. However, Kant is also in opposition to Plato, who
believed that true knowledge is limited to the world of Ideas or Forms—
the suprasensible world in which things exist in their pure, unmediated
state. Like the empiricists, Kant argued that it is impossible to know the
"thing-in-itself," that is, in its form or essence. Our knowledge is thus
confined to the world we experience.

Issues of epistemology have once again become central to theoretical debates, especially in discussions of the roles of IDEOLOGY or DIS-
COURSE in the constitution of the individual (or subject). Theorists
such as Jacques Derrida, Michel Foucault, and Jean Baudrillard have
argued that knowledge is ideologically or discursively bound and that
meaning does not issue from some originary source but rather is in a
state of INDETERMINACY and free play. These issues have been of special interest to cultural critics who study such phenomena as the
reporting of politics or wars. The possibility of an unproblematized
knowledge of these things, when mediated through the press, political
organizations, or the military, becomes ever more remote and the ways

in which such information is manipulated becomes one of the primary foci of investigation.

EPOCHÉ. Epoché (EPoSHAY) refers to the "bracketing" process in phenomenology, the keeping in abeyance of the natural mode or commonsense manner of observing phenomena. It is the suspension of the presuppositions and preconceptions about the "real" status of objects and subjects in order to analyze phenomenologically the operation of consciousness. Edmund Husserl describes the phenomenological epoché as the "methodology through which I come to understand myself as that ego and life of consciousness in which and through which the entire objective world exists for me, and is for me precisely as it is." See also PHENOMENOLOGY, SUSPENSION.

Husserl, Edmund. *The Paris Lectures.* Trans. Peter Kostenbaum. The Hague: Martinus Nijhoff, 1975.

ERASURE (*SOUS RATURE*). In his 1967 work, *Of Grammatology*, philosopher Jacques Derrida began the practice of placing under suspicion certain notions he links to the metaphysics of presence (see ABSENCE/PRESENCE). Words that signify appeals to authority, systemetizing, citations, or other interpretive conventions that he believes rely on conceptions of recoverable origins, the revelation of truth, or decidable and univocal meaning are marked through typographically with a large black *X*. It is important that Derrida chooses to term this practice "erasure," since metaphorically erasure often leaves traces of the marks that were once completely and totally visible. Such traces, however, do not indicate the marks themselves but the absence of the marks. And when Derrida places a term "under erasure," he is doing precisely the same thing—calling attention to the absence of univocal meaning, truth, or origin. Unlike the German philosopher Martin Heidegger, from whom he borrowed the device of crossing through the word, Derrida does not assume that concealed or forgotten Being (or meaning) is recoverable. Heidegger's philosophical project depended upon this assumption. For Derrida all we ever have of meaning or truth are traces, which suggest all the non-present meanings of the words, all the possible DIFFÉRANCE of the word.

Derrida, Jacques. *Of Grammatology*. Trans. Gayatri Chakravorty Spivak. Baltimore: Johns Hopkins University Press, 1976.

ESSENTIALISM. In its philosophical usage, *essentialism* can denote any one of three possible and distinct positions. The first is allied to a particular aspect of platonism which argues that physical objects are imperfect copies of their abstract forms, their *noumenal* or irreducible existence. Another use of *essentialism* is tied to linguistic practice and asserts that an object may have irreducible or essential qualities only in as much as those qualities are necessary for the object's existence. Thus, a person may be essentially two-legged only if described as an entity that relies on two-leggedness for existence, such as a bicyclist or a runner. The third use of the term is, like the first, metaphysical. According to this position, some objects, no matter what their definition or description, have properties that are timeless and immutable, and these properties not only are requisite to their existence but are *expressed* in their definitions or descriptions.

In theoretical discussions essentialism has come under considerable attack from certain POSTSTRUCTURALIST positions, especially in regard to issues of meaning. It is argued that since meaning is never completely ascertainable, to rely upon a concept of fixed and unchanging—essential—meaning for texts rather than to explore the effects of a plurality of meanings imposes restrictions on interpretation that prohibit rather than engender textual investigation. Often described as "anti-humanist," such arguments deny the existence of an essential human nature, a metaphysical starting point (such as God), or the emancipatory claims of such political systems as liberalism or Marxism.

The difficulty of practical politics is intensified in light of such theories. On one hand, to accept an essentialist position that supports concepts such as human nature runs the risk of reproducing the same sort of race, gender, and class oppressions that have disfigured so many political systems. On the other hand, to abandon certain essentialist assumptions would seem to dismiss any standards for evaluating actions and effects, thus creating a relativized world in which the intrinsic value of an interpretation, argument, or action is no greater or less than any other. One way some theorists have attempted to negotiate this difficulty is through strategic essentialism, in which for the purpose of local, limited political activity an essentialist position is adopted. See also COGITO, HUMANISM.

Fuss, Diana. *Essentially Speaking*. New York: Routledge, 1990.

Rorty, Richard. *Contingency, Irony, and Solidarity*. Cambridge: Cambridge University Press, 1989.

Spivak, Gayatri Chakravorty. *In Other Worlds*. New York: Methuen, 1987.

—. "Can the Subaltern Speak?" In Cary Nelson and Lawrence Grossberg, eds., *Marxism and the Interpretation of Culture*. Urbana: University of Illinois Press, 1988.

ESTRANGEMENT. See ALIENATION, EPIC THEATER.

ETHNICITY. See RACE/ETHNICITY.

ETHNOCENTRIC/ETHNOCENTRISM. *Ethnocentrism* means interpreting and judging a country, ethnic group, or culture foreign to you on the basis of your own ethnicity, nationality, or culture; it often means considering your own group superior to all others. The term first appeared in W. G. Sumner's *Folkways* (1906) as a technical term for the "view of things in which one's group is the center of everything, and all others are scaled and rated with reference to it." Prominent among studies of ethnocentrism is Daniel J. Levinson's "The Study of Ethnocentric Ideology," which presents a scale for measuring degrees of ethnocentrism.

Levinson, Daniel J. "The Study of Ethnocentric Ideology." In T. W. Adorno et al., eds., *The Authoritarian Personality*. New York: Norton, 1982.

EUROCENTRISM. The term *eurocentrism* (coined on analogy with ETHNOCENTRISM) refers to the belief that European societies are superior to those of other continents, as well as to the assumption that the norms and presuppositions of European culture have universal validity. The term is most frequently used by those who have argued that American education is dominated by European history and ideas at the expense of African, Native American, and Asian values and perspectives.

EVOLUTION. Theories of evolution posit that historical changes occur not through dramatic revolutions but through a slow and steady filtering out of the weak, the ineffectual, the inferior. Each new generation is somehow stronger than the previous one because only the fittest of the previous generation managed to reproduce. Although evolution is about *change*, it also depends on some degree of continuity between generations. For example, a social evolutionist believes that modern society is related to ancient cave dwellers, but that social structures have "evolved" to a superior stage. Evolution came into widest usage in the nineteenth century, especially after the appearance of Charles Darwin's theories of evolutionary biology put forward in *The Origin of Species* in 1859 (and the subsequent development of social Darwinism). But the idea, in its barest essence, is at least as old as the practice of animal husbandry. Much as Darwin discussed the evolutionary origins of varieties of species of birds, the social Darwinist Herbert Spencer in 1867 argued that "social life has a natural tendency to develop from simpler to complex forms, and steadily to enrich its variety." A secondary meaning of the term, in the social/political context, is a belief in institutional reform rather than radical change— see, for example, Eduard Bernstein's *Evolutionary Socialism* of 1899, which upholds Marxist ideals but critiques active revolutionism.

EXCHANGE VALUE. A fundamental concept to Marx's controversial theory of value, *exchange value* refers to a COMMODITY's worth in terms of another commodity for which it can be traded or "exchanged." A commodity's exchange value is contingent upon a number of variables and is not determined by its intrinsic usefulness. The exchangeability of commodities is important to Marx's theory, since in the trading of one product of labor for a dissimilar product of labor (which is the nature of exchange), the difference in commodities is overcome by their similarity as products of labor. At this point all labor is expressed as homogenous. The homogeneous labor that produces commodities is identified by Marx as abstract labor. When abstract labor expresses itself materially it does so in terms of value, whose form of appearance is exchange value. Thus, when Marxists speak of the value of a commodity, they are speaking of its exchange value, exchange being the primary condition for relations in a capitalist society.

Marx, Karl. *Capital.* Vol. 1. Moscow: Progress Publishers, 1965.

EXEGESIS. Exegesis (EKsiJEEsis) is the explication or interpretation of a TEXT. The term originally denoted interpretations of mystical or religious writings, oracles, or visions, but has been adopted by modern literary critics to describe the close analysis of poetry and prose. See also HERMENEUTICS.

EXISTENTIALISM. Often incorrectly referred to as a philosophical "school," existentialism is more accurately described as a trend or current in European philosophy and literature. While historians of philosophy often locate its origins in the works of the Danish theologian Søren Kierkegaard (fl. 1840s), and to a lesser degree in the writings of Friedrich Nietzsche (fl. 1870s–90s), existentialism rose to intellectual prominence in the 1930s and 1940s in France and Germany. Associated in Germany with the work of Martin Heidegger and Karl Jaspers, and in France with the writings of Jean-Paul Sartre, Albert Camus, Simone de Beauvoir, and Maurice Merleau-Ponty, the varieties of existentialism articulated by these thinkers, though widely divergent, emphasize the philosophical problem of being (ONTOLOGY) over that of knowledge (EPISTEMOLOGY). This emphasis on individual being and experience opposes existentialism to doctrines that situate reason as the impetus driving all human activity or that assume the universe to be an ordered system whose laws can be discovered through objective observation. For existentialists, society has overvalued rationality and technology at the expense of losing from consciousness a fundamental sense of "authentic" being; individuals thus live in a world that has no more than an absurd, superficial meaning and that threatens always to devolve into nothingness (see ABSURDISM).

For theistic existentialists like Martin Buber, Karl Jaspers, and Søren Kierkegaard, the anxiety or angst that is the product of recognizing and experiencing absurdity leads to the possibility of various kinds of redemption. Basic to these arguments is the assumption that the essence of an individual is discoverable and meaningful, transcending the nothingness that threatens to consume everyday existence.

In the atheistic existentialism of Jean-Paul Sartre, "existence precedes essence," implying that whatever meaning one's life attains is generated not by some inherent inner meaning but by the choices one makes in life to create one's values. For Sartre, as for Camus, this meant confronting one's angst rather than acting in "bad faith" by avoiding that responsibility and giving in to the absurdity of conventions. Essence, then, is unique, individual, and created through the "authentic" existence entailed in confronting the anguish of living in an absurd, meaningless world.

The social consequences of these two basic approaches to existential thought differ significantly. For those with theistic influences, existentialism can lead to a sort of mysticism that stresses introspection. Atheistic existentialism, on the other hand, directs the individual toward engagement with the world, especially in the form of defiance, as a means of redemption (for example, Camus's involvement with socialism or Sartre's with Marxism). See also ESSENTIALISM, PHENOMENOLOGY.

Barrett, William. *Irrational Man: A Study in Existential Philosophy.* New York: Doubleday, 1958.

Buber, Martin. *I and Thou.* Trans. Walter Kaufman. New York: Scribner's, 1970.

Heidegger, Martin. *Existence and Being.* London: Vision Press, 1949.

—. *Being and Time.* Trans. John Macquarrie and E. S. Robinson. New York: Harper, 1962.

Jaspers, Karl. *The Perennial Scope of Philosophy.* Trans. Ralph Manheim. New York: Philosophical Library, 1949.

Kierkegaard, Søren. *Fear and Trembling.* Trans. and ed. Howard V. Hong and Edna H. Hong. Princeton: Princeton University Press, 1983.

Sartre, Jean-Paul. *Existentialism and Humanism.* Trans. Philip Mairet. London: Methuen, 1948.

—. *Being and Nothingness.* Trans. Hazel E. Barnes. New York: Washington Square Press, 1956.

EXPRESSIONISM. Centered in Germany, expressionism was an early twentieth-century AVANT-GARDE movement in art, architecture, literature, theater, music, and film. Expressionist artists were concerned with the projection of personal emotions—often anguished—that would cut through the inhibiting and repressive bourgeois society that they perceived around them. Defined most narrowly, the movement's heyday ran from approximately 1910, the year when Herwarth Walden founded the weekly review *Der Sturm* (*The Storm*) in Berlin, to 1922. The roots of expressionism can be found, however, in such groups as *die Brücke* (the Bridge, founded in Dresden in 1905) and *der Blaue Reiter* (the Blue Rider, founded in Munich in 1911); and it continued to exist as a vital style until it was condemned by the Nazis during the thirties, particularly in their *Entartete Kunst* ("Degenerate Art") exhibition of 1937. Expressionist artists absorbed the influence of earlier movements like fauvism, cubism, and FUTURISM, although the expressionist style in painting was distinguished by its greater emotional vehemence. Unlike the dadaists or surrealists (see DADA, SURREALISM), the artists who have been grouped under the rubric of expressionism did not constitute a self-conscious movement. Instead, it has been used to label German artists who at the time simply considered themselves to be working in a modern style, and the term is often applied to German literature of the same period, as well as philosophical works like Ernst Bloch's *Geist der Utopie* (*Spirit of Utopia*, 1918).

Raabe, Paul, ed. *The Era of German Expressionism.* Trans. J. M. Ritchie. Woodstock, N.Y.: Overlook Press, 1974.
Solomon R. Guggenheim Museum. *Expressionism: A German Institution, 1905–1920.* New York: Solomon R. Guggenheim Foundation, 1980.
Willett, John. *Expressionism.* New York: McGraw-Hill, 1970.

EXPRESSIVE CRITICISM. Expressive criticism emphasizes the author as creator of the work, stresses the artist's emotions and beliefs, and presumes that the work contains, inadvertently or not, revelations of the author's life and personality. The theory judges a work's quality on the basis of the artistic vision and the quality of the mind or soul displayed in the work. Expressive theory flourished under the romantics, who viewed art as an overflow of emotion and a product of an inspired imagination. It continues to be evidenced in psychoanalytic criticism and the phenomenological criticism of Poulet. See INTENTIONAL FALLACY, OBJECTIVE CRITICISM, PHENOMENOLOGY.

EXTRACODING. *Extracoding* refers, in Umberto Eco's theories of interpretation and meaning, to the process of augmenting and enriching linguistic CODES (the institutional conventions that constitute linguistic competence). It is the process by which interpretations of sign sequences produce senses not predicted by the established codes. A code extends itself in order to adapt to new situations, and when the resulting modifications are accepted and become standard, the result is the overall enrichment of codes. According to Eco, overcoding and undercoding, the two components of extracoding, are the mechanisms by which codes modify themselves. Overcoding is accomplished when an interpreter proposes a new rule of interpretation to govern a rare and innovative application of a previous rule or convention. Eco relates it to the deductive process by which adults usually acquire a foreign language—by learning the rules governing codes. Undercoding, on the other hand, is related to the inductive way children learn a new language, by being exposed to preestablished strings of the language without knowledge of the governing rules. Undercoding may thus be defined as the operation in which portions of texts are provisionally assumed to be pertinent units of a code for which prefabricated rules are unknown.

While codes may be enhanced whenever confronted with a new semiotic item, Eco stresses the role of innovative aesthetic texts in the expansion of codes. Because an aesthetic text self-consciously foregrounds its own deployment of codes, the reading of such a text forces the reader's semantic universe to expand, thus leading to code modification.

F

FABULA/SUJET. The narrative theory of RUSSIAN FORMALISM distinguishes between STORY (*fabula*) and PLOT (*sujet*), between the story and the way it is told. *Fabula* (FAHByooluh) thus refers to the story as it might have occurred in real time and constitutes the raw narrative material awaiting the formal manipulation of the author. *Sujet* (SOOzhai) designates the authorial transformation worked upon the story. For example, in William Faulkner's famous short story, "A Rose For Emily," the narration moves back and forth in time to present its account of the title character's life; it does not present the events of Emily's life in the order that they happened. The chronological sequence of these events—the fabula—is left to the reader to reconstruct.

The practice of separating narrative structure into fabula and sujet derives from Alexander Veselovsky's techniques of thematic analysis. He defined *plot* as a complex array of irreducible story-motifs modified and arranged by art. This notion was later adopted in Boris Tomashevsky's "Thematics" and Vladimir Propp's *Morphology of the Folktale*. More recently, critics working within the traditions of French STRUCTURALISM and NARRATOLOGY have adopted this distinction, using the French *histoire* (or *récit*) and *discours*. These terms can be confusing because linguists also employ them, although in their usage *histoire* refers to the "objective" relation of events without reference to the narrator, the receiver of the narration, or the situation in which the events are related. This usage, which characterizes most historical writing and third-person narration, is contrasted with *discours* ("conversation"), which denotes a "subjective" form of speech or writing. *Discours* thus refers to the situation of the telling, the narrator, and the listener (or reader), through such signs as the pronouns *I*, *you*, or *we*, and adverbs such as *here* or *now*. In this sense, *discours* draws attention to the relationship between teller and receiver, whereas *histoire* attempts to hide its enunciative function. See also DIEGESIS.

Benveniste, Emile. *Problems in General Linguistics.* Trans. Mary Elizabeth Meek. Coral Gables, Fla.: University of Miami Press, 1971.

Propp, Vladimir. *Morphology of the Folktale.* Trans. Lawrence Scott, ed. Louis A. Wagner. Austin: University of Texas Press, 1968.

(THE) FANTASTIC. As Tzvetan Todorov has used the term, the fantastic is a type of narrative in which the reader is caught between interpreting plot events as natural or supernatural in origin. For instance, the spectral appearances in Henry James's *The Turn of the Screw* can be seen as psychotic projections of the characters or as ghostly apparitions. Because neither view can be supported with absolute certainty, the reader must settle for both.

Todorov, Tzvetan. *The Fantastic: A Structural Approach to a Literary Genre.* Trans. Richard Howard. Cleveland: Press of Case Western Reserve University, 1973.

FANTASY. *Fantasy* has two common usages in contemporary theory and criticism. The first is as a general description of any literary work whose action takes place in an extravagantly imaginary world, partakes of the supernatural, or generally flouts expectations about what can and cannot happen. The second and slightly more technical usage comes from psychoanalysis, where fantasy is roughly synonymous with "daydream"— that is, a meditation in which consciousness gives "free" rein to imagination and desire—insofar as the censoring mechanisms will allow it (conscious fantasies always express unconscious wishes in a disguised or distorted manner). There is, of course, a similarity between these two uses of the word, which is touched on by Freud in his 1908 essay "Creative Writers and Day-Dreaming." In psychoanalysis, fantasy is therefore used for both conscious fantasies, like daydreams, and UNCONSCIOUS fantasies expressing repressed desires that analysis attempts to uncover. While some critics prefer the spelling "phantasies" for those scenarios that are unconscious, others argue that Freud is concerned with showing how the latter always structure (as LATENT CONTENT) the MANIFEST CONTENT of conscious fantasies, so that a distinction in kind is not justified.

Freud, Sigmund. "Creative Writers and Day-Dreaming." In *Standard Edition of the Complete Psychological Works of Sigmund Freud*, vol. 9. Trans. James Strachey. London: Hogarth Press and Institute of Psycho-Analysis, 1974.

FEMININE READING COMPETENCE. Feminine reading competence means reading with the competence of a woman or women; the term is most associated with those critics engaged with GENERATIVE POETICS. According to Jonathan Culler, reading competence results from the reader's understanding of the "grammar of literature," an understanding necessary to observe literary structures and meanings. The usefulness of conceiving of a unique feminine reading competence depends on one's acceptance of the idea that reading as a woman is essentially or culturally different from reading as a man. See also COGNITIVE COMPETENCE/PERFORMANCE, COMPETENCE, LITERARY.

Culler, Jonathan. *Structuralist Poetics: Structuralism, Linguistics, and the Study of Literature*. London: Routledge, 1975.

FEMINIST CRITICISM. See CULTURAL FEMINISM, GENDER STUDIES, LESBIAN CRITICISM, LIBERAL FEMINISM, RADICAL FEMINISM.

FEMINIST CRITIQUE. According to Elaine Showalter, feminist critique is an interpretation of texts from a feminist perspective to expose clichés, stereotypes, and negative images of women. Generally focusing on male literary and theoretical texts, it also calls attention to the gaps in a literary history that has largely excluded writing by women. This approach dominated feminist criticism when it first emerged in the 1970s and is strongly linked to the decade's political agendas; Kate Millett's *Sexual Politics* (1970), for example, ties the mistreatment of women in fiction by Henry Miller and others to the oppression of women in a patriarchal society. As early as 1975, Carolyn Heilbrun and Catherine Stimpson associated such readings with the "righteous, angry" first stage of feminist criticism. Showalter would go on to suggest (in 1979 and 1981) that by continuing to emphasize writing by men, the strategy of feminist critique remained dependent "on existing models" of interpretation. It did, however, lay the foundation for what she identified as the second, "gynocritical" phase of feminist criticism, focusing on women as writers with values, methods, and traditions of their own. It has also led to more fully elaborated theories of women as readers, and continues to be an important tool in exposing the operation of sexism in culture and society. See also GYNOCRITICS, MISOGYNY, SEXUAL POLITICS.

Heilbrun, Carolyn G., and Catherine R. Stimpson. "Theories of Feminist Criticism: A Dialogue." In Josephine Donovan, ed., *Feminist Literary Criticism*. Lexington: University Press of Kentucky, 1975.
Millett, Kate. *Sexual Politics*. New York: Avon, 1970.
Showalter, Elaine. "Feminist Criticism in the Wilderness." In Elaine Showalter, ed., *The New Feminist Criticism*. New York: Pantheon, 1985.
—. "Toward a Feminist Poetics." In Elaine Showalter, ed., *The New Feminist Criticism*. New York: Pantheon, 1985.

FETISHISM. Fetishism is the endowment of an object or a body part with an unusual degree of power or erotic allure, as in the case of cultures that attribute magical powers to idols or human effigies. Use of the term often betrays a skeptical attitude toward such beliefs; thus, Karl Marx coined the term *commodity fetishism* to express the way that capitalist emphasis on the abstract value of commodities conceals the underlying social relations of their producers (see COMMODITY). The most common use of the term, however, is in psychoanalysis, which concerns itself with the sexual underpinnings of fetishistic behavior. According to Freud, sexual fascination with objects like shoes or garter belts is rooted in a compromise made by the male child upon discovering that the woman does not have a penis (see CASTRATION COMPLEX). Since this raises the intolerable possibility that his own penis may be lost, he partially refuses to accept what he has seen by turning some other object into a substitute for the missing organ (and simultanesouly developing a strong aversion to the female genitals). The idea that fetishism is a way of symbolically controlling an unacceptable truth has proven suggestive to some feminist critics, who have adopted psychoanalytic categories to describe the ways that men see women through the media of film and the visual arts (see MALE GAZE, VISUAL PLEASURE).

Freud, Sigmund. "Fetishism." In *Standard Edition of the Complete Psychological Works of Sigmund Freud*, vol. 21. Trans. James Strachey. London: Hogarth Press and Institute of Psycho-Analysis, 1974.

FICTION. Although most commonly used to describe a general category of literary texts within which one may distinguish GENRES such as the novel and the short story, *fiction* is actually a complex and somewhat ambiguous term that begs a number of questions about how we distinguish between truth and falsity, as well as how we order our world. Problems arise when one attempts to formulate a rigorous definition of fiction, since a text that describes imaginary events and characters may nevertheless contain many utterances that are not necessarily fictional statements. Thus, when a narrator comments in a general way about the death of a character, drawing conclusions about the universality of mortality, that statement may be integral to the fiction but also possess truth value for the reader. Similarly, when the wicked queen gives Snow White the poisoned apple, we recognize the act (and the apple) as existing only in fiction, yet this gesture of spiteful jealousy corresponds to what we know about the world of experience we inhabit. As Barbara Herrnstein Smith points out, "To say that an artist has represented a certain object or event is to say that he has constructed a fictive member of an identifiable class of natural (real) objects or events."

In another sense, philosophers and literary theorists speak of fictions as instruments for organizing our experiences. One may know something to be a provisional construction, yet "believe" it because it offers a useful means of proceeding. For example, in T. S. Kuhn's description of the PARADIGM, a scientist understands that an explanatory model may be replaced at some later date; nevertheless, he or she uses it as the best available tool, demonstrating that even the most rigorous truths offered by the physical sciences are dependent on the theoretical frameworks in which they are presented. From this perspective, it becomes possible to grasp the extent to which our ability to make sense of experience is inseparable from such frameworks, which often differ significantly from one culture to another. It is a basic tenet of much contemporary thought that our access to the world is inevitably mediated by linguistic and other culturally variable constructions—what Nelson Goodman has called "ways of worldmaking."

Goodman, Nelson. *Ways of Worldmaking*. Indianapolis: Hackett, 1978.

Kuhn, T. S. *The Structure of Scientific Revolutions*. Chicago: University of Chicago Press, 1962.

Smith, Barbara Herrnstein. *On the Margins of Discourse*. Chicago: University of Chicago Press, 1978.

FIGURATION. *Figuration* means the act of using figures of speech such as METAPHOR or METONYMY. Tzvetan Todorov uses the term to refer not to the act of a writer, but to that of the reader: for Todorov, figuration is one of several actions performed by readers upon literature. The reader looks for a certain repeated pattern or overall structure, beneath the surface of the text, in relation to which all the various elements that make up that text can be understood. This differs from finding a theme that the author may have placed in the text, because the figuration Todorov discusses doesn't produce a single meaning for the text but instead might support several readings. It may be understood by analogy to the common experience of seeing figures in clouds, cracks in the plaster, or the proverbial "figure in the carpet" of Henry James. Again, unlike theme, the figure in the text may not be articulated as an idea, but as a recurring figure of speech or linguistic pattern. See TROPE.

Hawkes, Terence. *Structuralism and Semiotics*. Berkeley: University of California Press, 1977.

Todorov, Tzvetan. "The Structural Analysis of Literature: The Tales of Henry James." In David Robey, ed., *Structuralism, an Introduction*. Oxford: Clarendon Press, 1973.

FILMIC. The filmic is that which is characteristic of film as a medium. Although film shares many characteristics with other media—e.g., narrative with literature, certain kinds of sound effects with recording, and certain methods of composition with the visual arts—the filmic resides in the combination of techniques unique to film. Techniques described as filmic generally originate in the mediation of the film camera and the fact that the film as a whole is assembled from a series of fragments shot from many different vantage points and at many different points in time. By contrast, the opposite of the filmic would be a film of the stage production of a play in which, except for providing a mixture of closeup and long shots, there is no use of the cutting, the juxtaposition of different vantage points, and the movement through time and space that can be employed in the medium of film.

FILM NOIR. The French phrase *film noir* (literally, black film) refers to a cinematic genre that flourished during the forties and fifties in America. These films, many of which were produced by major Hollywood studios, include such familiar titles as *Double Indemnity, Out of the Past,* and *Touch of Evil,* and stand in sharp contrast to much CLASSIC HOLLYWOOD CINEMA in their focus on fate, duplicity, manipulation, sexual obsession, and the figure of the *femme fatale.* They are also notable for their visual style, which features a prominent and very creative use of shadow and chiaroscuro effects.

Hirsch, Foster. *The Dark Side of the Screen: Film Noir.* New York: Da Capo Press, 1983.

Kaplan, E. Ann, ed. *Women in Film Noir.* Rev. ed. London: British Film Institute, 1980.

FILM THEORY. The cinema has been a subject of theoretical reflection from its beginnings, and more than one director or critic has doubled as a theorist of the medium, including such well-known figures as Sergei Eisenstein and Siegfried Kracauer. With the explosion of theoretical writing since the 1960s, however, film theory has grown enormously, becoming a vital area of debate in studies of many different facets of contemporary culture. During this period, film theory has accommodated a succession of theoretical models, which have roughly paralleled changes in fashion in such related disciplines as literary and art criticism. At first, structural linguistics and general SEMIOTICS were the strongest influence, followed by a period during the seventies in which Lacanian psychoanalysis and Althusserian Marxism came to the fore. This latter period saw the ascendence of the group of critics around the British journal *Screen* (see SCREEN GROUP), where a section of Christian Metz's influential book *The Imaginary Signifier* first appeared in English. In the past decade, film theory has exhibited considerable eclecticism, critiquing earlier approaches and—especially in the case of psychoanalysis—adapting them to new purposes. While much work has been done on the subjects of race, class, and sexuality in general, feminist work on the cinema has been especially fruitful, and several concepts, such as SCOPOPHILIA, VISUAL PLEASURE, and the MALE GAZE, have become regular points of reference in debates about REPRESENTATION.

Metz, Christian. *The Imaginary Signifier: Psychoanalysis and the Cinema.* Trans. Celia Britton, Annwyl Williams, Ben Brewster, and Alfred Guzzetti. Bloomington: Indiana University Press, 1982.

Mulvey, Laura. *Visual and Other Pleasures.* Bloomington: Indiana University Press, 1989.

Rosen, Philip, ed. *Narrative, Apparatus, Ideology: A Film Theory Reader.* New York: Columbia University Press, 1986.

FIXATION. In Freudian psychoanalysis, *fixation* refers to a failure to move from one set of objects and relationships to the next and, consequently, to the failure to let go of an early object of satisfaction. As children develop into adults, they find different ways to satisfy the demands of their INSTINCTS or DRIVES. At each of the three major stages of development, the subject psychically fixes or attaches him or herself to particular objects as well as relationships that pleasurably stimulate or excite the instincts (see INFANTILE SEXUALITY). Thus, according to Freud, in the early stages of development, the infant is stimulated orally: the activity of sucking upon the mother's breast or the bottle's nipple provides pleasure, as does the activity of sucking on a pacifier or a thumb. A traumatic experience during this phase of development may cause him or her to remain attached to the activity of sucking and to resist transferring the pleasure derived from sucking to another activity and object. In this case, the person may be said to have a fixation deriving from the oral stage of libidinal development. The most common forms of such fixations in adult life are eating disorders. When the child moves successfully into the second, anal, stage of development, pleasure is derived from the activities of expulsion and retention, or muscular control. This pleasure is initially experienced through the elimination and withholding of fecal matter, but in later life any object that can be offered or withheld may be substituted. Thus, in his essay "On Transformation of Instinct as Exemplified in Anal Eroticism," Freud introduces the symbolic equation: feces = gift = money.

Freud, Sigmund. *Introductory Lectures on Psycho-Analysis.* Trans. James Strachey. New York: Norton, 1965.

FLOW. *Flow* is a term introduced by the British critic Raymond Williams to describe the sequence of images and information he saw while watching American television in the 1970s. Typically, television provides a wide range of different types of programming—which Williams classifies as news and public affairs, features and documentaries, education, arts and music, children's programs, drama, movies, general entertainment, sports, religion, internal publicity, and commercials. *Flow* refers to both the order in which these programs are presented and the moments of transition between them. Because the movement from one to another type of programming is "the characteristic organization, and therefore the characteristic experience" of television broadcasting, the phenomenon of "planned flow . . . is the defining characteristic of broadcasting, simultaneously as a technology and as a cultural form." The analysis of flow permits us to see how commercial broadcasters manipulate the sequence and frequency of repeated images to affect the messages we receive. For example, when a dramatic show about auto racing is followed by an advertisement for a new model of car, the viewer's emotional response to the drama may prepare him or her to be more receptive to the message of the commercial. The term *flow* is also used, in a rather different sense, in the collaborative work of Gilles Deleuze and Félix Guattari. See SCHIZOANALYSIS.

Williams, Raymond. *Television: Technology and Cultural Form.* New York: Schocken, 1975.

FORCES OF PRODUCTION. Sometimes referred to in MARXIST CRITICISM as the means of production, the forces of production include raw materials, tools, machinery, techniques, and labor power (and, therefore, populations). Together with the RELATIONS OF PRODUCTION, they constitute the economic BASE or MODE OF PRODUCTION of a social formation.

FORECLOSURE. This English word is a translation of the French *forclusion*, a term introduced by the French psychoanalyst Jacques Lacan, who meant it as an equivalent of the German *Verwerfung* (repudiation), used by Freud in some of his discussions of psychosis. In Lacanian theory, foreclosure is the defense mechanism specific to psychosis and consists in the repudiation of the phallus as signifier of the CASTRATION COMPLEX and with it the entire realm of social reality (see also SYMBOLIC). Foreclosure differs from repression in that the foreclosed signifier does not enter and then return from the unconscious, but rather reappears "from without" in hallucinations. Although Freud's own use of the terms *Verwerfung* and *Verdrängung* (repression) is inconsistent, he did express doubts about whether the psychotic mechanism had anything to do with the more common phenomenon of repression, and so in this respect Lacan was justified in claiming a Freudian background for his thought. Lacan focused especially on Freud's use of *Verwerfung* in the so-called Wolf Man case history and on the essay on "Negation," where Freud opposes the two primary mechanisms of "introduction into the ego" and "expulsion from the ego." Lacan identifies the first of these with the process of symbolization and the latter with his concept of foreclosure.

Freud, Sigmund. "From the History of an Infantile Neurosis." In *Standard Edition of the Complete Psychological Works of Sigmund Freud*, vol. 17. Trans. James Strachey. London: Hogarth Press and Institute of Psycho-Analysis, 1974.

—. "Negation." In *Standard Edition of the Complete Psychological Works of Sigmund Freud*, vol. 19. Trans. James Strachey. London: Hogarth Press and Institute of Psycho-Analysis, 1974..

—. "Neurosis and Psychosis." In *Standard Edition of the Complete Psychological Works of Sigmund Freud*, vol. 19. Trans. James Strachey. London: Hogarth Press and Institute of Psycho-Analysis, 1974.

Lacan, Jacques. "On a Question Preliminary to Any Possible Treatment of Psychosis." *Ecrits: A Selection*. Trans. Alan Sheridan. New York: Norton, 1977.

FOREGROUNDING. The members of the PRAGUE CIRCLE of linguistics used *foregrounding* to refer to the way that literary texts emphasize—or place in the foreground—some linguistic elements at the expense of others. Poems, for instance, tend to foreground metaphorical language. Jan Mukarovsky expanded on this notion, arguing that the use of language foregrounds the act of expression itself.

Garvin, Paul, ed. *A Prague School Reader on Esthetics, Literary Structure and Style*. Washington, D.C.: Washington Linguistics Club, 1955.

FORM. Form is a concept that is inseparable in the history of criticism from the concept of FORMALISM; however, its various uses do offer some insights into the assumptions underlying formalism. Throughout the history of its usage, from Renaissance religious writers to the present, form has been associated either with the inessential or external, or the essential or determining, depending on the context. Either way, it is understood to constitute one half of a binary opposition, the other half of which is usually content (in this respect, form is a crucial concept in the history of Western METAPHYSICS). Thus, while it is common to hear the word formalist used pejoratively, suggesting a bloodless concern with surface pattern or abstract design, those who have thought of themselves as formalists, like the RUSSIAN FORMALISTS of the early part of the twentieth century, and their STRUCTURALIST heirs, have understood themselves to be focusing precisely on that which is crucial to literature and the aesthetic effect. They even see it as determining of content, which cannot be extracted from it like a nut from its shell, but is instead "informed" or constituted by its formal elaboration like the two-dimensional patterning of pigment in painting.

FORMALISM. In its broadest sense, *formalism* or *formalist criticism* refers to the critical practice of focusing on the artistic technique of the text or object under consideration at the expense of the subject matter. The term has often been applied pejoratively to a number of types of criticism that emphasize a work's structural design or pattern, or its style and manner—its FORM—in isolation from its content. In formalism, it is usually these formal characteristics upon which aesthetic evaluations are based. The concept of form itself has played a somewhat troubled role in critical discussions of art and literature at least since Plato and the *Phaedrus*, when the notion was poorly defined for the first, but by no means last, time. In recent years charges of formalism have been leveled at NEW CRITICISM, DECONSTRUCTION, some PSYCHOANALYTIC CRITICISM, and even some varieties of NEW HISTORICISM. Primarily these accusations come from leftist or liberal critics who believe that literary criticism should be oriented toward social criticism more than a discussion of aesthetic abstractions. The term *formalism* also is often used in contemporary theoretical parlance to denote the RUSSIAN FORMALISTS, especially Victor Shklovsky, Vladimir Propp, and Roman Jakobson, whose work became important to later movements like the PRAGUE CIRCLE, French STRUCTURALISM, and SEMIOTICS.

Bennett, Tony. *Formalism and Marxism*. London: Methuen, 1979.

Jakobson, Roman. *Language in Literature*. Eds. Krystyna Pomorska and Stephen Rudy. Cambridge, Mass.: Belknap Press, 1987.

Jameson, Fredric. *The Prison-House of Language*. Princeton: Princeton University Press, 1972.

Lentricchia, Frank. *After the New Criticism*. Chicago: University of Chicago Press, 1980.

Wellek, René, and Austin Warren. *Theory of Literature*. London: J. Cape, 1955.

FORT-DA. See OTHER.

FRAGMENTATION. The idea of fragmentation has often been invoked
as a general description of life in the modern era, encompassing all
aspects of experience from social traditions to religious and philosophical systems to aesthetic forms. The concept itself is opposed to that of
TOTALITY—whether as a description of the self or SUBJECT, the system of
values we inhabit, or the material experiences of everyday life. Fragmentation is often linked to the conditions of a POSTMODERN, postindustrial
world. For many, especially those invested in particular forms of ESSEN-
TIALISM, or belief in transcendent forms of aesthetics, morals, or political action, fragmentation is much lamented. For others, especially those
who espouse notions of DECENTERING or INDETERMINACY—that is, for
those who perceive all meaning to be contingently produced and without any absolute foundation—fragmentation is seen as the inevitable
consequence of capitalism and the proliferation of technology, especially
information technology. For this latter group, fragmentation is not necessarily in and of itself a deleterious state of affairs and can even be celebrated. At the same time, however, it can also be used by existing institutions (such as governments, the military, education, or corporations) to
exercise power over people by emphasizing the increasing alienation of
the individual and the ultimate futility of any sort of attempted unity or
totality.

Lyotard, Jean-François. *The Postmodern Condition: A Report on Knowledge.* Trans.
Geoff Bennington and Brian Massumi. Minneapolis: University of Minnesota
Press, 1984.

FRAME/FRAMING. A frame is a single "still" image on the strip of film in
a SHOT that, when projected in series, creates the illusion of movement
(hence "motion pictures"). It is also a unit of composition in that its
edges are used to select and arrange what will be presented to the spectator, just as a window frames a landscape. The frame, that is, offers the
viewer a certain perspective on what it presents, controlling the distance,
angle, height, and levelness of the vantage point on what is seen, as well
as determining what is seen at all (what part of a scene is framed out of
the picture altogether). Framings may also be static (fixed) or, when a
shot includes more than one frame of film, mobile, changing camera dis-

tance, angle, or height on what is onscreen (for example, zooming into a close-up, craning to an overhead view or rolling to a canted or "off-kilter" angle). A mobile camera may also reframe onscreen space to include what has previously been offscreen, as when the camera pans to reveal the respondent to a question, tilts down from a light to what it illuminates, or tracks or zooms out from a character to reveal the space in which the character moves. Framings can help determine our response to what is filmed. In *Citizen Kane,* the repeated low-angle views of Charles Foster Kane, so that the spectator is positioned as looking up at him, frequently help reinforce an impression of Kane's power and stature (although at times such framing seems to be used ironically, to comment on his fall from power and his reduced stature—there is no predetermined meaning of any camera positioning or movement). See also ANGLE/CAMERA ANGLE, SCALE/SHOT SCALE, SHOT.

Bordwell, Kristen, and David Thompson. *Film Art: An Introduction.* Reading, Mass.: Addison-Wesley, 1979.

Monaco, James. *How to Read a Film: The Art, Technology, Language, History, and Theory of Film and Media.* New York: Oxford University Press, 1977.

Turner, Graeme. *Film as Social Practice.* London: Routledge, 1988.

FRANKFURT SCHOOL. See CRITICAL THEORY.

FREE INDIRECT DISCOURSE. A concept developed by narrative theorists, free indirect discourse refers to those moments in narrative that blur the difference between, as Brian McHale puts it, "the representation of an action (diegesis) [and] the repetition of a character's words (mimesis)." For example, direct discourse would use the form: He said, "I'll leave for the coast next week." Simple indirect discourse would subordinate the direct quotation: He said that he would leave for the coast next week. Free indirect discourse, however, by combining aspects of the character's direct speech (the coast next week) with the tense and mode of the narrator's report (he would leave) creates a sentence that partakes of both the MIMETIC and the DIEGETIC: He would leave for the coast tomorrow. As a model of bivocal writing, free indirect discourse offers a way of theorizing the frequent slippage in narrative fiction between first-person action and third-person narration. Frequently thought of as a distinctly modern mode, free indirect discourse represents the psycholinguistic predicament of the twentieth-century divided self in dramatic terms. Critics such as Henry Louis Gates, Jr. have appropriated the notion for African-American literary criticism, exploring the ways in which it usefully describes the double-voiced nature of a minority literature struggling to articulate itself within a hostile dominant culture. See also BLUES AESTHETIC, SIGNIFYIN(G).

Gates, Henry Louis, Jr. *The Signifying Monkey: A Theory of African-American Literary Criticism.* New York: Oxford University Press, 1988.

McHale, Brian. "Free Indirect Discourse: A Survey of Recent Accounts." *Poetics and Theory of Literature* 3.

FRENCH "NEW WAVE." See "NEW WAVE" CINEMA.

FUTURISM. Futurism was an Italian AVANT-GARDE movement that flourished from approximately 1909 to 1916. Visually, the futurists were influenced by cubism; however, unlike the cubists, they were more interested in a directly kinetic appeal that conveys the exhilaration of modern urban life, especially the sensations of industry, energy, speed, and light. Thus, the future they envisioned was to be founded on a dynamism that would break completely with the cultures and societies of the past. These ideas—some of which were to have an influence on the aesthetics of fascism—were first defined by the Italian poet Filippo Tommaso Marinetti in "The Founding and Manifesto of Futurism," which he published in 1909. After Marinetti joined forces with the painters Carlo Carra, Gino Severini, and Gioacomo Balla, the group published their "Manifesto of the Futurist Painters" in 1910. Also prominent in the futurist movement were the sculptor Umberto Boccioni and the architect Antonio Sant'Elia. An unrelated futurist movement also appeared in Russia in 1912. Led by poet and playwright Vladimir Mayakovsky, this group's politics were decidedly revolutionary rather than reactionary. Although Russian futurism had limited impact on Western European aesthetic theories, the Italian futurists were considerably influential for French poet Guillaume Apollinaire, those involved in DADA, and Ezra Pound, whose theory of vorticism owes much to their work.

Appollonio, Umbro, ed. *Futurist Manifestos.* London: Thames and Hudson, 1973.

Perloff, Marjorie. *The Futurist Moment: Avant-Garde, Avant Guere, and the Language of Rupture.* Chicago: University of Chicago Press, 1986.

G

GAPS. *Gaps* is a term that refers in Wolfgang Iser's READER-RESPONSE criticism to the blanks or spaces in a sequence of signs that a reader must fill in so that meaning can be generated. Gaps occur at a point when the reader perceives indeterminacies or an absence of meaning between any units of text, such as words, sentences, chapters, stanzas, etc. Gaps constitute the unwritten aspect of texts, which allow readers to use their imaginations in constructing meaning to supply missing information, to resolve ambiguities, or to account for inconsistencies in a text. A given text is in and of itself unfinished, replete with blanks that require the interactive participation of the reader to repair its indeterminacies. Just how much freedom a reader has in filling in gaps remains an open question. See also CONCRETIZATION, PHENOMENOLOGY.

GAY CRITICISM. The term *gay criticism* describes a broad field of inquiry embracing both feminist investigations into the historical constructions of gender and distinctively antihomophobic theories of the historical production and reproduction of sexuality. By investigating literary and social texts, gay criticism questions the assumptions behind, and the historical importance of, categories and dichotomies such as "masculinity," "homo/heterosexual," and "female/male." It focuses on issues of sexuality, refusing to reduce desire to the terms and relations of gender. It is particularly concerned with the ways that sexuality and same-sex desire—the operations of homosocial, homosexual, and homophobic themes—inscribe cultural and literary artifacts. Like MEN'S STUDIES and LESBIAN CRITICISM, gay criticism is political in its interrogations of marginalized and minority discourses, the status and formation of the canon, and the forms and effects of oppression.

Although a relatively recent academic presence, gay-centered criticism has produced wide-ranging studies of the history and politics of sexuality and gender in religion, legal studies, literary criticism, history, and psychoanalysis. See also FEMINIST CRITICISM, GAY AND LESBIAN STUDIES, WOMEN'S STUDIES.

Altman, Dennis. *The Homosexualization of America, the Americanization of the Homosexual.* New York: St. Martin's, 1982.

Butters, Ronald R., John M. Clum, and Michael Moon, eds. *Displacing Homophobia: Gay Male Perspectives in Literature and Culture.* Durham, N.C.: Duke University Press, 1989.

Sedgwick, Eve Kosofsky. *Between Men: English Literature and Male Homosocial Desire.* New York: Columbia University Press, 1985.

—. *Epistemology of the Closet.* Berkeley: University of California Press, 1990.

GAZE. See MALE GAZE.

GEISTESWISSENSCHAFTEN. Difficult to translate literally since *Geist* and *Wissenschaft* each have a number of possible English renderings depending upon context, *Geisteswissenschaften* (GEIStesVEEZenshaften) refers to disciplines within the humanities and the social sciences that are specifically concerned with the human condition; thus, *Geisteswissenschaften* is often translated as "human studies" and includes philology, history, sociology, anthropology, comparative religion, communication theory, comparative jurisprudence, and the like. German tradition divided all scholarly disciplines into two distinct categories: *Geisteswissenschaften* and NATURWISSENSCHAFTEN, which are roughly comparable to the English division of the arts and sciences. Originally coined in Germany in the nineteenth century to refer to what John Stuart Mill called the "moral sciences," *Geisteswissenschaften* is today most often connected with the thought of Wilhelm Dilthey (1833–1911). Dilthey argued that disciplines should be classified by their subject matters rather than their method, and that the nature of *Geisteswissenschaften* is profoundly different from that of the physical sciences, since its subject matter is the human rather than the physical world. For Dilthey, the human world was one pervaded with expressions of meaning that are objectified in language, institutions, beliefs, and actions; and the disciplines that study the human world necessarily impinge upon one another. Dilthey argued that fruitful study of human activity depended on a cognitive process he called "understanding" (*das Verstehen*), which involved interpretive as well as empirical methods. Thus, while one may indeed emulate the empirical sciences by collecting and sorting data, as a sociologist might by collecting responses to a survey, the responses themselves require interpretation and understanding that goes beyond merely recording them. See also HERMENEUTICS, POSITIVISM.

Cassirer, Ernst. *An Essay on Man: An Introduction to a Philosophy of Human Culture.* New Haven: Yale University Press, 1945.

Dilthey, Wilhelm. *Meaning in History.* Ed. H. P. Rickman. London: Allen and Unwin, 1961.

Palmer, Richard. *Hermeneutics: Interpretation Theory in Schleiermacher, Dilthey, Heidegger, and Gadamer.* Evanston, Ill.: Northwestern University Press, 1969.

GENDER STUDIES. An interdisciplinary field of inquiry increasingly prominent since the second half of the 1980s, gender studies arose from and is closely tied to WOMEN'S STUDIES and also gay, lesbian, and MEN'S STUDIES. Starting with the premise that the gender of an individual does not flow naturally or inevitably from her or his anatomical sex, gender studies analyzes the way gender identity is constructed, in literature and in society, for both women and men. Turning away from women's studies' exclusive focus on women and women's writing, work in gender studies examines the way "masculinity" and "femininity" come to have certain meanings at a particular place and time, stressing the necessary interrelatedness of these meanings. What is considered typically masculine in a given society depends in part on being different from what is feminine, and what is feminine on not being masculine. Gender studies also points out that what is considered gender-neutral or "universal" is often, in fact, implicitly male and exclusive of the female. Ironically, some feminists have worried that gender studies itself, by rejecting the polemical, compensatory attention to women characteristic of women's studies, may itself run the risk of slipping back into a bias that favors men.

Boone, Joseph A., and Michael Cadden, eds. *Engendering Men: The Question of Male Feminist Criticism.* New York: Routledge, 1990.

Showalter, Elaine, ed. *Speaking of Gender.* New York: Routledge, 1989.

Spector, Judith, ed. *Gender Studies: New Directions in Feminist Criticism.* Bowling Green, Oh.: Bowling Green State University Popular Press, 1986.

GENEALOGY. A form of historical analysis, genealogy opposes the traditional impulses of historical methods that attempt to discover continuities and patterns of development. Instead, genealogy concerns itself with ruptures, discontinuity, and surfaces, attempting, as Michel Foucault has written, to "record the singularity of events outside of any monotonous finality."

Genealogy in this sense was first practiced by the nineteenth-century German philosopher Friedrich Nietzsche, a figure of extreme importance to contemporary theoretical endeavors. The French philosopher/historian Michel Foucault adopts many of Nietzsche's antisystematic methods and presuppositions in his attempts to demonstrate that the "deep meanings" that philosophy and history try to uncover are merely constructions, existing as inventions of DISCOURSE and not as the absolute underpinnings of all thought and existence. Foucault argues that genealogy is more of an overview and that the genealogist's aim is to demonstrate that things "have no essence" or rather that "their essence was fabricated in a piecemeal fashion from alien forms." Thus, closure, finality, the end of interpretation are anathema to genealogy. Instead, genealogy is more concerned with examining the surface of discursive events and is a record of the innumerable attempts to direct history through interpretation, even as history pretends to objectivity. See also ARCHAEOLOGY, EPISTEME, POWER.

Dreyfus, Hubert L., and Paul Rabinow. *Michel Foucault: Beyond Structuralism and Hermeneutics.* 2d ed. Chicago: University of Chicago Press, 1983.

Foucault, Michel. *The Archeology of Knowledge.* 1969. Trans. A. M. Sheridan Smith. New York: Pantheon, 1972.

—. "Nietzsche, Genealogy, History." In *Language, Counter-Memory, Practice: Selected Essays and Interviews.* Trans. Donald F. Bouchard and Sherry Simon. Ithaca, N.Y.: Cornell University Press, 1977.

—. "Nietzsche, Freud, Marx." Trans. Jon Anderson and Gary Hentzi. *Critical Texts* 3(2) 1986.

Nietzsche, Friedrich. *The Genealogy of Morals.* Trans. Francis Golffing. New York: Doubleday, 1956.

GENERATIVE POETICS. Generative poetics attempts to describe the rules or processes that enable authors to construct texts and that permit readers to understand them. As with the generative grammar developed by Noam Chomsky, which tries to explain sentences by examining the sets of rules that make it possible to form and transform sentences, a generative analysis of texts seeks to explain literary phenomena by providing a theory or "grammar" of the process of text production. In this way, generative poetics is related to cybernetics and artificially generated poetry:

to program a computer to produce new texts requires an understanding of the way already existing texts were produced. However, some critics point out that much work on generative poetics does not produce logical rules for forming a text, but instead describes the way that a text might be seen to be constructed.

Culler, Jonathan. *Structuralist Poetics: Structuralism, Linguistics and the Study of Literature.* London: Routledge, 1975.

Shukman, Ann. *Literature and Semiotics.* New York: North-Holland Publishing, 1977.

GENEVA SCHOOL. A school of criticism founded in Geneva and deeply rooted in PHENOMENOLOGY and EXISTENTIALISM, the Geneva School critics are sometimes known as critics of consciousness or critics of experience; they include Marcel Raymond, Albert Béguin, Georges Poulet, Jean Rousset, Jean-Pierre Richard, Jean Starobinski, and the early Hillis Miller. There is great diversity among the school; however, Hillis Miller, in an influential essay entitled "The Geneva Critics," notes that the practitioners would all define literary criticism as "consciousness of consciousness." The Geneva Critics view literature as a form of consciousness; the literary text is an embodiment of the author's unique state of mind or LEBENSWELT, which in its textual form is made available to the consciousness of others. Miller states that the task of the critic is to transpose the consciousness of the author into the receptive interior space of the critic's mind. To gain access to the author's consciousness, the critic must attempt to achieve complete neutrality and openness through what Miller describes as an act of renunciation of the self. The critic becomes lost in the text to the extent of totally identifying with and becoming united with the consciousness duplicated in the words of the text. The Geneva critics attempt to read the work with such commitment and objectivity that they "live" the consciousness of the author, and are then able to convey this consciousness in the critical text. Poulet, for example, states that the thought of the critic must *become* the thought of the writer by re-feeling, re-thinking, and re-imagining the author's thought from the inside. Paradoxically, Poulet also holds that the critic suffers no deprivation of consciousness as a result of this abdication of self; rather, a common consciousness is established between author and critic.

While Geneva School criticism is distantly related to romantic expressive criticism with its conviction that gaining access to the personality of the author is the primary concern of reading, it is an ahistorical, subjective criticism with little concern for matters external to the literary text. It is the unique consciousness of the author as it is duplicated within the confines of the text that is sought, not the historical, biographical self that exists outside the work. Because the author's consciousness is the unifying principle in a given work and because this consciousness suffuses all the author's texts, the Geneva critics display a tendency to focus on the author's oeuvre and to disregard the individual work as an autonomous entity, freely glossing one text with another.

Rather than viewing criticism as an objective science, Geneva critics view criticism as literature about literature. Because it examines literature ahistorically from the inside and because it mediates and reconstitutes in a new critical form the consciousness of the text, it is itself therefore a form of literature once removed.

Lawall, Sarah N. *Critics of Consciousness: The Existential Structures of Literature.* Cambridge, Mass.: Harvard University Press, 1968.

Miller, J. Hillis. "The Geneva Critics." In John K. Simon, ed., *Modern French Criticism: From Proust and Valéry to Structuralism.* Chicago: University of Chicago Press, 1972.

Poulet, Georges. *Proustian Space.* Trans. Elliott Coleman. Baltimore: Johns Hopkins University Press, 1977.

Simon, John K., ed. *Modern French Criticism: From Proust and Valéry to Structuralism.* Chicago: University of Chicago Press, 1972.

GENOTEXT/PHENOTEXT. According to Julia Kristeva, any text is composed of a phenotext (**FEE**noTEKST), or the text's surface structure (sound patterns, grammar, syntax, diction) and the genotext (**JEE**noTEKST), or the DEEP STRUCTURE and source of all meaning. Analysis involves a "dissolution" or separation of phenotext from genotext, and discovers hidden dimensions of meaning. However, since the genotext—containing all the possibilities of language, past, present, and future—is never present and is always "masked" by the phenotext, it would be impossible to verify what it contains. Jonathan Culler notes that the genotext's effect "is to prevent one from ever rejecting any proposal about the verbal structure of the text," so that there "is nothing to limit the play of meaning."

Culler, Jonathan. *Structuralist Poetics: Structuralism, Linguistics, and the Study of Literature.* Ithaca, N.Y.: Cornell University Press, 1975.

Kristeva, Julia. *The Kristeva Reader.* Ed. Toril Moi. New York: Columbia University Press, 1986.

GENRE. *Genre* is a French word that means "kind" or "type"; it is used in many disciplines to refer to the various categories in which works are classified, for example, whether a piece of writing is a drama, novel, or short story, or whether a painting is a landscape or portrait. Genre classifications can be purely formal (whether a poem is an ode or a sonnet), or they can be made according to other categories, like theme or setting. For example, the pastoral can include any work whose setting is rural, regardless of other formal characteristics. Thus, John Milton's elegy *Lycidas*, the Greek romance *Daphnis and Chloë*, and the medieval English drama *The Second Shepherd's Play* all qualify as pastorals.

Structural analysis, as a FORMALISM, has frequently concerned itself with isolating the basic elements that characterize various literary genres, and the codes or rules governing the relationships of those elements (see STRUCTURALISM). Other kinds of analysis such as feminist or African-American have focused on how sexism or racism can be encoded in genres. For instance, the nineteenth-century bildungsroman (the novel of education) often ends with the integration of the protagonist into society through marriage (e.g., *Jane Eyre*), thus reinforcing heterosexuality as a social norm and goal.

GESTURE. In discussions of sign systems, gestures are often considered to be the first form of language, and as such teach us about the nature of language in general. In their most primitive state, gestures may be either indicative (pointing) or imitative (imitating the motion of the object they seek to represent). Ernst Cassirer noted that more developed sign languages show a transition from imitative to representative gesture (where the bodily motion is arbitrarily connected to the thing to which it refers). The concept of gesture is also used as a metaphor to explain linguistic effects, such as in the description of DEIXIS.

Cassirer, Ernst. *A Philosophy of Symbolic Forms*. Trans. Ralph Manheim. New Haven: Yale University Press, 1953–57.

GLANCE. According to Norman Bryson, the glance differs from the GAZE in that the glance is temporal whereas the gaze transcends time. The glance is the look of a viewer still aware of his or her own position in time and place; the gaze is "vision disembodied," vision that is capable of

assessing the deeper structures incorporated in a work of art (see THE-
ATRICALITY for Michael Fried's similar distinction between theatricality
and absorption).

Bryson, Norman. *Vision and Painting: The Logic of the Gaze.* New Haven: Yale Univer-
sity Press, 1983.
Sartre, Jean-Paul. *Being and Nothingness.* 1943. Trans. Hazel E. Barnes. New York:
Washington Square Press, 1956.

GRAND RÉCIT. See MASTER NARRATIVE.

GRID. The grid, a two-dimensional framework of parallel horizontal and
vertical lines, has functioned in the history of art as both a technical and
a conceptual tool. Historically, grids were used to transcribe three-
dimensional scenes or objects onto the two-dimensional plane of paper
or canvas. The development of the grid as a technical tool is therefore
closely related to the development of single-point perspective during the
fifteenth century. More recently, the grid has been used by Rosalind
Krauss as a conceptual tool for the analysis of certain types of twentieth-
century abstract art, in which the surface of the work is in a sense doubled by the use of a grid-like structure. Whereas much modernist painting (see MODERNISM) incorporates a tension between flatness and depth,
the grid resolves this tension through its inherently flat structure, like the
surface of the canvas that provides its support.

Krauss, Rosalind. "Grids." In *The Originality of the Avant-Garde and Other Modernist
Myths.* Cambridge, Mass.: MIT Press, 1985.
Panofsky, Erwin. *Perspective as Symbolic Form.* Trans. Christopher S. Wood. Cam-
bridge, Mass.: MIT Press, 1991.

GROTESQUE. *Grotesque* once usually referred to a fresco or sculptural
decoration that combined hybrid human and animal forms (gargoyles,
etc.) with swirling vines and flowers. Now the term has come to be used
for a fascination with the unnatural, ugly, distorted, or bizarre, as in the
nineteenth-century gothic fictions of Edgar Allan Poe.

In the twentieth century, the term *grotesque* has been used to describe
a merging of the traditionally grotesque with the comic, as in black

humor (e.g., the novelist Nathanael West's *Miss Lonelyhearts*) and the theater of the ABSURD (Eugène Ionesco's *The Bald Soprano*). Moreover, it has received considerable attention in recent theory and criticism as a result of interest in the work of Mikhail Bakhtin, who in *Rabelais and His World* described the subversive function of grotesque folk humor in relation to the power of the late medieval church. Bakhtin presented Rabelais's "grotesque realism" as the literary exemplification of such humor and argued that its central principle is "degradation, that is, the lowering of all that is high, spiritual, ideal, abstract; it is a transfer to the material level, to the sphere of earth and body in their indissoluble unity." The strongly populist and anti-authoritarian cast of these ideas, which were developed at the height of Stalinist repression in the Soviet Union, has proven highly influential for both MARXIST and FEMINIST CRITICISM.   See also ABJECTION, CARNIVAL.

Bakhtin, Mikhail. *Rabelais and His World.* Trans. Helene Iswolsky. Cambridge, Mass.: MIT Press, 1968.
Stallybrass, Peter, and Allon White. *The Politics and Poetics of Transgression.* London: Methuen, 1986.

GYNESIS. A term coined by Alice Jardine in 1985, *gynesis* (geiNEEsis) refers to the process by which poststructuralist thought turns to the concept of "woman" to resolve the crises generated by modernity and by the radical rethinking of such traditional concepts as Truth, Identity, and History. This process is evident at a symbolic level in texts by several French male theorists: Derrida's *écriture*, Lacan's *jouissance*, and Foucault's "madness" are all associated with a notion of the female suggesting disruption and unknowability. In texts by American men, gynesis tends to occur at the level of representation. For example, in Thomas Pynchon's *V*, the title character is a woman, but a woman who may not exist and about whom nothing can be known, so that she remains theoretical only. While women theorists (such as Kristeva) also engage in gynesis, Jardine associates it with anti-feminism as well as feminism; for despite its "valorization of the feminine," gynesis tends to invoke an abstract idea of Woman, not the interests and experiences of women as a historical class, and to rely on the conventional view of women as passive, mute—the instruments of male redemption. Jardine urges French and American feminists to work together in making gynesis function on behalf of women.

Jardine, Alice A. *Gynesis: Configurations of Women and Modernity.* Ithaca, N.Y.: Cornell University Press, 1985.

GYNOCRITICS. *Gynocritics,* a term introduced by Elaine Showalter in her 1979 "Toward a Feminist Poetics" and elaborated in her 1981 "Feminist Criticism in the Wilderness," focuses on images, themes, plots, and genres, on individual authors and patterns of influence among women, in an effort to identify what is specifically characteristic of women's writing and to construct "a female framework for the analysis of women's literature." Associated primarily with Anglo-American feminist criticism of the late 1970s and 1980s, gynocritics seeks to recover unknown, and to reread known, writing by women in order to "map the territory" of a female literary tradition. Early examples include Patricia Spacks's *The Female Imagination* (1975), Ellen Moers's *Literary Women* (1976), and Showalter's *A Literature of Their Own* (1977). These were followed by such discussions and theories of women's writing as Sandra Gilbert and Susan Gubar's *The Madwoman in the Attic* (1979), Barbara Christian's *Black Women Novelists* (1980), and Nancy Miller's "Emphasis Added: Plots and Plausibilities in Women's Fiction" (1981), to name only a few. Showalter called gynocritics the "second phase" of feminist criticism, because it succeeded and built upon an earlier phase of "feminist critique," which had focused on women as the readers of male texts. The shift toward gynocritics in the U.S. and England was paralleled by the celebration of women's writing by French feminists such as Hélène Cixous and Luce Irigaray. Its rise also coincided with the rise of CULTURAL FEMINISM, and, as with cultural feminism, its focus on women has recently begun to give way to studies of "gender." See also BLACK FEMINIST CRITICISM, ÉCRITURE FEMININE, FEMINIST CRITIQUE.

Christian, Barbara. *Black Women Novelists: The Development of a Tradition: 1892–1976.* Westport, Conn.: Greenwood Press, 1980.

Gilbert, Sandra J., and Susan Gubar. *The Madwoman in the Attic: The Woman Writer and the Nineteenth-Century Literary Imagination.* New Haven: Yale University Press, 1979.

Miller, Nancy K. "Emphasis Added: Plots and Plausibilities in Women's Fiction." In Elaine Showalter, ed., *The New Feminist Criticism.* New York: Pantheon, 1985.

Showalter, Elaine. "Feminist Criticism in the Wilderness." In Elaine Showalter, ed., *The New Feminist Criticism.* New York: Pantheon, 1985.

—. "Toward a Feminist Poetics." In Elaine Showalter, ed., *The New Feminist Criticism.* New York: Pantheon, 1985.

H

HARLEM RENAISSANCE. The Harlem Renaissance was a flourishing period of artistic and literary creation in African-American culture generally and among the "New Negroes" of Harlem in particular. Most chroniclers of the renaissance—e.g., Anderson, Huggins, Lewis—define the period as beginning with the increased militancy and racial pride symbolized by the 1919 parade of black veterans through Harlem and ending with the economic collapse of the Great Depression. Houston Baker has argued for an expanded view of "renaissancism" as characteristic of the modernist "mastery of form" and "deformation of mastery" in African-American art from the turn of the century to World War II. Participants in the renaissance saw it as a period of realist, non-stereotyped art, which broke with the genteel and didactic Negro writing of the previous century. Despite the contributions of various musicians, painters, actors, and other artists, most critics of the renaissance have focused on the writers who were drawn to Harlem: Countee Cullen, Langston Hughes, Zora Neale Hurston, Nella Larsen, Claude McKay, and others. The artists of the period were supported and influenced by black editors—W. E. B. Du Bois, Jessie Fauset, Charles Johnson, Alain Locke—and white patrons—Charlotte Osgood Mason, the Spingarn family, and Carl Van Vechten—who have been variously referred to as "midwives" of the renaissance. The period can be seen as a precursor of later movements for African-American cultural autonomy and race consciousness. See also NEW NEGRO.

Anderson, Jervis. *This Was Harlem: A Cultural Portrait, 1900–1950.* New York: Farrar, Straus, Giroux, 1982.

Baker, Houston A., Jr. *Modernism and the Harlem Renaissance.* Chicago: University of Chicago Press, 1987.

Huggins, Nathan Irvin. *Harlem Renaissance.* New York: Oxford University Press, 1971.

Hull, Gloria T. *Color, Sex, & Poetry: Three Women Writers of the Harlem Renaissance.* Bloomington: Indiana University Press, 1987.

Lewis, David Levering. *When Harlem Was in Vogue.* New York: Knopf, 1981.

HEGEMONY. In its most common sense, *hegemony* (heJEMoNEE) refers to the dominance of one group, nation, or culture over another. In the twentieth century, it has acquired the connotation of political dominance, especially in regard to the activities of superpowers like the United States and the former Soviet Union.

Though many theorists and critics often casually (and confusingly) use hegemony in this general way, for Marxist and poststructuralist criticism it actually has a complex and specialized meaning. As a theoretical concept, hegemony became important through the writings of the Italian Marxist Antonio Gramsci (1891–1937), who uses the term in at least two distinct ways. At first, Gramsci used *hegemony* to describe a revolutionary strategy that depended upon a structure of alliances within the working class that could serve as a unitary base for the overthrow of bourgeois capitalism. Later, in his *Prison Notebooks, hegemony* refers to relationships between classes, specifically the control that the bourgeoisie exerts over the working classes. For Gramsci, hegemonic control is not maintained merely by force or the threat of force, but by consent as well. That is, a successful hegemony not only expresses the interest of a dominant class (see IDEOLOGY), but also is able to get a subordinate class to see these interests as "natural" or a matter of "common sense." For Gramsci, this attitude of consent to the social order permeates all aspects of social existence: institutions, relationships, ideas, morals, etc. Gramsci further argues that the basis of hegemony is not purely economic, but also exists within the cultural life of any society. Therefore, a strategy of working-class revolution that depends solely on economistic models of analysis is inadequate and doomed to failure.

The concept of hegemony as a unifying web of relations that function as natural or evident shares much with poststructuralist discussions of IDEOLOGY, DISCOURSE, and POWER, which are also often seen as irreducible to a determinate origin and as constitutive of lived experience. While such formulations have proven a problem for discussions of resistance, especially in the works of Louis Althusser and Michel Foucault, Gramsci actually formulates hegemony in terms of resistance. He proposes that in order to overthrow bourgeois hegemony—in order to perceive it as primarily (though not exclusively) self-interested—it is necessary to form a "new" hegemony, which will have an even greater basis of consent and which will address the needs and interests of a larger number of groups. This fully extended society realizes itself in a democracy that will allow various groups to unite at various times and according to their perceived shared social and political needs and goals. Such a new hegemony can only be fashioned in opposition to the dominant one, which is perceived as hegemony and not common sense when its unified, coherent worldview is no longer able to explain satisfactorily events and experiences that contradict that unity. See also BASE/SUPERSTRUCTURE, DETERMINISM, MARXIST CRITICISM.

Gramsci, Antonio. *Selections from the Prison Notebooks, 1921–1935.* Trans. and ed. Quintin Hoare and Geoffrey Nowell Smith. New York: International Publishers, 1971.

—. *Selections from Political Writings, 1921–1926.* Trans. and ed. Quintin Hoare. New York: International Publishers, 1978.

—. *Prison Notebooks*, vol. 1. New York: Columbia University Press, 1992.

Laclau, Ernesto, and Chantal Mouffe. *Hegemony and Socialist Strategy: Towards a Radical Democratic Politics.* Trans. Winston Moore and Paul Cammack. London: Verso, 1985.

Sassoon, Anne Showstack. *Gramsci's Politics.* New York: St. Martin' Press, 1980.

HERMENEUTIC CIRCLE. A spatial model of the process of interpretation as it is formulated in HERMENEUTICS, the hermeneutic circle describes the circular relation between part and whole. In order to understand the whole of any TEXT, one must first have an understanding of the constituent parts; yet to understand the parts, one must have a workable comprehension of the whole. Not just emblematic of interpretation, the hermeneutic circle has also been the primary problem and focus of hermeneutics since 1819, when Friedrich Schleiermacher first proposed a general theory of hermeneutics that would apply to texts other than scripture or other religious writings. In the twentieth century, theorists like Martin Heidegger and Hans Georg Gadamer have extended the problematics of language and interpretation beyond written texts to one's very existence in time. Gadamer's conception of the hermeneutic circle asserts that we can understand the present only in the context of the past and that we can only understand the past in relation to our existence in the present. See also HISTORICISM, READER-RESPONSE THEORY.

HERMENEUTICS. Originally *hermeneutics* (HERmenOOtiks) referred to theories of biblical interpretation, but later the term came to designate the theory of interpretation in general. At the heart of all hermeneutic enterprises is the presupposition that a TEXT, whether legal, religious, historical, or literary, contains a determinate meaning, whose recovery, whether possible or not, is the goal of interpretation. In 1819 Friedrich Schleiermacher, a German philosopher and theologian, proposed a theory of general hermeneutics that could extend to all texts. In the 1890s, Wilhelm Dilthey adopted and expanded upon Schleiermacher's ideas, proposing hermeneutics as the basis for understanding all works in the humanities and social sciences or GEISTESWISSENSCHAFTEN, which he saw as "expressions of inner life." His theory of hermeneutics attempted to establish principles for "valid" and "objective" interpretations of these texts but disdained the simple adoption of the methods of the natural sciences (*Naturwissenschaften*) as the means to obtain such objectivity. Since for Dilthey *Geisteswissenschaften* were based on concrete, historical, lived experience, the static, categorizing of the natural sciences would not serve for the study of humanity and its institutions. Rather, Dilthey proposed that a text can be understood in its particulars only when the interpreter has a predetermined sense of the meaning of the whole. Yet one can only know the meaning of the whole by understanding the meanings of the constituent parts. This HERMENEUTIC CIRCLE appears vicious, but Dilthey insisted that a reader can come to a determinate meaning by continually moving between his or her emerging sense of the whole and his or her retrospective understanding of the parts.

This movement between the poles of part-whole relationships is characteristic of the two major schools of hermeneutics that have been influential in recent years. The first is grounded in authorial intention and came to some prominence with the publication of E. D. Hirsch's 1967 book, *Validity in Interpretation*. Starting from Dilthey's assertion that a reader can arrive at an objective interpretation of an author's expressed meaning, Hirsch argues that this expressed meaning refers to the author's intention to produce a meaning through the conventions of language that can be shared. For Hirsch, an author's intention may be informed by his or her cultural milieu, idiosyncrasies, the availability of particular genres or forms, and other factors "external" to the text, but to read the text without any consideration of authorial intention is to render a text indeterminate—that is, capable of an indefinite diversity of meanings. Hirsch's application of the hermeneutic circle depends on the reader's formation of a "hypothesis" as to the meaning of a text, or a portion of it. This hypothesis is "corrigible," and may be either confirmed by continuing reference to the text, or invalidated, in which case an alternative hypothesis is posited that better conforms to all the demands of the text. According to Hirsch, it is in this way that the reader, though never entirely sure of the author's intended verbal meaning, moves toward an ever-increasing probability of authorial intention and is able to limit the possibilities of meaning and to corroborate his or her interpretation by comparing it to the findings of other competent readers. For Hirsch, this process can, and does, yield objective knowledge of the determinate and stable meanings of texts.

In contrast to Hirsch is the second major school of hermeneutic theory. Following from Dilthey's notion that authentic understanding of texts that fall within the domain of *Geisteswissenschaften* requires the reader's re-experience of the "inner life" expressed by those texts, and working from the premises informing the EXISTENTIALIST philosopher Martin Heidegger's concept of DASEIN as a temporal and interpretive "being-in-the-world," Hans Georg Gadamer developed a hermeneutic theory that extends beyond texts to a notion of existence itself as an interpretive enterprise. Gadamer, in his important *Truth and Method*, argues that all experience, not just literary texts, is subject to interpretation and that language permeates all aspects of that experience. For Gadamer, an interpreter is defined by "horizons" of time and experience that shape the presuppositions he brings to the text. But rather than approaching the text as an autonomous object, the reader must be aware that the text, too, has temporal horizons; therefore, he must enter into "dialogue" with the text, asking questions of it but also allowing it to question his own assumptions. This is Gadamer's version of the hermeneutic circle, and one can only escape it when the horizons of the text and the interpreter "fuse" in understood meaning.

Unlike Hirsch, Gadamer concedes the irrecoverable, relative nature of textual meaning. And since, as the reader experiences the text, that experience becomes a part of the reader's horizon, subsequent readings of the same text will necessarily be affected, for his presuppositions will have changed. For Gadamer, then, textual meaning and significance are hardly distinct; the meaning of a text is perhaps most importantly what it means now, at this moment, to the reader. Hirsch, in contrast, argues that verbal meaning, based in authorial intention, is stable, determinate, and atemporal, while a text's *significance* is always relative, changing with every reader. Ultimately the difference between these two theories lies in their conceptions of the production of understanding. For Gadamer, as in much of the READER-RESPONSE THEORY that has derived from his philosophical work, the reader is privileged as the site where meaning resides; for Hirsch, meaning is in the text, and thus is recoverable. See also AUTHOR, PHENOMENOLOGICAL CRITICISM, POSTSTRUCTURALISM, REZEPTIONSÄSTHETIK.

Gadamer, Hans-Georg. *Truth and Method.* 1960. Translation edited by Garrett Barden and John Cumming. New York: Continuum Press, 1975.

Heidegger, Martin. *Being and Time.* Trans. John Macquarrie and E. S. Robinson. New York: Harper, 1962.

Hirsch, E. D. *Validity in Interpretation.* New Haven: Yale University Press, 1967.

Hoy, David Couzens. *The Critical Circle.* Berkeley: University of California Press, 1978.

Palmer, Richard. *Hermeneutics: Interpretation Theory in Schleiermacher, Dilthey, Heidegger, and Gadamer.* Evanston, Ill.: Northwestern University Press, 1969.

Ricoeur, Paul. *The Conflict of Interpretations: Essays in Hermeneutics.* Evanston, Ill.: Northwestern University Press, 1974.

HETEROGLOSSIA. In the writings of Mikhail Bahktin and his followers, the term *heteroglossia* designates the fundamental condition under which meaning is created. For Bahktin, the meaning of any word is governed by the entire set of circumstances in which that word is uttered. These circumstances, both material and intellectual, are understood to be unique, complex, and fleeting; thus, heteroglossia represents an attempt to conceptualize that which formalized linguistic theories such as STRUCTURALISM cannot accomodate: the perception that meaning depends on a host of factors unique to a given moment, rather than merely to structures inherent in language itself.

Bahktin, Mikhail. *The Dialogic Imagination: Four Essays.* Trans. Caryl Emerson and Michael Holquist, ed. Michael Holquist. Austin: University of Texas Press, 1981.

HIGHER CRITICISM. *Higher Criticism* refers to a branch of nineteenth-century biblical scholarship that rigorously examined the historical contexts of the Bible, attempting to accurately establish dates, authors, sources, and circumstances of composition of the scriptural texts. The term "higher" was applied not to suggest its superiority to orthodox studies (which it challenged) but rather to distinguish it from "lower" criticism—the establishment of definitive texts—on which it was based.

HISTOIRE/DISCOURS. See FABULA/SUJET.

HISTORICISM. Historicism is a concept whose basic principles are at least as old as Giambattista Vico's *Scienza Nuova* (1725) and J. G. Herder's *Ideen zur Philosophie der Geschichte der Menschheit* (1774), and has traditionally been associated with the development in the nineteenth century, and particularly in Germany, of the "historical sense"—the recognition that the past is fundamentally different from the present and can be understood only in terms of its own context. In *Der Historismus und Seine Probleme* (1922), the first extended analysis of historicism, Ernst Troeltsch saw historicism, which he defined as the tendency to view all knowledge and all experience as subject to historical change, as the dominant mode of nineteenth-century historical thought, and he contrasted historicism with the generalizing, quantitative study of nature, which he called *Naturalismus.* For Troeltsch, as for Friedrich Meinecke, who extended and emphasized the importance of the concrete, the unique, and the individual, historicism represented not simply a methodology for historical studies, but a worldview fundamentally different from a "naturalistic" or "positivistic" understanding of reality that relied upon the concept of an unchanging and universal natural law. Since these studies, *historicism* has been used in a variety of senses and, in the work of Karl Popper and F. A. von Hayek, for example, has been defined in ways clearly opposed to the use given to the term by Troeltsch. But if there is a single definition that succeeds in uniting the various aspects of historicism, it is Maurice Mandelbaum's in *History, Man, and Reason* (1971): "Historicism is the belief that an adequate understanding of the nature of any phenomenon and an adequate assessment of its value are to be gained through considering it in terms of the place which it occupied and the role which it played within a process of development."

The possible applications of historicist principles to literary studies are clear, and they have been pursued in a number of ways, from a sort of "metaphysical" historicism often associated with Hegel, which assumes the continuity of historical development and seeks to understand the work of literature within that development, to a conflation of positivistic and historicist principles, such as in some Marxist criticism, which perceives the literary text as a historical and sociological document, to a form of "aesthetic" historicism (deriving from the philosophy of Benedetto Croce), which transfers the critic's attention from the historical and cultural context to the intuitive re-performance of the creative act of the author. In all of these applications, however, the underlying assumption is that the work is determined by (and in turn determines) its context in history and can be understood only historically. Such an assumption implies that the work of art can be understood not in terms of some transcendental, eternal scheme of value, but solely in terms of its cultural and historical context.

This assumption also opens historicism to critique from at least two angles. The first, and more traditional, is that a historicist approach leads, to use René Wellek's phrase, to a "crippling relativism and an anarchy of values." This problem of historicism's denial of a timeless, aesthetic value to the work of art has been addressed most effectively in the work of Leo Spitzer and Erich Auerbach, who attempt to establish the historical and cultural context of the work and to place that work within a larger, continuous historical tradition. Thus, in *Mimesis* (1953), Auerbach seeks to place Boccaccio's story of Frate Alberto from the *Decameron* solidly within the historical context of the development of a style of prose fiction growing out of and away from both the earlier fabliaux tradition and the antique genre of the novel of love, the *fabula milesiaca*, and into the "first literary prose of postclassical Europe"; at the same time, Auerbach's analysis places Boccaccio's story, which incorporates the sensory realism heralded by Dante's *Commedia*, in the larger historical context of a continuous tradition of REALISM extending from Homer to Virginia Woolf.

The second, and diametrically opposed, angle of critique is presented by deconstruction's presumption of the ultimate indeterminacy of meaning, historical and otherwise, and the infinite play of signification. Thus, while Derrida, for example, declares that meaning is determined by context, including historical context, he also maintains that "no context permits saturation"—that is, context is unlimited. Furthermore, the historical ground upon which, and only upon which, the historicist would base the meaning of a text is, according to the principles of DECONSTRUCTION, itself constantly shifting and disappearing. So the meaning of a literary text can never be fixed according to a historical context that is itself approachable only as a text. Historicism, however, remains an active interpretive practice; the issues raised by POSTSTRUC-TURALISM are currently being addressed by a historical methodology that sees itself as a NEW HISTORICISM. See also HERMENEUTICS, MARX-IST CRITICISM, NEW CRITICISM.

Collingwood, R. G. *The Idea of History.* Oxford: Clarendon Press. 1951.
Croce, Benedetto. *Philosophy, Poetry, History: An Anthology of Essays.* Trans. Cecil Sprigge. London: Oxford University Press, 1966.

—. *The Essence of the Aesthetic.* Trans. Doublas Ainslie. Folcraft, Pa.: Folcraft Library Editions, 1974.

Hayek, F. A. von. *The Counter-Revolution of Science: Studies in the Abuse of Reason.* Glencoe, Ill.: Free Press, 1952.

Mandelbaum, Maurice. *History, Man, and Reason: A Study in Nineteenth-Century Thought.* Baltimore: Johns Hopkins University Press, 1971.

Meinecke, Friedrich. *Die Enstehung des Historismus.* 2 vols. Munich: Oldenbourg, 1936.

Popper, Karl. *The Poverty of Historicism.* New York: Basic Books, 1960.

Spitzer, Leo. *Linguistics and Literary History: Essays in Stylistics.* Princeton: Princeton University Press, 1948.

—. *A Method of Interpreting Literature.* Northampton, Mass.: Smith College, 1949.

Troeltsch, Ernst. *Der Historismus und Seine Probleme.* Tübingen: Mohr, 1922.

HISTORY OF EVERYDAY LIFE. The term *history of everyday life* is often used to label histories that attempt to document, describe, and analyze the history of human experience as it was lived, at the most mundane levels. In most cases, this has meant writing case studies of life in villages and other small communities, or studies of the impact of seemingly simple innovations on the way life was led (e.g., how did life change after coffee was imported? after the invention of indoor plumbing?). On one hand, the historians of everyday life are responding to an inadequacy of traditional history, which tended to focus on kings and conquerors, and sought large generalizations about historical trends. On the other hand, the rise of interest in the history of everyday life reflects shifts in other intellectual disciplines and cultural/political orientations—psychoanalysis focused great interest on the history of the family and child-rearing practices; Marxism generated an interest in the daily lives of workers and peasants; feminism brought attention to the lives of women; African-American scholars sought information about the lives of slaves in the antebellum South, etc. The term is most closely associated with the members of the "Annales school" (including Fernand Braudel, Philippe Aries, and Emmanuel Le Roy Ladurie), centered in France in the 1950s, but it has also been applied to the work of the American historian Natalie Zemon Davis, the Italian Carlo Ginsburg, and the English "History Workshop" group of the 1970s and 1980s, etc.

HOMOSOCIAL. A term referring to social bonds between people of the same sex, *homosocial* was popularized by Eve Sedgwick in her discussion of "male homosocial desire." By speaking of "homosocial desire," Sedgwick places "male bonding" and male homosexuality on the same continuum. Yet in our society, she observes, this continuity is denied: relationships among male politicians, business partners, athletes, and soldiers—the many alliances between men on which patriarchy is based—are thought to preclude "homosexual" ones. In fact, the more closely men associate, the more they are apt to express a hatred and fear of homosexuality; male homosociality seems to require extreme homophobia. Sedgwick's analysis goes on to suggest that we look again at the love triangle in which two men appear to be competing for a woman's love. In *Between Men,* she develops René Girard's claim that such a triangle may disguise as rivalry what is actually an attraction between men. This pattern has two major effects: to deny that male homosocial relations may have a sexual component and to reduce women to a middle term, mediating between men.

According to Sedgwick, female homosocial ties, on the other hand, are not so emphatically opposed to homosexual ties between women. Lesbian relations, in her view, are seen in our society as more continuous with the sanctioned relations between mothers and daughters, between female friends and coworkers. It is precisely this broad spectrum of women's homosocial loyalties that Adrienne Rich has referred to and celebrated as the "lesbian continuum." Unlike Sedgwick, however, Rich argues that lesbian desire is not tolerated but severely punished, and that female homosociality in general is devalued. The work of historian Carroll Smith-Rosenberg suggests that passionate friendships between women—in which homosocial ties include intensely erotic feelings— were somewhat more socially acceptable in the nineteenth century. See also GAY CRITICISM, LESBIAN CONTINUUM, LESBIAN CRITICISM.

Rich, Adrienne. "Compulsory Heterosexuality and Lesbian Existence." In *Blood, Bread, and Poetry: Selected Prose 1979–1985.* New York: Norton, 1986.

Sedgwick, Eve. *Between Men: English Literature and Male Homosocial Desire.* New York: Columbia University Press, 1985.

——. *Epistemology of the Closet.* Berkeley: University of California Press, 1990.

Smith-Rosenberg, Caroll. "The Female World of Love and Ritual: Relations Between Women in Nineteenth-Century America." In *Disorderly Conduct: Visions of Gender in Victorian America.* New York: Knopf, 1985.

HORIZON.   Derived from PHENOMENOLOGY, the term *horizon* is associated with the philosophical HERMENEUTICS of Hans-Georg Gadamer and with the REZEPTIONSÄSTHETIK that developed from Gadamer's theories of interpretation, especially in the work of Hans Robert Jauss. For

Gadamer, horizons signal the boundaries of meaning and understanding for a text or a reader, boundaries that are historically contingent and thus always changing in relation to both the spatial and temporal connections between text and reader. Jauss focuses more exclusively on horizons as those sets of expectations established by cultural norms, conventions, and presuppositions that inform how a reader understands and evaluates a literary work at any given time. Like Gadamer, Jauss sees these horizons of expectations as historically determined and thus subject to change as social mores and assumptions change.

Gadamer, Hans-Georg. *Truth and Method*. Translation edited by Garrett Barden and John Cumming. New York: Continuum Press, 1975.

Jauss, Hans Robert. *Aesthetic Experience and Literary Hermeneutics*. Trans. Michael Shaw. Minneapolis: University of Minnesota Press, 1982.

—. *Toward an Aesthetic of Reception*. Trans. Timothy Bahti. Minneapolis: University of Minnesota Press, 1982.

—. "Literary History as a Challenge to Literary Theory." *New Literary History* 2, 1970.

HUMANISM. While in current critical debates *humanism* usually refers to an anthropocentric view of the world that asserts the existence of a universal human nature informing all actions and decisions, the term has a long and complex history. Modern humanism has its origins in Renaissance Italy, although the word itself is derived from the Latin *humanitas* and includes the sense expressed in the Greek word *paideia*: that is, education in the liberal arts, understood as forms of learning that separate human beings from animals and barbarians. By the second half of the fourteenth century, the concept of *humanitas* implied two distinct meanings, one of which was precisely this distinction between *homo humanus* and *homo barbaritas* or animality. The other important meaning of the word is derived from the medieval distinction between humanity and divinity; in contrast to the ancient usage, it emphasizes the *limitations* of humans, above all their frailty and impermanence. A major current in Renaissance thought, humanism defended the study of classical letters as the means to effect a rebirth of the human spirit manifested in ancient Greece and Rome but lost during the Middle Ages. Renaissance humanists like Pico Della Mirandola and Marsilio Ficino emphasized human freedom and the responsibility of human beings to shape and better their world, while accepting and incorporating the general awareness of natural human limitations inherited from medieval thought. Opposing dogma, asceticism, and intolerance, they placed human nature at the center of all human endeavors, making humans "the measure of all things."

The heritage of Renaissance humanism is extensive and has shaped many aspects of modern society, including the organization of the disciplines in the modern university and many of their most cherished tenets, especially that of the importance of a liberal arts education. While humanism has never been by definition unfriendly to religious belief, contemporary usage often favors the phrase "secular humanism," largely as a result of nineteenth-century efforts to promote the monuments of secular culture as a modern replacement for the waning influence of religion. Understood in this way, humanism is a frequent target of fundamentalist religious groups.

In much contemporary theoretical writing, humanism has been the object of a highly sophisticated critique. Anti-humanist critics have questioned the humanist exaltation of human freedom and self-determination, and opposed the habit of placing humanity at the center of the universe, viewing humanism as an apology for INDIVIDUALISM. For example, many poststructuralist thinkers have maintained that humanity's supposed freedom of thought and action (see AGENT) is limited by the linguistic, psychological, or socioeconomic conditions of our existence (see POSTSTRUCTURALISM). And feminists, black activists, postcolonial critics, and gay and lesbian critics have argued that the "man" at the heart of humanism is not free of the limitations or limiting interests resulting from the specifics of a particular gender, class, race, or sexual orientation; on the contrary, this "man" is male, white, middle-class, Anglo, and heterosexual. For these critics, the attempt to pass off such a limited viewpoint as universal is covertly, if not overtly, oppressive.

Althusser, Louis. "Marxism and Humanism." In *For Marx.* Trans. Ben Brewster. New York: Pantheon, 1969.

—. "Ideology and Ideological State Apparatuses: Notes Towards an Investigation." In *Lenin and Philosophy.* Trans. Ben Brewster. New York: Monthly Review Press, 1971.

Carby, Hazel. "White Women Listen . . ." *The Empire Strikes Back: Race and Racism in 70s Britain.* London: Hutchinson and University of Birmingham, 1982.

Cassirer, Ernst. *The Individual and the Cosmos in Renaissance Philosophy.* Trans. Mario Domandi. New York: Harper and Row, 1963.

Derrida, Jacques. "Structure, Sign, and Play in the Discourse of the Human Sciences." In *Writing and Difference.* Trans. Alan Bass. Chicago: University of Chicago Press, 1978.

Foucault, Michel. *The Order of Things: An Archaeology of the Human Sciences.* New York: Vintage, 1970.

—. *Language, Counter-Memory, Practice: Selected Essays and Interviews.* Trans. Donald
     F. Bouchard and Sherry Simon. Ithaca, N.Y.: Cornell University Press, 1977.
Fuss, Diana. *Essentially Speaking.* London: Routledge, 1990.
Moi, Toril. *Sexual/Textual Politics: Feminist Literary Theory.* New York: Routledge, 1985.
Panofsky, Erwin. "The History of Art as a Humanistic Discipline." In *Meaning in the
     Visual Arts.* Garden City, N.Y.: Doubleday, 1955.

HYPERREAL. A term coined by the French theorist Jean Baudrillard, *hyperreality* describes a common phenomenon in the late twentieth century and refers to his idea that it has become impossible to tell the difference between the "real" and reproductions of the real. When reproductions of things seem more real, authentic, and powerful to us than the thing being reproduced, then we are in the realm of hyperrealism. For example, many people find viewing postcard reproductions of famous paintings such as the *Mona Lisa* more satisfying than seeing the painting itself. See also SIMULACRUM, SIMULATION.

Baudrillard, Jean. *Simulations.* Trans. Paul Foss, Paul Patton, and Philip Beitchman.
     New York: Semiotext(e), 1983.
Eco, Umberto. *Travels in Hyperreality.* Trans. William Weaver. San Diego: Harcourt
     Brace Jovanovich, 1986.

HYPERTEXT. Coined in the 1960s by the computer pioneer Theodor H. Nelson but only recently introduced into common usage, *hypertext* refers to the new, computer-created possibilities of access to and linkage of texts. Above all, it emphasizes the ways that computers allow the reader to escape from the constrictions of linearity, fixity, and boundedness that characterize the traditional written text. Of course, the act of reading has never been simply determined by those qualities; in practice, readers have always been able to skip around within a text, jump to footnotes, stop to consult other texts, or simply abandon one text in favor of another. With the introduction of the computer and modern software, however, the ability to move from one block of text to another has been greatly enhanced; and writers such as George P. Landow view this development as a technological complement to such theoretical concepts as the project of DECENTERING, the concepts of INTERTEXTUALITY and the WRITERLY text, and the POSTMODERN rejection of linear narrative.

Landow, George P. *Hypertext: The Convergence of Contemporary Critical Theory and
     Technology.* Baltimore: Johns Hopkins University Press, 1992.

I

ICON. In the most general use of the term, an icon is simply an image, figure, or likeness. Bound up in this definition is the concept of resemblance. Icons are signs that resemble what they denote, and often come to be identified with the object they denote. This resemblance between an icon and its referent may be pictoral or it may be a feature—such as shape—that the icon shares with the object it represents. A common example is the Christian cross. The American semiologist Charles Sanders Peirce uses this sense of icon to describe one of three types of relations between SIGNIFIER and SIGNIFIED in their formation of the SIGN. Peirce's other two types of signs are the indexical and symbolic: the former is distinguished by a concrete relationship—usually of cause and effect—between the sign and the object it signifies, such as smoke as an index of fire or fever as an index of infection. The symbolic sign's connection to its REFERENT is arbitrary and thus is analogous to Ferdinand de Saussure's conception of the linguistic sign.

Because the iconic sign's function is grounded in resemblance, a good deal of the theoretical considerations of the icon have occurred in art criticism. In medieval and early modern art most of the discussion surrounding iconic representations was highly formalized, dependent upon complex systems of signification that were articulated in treatises, contracts, or programs that the artist would follow and that acted as a guide for understanding the works. By the mid-eighteenth century, thinkers such as G. E. Lessing, Friedrich Schlegel, and Johann Herder, influenced by the period's infatuation with myth and symbol, moved from *ekphrastic*, or descriptive, analyses of art to *hermeneutic*, or interpretive, analyses. In the early twentieth century (1912), Aby Warburg broke with the main tenets of nineteenth-century iconography, which had primarily sought to establish the links between religious art and religious texts and the liturgy. Warburg argued that the study of images was the study of their relations to the complex structure of historical life—including religion of course, but extending as well to poetry, myth, science, politics, and society.

Following upon Warburg's assertions and informed by his contemporary Ernst Cassirer's philosophy of symbolic forms, Erwin Panofsky first articulated the twentieth-century's most influential theory and method of inconographic interpretation in his *Herkules am Schweidewege* (1930), and again in 1939 in his best-known book, *Studies in Iconology*. It is at this point that the term *iconology* comes to prominence, displacing the older *iconography* and differing significantly from it in meaning. Increasingly, *iconography* denoted the descriptive practice of identifying themes, whereas *iconology*, as G. J. Hoogewerff put it, aimed at understanding "symbolic, dogmatic, or mystical meaning which is expressed (or hidden) in figurative forms."

Panofsky's method of analysis moves through three distinct levels. The first, pre-iconographical analysis is the level of pure description, of information not yet codified. The second, or iconographic, is the level of conventional meaning. The third level is the iconological—the level of what Panofsky calls "symbolic" values. Panofsky demonstrates these distinctions with the example of hat-lifting, a conventional gesture of politeness in Western society. The pre-iconographic would consist of a description of the series of movements that make up the gesture. On the iconographic level, the arbitrary gesture of lifting the hat is understood to have the conventional meaning of politeness. The various inflections that particular circumstances might give the gesture would constitute the iconological level.

Although there is some similarity between this formulation and certain structuralist theories of signification (for example, the distinction between the DENOTATIVE and the CONNOTATIVE) Panofsky does not give as much consideration to the ways that one's perception of the pre-iconographic is already structured by the system through which one's knowledge is organized. In this regard, he is not far removed from his Kantian antecedents and Cassirer. Panofsky is not primarily concerned with the epistemological status of the icon in its structuring of thought but rather with its function as an amalgam of historically specific conventions, themes, and symbols that represent some aspect of the history of the human mind. For Panofsky a work of art always contains what he refers to as *intrinsic* meaning that can be uncovered and shared.

In recent years, W. J. T. Mitchell has done important work on iconology. Going beyond Panofsky's separation of iconology from iconography, Mitchell attempts to further generalize iconology's interpretive functions by "asking it to consider the idea of the image as such." By this,

Mitchell means to demonstrate the ways that "the notion of image serves as a kind of relay connecting theories of art, language, and the mind with conceptions of social, cultural, and political value." Of vast importance to Mitchell is the consideration of the image as an ideologically informed and informing entity—one that relies upon its social context for its force, even as it shapes that context.

Mitchell, W. J. T. *Iconology: Image, Text, Ideology*. Chicago: University of Chicago Press, 1986.

Panofsky, Erwin. *Studies in Iconology*. Oxford: Oxford University Press, 1939.

ICONIC SIGN. See SIGN.

ID. A (frequently criticized) translation of the German neuter pronoun *das Es* (the "it"), this term designates one of the three agencies of the human psyche in what has come to be known as Freud's "second topography," developed in the later part of his career (the earlier one divides the psyche into the preconscious-conscious and UNCONSCIOUS systems). The id is the primitive, instinctual part of the mind, and its contents are unconscious and partially innate. As the primary source of psychic energy, the id comes in conflict with the other two agencies that make up the psychic apparatus, the EGO and the SUPEREGO, although it cannot be seen as entirely distinct from those other agencies either.

Freud, Sigmund. *The Ego and the Id*. Ed. James Strachey, trans. Joan Riviere. New York: Norton, 1960.

IDEALISM. The difficulty with defining *idealism* is that the term has at least two distinct meanings that are often confused even in careful critical prose. The most common use of *idealism* denotes behavior or thought based upon a notion of how things should be or how one would like them to be. Used in this sense, *idealism* may be either complementary— indicating one's devotion to one's ideals—or pejorative—indicating a naiveté that refuses to deal with "reality."

Philosophically, the term refers to a theory which either posits that the objects one perceives are ideas the mind knows directly and are not objects themselves, or argues that the objects one perceives are manifestations of an independent realm of essences or forms that are unique and changeless. The most important antecedent to all modern idealisms is Plato's theory of Forms or Ideas. These are eternal, transcendental realities that are knowable only through thought and are directly opposed to the changing empirical existence of humans.

Three strains of idealism have exerted considerable influence on philosophical and critical thought since the eighteenth century. The first, which was held by the eighteenth-century Anglo-Irish philosopher George Berkeley (1685–1753), proposed that all material objects are composed of nothing but ideas, which are either in the mind of God or the AGENTS he created. Thus, for Berkeley, there is no "reality" without perception. Berkeley's philosophy, which he called "immaterialism," is sometimes referred to as "empirical idealism," since his theory supposes that sense perception is basically reliable. What we must understand, according to Berkeley, is that what we are perceiving are not *material* objects, but ideas. Dr. Johnson's famous response to this position was to assert his own material empiricism by kicking a stone and saying, "I refute *it* thus!"

The second important variety is transcendental idealism or Kantian idealism. For the German philosopher Immanuel Kant (1724–1804), it is not possible to gain knowledge of the world through rational thought alone; nor can sense perception be relied upon to give us that knowledge, since without interpretation, sense perception is "blind." Kant argued that without the a priori intuitions of time and space, we would not be able to know the material world, however much we might experience fluctuations of sensation about it. Unlike Berkeley, for whom space and time existed as part of the objects perceived, Kant argued that space and time were categories of understanding that are inherent in the perceiving SUBJECT. For Kant, the synthesizing of one's perceptions into these a priori categories was not undertaken by a self such as we are aware of in ourselves and in others but by a transcendental self, which is not an object of knowledge but a condition of knowledge. This transcendental self can know nothing of itself except that it is. According to Kant, we can only account for our a priori categories of understanding by accepting this concept of the transcendental self, since we can never know it.

The third important idealism is objective or absolute idealism and is associated with the work of the German philosopher G. W. F. Hegel (1770–1831) and his followers. Whereas Berkeley's and Kant's idealisms, despite their vast differences, are pluralistic, insisting upon the existence of a multiplicity of ideas or forms in the noumenal realm, Hegel argued that all that exists is a form of the Absolute Mind. This type of idealism is also sometimes called objective idealism, and its proponents often refer to Kantianism as subjective idealism, to emphasize the role played by the perceiving subject and the a priori knowledge he or she must exercise in the act of perception.

Arguments over idealism still abound in contemporary theoretical debates. Much of the discussion surrounding ESSENTIALISM is centered in attitudes toward idealism in criticism. Confusion often arises when critical discussions merge judgments of political principles with analyses of philosophic principles. For example, it is not unusual for Marxism, which in its orthodox forms insists upon a material first instance, to be accused of being idealistic for the political agenda it espouses. See also SUBJECT/OBJECT.

Berkeley, George. *Three Dialogues Between Hylas and Philonous.* Ed. Colin M. Turbayne. New York: Liberal Arts Press, 1954.

Hegel, G. W. F. *Lectures on the Philosophy of History.* Trans. J. Sibree. London: G. Bell and Sons, 1894.

—. *Science of Logic.* Trans. A. V. Miller. London: Allen and Unwin, 1969.

Kant, Immanuel. *Critique of Pure Reason.* Trans. Norman Kemp Smith. New York: St. Martin's, 1965.

IDEATIONAL REPRESENTATIVE. A translation of the German *Vorstellungsrepräsentanz*, this Freudian term refers to the idea or mental impression that represents an INSTINCT in the psyche (the German word *Repräsentanz* implies the idea of delegation). The concept is an attempt to understand the relationship of body to mind as that of the instinct, which is biological, to its psychic representatives. Freud conceived of these representatives as ideas on which the instinct becomes fixated in the course of development (see FIXATION). Only the ideational representatives, rather than the instinct itself, enter the unconscious in a process that Freud described as an inscription in several layers. Moreover, the ideational representative is to be understood as distinct from the emotion or "affect" that was originally attached to it. This latter may be displaced onto another idea, transformed into another emotion, or suppressed altogether with the repression of the ideational representative into the UNCONSCIOUS.

Freud, Sigmund. "Repression." In *Standard Edition of the Complete Psychological Works of Sigmund Freud,* vol. 14. Trans. James Strachey. London: Hogarth Press and Institute of Psycho-Analysis, 1974.

—. "The Unconscious." In *Standard Edition of the Complete Psychological Works of Sig-*

mund Freud, vol. 14. Trans. James Strachey. London: Hogarth Press and Institute of Psycho-Analysis, 1974.

IDENTIFICATION. Identification is a process in which one takes aspects of another as a model for oneself. Although the primary usage of the term is "to identify oneself with something," it also includes the more common meaning "to recognize," since the process of identification may have the feeling of a recognition or discovery of what one has been looking for without knowing it. The effect of identification is to bring about a transformation of the personality according to the prototype with which one identifies, and for this reason it occupies a position of crucial importance in the Freudian theory of psychic development.

Freud, Sigmund. *The Interpretation of Dreams*. Trans. and ed. James Strachey. London: Hogarth Press, 1953.

IDENTITY. The word *identity* has two related but somewhat different uses in contemporary criticism and theory, the first of which is part of the more general problem of the SUBJECT. Thus, much contemporary theory has sought to question the traditional belief that human identity is present to the conscious mind or at least an accessible piece of self-knowledge. Rather, many theorists describe the subject as perpetually in flux, pursuing an illusion of wholeness and selfhood that is ultimately unattainable, however necessary it may be to human functioning. (One of the most influential positions on this topic is Jacques Lacan's concept of the MIRROR STAGE and his thesis that the subject is constituted in and by its language.) The other common use of the term *identity* is in reference to group identity, as in the phrase *identity politics*. The sense of identity offered by one's membership in groups that have suffered oppression on the basis of gender, race, class, or sexual preference is a major area of investigation in contemporary criticism and CULTURAL STUDIES. See also DECENTERED SUBJECT, DECENTERING.

IDENTITY THEME. American ego psychology postulates that an individual's life is held together, like a novel, by a single recurring element—an "identity theme"—which is unique to the individual. The reader-response critic Norman Holland has used "identity theme" to explain and systematize why different readers see different things in the same text. According to Holland, readers derive pleasure from reading, even though at first some texts may challenge their sense of self or worldview. Readers, Holland speculated, ultimately find ways of understanding the text in their own terms, so that the text reinforces and assures their identity theme. Terry Eagleton contrasts Holland's work with classical Freudian reading theories, which posit a "split subject" or divided ego, and challenges the idea that literature always leaves the reader reassured and unaltered. See also READER-RESPONSE CRITICISM.

Eagleton, Terry. *Literary Theory: An Introduction.* Minneapolis: University of Minnesota Press, 1983.
Holland, Norman. *5 Readers Reading.* New Haven: Yale University Press, 1975.

IDEOLOGY. *Ideology,* in its current critical usage, has at least four possible meanings, which have evolved as a result of various political and philosophical attempts to define the relation of ideas to their social context. First, ideology is a form of misrepresentation that distorts social reality and seeks symbolically to resolve social contradictions that elude real solutions. Second, ideology is the combination of all forms of social consciousness, such as law, philosophy, ethics, art, etc. Third, ideology is simply the political ideas ascribed to a social or economic class, such as bourgeois ideology. Finally, poststructuralist thinking has used elements from all three of these definitions to construct a theory of ideology as the system of representations, or stories, that define the possibilities of existence for all individuals.

Coined by Destutt de Tracy in 1796, the term *ideology* referred to his science of ideas, which analyzed ideas empirically in the tradition of Locke. The ideologists believed that ideas arise from human experience; they begin as sensations that are transformed and organized within a formal system of linguistic signs. Their very abstract conception of human experience and their insistence on the formal aspect of language did not allow them to analyze the social relationships that govern human experience and its meaning. When Napoleon reorganized the Institut National, he dismissed the ideologists, whose reforms and theories he saw as a threat, and he criticized them as ideologues—thus introducing the term and the pejorative sense of ideology as illusion or impractical theory.

Marx and Engels defined ideology as a false consciousness that fails to recognize the true motives underlying its view of the world and imagines false ones instead, thus distorting social reality and providing symbolic resolutions to social problems that have not been resolved in practice. After Marx's death the concept of ideology was broadened to include neutral usages that conflict with this theory of ideology as misrepresentation. On the one hand, Marxist theorists borrowed from Engels his concept of culture as an ideological superstructure. Taken together, ideas form a coherent structure that is determined by and reflects the economic BASE. Antonio Gramsci, in his *Prison Notebooks*, argues for historically organic ideologies that organize masses of people and create the terrain on which persons move, acquire consciousness of their position, struggle, etc. For him, ideology is crucial to HEGEMONY, whereby a class maintains its control not simply by force but by manufacturing consent within a network of institutions, social relations, and ideas. On the other hand, Lenin in particular was responsible for redefining ideology as the political beliefs of a class, so that we can now speak of a socialist ideology as well as a bourgeois ideology. Georg Lukács argues then that the falseness of a particular ideology lies not in its being ideology per se, but in the structural limitations of the class whose thought it represents.

Louis Althusser's theory of ideology elaborates further upon these notions. In *For Marx*, Althusser argues that no society—not even a communistic one—could exist without ideology, and that ideology, like Freud's UNCONSCIOUS, has no history. Although specific ideologies may come and go, the realm of ideology in general is eternal; for it is the universal means by which individuals are defined as subjects within a prevailing social system. Thus, rather than a mere set of ideas or political beliefs, ideology is, in Althusser's view, inseparable from the process by which human beings acquire identities (see INTERPELLATION).

Althusser's most famous dictum provides the elements of a narrative model of ideology that is of particular importance to literary critics. Althusser argues that ideology is a system of representations that express the *lived* relation between human beings and their conditions of existence, and that this imaginary or lived relation implicitly takes a narrative shape. Thus, says Althusser, subjects live their lives in hopeful, nostalgic, or other ways according to the specifics of that imagined relation. Ideology is distinct from science, which gives us a superior knowledge of things because of its greater methodological rigor. Ideology is also distinct from art, which does not give us knowledge but instead makes us see the ideology from which it is born and to which it *alludes*. Taking his cue from these formulations, Fredric Jameson explicitly defines ideology in terms of a narrative model. He sees art as an ideological form of consciousness and believes that art's power lies in its allusiveness: any symbolic act, such as a poem, novel, or speech, produces its social context even as it reacts against it, and thus it provides a textual avenue toward the recovery of history. Jameson argues that aesthetic forms are inherently ideological because they formally resolve antinomies or aporias that are the textual equivalents of real social conditions. This notion is not far removed from Marx's own view of ideology, but Jameson takes it further by providing a working model of the narrative elements of ideology. Moreover, he sees ideology as a form of closure, or strategy of containment, that simultaneously implies and represses an ideal of TOTALITY, and he thus privileges narratives that render history as a whole. See also MARXIST CRITICISM, POSTMODERNISM, SEMIOTIC RECTANGLE, STRUCTURALISM, SUBJECT.

Althusser, Louis. *For Marx.* Trans. Ben Brewster. New York: Pantheon. 1969.
—. "Ideology and Ideological State Apparatuses." In *Lenin and Philosophy and Other Essays.* Trans. Ben Brewster. New York: Monthly Review Press, 1971.
Eagleton, Terry. *Ideology: An Introduction.* London: Verso, 1991.
Jameson, Fredric. *The Political Unconscious: Narrative as a Socially Symbolic Act.* Ithaca: Cornell University Press, 1981.
Lichtheim, George. *The Concept of Ideology and Other Essays.* New York: Vintage, 1967.
Lukács, Georg. *History and Class Consciousness.* Trans. Rodney Livingstone. Cambridge, Mass.: MIT Press, 1971.
Marx, Karl, and Friedrich Engels. *The German Ideology.* Trans. S. Ryazanskaya. Moscow: Progress Publishers, 1968.
Williams, Raymond. *Marxism and Literature.* Oxford: Oxford University Press, 1977.

IMAGINARY. The Imaginary is one of the three cognitive dimensions or "orders" (the other two being the SYMBOLIC and the REAL) in the psychoanalytic theory of Jacques Lacan; it is, quite simply, the dimension of images, whether conscious or unconscious, insofar as they can be conceived apart from the linguistic categories that shape and define them. Although all three orders function together to constitute consciousness, human beings exist in the Imaginary from their earliest years, when experience is dominated by visual and spatial relationships, the most important of which is the relationship to the image of one's own body that Lacan described in the concept of the MIRROR STAGE. This initial process of coming to terms with the unity of the body by grasping it as a vision of wholeness from which one is nevertheless alienated is the prototype for all of the dual relationships that characterize the Imaginary; these are marked by attitudes of IDENTIFICATION or aggressiveness toward a counterpart. While it is only in the early years of childhood that human beings live entirely in the Imaginary, it remains distinctly present throughout the life of the individual.

Lacan, Jacques. "Aggressivity in Psychoanalysis." In *Ecrits: A Selection*. Trans. Alan Sheridan. New York: Norton, 1977.
—. "The Mirror Stage." *Ecrits: A Selection*. Trans. Alan Sheridan. New York: Norton, 1977.

IMAGO. For Jung and later psychoanalysts, the imago is an UNCONSCIOUS figure or stereotype that forms the basis for relationships. Although imagos are originally based on figures in the family environment, they are not reflections of real individuals so much as fantasy representations. For example, a patient may describe an imago of a fearsome parent, when the parent in question is actually relatively mild-mannered. The term *imago* has reacquired currency among psychoanalytic critics largely as a result of its use by Jacques Lacan in his influential essay on the MIRROR STAGE, which demonstrates the significance of the imago of the young child's own body in his or her experiential world.

Jung, Carl. *Psychology of the Unconscious*. Trans. Beatrice M. Hinkle. Princeton: Princeton University Press, 1991.
Lacan, Jacques. "The Mirror Stage as Formative of the Function of the 'I' as Revealed in Psychoanalytic Experience." In *Ecrits: A Selection*. Trans. Alan Sheridan. New York: Norton, 1977.

IMPERIALISM. See COLONIALISM.

IMPRESSIONISM. In painting, impressionism is associated most closely with the work of a group of French painters who exhibited together in Paris between 1874 and 1886, first under the label "intransigents" and then as "impressionists." Impressionism was an outgrowth of realism in that the impressionists focused on aspects of contemporary life. Impressionist artists such as Claude Monet, Auguste, Renoir, and Alfred Sisley were, however, much more concerned than their immediate predecessors with capturing fleeting effects of light under different atmospheric conditions through the use of color, often in works painted out of doors rather than in the studio on the basis of earlier sketches. The impressionist artists also continued the realist rebellion against traditional academic training—in which painting from the live model was prefigured by many years of drawing from plaster casts—and the French Academy's official exhibition, the Salon, though some artists from the group did occasionally participate in the official exhibition. Though associated primarily with France, impressionist techniques were also adapted by artists in various other countries by the end of the nineteenth century.

Herbert, Robert . *Impressionism: Art, Leisure, and Parisian Society.* New Haven: Yale University Press, 1988.

Moffett, Charles S., ed. *The New Painting: Impressionism 1874–1886.* San Francisco: Fine Arts Museums of San Francisco, 1986.

Rewald, John. *The History of Impressionism.* New York: Museum of Modern Art, 1973.

INDEXICAL SIGN. See SIGN.

INDIVIDUALISM. The word *individualism* is a nineteenth-century coinage describing the central tradition of liberal political and economic thought. Drawing on several major contributions of the ENLIGHTENMENT, including the political theory of John Locke and the economic ideas of Adam Smith, individualism posits the individual human being as the basic unit out of which all larger social groups are constructed, grants priority to his or her rights and interests over those of the state or social group, and aims to minimize restrictions on his or her economic initiatives. During much of its history, individualism has been attacked from both the right and the left—in the first case, for undervaluing the wisdom of the traditions represented by established social forms, and in the second, for underestimating the extent to which the individual is shaped by the social relationships into which he or she is born.

Dewey, John. *Individualism, Old and New.* New York: Minton, Balch and Co., 1930.

Hampshire, Stuart. *Freedom of the Individual.* London: Chatto and Windus, 1975.

Mill, John Stuart. *On Liberty.* Ed. John Gray. Oxford: Oxford University Press, 1991.

INFANTILE SEXUALITY. Psychoanalysts since Freud have recognized that the sexuality of children is neither nonexistent, as the common wisdom of the nineteenth century had it, nor simply identical to that of adults, but rather progresses through a series of phases. At first, the sexual feelings of infants are simply a general feature of their relation to the world and are not bound to any organ (see NARCISSISM, POLYMORPHOUS PERVERSITY); however, as they grow, they move through periods in which their sexuality is centered on a specific erotogenic zone: the mouth (oral phase), the sphincter muscle (anal phase), and the penis or clitoris (genital phase). In each phase, the dominance of a given erotogenic zone indicates a preferred mode of sexual contact between the child and his or her surroundings. See also FIXATION.

Freud, Sigmund. *Three Essays on the Theory of Sexuality*. Trans. and ed. James Strachey. London: Hogarth Press, 1962.

INFOLDING/UNFOLDING. In Roland Barthes's account of reading in *S/Z*, two inverse impulses work together in the interpretive act, one reducing the text to a single meaning, the other disrupting the effort by reveling in the plurality of possible meanings. Infolding is the act of consolidating or gathering in meaning through the process of naming, enclosing meaning by substituting a single generic term for a multitude of significations. Unfolding arises out of the limitless play of meanings associated with naming. It disperses meaning in a process of connotative expansion rather than the denotative compression associated with infolding. See also CONNOTATION/DENOTATION.

Barthes, Roland. *S/Z*. Trans. Richard Miller. New York: Hill and Wang, 1974.

INSTINCT. *Instinct* traditionally refers to a hereditary behavior pattern that is peculiar to a species and resists change; however, the word also has a more specific usage in psychoanalysis, where it serves as a translation of the German *Trieb* (DRIVE). Here it refers to a force or internal pressure that directs the individual toward an object. Although instincts have biological origins and aim to eliminate the tension created at this source, the acts that they inspire vary greatly from person to person, as well as from one occasion to another. Freud distinguished among *source, pressure, aim,* and *object* in his description of the instincts and emphasized the variable character of the object, which is chosen in accord with arbitrary factors in the individual's history. The choice of an object is by no means constant throughout the life of the individual and least of all during childhood, when the sources of instinctual excitation are multiple and one or another predominates at different times (see INFANTILE SEXUALITY). Moreover, since these choices are affected by external contingencies, physical maturity does not necessarily ensure a comparable development of instinctual behavior (see FIXATION). Freud did, however, attempt to classify the instincts according to a fundamental dualism, which he altered during the latter part of his career. Originally, he spoke of the instincts of pleasure and self-preservation (see PLEASURE PRINCIPLE, REALITY PRINCIPLE), but later revised this formulation to include simply LIFE INSTINCTS and DEATH INSTINCTS.

Freud, Sigmund. *Beyond the Pleasure Principle.* Rev. ed. Trans. and ed. James Strachey. New York: Liveright Publishing, 1961.
—. *Three Essays on the Theory of Sexuality.* Trans. and ed. James Strachey. London: Hogarth Press, 1962.
—. "Instincts and Their Vicissitudes." In *Standard Edition of the Complete Psychological Works of Sigmund Freud,* vol. 14. Trans. James Strachey. London: Hogarth Press and Institute of Psycho-Analysis, 1974.

INSTITUTION. The term *institution* designates an established, self-contained, well-defined, unified network of beliefs and practices. According to Wlad Godzich, one view holds that institutions are "apparatuses," "constituted bodies with their internal procedures and delimited field of intervention." He amends this notion, suggesting that an institution is preeminently a "guiding idea," a defined goal to be reached for the common good and to be achieved by following set procedures.

Because of the conservative nature and authority of an institution, the term is most often used pejoratively to suggest the status quo, the established system. Richard Rorty objects to the illogical radical position that draws upon such negative concepts to justify categorical rejection of all institutions, as if "escaping from institutions [were] automatically a good thing, because it ensures that one will not be 'used' by the evil forces which have 'co-opted' these institutions." While the negative usage has much currency today, it is reductive. René Lorau distinguishes two components of the term: "instituted," which refers to its static quality, and "instituting," which designates its dynamic, transformative aspect. Summarizing the present state of the term, he concludes, "By emptying the concept of institution of one of its primordial components (that of instituting, in the sense of founding, creating, breaking with an old order and creating a new one), [we have] finally come to identify the institution with the status quo."

Godzich, Wlad. "Afterword." In Samuel Weber, *Institution and Interpretation*. Minneapolis: University of Minnesota Press, 1987.

Lorau, René. *L'Analyse institutionnelle*. Paris: Editions de Minuit, 1970.

Rorty, Richard. "Habermas and Lyotard on Postmodernity." In Richard J. Bernstein, ed., *Habermas and Modernity*. Cambridge, Mass.: Polity Press, 1985.

INSTITUTIONALIZATION. *Institutionalization* refers to the process by which ideas, theories, interpretations, or other forms are made conventional and assimilated into an existing framework or established system. The term is used negatively in academia (itself an INSTITUTION responsible for institutionalization) to designate the appropriation of innovative or radical ideas and their subsequent domestication into politically nonthreatening forms. Like the term *co-optation*, which it resembles, it is a paradoxical concept, made so, as Gerald Graff has pointed out, by "the negative value it assigns to something that we usually think of as desirable—being accepted or successful, persuading others to one's point of view." The source of the paradox lies in a misuse of the term *institution*, which consists of two components: the overly emphasized "instituted" (status quo) and the forgotten "instituting" (founding, breaking with the old). Resistance to institutionalization is possible through the process of MARGINALIZATION but always with the risk of a loss of effectiveness.

Graff, Gerald. "Co-optation." In H. Aram Veeser, ed., *The New Historicism*. New York: Routledge, 1989.

INSTRUMENTALITY. Most commonly, this term is used to describe a view of pre-Saussurian linguistics that regards the relations of signified and signifier as other than arbitrary. In other words, instrumentalism suggests that a word, uttered or written, has some close and special relationship with the thing it stands for. An important example of instrumentalism is REALISM, the dominant British linguistic philosophy and literary style in the eighteenth and nineteenth centuries, which held that language always reflects reality. The "instrumentality" of the realists was often associated with questions of ethical behavior. Indeed, a modern form of linguistic instrumentalism, SPEECH ACT THEORY, focuses on how language is used to do things—that is, how language can alter reality (create expectations, disseminate information, etc.). However, describing speech act theory as instrumentalism has less to do with ethical behavior than with the more general definition of "instrumentality" as the means or agency through which some function is performed.

Austin, John Langshaw. *How to Do Things with Words.* Cambridge, Mass.: Harvard University Press, 1962.

INTENTIONAL FALLACY. A key concept in American NEW CRITI-CISM and formulated by W. K. Wimsatt and Monroe Beardsley in an important 1952 essay, the intentional fallacy is an appeal to the supposed intentions of the author in the reading of a poem or other literary work. For the New Critics, a poem is an autonomous structure that contains within itself everything necessary to its own reading, and they rejected appeals to authorial intention as irrelevant. See also AUTHOR.

Wimsatt, W. K., and Monroe Beardsley. "The Intentional Fallacy." In *The Verbal Icon.* Lexington: University of Kentucky Press, 1954.

INTENTIONALITY. The word *intentionality* was first used by Jeremy Bentham to designate any intentional or willed activity of the mind; however, its technical philosophical usage is associated with the PHE-NOMENOLOGY of Edmund Husserl, who reintroduced the term in his discussions of his teacher Franz Brentano's conception of mental phenomena. Briefly, intentionality refers to the state of existence of objects in the mind and is, for Husserl, the defining characteristic of consciousness. Husserl's point is that thought is always thought *of* something, and the description of these mental objects is the province of phenomenology.

Brentano, Franz. *Psychology from an Empirical Standpoint.* Trans. Antos C. Rancurello, D. B. Terrell, and Linda L. McAlister, ed. Linda L. McAlister. New York: Humanities Press, 1973.
Husserl, Edmund. *Ideas: General Introduction to Pure Phenomenology.* Trans. W. R. Boyce-Gibson. New York: Humanities Press, 1967.
—. *Logical Investigations.* Trans. J. N. Findlay. New York: Humanities Press, 1970.

INTERPRETIVE COMMUNITY. A term introduced by Stanley Fish in his 1980 book, *Is There a Text in This Class?*, *interpretive community* refers to a group of readers (or interpreters of signs) who share common assumptions about the nature of meaning and who employ common strategies in their reading. For Fish, reading and understanding can only take place within such a community, and the strategies one employs are as constructive as they are interpretive. Thus, Fish argues, the features of a text that one may see as objective, as well as the "intentions, speakers, and authors" of the text are in fact created by the assumptions asserted by the community and employed by the reader. Such an argument, often linked philosophically with recent work in PRAGMATISM, asserts that a universally valid reading of any text is impossible, since all readings are relative to the "principles of noticeablity and relevance" that function within a specific community and that inform a reader's interpretive strategy.

Fish, Stanley. *Is There a Text in this Class? The Authority of Interpretive Communities.* Cambridge, Mass.: Harvard University Press, 1980.

INTERNALIZATION. Although *internalization* is frequently used as a synonym for INTROJECTION, it sometimes refers more specifically to the taking of a relationship into the psyche, as when a child internalizes his/her relationship to his/her father by transforming it into the relationship between EGO and SUPEREGO.

Freud, Sigmund. *The Ego and the Id.* Trans. Joan Riviere, ed. James Strachey. New York: Norton, 1960.

INTERPELLATION. In the theory of IDEOLOGY developed by the French Marxist philosopher Louis Althusser, the word *interpellation* refers to the central operation by which ideology assigns to the individual human being an identity as a SUBJECT. To interpellate means, among other things, to interrupt or break in upon someone with a formal address or series of questions. In Althusser's theory, however, the process of interpellation is a moment of recognition, which, to use Althusser's somewhat loaded example, "can be imagined along the lines of the most commonplace everyday police (or other) hailing: 'Hey, you there!' " This process, whether literal or not (a teacher can recognize a student, but a book cannot recognize its readers), is also the addressee's recognition that it is he or she who is being addressed: hailed by the forces of authority, the individual involuntarily turns around, thus acknowledging his or her identity as a subject. Although the example presents these operations for convenience as a sequence, Althusser suggests that we have always existed in ideology and cites the ritual of anticipation that surrounds the birth of a child. Moreover, his understanding of the individual's self-recognition is heavily influenced by Jacques Lacan's account of the beginnings of human identity in the MIRROR STAGE of psychic development, as well as the Lacanian concept of the OTHER. In Althusserian parlance, the latter is known as the Absolute Subject and imagined as a kind of supreme figure or model with which one identifies, and to which one is at the same time "subjected." Thus internalized, the Absolute Subject infuses the world of social relations and its history with meaning, and the existence of each individual becomes an ever-renewed attempt to live up to his or her own role in this collective social process.

Althusser, Louis. "Ideology and Ideological State Apparatuses." In *Lenin and Philosophy and Other Essays*. Trans. Ben Brewster. New York: Monthly Review Press, 1971.

INTERPRETATION. See HERMENEUTICS.

INTERTEXTUALITY. According to theorists such as Roland Barthes and Julia Kristeva, no text can be read outside its relations to other, already extant texts. Neither the text nor its reader can escape this intertextual web of relationships that causes the reader to have certain expectations about both the content and the form of the work(s) he or she is reading. These relationships may take many forms, including parody, PASTICHE, allusion, imitation, etc. In STRUCTURALIST and POSTSTRUCTURALIST accounts of the relationships between texts, texts are assumed to refer only to other texts and not to any empirical, nontextual reality. See also ANXIETY OF INFLUENCE, MISPRISION, TEXT.

INTROJECTION. *Introjection* refers to the fantasy incorporation of objects into the EGO. Introduced into psychoanalytic theory by Sandor Ferenczi, who understood it as the opposite of PROJECTION, introjection is closely related to the fantasy of oral incorporation into the body; however, it also refers more broadly to any fantasy situation in which the object is taken into the psychic apparatus.

Ferenczi, Sandor. "Introjection and Transference." In *Selected Papers*. New York: Basic Books, 1950–55.

Freud, Sigmund. *Civilization and Its Discontents*. Trans. and ed. James Strachey. New York: Norton, 1962.

—. "Instincts and Their Vicissitudes." In *Standard Edition of the Complete Psychological Works of Sigmund Freud*, vol. 14. Trans. James Strachey. London: Hogarth Press and Institute of Psycho-Analysis, 1974.

—. "Mourning and Melancholia." In *Standard Edition of the Complete Psychological Works of Sigmund Freud*, vol. 14. Trans. James Strachey. London: Hogarth Press and Institute of Psycho-Analysis, 1974.

IRONY. Irony is a rhetorical TROPE that involves the creation of a meaning different from—and often opposite to—the meaning one would normally expect in a certain situation or associate with a given word or phrase. According to this most basic definition, to be ironic is to say one thing and mean another. The word has its origins in Greek comedy, where the *eiron* was traditionally a powerless but shrewd character whose cleverness allowed him to triumph over the proud but slow-witted *alazon*. This association is also present in the Socrates of the Platonic dialogues, who claims not to know in order to get at the truth in exchanges with less humble conversationalists (a technique that is sometimes called Socratic irony), and in Aristotle, who describes *eironeia* as a form of self-deprecation for the purpose of concealing one's powers.

In more recent centuries, the rhetorical definition of irony has been supplemented by a number of further elaborations of the concept. Thus, the German philosopher Friedrich Schlegel spoke of *romantic irony*, which involves the sense of a discrepancy between the desire for unity and infinity, on the one hand, and the perception of a chaotic and finite world on the other. Romantic irony arises out of the endless, ever-renewed attempt to establish distance from this predicament and to resolve its contradictions through acts of imagination. Similarly, although he rejected the concept of romantic irony, the philosopher G. W. F. Hegel proposed the term *cosmic irony* to describe the contrast between a totalizing view of the world and the perspective of the individual; and Hegel's term was later adopted by the Danish philosopher Søren Kierkegaard, who defined it as the irreconcilability of the subjective and the objective.

The idea of a discrepancy between the individual and the machinations of an unyielding or impersonal fate is central to the notion of *tragic irony*, which can be thought of as a special case of *dramatic irony*. The latter refers generally to a theatrical situation in which a gap is opened up between a character's own understanding of his or her actions and what the audience knows about them or what the play eventually reveals about them, as in the classic example of *Oedipus Rex*. This sort of irony is itself a special case of what is sometimes called *situational irony*, in contrast to *verbal irony*, where the ironic effect is concentrated in specific statements.

In modern literary criticism, irony has been especially important to the American NEW CRITICISM, whose proponents viewed it as the literary device most characteristic of poetry as such, reconciling contradictory elements into a meaningful whole (see also PARADOX). By contrast, in an influential essay on the subject, Paul de Man has assimilated the concept of irony to the project of DECONSTRUCTION (see also APORIA).

Aristotle. *Nicomachean Ethics*. Trans. H. Rackham. New York: Putnam, 1926.

De Man, Paul. "The Rhetoric of Temporality." In *Blindness and Insight: Essays in the Rhetoric of Contemporary Criticism*, 2d rev. ed. Minneapolis: University of Minnesota Press, 1983.

Hegel, Georg Wilhelm Friedrich. *Lectures on the History of Philosophy*. Trans. J. Sibree. London: G. Bell and Sons, 1894.

Kierkegaard, Søren. *The Concept of Irony, with Constant Reference to Socrates*. Trans. Lee M. Capel. New York: Harper, 1965.

Schlegel, Friedrich von. *Philosophical Fragments*. Trans. Peter Firchow. Minneapolis: University of Minnesota Press, 1991.

ISOTOPY. Introduced by A. J. Greimas, the term *isotopy* (EIsoTopee) refers to the synonymous nature of the four terms of the SEMIOTIC RECTANGLE and more broadly to the repetition of an idea in a text on different levels and through different signs. In the following description of Coketown from *Hard Times*, for example, Dickens employs an isotopy of "sameness" or "monotony": "All the public inscriptions in the town were painted alike, in severe characters of black and white. The jail might have been the infirmary, the infirmary might have been the jail, the town hall might have been either, or both, or anything else, for anything that appeared to the contrary in the graces of construction. Fact, fact, fact, everywhere in the material aspect of the town; fact, fact, fact everywhere in the immaterial." Here both the descriptive terms ("sever," "alike," and "contrary in the graces of construction") and the rhetorical structures (the interchangeability of the terms "jail," "infirmary," and "townhall" and the insistent repetition of the word "fact") contribute by isotopy to the characterization of Coketown as a monotonously ugly place. The isotopy—the deployment of synonymous terms and figures of speech throughout the description—gives the text its coherence. However, Umberto Eco and others have argued that what Greimas and his followers call isotopies have different structures and relationships and are therefore not properly synonymous.

Eco, Umberto. *A Theory of Semiotics.* Bloomington: Indiana University Press, 1979.
Greimas, A. J. *Structural Semantics: An Attempt at a Method.* Trans. Daniele McDowell et al. Lincoln: University of Nebraska Press, 1983.

J

JEREMIAD. A jeremiad (JAIRiMEIad) is a prediction of destruction because of a people's evil or disobedience to God (see Jeremiah 1:14, 16), or, more generally, any expression of extreme grief. The American critic Sacvan Bercovitch has pointed to the New England Puritans' use of the term to mean "political sermon," which Bercovitch understands as indicative of the Puritans' theocratic governance. Bercovitch, following Perry Miller, identifies the New England jeremiad as "America's first distinctive literary genre"—it differed from the European jeremiad, Bercovitch argues, because whereas the latter was used to assert that God's wrath would descend to wreak vengeance upon these evil times, the "American jeremiad" viewed God's anger as an act of love that would bring into existence a new and better community.

Bercovitch, Sacvan. *The American Jeremiad.* Madison: University of Wisconsin Press, 1978.
Miller, Perry. *Errand into the Wilderness.* Cambridge, Mass.: Harvard University Press, 1956.

JOUISSANCE. From the French verb *jouir,* "to enjoy," *jouissance* (zhweeSANS) is usually translated as "delight," "enjoyment," "sexual pleasure," or "orgasm." Among critical theorists, however, its meaning is more complicated. In Roland Barthes's theory of textual pleasure, *jouissance* is the name given to that which is indeterminate, mobile, blank— it is the explosion of language, when language no longer has meaning. For the psychoanalyst Jacques Lacan, it refers both to specifically female sexual pleasure (various and diffuse as opposed to the singular male orgasm) and to the realm of the Imaginary, a prelinguistic state in which the infant is not yet differentiated from his or her mother or from the world. Like female sexual pleasure, the Imaginary is a realm of multiple rather than individual identity, of excess rather than limit. French feminists Hélène Cixous and Luce Irigaray have suggested that *jouissance* in this sense is characteristic of what they call "feminine" writing. The term also has an economic meaning. Lacan contrasts it to "possession," for *jouissance* is fluid and unending; it involves using without using up, and as such exceeds a notion of possession based on some fixed value. Cixous agrees that *jouissance* as an economy of female pleasure is prodigal, giving freely and undermining notions of thrift or profit. See also ÉCRITURE FEMININE, IMAGINARY.

Barthes, Roland. *The Pleasure of the Text*. Trans. Richard Miller. New York: Hill and Wang, 1975.

Cixous, Hélène. "The Laugh of the Medusa." Trans. Keith Cohen and Paula Cohen. In Elaine Marks and Isabelle de Courtivron, eds., *New French Feminisms*. Amherst: University of Massachusetts Press, 1980.

Irigaray, Luce. *This Sex Which is Not One*. Trans. Catherine Porter. Ithaca, N.Y.: Cornell University Press, 1985.

Kristeva, Julia. *Desire in Language: A Semiotic Approach to Literature and Art*. Trans. Alice Jardine et al., ed. Leon S. Roudiez. Oxford: Blackwell, 1980.

Lacan, Jacques. *Ecrits: A Selection*. Trans. Alan Sheridan. New York: Norton, 1977.

JUMP CUT. A jump cut is a cut within a scene, rather than between scenes, that has the effect of condensing the SHOT so that a certain amount of time devoted to character action is not represented. The ellipsis may be achieved by retaining the same FRAMING on the background but instantly changing the figure, or by retaining the same framing on the figure but instantly changing the background. This interruption of the action may not be perceived as obtrusive or as a violation of continuity editing and its effect of REALISM if it is narratively motivated (if the time elided is "dead time," taken up by unimportant character actions like getting to the top of a flight of stairs), or if it is the basis for such cinematic illusions as characters walking on walls or objects turning into other objects. Generally, however, ellipses are achieved by changing the framing on both figure and background, cutting out "dead time" by cutting away to something else in a scene before returning to the character at a different point in the action. Ellipses are also routinely produced by changing the CAMERA ANGLE on the character more than 30 degrees, so that the second shot is obviously from a different camera position (in fact, this is so routine that it is called " the 30 degree rule"), or by shifting SHOT SCALE (camera distance), for example, by cutting in for a close-up. When two shots of the same characters are cut together without significantly varying camera angle or distance, a jump cut will be perceived as such—the character will appear to "jump" across part of the screen. This is exactly what happens when a film has been repaired by splicing together two sections of a single shot but with several frames missing from the action filmed. In effect, two shots of the same action from the same camera angle and distance have been edited together and the action appears to be interrupted illogically, thereby calling attention to the editing itself. Obtrusive jump cuts tend to achieve an ALIENATION EFFECT, weakening narrative continuity by disrupting the illusion of realism as they remind the viewer of the constitutive presence of the cinematic apparatus, whose conventions mediate and produce that reality for the spectator. Jump cuts have sometimes been used for just this reason in anti-realist avant-garde or alternative cinemas, which often reflect on the medium itself in order to promote reflection on reality and the CODES (including cinematic codes) that mediate it for its consumers.

K

KINSHIP. The study of kinship relations is a major area of anthropology; it attained special prominence with the advent of STRUCTURALISM and the appearance of Claude Lévi-Strauss's influential book *The Elementary Structures of Kinship* (1949), which brought a new level of scientific precision to the subject. Briefly, the major controversy concerns the question of whether kinship structures can be shown to be systems that conform to the pattern of a universal human psychology or logical structure of the human mind, as structuralist anthropologists often imply, or whether they must be understood as responses to local forms of social organization, as the tradition of British functionalist anthropology has maintained. Anthropological study of kinship relations has also been of considerable interest to feminist theorists, who focus on the ways that women often serve as materials for barter in various societies.

Lévi-Strauss, Claude. *The Elementary Structures of Kinship*. Trans. James Harle Bell and John Richard von Sturmer. Boston: Beacon Press, 1969.

KULTURWISSENSCHAFT. See NATURWISSENSCHAFT.

L

LANGUE/PAROLE. *Langue* (LAHNG) is French for "language" or "tongue" and is used by Ferdinand de Saussure in his *Cours de linguistique générale* to denote the entire system of a language, its rule of combination and its system of differentiations. *Parole* (pahROL) refers to a particular utterance within that system. For Saussure, it is the *langue* that makes all individual utterances possible. Thus, he argued, the appropriate study of linguistics is not specific utterances but the system out of which they emerge. See also DIACHRONY, PARADIGM, STRUCTURALISM, SYNCHRONY, SYNTAGM.

LATENT CONTENT. *Latent content* is a psychoanalytic term that refers to the meanings of a dream or other psychological document, which are revealed through analysis. In contrast to the usually cryptic MANIFEST CONTENT of the dream, the latent content is an organized discourse in which the unconscious wishes of the dreamer are given undisguised expression (see WISH-FULFILLMENT). Although this analytic discourse is inevitably a construction and may not be complete, Freud uses the term *latent content* in such a way as to suggest that it actually precedes the manifest content, which encodes the former in order to escape the censorship to which all unconscious materials are subjected (see REPRESSION).

Freud, Sigmund. *The Interpretation of Dreams*. Trans. and ed. James Strachey. London: Hogarth Press, 1953.

LEBENSWELT. *Lebenswelt* (**LAY**benzVelt) is usually rendered as "life world" or the world of one's own immediate experience, which in PHENOMENOLOGY is regarded as the foundation of all knowledge. Edmund Husserl defines it as "the moving historical field of our lived existence." It refers to the world at hand as it is actually structured and experienced by the knowing subject. It is the matrix of experiential patterns that constitute the individual's subjectively apprehended history of consciousness. The significance of *Lebenswelt* for literary theory is that the author's self-world relation is duplicated in the literary work, where it can be recovered by the phenomenological critic. See also GENEVA SCHOOL.

LEGITIMATION. Legitimation is the process by which the governing obtain the acceptance of the governed. Jürgen Habermas uses the term to refer to the ways that those in power encourage the support of those for whom they make and administer laws. The usefulness of *legitimation* as a critical term is that it points to a fundamental question: do the people freely consent to those who have power, or is their submission to power coerced? Many Marxists see IDEOLOGY as the characteristic legitimation process of capitalist government: ideology "legitimates" existing power relations by making them seem natural and right. The French philosopher Jean-François Lyotard has broadened the term, introduced it to cultural studies, and used it to question the legitimation processes of separate compartments of knowledge. Disciplines like hard science, sociology, and psychology "legitimate" the "truths" they produce in varying ways. The postmodern era, according to Lyotard, has come about because we have suffered under regimes of knowledge that have claimed to explain and represent (and thus "legitimate") more than they can. See also AUTHORITY, POSTMODERNISM.

Habermas, Jürgen. *Legitimation Crisis.* Trans. Thomas McCarthy. Boston: Beacon Press, 1975.

Lyotard, Jean-François. *The Postmodern Condition: A Report on Knowledge.* Trans. Geoff Bennington and Brian Massumi. Minneapolis: University of Minnesota Press, 1984.

LEITMOTIF. Contemporary use of the term *leitmotif* (leading motif) can be traced to the theoretical writings of the composer Richard Wagner, although the term that Wagner actually used was *grund-motiv* (ground-motif). To organize the enormous operatic compositions that he called "music dramas," Wagner employed a system of germinal musical ideas, each only a few notes in length and consistently identified with a specific character, mood, or theme. The leitmotif is, then, a device for establishing unity and serves to link past, present, and future at a given moment in the action. This technique had considerable influence on writers like Thomas Mann, who employed it conspicuously in his early novel *Buddenbrooks* (1901).

Wagner, Richard. *Oper und Drama.* In *Gesammelte Schriften.* 14 vols. Ed. Julius Kapp. Leipzig: Hesse and Becker, 1914.

LESBIAN CONTINUUM. A term introduced by Adrienne Rich in her essay on COMPULSORY HETEROSEXUALITY, *lesbian continuum* refers to the broad spectrum of intimate relations between women, from those involving the experience of or desire for genital sexuality, to mother-daughter relationships and female friendships, to ties of political solidarity—all of them "forms of primary intensity between and among women." Rich associates such bonds, within each woman's life and throughout the course of history, with resistance to heterosexuality and male domination. The concept is similar to what Carroll Smith-Rosenberg and Eve Sedgwick describe as "female homosocial" ties, including but not limited to explicitly lesbian ones. It has been part of the feminist critical project to call attention to such ties as a theme in literary texts and as a pattern of influence among women writers. See also HOMOSOCIAL, LESBIAN CRITICISM.

Rich, Adrienne. "Compulsory Heterosexuality and Lesbian Existence." In *Blood, Bread, and Poetry: Selected Prose 1979–1985*. New York: Norton, 1986.

Sedgwick, Eve Kosofsky. *Between Men: English Literature and Male Homosocial Desire*. New York: Columbia University Press, 1985.

Smith-Rosenberg, Caroll. "The Female World of Love and Ritual: Relations Between Women in Nineteenth-Century America." In *Disorderly Conduct: Visions of Gender in Victorian America*. New York: Knopf, 1985.

LESBIAN CRITICISM. Lesbian criticism proceeds from two main axioms. First, it assumes that heterosexuality is an imposed political system rather than a biological mandate. What Adrienne Rich has called "compulsory heterosexuality" is a vast, elusive institution that ensures the dominance of heterosexual males, in part by obscuring, misrepresenting, and persecuting homosexuality, thereby perpetuating the notion that sexuality is natural and valid only between women and men. Lesbian critics look at the ways particular historical contexts shape perceptions of gender and sexuality. Second, lesbians experience their femaleness differently than nonlesbian women, because conventional definitions of femininity presuppose heterosexuality. Lesbians are oppressed not only as women but also as "perverts." When feminist critics began to speak out in the early to mid-1970s, most ignored issues of sexual preference, as well as race and class, overlooking the various and distinct ways that different groups of women are discriminated against. Though closely tied to the feminist movement and feminist criticism, much early lesbian criticism had to begin by calling attention to the heterosexism of feminism itself. Lesbian critics have also emphasized the commonality of lesbian identity and experience, yet work examining the ways that race, class, and nationality affect lesbianism has appeared from the beginning. A milestone essay written by Barbara Smith in 1977, for example, called for the establishment of both black feminist and lesbian criticism.

A precise definition of lesbianism and lesbian literature remains a matter of much fruitful debate. Some critics, like Catherine Stimpson in her study of the lesbian novel, define lesbianism narrowly as the presence of genital sexual desire between females. Others, like Rich, use *lesbian* to name a broader range of ties between women, including familial and friendship bonds as well as explicitly sexual ones. Both groups call attention to lesbian texts, whether narrowly or broadly defined, in order to recover a tradition of lesbian literature and culture. This project involves both the excavation of forgotten works and the re-reading of such canonical figures as Emily Dickinson, Willa Cather, and Virginia Woolf, emphasizing lesbian elements that have been willfully overlooked or never before recognized. It involves returning to texts that were ignored or censored because of their explicit treatment of lesbian themes as well as the decoding of texts whose lesbian content is less obvious, hidden for fear of persecution. Though lesbian criticism continues to gain legitimacy and authority, particularly with the emergence of gay and lesbian studies as a field, it must still struggle against the tendency of straight feminist and gay criticism to subsume lesbian criticism either as the same or as a minor variation of themselves. See also COMPULSORY HETERO-SEXUALITY, LESBIAN CONTINUUM.

Faderman, Lillian. *Surpassing the Love of Men: Romantic Friendship and Love between Women from the Renaissance to the Present.* New York: Morrow, 1981.

Rich, Adrienne. "Compulsory Heterosexuality and Lesbian Existence." In *Blood, Bread and Poetry: Selected Prose 1979–1985.* New York: Norton, 1986.

Smith, Barbara. "Toward a Black Feminist Criticism." In Elaine Showalter, ed., *The New Feminist Criticism.* New York: Pantheon, 1985.

Stimpson, Catherine. "Zero Degree Deviancy: The Lesbian Novel in English." *Critical Inquiry* 8, 1981.

Zimmerman, Bonnie. "What Has Never Been: An Overview of Lesbian Feminist Criticism." In Elaine Showalter, ed., *The New Feminist Criticism.* New York: Pantheon, 1985.

LIBERAL FEMINISM. The oldest identifiable feminism, liberal feminism grows directly out of eighteenth-century liberal philosophy. Mary Wollstonecraft's *A Vindication of the Rights of Woman* in 1792 and John Stuart Mill's *The Subjection of Women* in 1869 have been among the most influential texts, with their emphasis on traditional liberal conceptions of autonomy and self-fulfillment for the individual. Late twentieth-century liberal feminism, typified by the National Organization for Women (NOW), champions equal rights, equal access, and equal pay for women; works for judiciary, economic, and social fairness; and uses methods such as education, legislation, and litigation. The liberal feminist impulse in literary studies is to demand that certain "great" women writers be included in the canon, and to seek equal opportunities for women within the academy. Because it operates within established political and social spheres and, in regard to literature, within traditional interpretive frameworks (e.g., invoking "greatness" and "the canon"), liberal feminism is a revisionist and not a revolutionary philosophy. More interested in reforming existing structures so as to accommodate women than in dismantling these structures altogether, it is accused by radical feminists of not going far enough. See also RADICAL FEMINISM, SOCIALIST FEMINISM.

Eisenstein, Zillah R. *The Radical Future of Liberal Feminism.* New York: Longman, 1981.

Mill, John Stuart. *The Subjection of Women.* Ed. Sue Mansfield. Arlington Heights, Ill.: AHM Publishing, 1980.

Wollstonecraft, Mary. *A Vindication of the Rights of Woman.* Ed. Carol H. Poston. New York: Norton, 1975.

LIBIDO. The term *libido* (liBEEdo), a Latin word meaning "wish" or "desire," is used by psychoanalysts beginning with Freud to refer to the energy involved in the various manifestations of the sexual instinct in mental life (see DESIRE). In Freud's own work, the libido does not underlie all instinctual activity but only what he called the LIFE INSTINCTS. During the earlier part of his career, Freud argued that this group of instincts was opposed to the self-preservative instincts, although he eventually came to view the latter group as simply another manifestation of the life instincts, the whole of which were then contrasted to the DEATH INSTINCTS. Thus, in both formulations, Freud showed a preference for a dualistic theory of the instincts (see DUALISM), whereas Carl Jung attempted to develop a monistic theory (see MONISM) in which the libido does not have its source in the sexual instinct. For Jung, the libido is a generalized psychic energy that underlies every kind of wish or desire.

Freud, Sigmund. *Beyond the Pleasure Principle.* Rev. ed. Trans. and ed. James Strachey. New York: Liveright, 1961.

—. *Introductory Lectures on Psychoanalysis.* Trans. James Strachey. New York: Norton, 1965.

—. *Three Essays on the Theory of Sexuality.* Trans. and ed. James Strachey. London: Hogarth Press, 1962.

LIFE INSTINCTS. In Freud's work, the concept of the life instincts undergoes a substantial modification from his original formulation, which sought to understand this group of instincts as driven by the LIBIDO in opposition to the self-preservative instincts. This early formulation opposes the sexual instinct, which underlies the life instincts, to those other instincts that aim specifically at the perpetuation of the individual organism, like hunger, which is the model self-preservative instinct. Following his elaboration of the concept of NARCISSISM, however, Freud eventually came to classify the self-preservative instincts with the life instincts, creating a large group of instincts that he now saw as being in opposition to the DEATH INSTINCTS. The common characteristic of the life instincts is that they aim to create and maintain new unities, whereas the death instincts aim to destroy unities. See also PLEASURE PRINCIPLE.

Freud, Sigmund. *Beyond the Pleasure Principle*. Rev. ed. Trans. and ed. James Strachey. New York: Liveright, 1961.

—. *Three Essays on the Theory of Sexuality*. Trans. and ed. James Strachey. London: Hogarth Press, 1962.

—. *Introductory Lectures on Psychoanalysis*. Trans. James Strachey. New York: Norton, 1965.

—. "On Narcissism." In *Standard Edition of the Complete Psychological Works of Sigmund Freud*, vol. 14. Trans. James Strachey. London: Hogarth Press and Institute of Psycho-Analysis, 1974.

LITERARY MODE OF PRODUCTION.

LITERARY MODE OF PRODUCTION. Used somewhat ambivalently by late twentieth-century Marxist critics, the concept of the *literary mode of production* serves to underline the extent to which literary works are ideological productions brought into existence under the pressure of determinate historical forces, rather than the uncircumscribed creations of individual genius, although most Marxist critics resist the dogmatism and pseudo-scientificity that the term implies. These critics insist that literary works must be understood as produced by the particular ideological configuration of a given historical moment (see IDEOLOGY), and in their use of the term have relied heavily on the rejuvenation of the classical Marxist concept of the MODE OF PRODUCTION in the work of Louis Althusser and his French and British followers. While the Althusserian view of historical determination allows for the relative autonomy of political and ideological practices, it stipulates that the economic sets limits on the activities of those other levels by assigning them the task of reproducing social practices congenial to the mode of production. Thus, Terry Eagleton, in his avowedly Althusserian book *Criticism and Ideology*, defines literary mode of production as "a unity of certain forces and social relations of literary production in a particular social formation," but adds the proviso that "in any literate society there will normally exist a number of distinct modes of literary production, one of which will normally be dominant."

Althusser, Louis, and Etienne Balibar. *Reading "Capital."* Trans. Ben Brewster. New York: Schocken, 1970.

Eagleton, Terry. *Criticism and Ideology: A Study in Marxist Literary Theory.* London: Verso, 1976.

Feltes, N. N. *Modes of Production of Victorian Novels.* Chicago: University of Chicago Press, 1986.

Macherey, Pierre. *A Theory of Literary Production.* Trans. Geoffrey Wall. Boston: Routledge and Kegan Paul, 1978.

LOCUTION. In the SPEECH ACT THEORY of J. L. Austin, *locution* refers to the simplest form of speech act, the utterance of a sentence. Austin defined two broad categories of locutions: the CONSTATIVE and the PER-FORMATIVE. The former is a statement that can be judged either true or false, while the latter accomplishes something in its utterance, such as promising, threatening, interrogating, etc. See also ILLOCUTIONARY ACT, PERLOCUTIONARY ACT.

Austin, J. L. *How to Do Things With Words.* Cambridge, Mass.: Harvard University Press, 1962.

LOGOCENTRISM. *Logocentrism* is a word coined by Jacques Derrida on the analogy of ETHNOCENTRISM to describe the form of METAPHYSICS that understands writing as merely a representation of speech, which is privileged because the utterance is present simultaneously to both speaker and listener, a situation that seems to guarantee the transmission of meaning. In Derrida's view, the opposition between speech and WRITING functions like all such metaphysical oppositions in that speech is seen as embodying presence, whereas writing is considered secondary, a weak copy or SIMU-LACRUM of the original embodied by speech. It is one of the major projects of DECONSTRUCTION to undo this opposition. See also SUPPLEMENT.

Derrida, Jacques. *Of Grammatology.* Trans. Gayatri Chakravorty Spivak. Baltimore: Johns Hopkins University Press, 1976.

LOGOS. *Logos* is Greek for "word," as well as truth, reason, logic, law. Since Plato, logos has stood as the transcendent grounding principle of order and reason that confers meaning on discourse. It constitutes the origin of truth. The New Testament appropriates this Hellenistic principle, referring to God as logos or The Word, reflecting Christianity's move to absorb and supersede classical philosophy. Thus, God as logos is viewed as the self-sufficient ground and measure of all meaning and truth. Linguistically, logos is the meaning, presence, idea, intention that is assumed to reside behind a text and for which language is a subservient means of expression. Moreover, logos is the meaning to which the sign refers, to which the sign is always secondary. Logos privileges the primary or "superior" aspect of a given hierarchy such as speech/writing. It is against such a metaphysics of presence or LOGOCENTRISM that Derrida poses the philosophical activity of DECONSTRUCTION.

LUDISM. See PLAY.

M

MAGIC REALISM. See REALISM.

MALE GAZE. Film theorists have used this term to describe the way that mainstream cinema constructs the vision of the spectator. To engage the viewer's interest, these films rely on two conventions: narrative (the logical progression of events and actions featuring a central protagonist) and spectacle (the interruption of narrative progress for the sake of visual show). Representations of women have traditionally been essential to moments of spectacle in mainstream film, from the showgirl's dazzling number in musicals to the fragmenting images of parts of the body in cinematic close-ups. Women are objectified and exhibited, to be looked at by men in the film—and, correspondingly, by members of the audience. In terms of narrative, viewers identify with the active male protagonist these films predominantly cast. Not subject "to being looked at," this character rather carries the look and pushes forward the story's action. Spectators are given a sense of control, a command over the world of the film's story, through the male figure. Critics have worked against such a monolithic approach, proposing theories of female spectatorship and bisexual identification; but this version of the gaze—central as it is to the Western visual arts tradition—still forcefully explains many of the dominant forms of narrative cinema. See also SCOPOPHILIA, VISUAL PLEASURE, VOYEURISM.

Berger, John. *Ways of Seeing*. Harmondsworth, U.K.: Penguin, 1972.

Kaplan, E. Ann. "Is the Gaze Male?" In E. Ann Kaplan, ed., *Women and Film: Both Sides of the Camera*. New York: Methuen, 1983.

Mulvey, Laura. "Visual Pleasure and Narrative Cinema." In Constance Penley, ed., *Feminism and Film Theory*. New York: Routledge, 1988.

MANIFEST CONTENT. *Manifest content* is a psychoanalytic term that refers to the the material presented in a dream, or other psychological "document" before it is interpreted. It is simply the content of the dream as the dreamer has experienced and recounted it. The term is in contrast to LATENT CONTENT.

Freud, Sigmund. *The Interpretation of Dreams*. Trans. and ed. James Strachey. London: Hogarth Press, 1953.

MARGINAL/MARGINALIZATION. Anything "marginal" is outside of what is central and therefore dominant. Marginalization is the process through which an individual, group, thing, or activity is made "marginal," stripped of any claim to centrality and the power that position implies. The industrial revolution, for instance, marginalized manual crafts because factory goods were much cheaper and more quickly manufactured. Recent interest in the marginal has come about for two different but closely related reasons. First, there has been a politically motivated rise of studies of the words and behavior of the poor, the criminal, the subaltern, women, blacks, and other groups excluded from traditional history. This development is predicated on the assertions that the lives of the marginal classes are also worth including in the writing of history, and that one can best see the weaknesses and contradictions in the larger power structure from the perspective of the margin (the latter a central idea in the work of Michel Foucault). The second interest in the "marginal" is more textual in nature, and is central to deconstructionist criticism (see DECONSTRUCTION). In *Marges* ("Margins"), Jacques Derrida presents rereadings of major figures such as Heidegger, Kant, and Freud by focusing on their footnotes, lesser-known writings, and other "marginal" moments, and bringing these "margins" to bear upon the more visible and central text. This procedure, Jonathan Culler writes, allows us to see that "what has been relegated to the margins or set aside by previous interpreters may be important precisely for those reasons that led it to be set aside." "Reading the margin" is thus a primary activity of deconstructionist critics, who aim to analyze what a text advances as dominant and important in relation to what a text tries to exclude, bury, suppress, conceal, "marginalize."

Culler, Jonathan. *On Deconstruction: Theory and Criticism after Structuralism.* Ithaca, N.Y.: Cornell University Press, 1982.

MARXIST CRITICISM. Marxist criticism has a long and appropriately contradictory history beginning with the scattered literary writings of Marx and Engels themselves. Despite the variety of Marxisms that have arisen over the years, most Marxist criticism assumes that the objects we view as works of literature or art are the products of historical forces that can be analyzed by focusing on the material conditions in which they are formed. For Marxist critics these conditions are discussed in terms of the control of capital or MEANS OF PRODUCTION by classes—specific groups with similar or shared interests. Control of the means of production of material items also usually entails the control of intellectual and cultural production as well. Such dominance is not passively assumed or accepted by the classes, however, and all historical epochs are marked by class conflict and dissension. Thus, for Marxists, history is seen not as a seamless unity or whole but as a site of contestation and contradiction. What is often accepted as characteristic of an age (as when we talk about a "Victorian frame of mind" or a "Renaissance worldview") are actually articulations of the dominant class. As such they are ideological, attempting to produce a narrative of a unified social totality that, by Marxist accounts, is essentially contradictory and unstable.

The literary or artistic works that are produced in such an environment (from which there can be no escape) are also ideological. Literature or art signifies the class conflict, then, and it is the goal of Marxist criticism to bring to light this conflict as it is articulated in a text. Further,

Marxist criticism has a political agenda of its own, which is to bring about what it perceives to be progressive political and social change: usually configured as an overthrow of middle-class power (both materially and ideologically) to be replaced with a classless society.

While VULGAR MARXISM has argued that literary texts are "reflections" of the specific conflicts of particular eras and their political tendencies, most Marxist criticism has avoided this reductive position, contending instead that literature is "relatively autonomous," functioning within its own rules of production and reception. Thus, it both partakes of and contributes to IDEOLOGY and cannot be viewed as merely a reflection of specific class interests. For some Marxist critics, like the influential Georg Lukács, the autonomous demands of literature—formal, generic, and traditional—can enable a work to overcome the bourgeois ideology out of which it was shaped so that it might reflect an "objective" reality. This is Lukács's position in works such as his *The Historical Novel* and *Studies in European Realism.* Despite his abhorrence of the politics of authors like Walter Scott or Leo Tolstoy, Lukács argues that their novels, in their complexity, their representation of the multifarious contradictions of everyday life, and their use of "typical" characters to demonstrate the general tendencies of the age, achieve a reflection of the real world that may even be at odds with the authors' "conscious ideology" (see REALISM).

Lukács also decried modernist works for their emphasis on FRAGMENTATION and the alienation of the individual SUBJECT. He considered such work to be "decadent" and antithetical to a critical project that must concentrate on the totality of social connections. In contrast, theorists such as Theodor Adorno and Max Horkheimer of the FRANKFURT SCHOOL argued that such works are implicitly critical and establish and inform what Adorno labeled "negative knowledge" of capitalist society. It is at this point that theories of literature and their production move toward a kind of revolutionary practice. For example, Walter Benjamin, who was for a time associated with the Frankfurt School, supported a conception of literature and art that confronted the social formations that control their production and reception. In his essay, "The Work of Art in the Age of Mechanical Reproduction," he suggests that new technologies such as film and photography not only demystify the process of creating art, they also make available radical new roles for art. Because art can now easily (and cheaply) be reproduced in great quantities, it is no longer the exclusive province of the bourgeoisie. Such technologies, he argues, clear the way for "the formulation of revolutionary demands in the politics of art." Similarly, playwright Bertolt Brecht proposed EPIC THEATER as a means of laying bare the illusion of realism that, until his time, was the underpinning convention of all drama. Brecht's plays purposefully do not conform to Aristotelian notions of MIMESIS, unified plot, theme, action, and an identification of the audience with protagonists; instead, they call attention to their own artificiality and contrivedness, and strive for estrangement or an alienation effect. This, he argued, would move the audience to consider critically not only the conventions of theater but of life in a capitalistic society.

For Brecht and Benjamin, the concept of art itself was, at least in part, an object of reconsideration and criticism. In the work of Lukács, his follower Lucien Goldmann, and even more recent theorists such as Pierre Macherey and Louis Althusser, art (or more precisely, literature) exists as a relatively unproblematic category. Yet unlike Lukács and Goldmann, who retained many of the humanistic assumptions such as unity, truth, and beauty that inform bourgeois conceptions of art and literature, Althusser and Macherey have attacked these presuppositions, insisting instead on the work of art as essentially divided and contradictory. Complicit with ideology, it contains gaps and silences that, when explored, begin to unravel its overt claims and ultimately expose its more implicit ideological agenda. And rather than focus on works as creations of the "genius" of an AUTHOR, Althusser, Macherey, and their followers prefer instead to concentrate on the material and social conditions that combined to produce these texts.

For contemporary Marxist critics like Fredric Jameson and Terry Eagleton, these insights have been crucial. And while their particular critical methods and concerns differ significantly, each has incorporated aspects of Althusserian Marxism into their own approaches. For Jameson, perhaps the most influential American Marxist critic of the late twentieth century, Althusser's work has allowed him to utilize a highly politicized conception of the Lacanian UNCONSCIOUS, extending its application to an entire class. In his book *The Political Unconscious*, he argues that the political is "the absolute horizon of all reading and all interpretation." The "collective," "POLITICAL UNCONSCIOUS," the repository of the repression of history by ideology, can be brought to awareness through appropriately historicized and politicized readings that are aware of both current and previous historical ideological attempts to contain the meanings, implications, and contradictions of texts. To

British Marxist Eagleton, Althusser has contributed the conception of Marxism as a "scientific theory of human societies and of the practice of transforming them," though in recent years Eagleton has also explored the theoretical assumptions of other, more humanistic theorists such as Benjamin and the German Marxist social philosopher Jürgen Habermas.

Also closely allied to Marxist criticism, but somewhat at odds with the elitism still evident in the work of the Frankfurt School, is the social and literary critical work of Raymond Williams. Williams, whose Marxist affiliations have often been questioned by both Marxists and non-Marxists, was heavily influenced by the work of Italian Marxist Antonio Gramsci. Williams's work has been central in establishing the legitimacy of CULTURAL STUDIES as a discipline, greatly influencing the work, especially early on, of the BIRMINGHAM CENTER FOR CONTEMPORARY CULTURAL STUDIES. His work in texts like *The Country and the City* has been instrumental in rethinking the idea of "literary" as timeless and of exploring issues of canonicity (see CANON FORMATION). For Williams, as for the CULTURAL MATERIALISTS who follow him, the designations "literary" and "artistic" are functions of ideology and discourse, largely legitimated by institutions that have a vested interest in the specifics of these categories.

Most recently, with the collapse of Marxist governments in Eastern Europe and the former Soviet Union, and with the increasingly frequent accusations by many POSTSTRUCTURALISTS that Marxism is, if not humanistic, then at the very least ESSENTIALIST in its presuppositions, Marxist criticism has undergone a metamorphosis, at least to some degree. Though some like Eagleton still take a rather traditional Marxist line, others such as Ernesto Laclau and Chantal Mouffe prefer to appropriate certain aspects of Marxist analysis while repudiating the totalizing schema much Marxist criticism takes. Embracing the conceptions of the DECENTERED SUBJECT and constitutive power of DISCOURSE upon which so much poststructuralist criticism is based, these critics, sometimes labeled "post-Marxist," have attempted to formulate agendas for ameliorative social change that are not so much founded upon the destruction of class-based society as on the formation of broader-based, temporary political and social coalitions that can increase the political agency (see AGENT) of more and more individuals. See also HEGEMONY.

Adorno, Theodor W. *Noten zu Literatur.* 4 vols. Berlin: Suhrkamp Verlag, 1958–74.
Althusser, Louis. *Lenin and Philosophy and Other Essays.* Trans. Ben Brewster. New York: Monthly Review Press, 1971.

Benjamin, Walter. *Illuminations.* Trans. Harry Zohn, ed. Hannah Arendt. New York: Harcourt Brace and World, 1968.

Eagleton, Terry. *Marxism and Literary Criticism.* Berkeley: University of California Press, 1976.

—. *Against the Grain: Essays 1975–1985.* London: Verso, 1986.

Goldmann, Lucien. *The Hidden God: A Study of Tragic Visions in the Pensees of Pascal and the Tragedies of Racine.* Trans. P. Thody. New York: Humanities Press, 1964.

Jameson, Fredric. *The Political Unconscious: Narrative as a Socially Symbolic Act.* Ithaca, N.Y.: Cornell University Press, 1981.

Lukács, Georg. *Studies in European Realism.* Trans. E. Bone. London: Hillway, 1950.

—. *The Historical Novel.* Trans. Hannah Mitchell and Stanley Mitchell. New York: Humanities Press, 1965.

Macherey, Pierre. *A Theory of Literary Production.* Trans. Geoffrey Wall. Boston: Routledge and Kegan Paul, 1978.

Marx, Karl, and Frederick Engels. *The German Ideology.* Trans. S. Ryazanskay. Moscow: Progress Publishers, 1968.

Taylor, Ronald, ed. *Aesthetics and Politics: Ernst Bloch, Georg Lukács, Bertolt Brecht, Walter Benjamin, Theodor Adorno.* London: New Left Books, 1977.

Williams, Raymond. *The Country and the City.* New York: Oxford University Press, 1973.

—. *Marxism and Literature.* Oxford: Oxford University Press, 1977.

MARXIST FEMINISM. See SOCIALIST FEMINISM.

MASCON WORDS. This is a term invented by Stephen Henderson to describe certain words and phrases that, because of their significance in African-American history and culture, make an inordinate impact on the African-American reader. The U.S. National Aeronautics and Space Administration coined the acronym "mascon" to indicate "massive concentrations" of matter beneath the moon's surface that exert a strong gravitational pull on satellites. Henderson appropriates the term to describe seemingly ordinary words, such as "roll" or "train," that resonate with multiple meanings because they contain a "massive concentration of Black experiential energy." Both Henderson and Sherley A. Williams show that African-American poetry and songs use mascon words to connect disparate realms of experience and increase a work's emotional power. See also BLACK ARTS MOVEMENT.

Henderson, Stephen. *Understanding the New Black Poetry.* New York: William Morrow, 1973.

Williams, Sherley A. "The Blues Roots of Contemporary Afro-American Poetry." In

Michael S. Harper and Robert B. Stepto, eds., *Chant of Saints: A Gathering of Afro-American Literature, Art, and Scholarship*. Urbana: University of Illinois Press, 1979.

MASCULINIST. *Masculinist* is a term used by feminist and gender critics to identify a masculine bias underlying concepts or works that present themselves or have usually been seen as neutral or universal. Marlon Ross, for example, in his recent study of romanticism, uses *masculinist* to describe and critique a set of previously unrecognized masculine beliefs and values at work in the writings of the romantic poets and in much of the criticism about them. The notion enables Ross to argue that this poetry is not "timeless" so much as the product of a particular time, place, and gendered social position, and also to resurrect the women whose contemporaneous poetry has been obscured by interpretations of the period implicitly favoring men and manliness. See also ANDROCENTRIC, FEMINIST CRITIQUE, GENDER STUDIES.

Ross, Marlon B. *The Contours of Masculine Desire: Romanticism and the Rise of Women's Poetry*. New York: Oxford University Press, 1989.

MASOCHISM. Masochism is a sexual preference in which pleasure is linked to one's own experience of suffering or humiliation. It was first defined by Krafft-Ebing, who named it after the novelist Leopold von Sacher-Masoch, a devotee and prolific describer of masochistic practices. In Freudian psychoanalysis, masochism is understood as the counterpart of SADISM and explained as a condition in which the DEATH INSTINCTS are directed against the EGO and fused with the LIBIDO. It should be noted, however, that Freud eventually came to allow for the existence of different types of masochism, and the entire question has remained an area of contention. Notably, the French poststructuralist philosopher Gilles Deleuze has disputed the classical description of masochism as the opposite of sadism and celebrated it as a creatively subversive ritual.

Deleuze, Gilles. *Masochism: An Interpretation of Coldness and Cruelty*. Trans. Jean McNeil. New York: G. Braziller, 1971.

Freud, Sigmund. *Three Essays on the Theory of Sexuality*. Trans. and ed. James Strachey. London: Hogarth Press, 1962.

—. "Instincts and Their Vicissitudes." In *Standard Edition of the Complete Psychological Works of Sigmund Freud*, vol. 14. Trans. James Strachey. London: Hogarth Press and Institute of Psycho-Analysis, 1974.

—. "A Child is Being Beaten." In *Standard Edition of the Complete Psychological Works of Sigmund Freud*, vol. 17. Trans. James Strachey. London: Hogarth Press and Institute of Psycho-Analysis, 1974.

—. "The Economic Problem of Masochism." In *Standard Edition of the Complete Psychological Works of Sigmund Freud*, vol. 19. Trans. James Strachey. London: Hogarth Press and Institute of Psycho-Analysis, 1974.

Krafft-Ebing, Richard von. *Psychopathia Sexualis*. Trans. Franklin S. Klaf. New York: Bell Publishing, 1965.

MASTER NARRATIVE. The term *master narrative* or *grand récit* has become familiar in discussions of historicism; it refers to the organizing story that a philosophy of history tells, and that provides an explanatory framework in relation to which all historical events can be understood. Thus, to take a familiar example, history is, for Marxism, the story of the continual replacement of one mode of production by another and the resulting conflicts between social classes, culminating in socialist revolution. The concept of the master narrative has become an object of frequent attacks by postmodernist critics like Jean-François Lyotard, who see it as a remnant of nineteenth-century thinking and subject to its idealizing tendencies.

Lyotard, Jean-François. *The Postmodern Condition: A Report On Knowledge*. Trans. Geoff Bennington and Brian Massumi. Minneapolis: University of Minnesota Press, 1984.

MASTER SHOT. A master shot is the filming of one scene of a movie, usually with the camera fixed at middle range, to establish a scene's physical setting and the spatial arrangement of the actors. It may or may not appear in the final edited version of the film, and is almost always interedited with shots taken from different angles, with the camera at closer and farther distances from the action. See also CUT, FRAME/FRAMING, SHOT.

MATERIALISM. In philosophy materialism is the doctrine that all things exist either as physical matter or as directly dependent upon physical matter. In contemporary theory materialism has found its most important articulation in MARXIST CRITICISM, which connects all aspects of life and consciousness to the material conditions of existence. The problems with materialist explanations, especially of metaphysical and epistemological issues, are numerous and often fairly complex. Consider, for instance, the intricacies inherent in the arguments asserting that space and time, in which matter exists, are necessarily dependent upon it for their own existence. Despite the obvious objections to such arguments, however, materialism has found an important niche in current theoretical projects as a means of repudiating such concepts as the Cartesian "thinking substance" or mind as existing independently of material concerns. Not only Marxists, but some New Historicists have used varieties of materialism as a basis for their analyses of culture and DISCOURSE. See also CULTURAL MATERIALISM, DUALISM, IDEALISM, NEW HISTORICISM.

MEDIA STUDIES. With modern society's technological advances and the resulting production of TEXTS in a variety of new forms, such as film, video, computer bulletin boards and networks, as well as audio recordings and the more traditional print format of newspapers and magazines, a number of theorists have turned their attention to the critical investigation of the ways in which these informational media help to explain (and to order) our existence. Media studies borrows from many different theoretical venues, including several varieties of Marxist, feminist, and psychonalytic theory. Also, because it is still in the early stages of its formation as a discipline, it is difficult to draw any coherent picture of its overall project. Nevertheless, a few commonalities exist among its practitioners. For instance, these critics and theorists tend to repudiate distinctions between high and low culture as such. They often concentrate on popular cultural formations and the pressure such formations exert on how we understand ourselves and our place in the world. They are concerned mainly with the effects of the dissemination of texts, especially through technologically advanced means. Thus, a media studies expert may focus on texts as diverse as the reworking of a Shakespeare play in a film like Gus Van Sant's *My Own Private Idaho*, to Madonna, in all her manifestations, to the ideology of computer viruses.

Much of current media studies work can trace its influence back to at least two important antecedents. The first was the formation of the BIRMINGHAM CENTER FOR CONTEMPORARY CULTURAL STUDIES, which helped to establish the study of contemporary popular culture and subcultures as a serious and legitimate field of inquiry. The other precursor was the advent of sophisticated theoretical criticism that emerged in the journal *Screen* in the 1960s (see FILM THEORY). The theoretical positions that emerged from each of these sources has contributed to media studies' problematizing of the role of IDEOLOGY and the formation of the SUBJECT in mass culture and communication. See also CULTURAL STUDIES.

Brantlinger, Patrick. *Crusoe's Footprints: Cultural Studies in Britain and America.* New York: Routledge, 1990.

MELTING POT. *Melting pot* is a term that uses alchemical imagery to describe the process of cultural fusing. Israel Zangwill made the term famous in his 1909 play *The Melting Pot*, but the idea of America as "God's Crucible" has had a long history, from Jean de Crèvecoeur's description in *Letters from an American Farmer* of the United States as the place where "individuals of all nations are melted into a new race of men" (1782) to Alain Locke's race-specific idea in *The New Negro* of Harlem as the site for the merging and rebirth of a new African-American identity (1925). Writers inspired by the idea of the melting pot thought that the end of discrete races and ethnic groups would mean the end of discrimination, along with the creation of a new and vital American culture. With the renewed emphasis on MULTICULTURAL and ethnic identification in the past decades, the idea of the melting pot has become what Werner Sollors calls the "most favored scapegoat" of cultural criticism. Critics attack the term as static and homogeneous, and charge that such an idea demands that the various races and ethnic groups lose their separate identities in order to assimilate themselves to standard white culture. See also RACE/ETHNICITY.

Sollors, Werner. "Melting Pots." In *Beyond Ethnicity: Consent and Descent in American Culture.* New York: Oxford University Press, 1986.

MEN'S STUDIES. Men's studies is an emerging field that treats men, manhood, and masculinity itself—men qua men—as objects of inquiry. Like WOMEN'S STUDIES, men's studies is based on the notions that gender is a social construction and that sexual identity is historically contingent. The study of men focuses on the ways that male identities and subjectivities are defined within language and culture. It investigates discourses and cultural representations of masculinity, particularly men's gendered relations to language, culture, nature, women, other men, and modernity. With women's studies and gay studies, the field shares a sexual politics that recognizes the complex relation of personal and psychological changes to political ones. Men's studies assumes that masculinity is not necessarily complicitous in patriarchal oppression.

Men's studies incorporates various critical methods of analysis. Under this broad umbrella various scholars examine men and maleness with attention to social, historical, or discursive functions. The more empirical social sciences, sociology and demography, along with anthropology, literary criticism, history, and psychology, comprise men's studies. Specific topics include men in domestic settings, male-female relations, literary representations of masculinity, and maleness within the context of differences relating to age, race, sexual orientation, and class.

Brod, Harry, ed. *The Making of Masculinities: The New Men's Studies.* Boston: Allen and Unwin, 1987.

Kimmel, Michael S., ed. *Changing Men: New Directions in Research on Men and Masculinity.* Newbury Park, Calif.: Sage Publications, 1987.

Segal, Lynne. *Slow Motion: Changing Masculinities, Changing Men.* London: Virago, 1990.

Seidler, Victor. *The Achilles Heel Reader: Men, Sexual Politics and Socialism.* New York: Routledge, 1991.

—. *Recreating Sexual Politics: Men, Feminism and Politics.* New York: Routledge, 1991.

METALANGUAGE. *Metalanguage* refers to the special use of language either to talk about itself or another language. The linguist Roman Jakobson distinguishes six elements involved in communication—the addresser, the addressee, the message, the shared code, the "contact" or medium of communication, and the context to which the message refers—and classifies acts of communication according to their emphasis on one of those elements. A message that focused on the code itself would be considered metalinguistic. Literary criticism is traditionally considered a kind of metalanguage and, as such, separate from literature itself. Jonathan Culler, however, points out that literature very often also contains metalinguistic statements, as when a narrator in a novel comments on the structure of the tale.

Culler, Jonathan. *On Deconstruction: Theory and Criticism after Structuralism.* Ithaca, N.Y.: Cornell University Press, 1982.

Eagleton, Terry. *Literary Theory: An Introduction.* Minneapolis: University of Minnesota Press, 1983.

Jakobson, Roman. *Language in Literature*. Eds. Krystyna Pomorska and Stephen Rudy. Cambridge, Mass.: Belknap Press, 1987.

METAPHOR. Perhaps the most widely used figure of speech in both literary and everyday language, metaphor characterizes an action, concept, or object in terms usually used to denote something else, often quite different. Metaphor implies a comparison between the thing being described and the thing used to describe it, but is not articulated *as* comparison. For instance, the phrase "love is a dangerous game" suggests a comparison between the activity of loving and a competition where the stakes are high, but the comparison remains implicit. In contrast, a SIMILE depends not only on the metaphorical practice of describing something in terms of something else, but also on the explicit expression of the comparison. Thus, when Robert Burns writes, "My love is like a red, red rose" he stops short of the *identification* at work in metaphor, relying instead upon a partial similarity or resemblance. A dead metaphor is one that no longer draws attention to itself but has passed into everyday usage, such as "the long arm of the law." A mixed metaphor is one in which the combination of comparisons is illogical or ludicrous. For instance, to say, "those weasels pulled the rug out from under us," conjures up a rather cartoonish image, when the point is to express betrayal by untrustworthy characters.

Modern analysis of metaphor, beginning with I. A. Richards, has schematized analysis of metaphor by distinguishing between a metaphor's "tenor" and its "vehicle." The tenor refers to the primary literal term, while the vehicle is the figurative term applied to it. For example, in the metaphor above, "love is a dangerous game," the tenor is "love" while the vehicle is "game." See also CATECHRESIS, METONYMY.

Hawkes, Terence. *Metaphor*. London: Methuen, 1972.

Ortony, Andrew, ed. *Metaphor and Thought*. Cambridge: Cambridge University Press, 1979.

Ricoeur, Paul. *The Rule of Metaphor: Multi-Disciplinary Studies of the Creation of Meaning in Language*. Trans. Robert Czerny et al. Toronto: Toronto University Press, 1977.

METAPHYSICS. Although it is one of the primary divisions of the discipline of philosophy, metaphysics has a number of possible meanings.

The Greek word "meta," which is used as a prefix by English speakers and usually means "about," originally was a preposition, meaning "after." Aristotle's *Metaphysics* therefore was so named because it followed the *Physics*. In the case of metaphysics, however, the prefix does not mean "about" except in the most general sense. Rather, metaphysics usually refers to philosophical attempts to establish indisputable first principles as a foundation for all knowledge. It may also refer to attempts to explore those things that exist beyond the world of experience. Thus, studies investigating the existence of absolute entities, such as spiritual or religious questions, fall within the realm of metaphysics.

In the eighteenth and nineteenth centuries the subject matter of metaphysics included such issues as the possibility of a priori knowledge, the nature of memory and abstract thought, the reality of the external world and other questions that today are usually included in the study of EPISTEMOLOGY, or *how* we know and perceive. Contemporary metaphysics is concerned primarily with such things as the distinctions between particulars and universals, individuals and classes, and the nature of time, space, matter, and mind. In recent years, the work of philosophers such as Jacques Derrida, Michel Foucault, Jean Baudrillard, Gilles Deleuze, and Jean-François Lyotard has questioned the assumptions of Western metaphysics, arguing that its dependence on continuity, causality, presence, and structure limit the possibilities of investigation of fundamental issues, preordaining the form of both the questions and the answers of traditional studies. These philosophers, who are often grouped together as poststructuralists (see POSTSTRUCTURALISM), advocate concepts such as "free play" and "rupture," and repudiate systematic explanations of the nature of things. Although this approach to metaphysical inquiry has been widely articulated, especially in France, since the mid-1960s, it is only relatively recently that the works of these thinkers have found purchase in philosophy departments in the United States and Great Britain, primarily through the work of literary critics and theorists, and more recently by film and art theorists. See ESSENTIALISM.

Baudrillard, Jean. *Simulations*. Trans. Paul Foss, Paul Patton, and Philip Beitchman. New York: Semiotext(e), 1983.

Collingwood, R. G. *An Essay on Metaphysics*. Oxford: Oxford University Press, 1940.

Deleuze, Gilles. *Nietzsche and Philosophy*. Trans. Hugh Tomlinson. London: Athlone Press, 1983.

Derrida, Jacques. *Writing and Difference*. 1967. Trans. Alan Bass. Chicago: University of Chicago Press, 1978.

—. *Positions*. Trans. Alan Bass. Chicago: University of Chicago Press, 1981.

Foucault, Michel. *The Archaeology of Knowledge*. 1969. Trans. A. M. Sheridan Smith.
New York: Pantheon, 1972.

—. *Language, Counter-Memory, and Practice: Selected Essays and Interviews*. Trans.
Donald F. Bouchard and Sherry Simon. Ithaca, N.Y.: Cornell University Press, 1977.

Lyotard, Jean-François. *The Differend: Phrases in Dispute*. Trans. Georges Van Den
Abbeck. Minneapolis: University of Minnesota Press, 1988.

— and Jean-Loup Thebaud. *Just Gaming*. Trans. Wlad Godzich and Brian Massumi.
Minneapolis: University of Minnesota Press, 1985.

Wittgenstein, Ludwig. *Philosophical Investigations*. Trans. G. E. M. Anscombe. Oxford:
Blackwell, 1968.

METHODOLOGY. Despite its suffix, *methodology* is most often used as a synonym for *method*, not the study or science of methods. A scientist, anthropologist, sociologist, or literary critic who employs a methodology to study a subject has a conscious grasp of the general premises that support acting as a scientist, anthropologist, sociologist, or literary critic. Often, the adjective *methodological* is used to discuss concepts that may not be true or actually exist, but that are useful as working hypotheses— i.e., "methodological individualism" is a phrase used by those who may not be certain that individualism is possible but act as though it were.

METONYMY. Often discussed in contradistinction to METAPHOR, metonymy (muhTAHNuhMEE) is a figure of speech that substitutes the name of a thing with the name of another thing closely associated with it. Thus, when we say or write that "Washington today issued last quarter's balance of trade figures," the term *Washington* stands for the U.S. government. Other examples include *crown* for monarch, *the ring* for boxing, *Dickens* for the writings of Charles Dickens, and *jock* for athlete. One specific and often used type of metonymy is synecdoche, in which the name of a part is substituted for the whole (e.g., *sails* for ships or *head* for a cow or a horse), or less frequently the whole stands for a part. In recent years, literary criticism has broadened the scope of metonymy to indicate the ways that metonymies are understood and produced. Unlike metaphor, which establishes relationships of *similarity* between two things, metonymy in this broader sense relies on relationships of *contiguity*. For example, in the 1840s, social reformers often wrote of the working classes as becoming "of a piece" with their places of abode. Many of these homes were dilapidated, poorly ventilated, and extremely dirty. To speak, then, of the poor taking on the characteristics of their dwellings is to establish a metonymic connection between person and home that is based on contiguity. The distinction between metaphor and metonymy has often been discussed in connection to the contrast between PARADIGM and SYNTAGM.

MIMESIS. A particularly venerable term that has undergone a number of meaning changes since it was used by Plato, *mimesis* in its strictest sense means, simply, imitation. Plato uses it derogatorily in the *Republic* to describe the artist's "creations." For Plato, since all things of this world exist only transiently and already in imitation of their Idea, to copy the things of this world is to copy copies. The problem with this practice, which is the practice of all the arts, is that these imitations, despite their increased distance from Truth or the Idea, are taken for true or give their audiences the illusion of truthful representation.

In contrast to Plato, Aristotle in the *Poetics* argued that mimesis is a fundamental human instinct and that it is not a counterfeiting of reality but a representation of universals. By universals he did not mean the Platonic Ideas, but the "natural order" that is present in everyday experience. In literature, this order is bound up in plot—not simply in the sequence of events of a story, but a structure of events that are so firmly enmeshed that they form an organic whole. Thus, for Aristotle, the work is not merely a reflection of some pre-existent reality, but itself is an entity subject to the formal laws of nature.

In modern critical parlance, *mimetic* may refer to the Aristotelian concept of imitation, especially when it is used in conjunction with discussions of criticism by members of the CHICAGO SCHOOL, Kenneth Burke, or Erich Auerbach. Its most common use, however, is as a description of works of art that are understood to be reproductions of an external reality or some portion of it. A number of theoretical approaches, including some types of MARXIST CRITICISM, are known as MIMETIC CRITICISM for their insistence on the representational relationship of art to an empirical reality, and on their positing of reality as existing, at some level, outside the mediation of discourse. See also POSTSTRUCTURALISM, REALISM, REPRESENTATION, SIMULACRUM.

Abrams, Meyer H. *The Mirror and the Lamp: Romantic Theory and the Critical Tradition.* New York: Oxford University Press, 1953.

Auerbach, Erich. *Mimesis: The Representation of Reality in Western Literature.* Trans. Willard R. Trask. Princeton: Princeton University Press, 1953.

Crane, Ronald Salmon, ed. *Critics and Criticism, Ancient and Modern*. Chicago: University of Chicago Press, 1952.

Else, G. F. *Aristotle's "Poetics": The Argument*. Cambridge, Mass.: Harvard University Press, 1957.

MIMETIC CRITICISM. Mimetic criticism emphasizes a work's relationship to the world it depicts, and judges its quality in terms of its verisimilitude, the fidelity of its imitation or reflection of the world and life. Mimetic theories are associated with classical and neoclassical criticism, and particularly with Plato, who denigrated MIMESIS, and Aristotle, who extolled it. See also REALISM, REPRESENTATION, VERISIMILITUDE, VRAISEMBLANCE.

MIMETIC THEORIES. See MIMESIS.

MIRROR STAGE. The concept of the mirror stage is perhaps the most famous of Jacques Lacan's contributions to psychoanalysis. Between the ages of six and eighteen months, the child develops the capacity to recognize her or his image in a mirror and so demonstrates an awareness of the connection between her or his own movements and those of the specular counterpart. This specular image is not, however, a reflection in the strict sense of the word—that is, not an exact duplicate—but is rather a fantasy construction or *gestalt*, an ideal figure of bodily integration and unity with which the child identifies (see IDENTIFICATION, IMAGINARY, NARCISSISM). What is heralded by the mirror stage of psychic development is thus a kind of primary *alienation*, the opening of an unbridgeable gap between the child and her or his own self-image, which will be a feature of all of her or his future relationships. Henceforth, the child will only be able to conceive of her or his own identity in fictional terms, although this is, paradoxically, a necessary prelude to the even greater alienation that occurs with the acquisition of language and the child's entry into the SYMBOLIC order (see also NAME-OF-THE-FATHER, OEDIPUS COMPLEX).

Lacan's concept has had a wide influence in contemporary theory, beginning with the theory of IDEOLOGY developed by the French Marxist philosopher Louis Althusser, and continuing in the work of many feminist critics and others concerned with the problem of the relationship between the individual subject and the larger cultural structures into which he or she is born. See also DECENTERED SUBJECT, IDENTITY.

Lacan, Jacques. "The Mirror Stage as Formative of the Function of the 'I' as Revealed in Psychoanalytic Experience." *Ecrits: A Selection.* Trans. Alan Sheridan. New York: Norton, 1977.

MISOGYNY. A term in use in English from the first half of the seventeenth century to the present, with etymological roots extending directly to Latin and ancient Greek, *misogyny* (mis**AHJ**inee) means the hatred and fear of women. Recent feminist scholarship has attempted to analyze the psychological as well as social causes and manifestations of misogyny, arguing that a wide range of sources—from methods of childrearing to images in the media—produce a correspondingly vast array of misogynist behavior. On the part of men, examples of misogyny include sexual assault and harassment of women, economic discrimination, and demeaning portrayals of women in advertisements, movies, literary texts, etc. In the United States, feminist literary criticism began by calling attention to such portrayals in writing by men—Kate Millett's famous 1970 analysis of misogyny in the works of D. H. Lawrence, Henry Miller, and Norman Mailer, for example. In women, too, misogyny may be evident in the form of shame about the female body, anorexia and other eating disorders, sexual dysfunction, depression and pervasive feelings of inferiority and worthlessness tied to being female. Feminist critics Sandra Gilbert and Susan Gubar have suggested that nineteenth-century women's writing may be marked by such a sense of female inferiority in relation to authorship. See also ANXIETY OF AUTHORSHIP, COMPULSORY HETEROSEXUALITY, FEMINIST CRITIQUE.

Chodorow, Nancy. *The Reproduction of Mothering: Psychoanalysis and the Sociology of Gender.* Berkeley: University of California Press, 1978.
Gilbert, Sandra, and Susan Gubar. *The Madwoman in the Attic: The Woman Writer and the Nineteenth-Century Literary Imagination.* New Haven: Yale University Press, 1979.
Millett, Kate. *Sexual Politics.* New York: Avon, 1970.
Rich, Adrienne. "Compulsory Heterosexuality and Lesbian Existence." In *Blood, Bread, and Poetry: Selected Prose 1979–1985.* New York: Norton, 1986.

MISPRISION. In Harold Bloom's theory of poetic influence (see ANXIETY OF INFLUENCE), misprision is the act by which the later poet seeks to win imaginative space for him or herself by creatively "misreading" the work of a strong predecessor, so as to evade the crippling knowledge that the great poems he or she wishes to write have already been written. Bloom's use of the word is a playful derivative of its legal use, which refers to the misuse of a public office or the failure to report or prevent a crime.

Bloom, Harold. *The Anxiety of Influence: A Theory of Poetry.* New York: Oxford University Press, 1973.

MISREADING. See MISPRISION.

MODE OF PRODUCTION. A central concept in Marxist thought, the mode of production is the organization of economic relations in society at a given historical moment; its functioning is explained succinctly in Marx's preface to *A Contribution to the Critique of Political Economy:* "The mode of production [for instance, capitalism] in material life determines the general character of the social, political, and spiritual processes of life." *Capital* (vol. 3) provides a more elaborate (and less deterministic) explanation of the concept, as does Marx's intended chapter 6 for volume 1. The question for cultural theorists has traditionally been whether such thinking can provide an adequate explanation of cultural production in general. Charges of reductionism have frequently been leveled against writers committed to the concept, including even Louis Althusser, who tried to rescue some space for culture under the rubric of "relative autonomy" (see LITERARY MODE OF PRODUCTION, OVERDETERMINATION). Nevertheless, the concept has provided a useful corrective to the universalist and ahistorical tendencies of much cultural analysis.

Althusser, Louis, and Etienne Balibar. *Reading "Capital."* Trans. Ben Brewster. New York: Shocken, 1970.
Marx, Karl. "Preface." In *A Contribution to the Critique of Political Economy.* Trans. S. W. Ryazanskaya, ed. Maurice Dobb. New York: International Publications, 1970.
Marx, Karl. *Capital,* vol. 3. Moscow: Progress Publishers, 1965.

MODERNISM. Although it is very difficult to pin exact moments of conception and demise upon artistic movements, it is safe to say that some aspects of modernism emerged in France in the last quarter of the nineteenth century, while others linger in the writing and work of many of today's authors and artists. Despite its fuzzy origins and stubborn refusal to die out completely, modernism ism usually defined as the predominant artistic and literary movement between 1890 and 1945, with its most productive and innovative period being the 1920s and 1930s. Often seen as a reaction to the stringent aesthetic formulas and moralism of the Victorian period, modernism is associated with the AVANT-GARDE, bohemianism, experimentation with traditional genres and styles, and a conception of the artist as creator rather than preserver of culture. For critics such as Harold Rosenberg, modernist art participates in the "tradition of the new." Unconventional, often formally complex and thematically apocalyptic, modernist literary and artistic creations typically emphasize the artist's difference, even ALIENATION, from the masses. Thus, the artist occupies a privileged social position, but the redemptive possibilities of art are not assured. Ezra Pound wrote that "artists are the antennae of the race, but the bullet-headed many will never learn to trust their great artists."

Most literary historians identify 1922 as the apex of "high modernism." It was in that year that both James Joyce's *Ulysses* and T. S. Eliot's *The Wasteland* were published. Both texts were highly experimental, relying on FRAGMENTATION and a sense of alienation to achieve their effects. Joyce's novel is often singled out as the innovator of a narrative style, stream of consciousness, which placed the reader in characters' minds without benefit of the usual explanations and frames of REALIST literature. This technique, which Joyce pushed even further in his later work *Finnegans Wake*, was also used and experimented with by writers such as Virginia Woolf and William Faulkner. In literary theory, the "practical criticism" of I. A. Richards, together with the NEW CRITICISM, helped to emphasize the primacy of the text and to focus increasing attention on writing itself, just as emerging literary styles insisted that increased attention be paid to the ways in which a text can produce meaning.

The emergence of modernism as a dominant artistic and literary trend is often linked to the change in thinking that seemed to come about as an effect of the First World War. Faced with the dissolution of the outmoded political orders and the enormous casualties of the war, old ways of explaining and portraying the world no longer seemed either appropriate or applicable. Increasingly, alienation and isolation emerged as important themes, and even as techniques. Bertolt Brecht's EPIC THE-ATER, for example, deliberately attempted to achieve "alienation effects" that would break down the conventions of nineteenth-century realist theater—conventions that he believed encouraged passive reception on the part of audiences. Franz Kafka, on the other hand, as well as early existentialists like Jean-Paul Sartre, focuses on the absurd and isolated circumstances of the individual.

In recent years there has been much discussion as to whether modernism has been replaced by an even more fragmented, but ultimately more "playful" aesthetic, POSTMODERNISM. For a number of theorists and critics, the advent of atomic war and the horror of the Holocaust effectively ended modernism and gave rise to yet a new way of conceiving the world. Other critics have argued that modernism has outlived its anti-conventional status, its major texts having become canonized in anthologies and on syllabi and its major formal innovations having become the standard against which younger artists now rebel. On the other hand, theorists such as Jürgen Habermas have argued that modernism is the epitome of ENLIGHTENMENT thought, and that as long as we subscribe to enlightenment epistemology and the primacy of reason, we remain in the throes of modernism. See also CONSTRUCTIVISM, DADA, EXISTENTIALISM, FUTURISM.

MONAD. The concept of the monad is central to the philosophy of the ENLIGHTENMENT thinker Gottfried Wilhelm Leibniz (1646–1716), who attempted to isolate the most basic elements out of which all complex aggregates could be shown to be constructed. He argued that because empirical objects are divisible, there must be simple substances, which he called *monads*. Although each monad develops according to its own internal laws, it nevertheless reflects the whole of the total system of monads in its own way. This curious doctrine is chiefly of interest to contemporary criticism because the term *monad* has been adopted by Marxist philosophers like Walter Benjamin as analogous to the Hegelian doctrine of the relation between part and whole. Because Hegel also argued that the TOTALITY is present in each of its individual parts, the concept of the monad provided a model for understanding how cultural practices can develop in apparent autonomy while at the same time bearing a significant relation to the total historical development of the society.

Benjamin, Walter. *The Origin of German Tragic Drama*. Trans. John Osborne. London: New Left Books, 1977.

Leibniz, Gottfried Wilhelm. *Discourse on Metaphysics.* Trans. Peter Lucas and Leslie Grant. Manchester, U.K.: Manchester University Press, 1953.

——. *Monadology, and Other Philosophical Writings.* Trans. Paul Schrecker and Anne Martin Schrecker. Indianapolis: Bobbs-Merrill, 1965.

MONISM. In its broadest usage, *monism* refers to any METAPHYSICAL system that attempts to explain reality in terms of its unity or wholeness and the reducibility of all things to a common temporal, spatial, or compositional element. The first to actually coin the term was Christian Wolff (1679–1754), but developed forms of monism existed as early as the pre-Socratics and the philosophy of Parmenides. Modern philosophers usually identify Hegel's as the most influential monistic theory, though many of his assumptions are borrowed from Spinoza. For Hegel, mind and body, rather than being two entities that differ in substance, are in fact different modes of the same substance to which they are both reducible, although they are not reducible to each other. In the nineteenth century the term took on a rather ambiguous meaning, referring to any system that attempts to explain all of reality in terms of a single principle. This usage can be somewhat confusing, since within such systems a plurality of phenomena might exist that are mutually exclusive of each other in substance and effects, despite their traceability back to a common base or informing source. See also DUALISM.

MONOLOGIC. The Soviet critic Mikhail Bakhtin coined the term *monologic* in his 1929 work *Problems of Dostoevsky's Poetics* to distinguish between novels in which characters' voices are subordinated to a central, controlling authorial voice and novels that are DIALOGIC (or polyphonic) in form and allow a "plurality of independent and unmerged voices and consciousnesses." For Bakhtin, the primary example of the monologic form was the novels of Tolstoy, while he found Dostoevsky's works to be dialogical. Despite this distinction, Bakhtin asserts that no novel can be fully monological, for the narrator's articulations of another character's utterances are always DOUBLE-VOICED, that is, we can distinguish in that re-articulation the author's particular inflections and accents, since the author's voice and purpose are always reinforcing, altering, and contesting with the utterances of characters. See also AUTHOR, CARNIVAL.

Bakhtin, Mikhail. *Rabelais and his World.* Trans. Helene Iswolsky. Cambridge, Mass.: MIT Press, 1968.

—. *The Dialogic Imagination: Four Essays.* Trans. Caryl Emerson and Michael Holquist, ed. Michael Holquist. Austin: University of Texas Press, 1981.

—. *Problems of Dostoevky's Poetics.* Trans. and ed. Caryl Emerson. Minneapolis: University of Minnesota Press, 1984.

MOTHERHOOD.   *Motherhood* is a very important, and contested, term in feminist criticism and theory. Although feminists of the 1970s began by associating motherhood with women's oppression—their confinement to the domestic sphere, responsibility for childcare, etc.—they were later encouraged by such works as Adrienne Rich's *Of Woman Born* (1976) to distinguish between motherhood as a patriarchal institution and motherhood as a source of potential empowerment for women. In the social sciences, works by Dorothy Dinnerstein and Nancy Chodorow emphasized the early, PREOEDIPAL phase of infant development (named but neglected by Freud) during which the mother, not the father, is primary. While masculinity is defined largely as a successful separation from the mother, daughters, Dinnerstein and Chodorow agreed, continue into adulthood to remain attached to the mother and, generally, to view themselves in relational terms. These claims have had an enormous influence on subsequent feminist thinking about the mother-daughter relationship and its key role in making girls grow up differently from boys. Carol Gilligan and Sara Ruddick, for example, have described and celebrated women's "different" moral voice (Gilligan) and the practice of "maternal thinking" (Ruddick), both of which involve a sense of relation and responsibility to others, are specifically characteristic of women, and derive from the mother's role as primary caretaker in modern Western society. Attention to and appreciation for the mother-daughter relationship as a defining aspect of women's culture has also influenced feminist literary criticism, producing a wealth of readings informed by this motif. Cathy Davidson and Esther Broner, for example, have used it to define and recover a "lost tradition" of women's texts, while Marianne Hirsch has argued that in the works of early women novelists the mother is repressed. Like other feminist critical concepts, notions of motherhood have recently begun to be complicated by the realization that Chodorow's model and many of those inspired by it describe not all mothers but only a narrow group. Future work on motherhood promises to explore the ways that motherhood and mother-daughter relations are differently shaped by the facts of race, class, and other social variants. See also LESBIAN CONTINUUM.

Chodorow, Nancy. *The Reproduction of Mothering: Psychoanalysis and the Sociology of Gender.* Berkeley: University of California Press, 1978.

Gilligan, Carol. *In a Different Voice: Psychological Theory and Women's Development.* Cambridge, Mass.: Harvard University Press, 1982.

Davidson, Cathy, and Esther Broner, eds. *The Lost Tradition.* New York: Frederick Ungar, 1980.

Hirsch, Marianne. *The Mother/Daughter Plot: Narrative, Psychoanalysis, Feminism.* Bloomington: Indiana University Press, 1989.

Rich, Adrienne. *Of Woman Born: Motherhood as Experience and Institution.* New York: Norton, 1976.

Ruddick, Sara. *Maternal Thinking: Toward a Politics of Peace.* New York: Ballantine, 1989.

MULTICULTURALISM. *Multiculturalism* is a catchall term that refers generally to the project of making education more inclusive of the perspectives of women, minorities, and non-Western cultures in recognition of the increasingly diverse character of life in modern Western societies. To this end, textbooks, anthologies, curricula, and course syllabi have been revised to incorporate material previously excluded from study in elementary and secondary schools as well as colleges (see also CANON FORMATION). The term does not, however, describe a single ideological position; and multiculturalism incorporates views that can be described at one extreme as simply an extension of liberal PLURALISM or cosmopolitanism, and at the other as a form of radical separatism according to race, gender, or sexual preference. The strong element of political advocacy in many versions of multiculturalism has inspired a conservative backlash, which has made effective use of the derogatory epithet "political correctness," sometimes to describe the humorless or dictatorial attitudes displayed by certain advocates of multiculturalism and other times merely to justify conventional exclusions.

Bloom, Allan. *The Closing of the American Mind.* New York: Simon and Schuster, 1987.

D'Souza, Dinesh. *Illiberal Education: The Politics of Race and Sex on Campus.* New York: Free Press, 1991.

Gates, Henry Louis, Jr. *"Race," Writing, and Difference.* Chicago: University of Chicago Press, 1986.

MYTH. One usage of *myth* is as a story in a set of stories (a mythology) that at one time functioned to explain the ways of the world, establish rituals, or provide justification and rationales for the observance of rituals. Importantly, a myth was at one time regarded as true by a specific cultural group, but is only discussed *as* myth if it is not held as true by those involved in the discussion. Myths are often distinguished from legends in that the latter are usually more attributable to some historical basis, although their transmission (usually oral) and literary adaptation are quite similar. In literary analysis, myths are often discussed as representative of certain fundamental human concerns such as life and death, fear of the unknown, and the supernatural (see MYTH CRITICISM). With the publication of Claude Lévi-Strauss's *The Savage Mind* (1966), myth has taken on new resonances. For Lévi-Strauss, myth is a type of language that communicates thought, and the appropriate study of myth should focus on its structure rather than content. According to this view, myth attempts to mediate irresolvable PARADOXES within cultures. From this view of myth as language—an abstract series of signs—myth (and literature) can be characterized as "mediators rather than media," which are always assuming something absent (nature, God, eternity, reality) and attempting to close that gap between presence and absence. See STRUCTURALISM.

Frazer, James G. *The Golden Bough.* New York: Macmillan, 1922.
Frye, Northrop. *Anatomy of Criticism.* Princeton: Princeton University Press, 1957.
Hartman, Geoffrey. "Structuralism: The Anglo-American Adventure." In Jacques Ehrmann, ed., *Structuralism.* New York: Anchor, 1970.
Ruthven, K. K. *Myth.* London: Methuen, 1976.

MYTH CRITICISM. Often used interchangably with *archetypal criticism,* myth criticism argues that literary works embody recurrent mythic patterns or ARCHETYPES, which are fundamentally unaffected by historical change. Myth critics, who saw their heyday in the 1950s and 1960s, focus on a work's symbolism or narrative structure in order to connect it to ancient myths and religions or such fundamental human experiences as the change of the seasons. By insisting that even the most innovative modern writers simply retell old stories in new ways, they aim to enforce a sense of the continuity of human existence from the earliest times to the present. Influenced by anthropological work like James G. Frazer's *The Golden Bough* (1890–1915) and the psychology of Carl Gustav Jung, prominent practitioners of myth criticism include Maud Bodkin, Robert Graves, Joseph Campbell, Leslie Fiedler, and Northrop Frye, whose *Anatomy of Criticism* (1957) is perhaps the most well-known and influential work of myth criticism. In recent years, myth criticism has been attacked as reductionist by HISTORICIST and FORMALIST critics for ignoring the historical and cultural context of literary works as well as their specific formal premises. See also MYTH.

Frazer, James G. *The Golden Bough.* New York: Macmillan, 1922.

Frye, Northrop. *Anatomy of Criticism.* Princeton: Princeton University Press, 1957.

Jung, Carl Gustav. "On the Relation of Analytical Psychology to Poetic Art." In *Contributions to Analytical Psychology.* Trans. H. G. and Cary F. Baynes. New York: Harcourt Brace, 1928.

—. *The Archetypes and the Collective Unconscious. Collected Works,* vol. 9. Trans. R. F. C. Hull. New York: Pantheon, 1959.

N

NAME-OF-THE-FATHER. In the psychoanalytic theory of Jacques Lacan, the Name-of-the-Father (in French, *Nom-du-Père*) is a concept derived from the mythical figure of the father described in Freud's *Totem and Taboo.* This is the stern, primeval father whose name is inseparably associated with the law governing interpersonal relations, to which the child becomes subject upon entry into the SYMBOLIC order. For Lacan, the experience of the OEDIPUS COMPLEX is mediated by the linguistic structures to which the child is simultaneously being introduced, so that the dominant figure of the father is conceived not as a particular individual, but rather as an abstraction of the paternal role, which is characterized by its privileged possession of the mother and its function as the enforcer of the law. This latter capacity of prohibition ultimately determines the child's social identity, for in Lacan's conception of the symbolic order, the power of the law is above all the power to establish relationships through speech and the act of naming. Moreover, the nature of the paternal role as a function distinct from any one individual is what allows the male child, even in his resentment, to identify with the father's role himself. Forced to give up his claim to the mother, he receives in exchange his own claim to a place within the order of language and culture.

Freud, Sigmund. *Totem and Taboo*. Trans. James Strachey. London: Routledge, 1961.
Lacan, Jacques. *Ecrits: A Selection*. Trans. Alan Sheridan. New York: Norton, 1977.

NAMING. A central concept in marginalized American cultures, naming describes and therefore expresses the identity of the named. Under the dominant Anglo-American culture, naming became a tool of domination through its power to symbolically confine the named within the parameters of an imposed racial identity. As Kimberly W. Benston puts it, naming functions as "the means by which the mind takes possession of the named." But naming can also function as the site of an empowering self-definition, a means by which to revise one's own identity and reject imposed descriptions of the self. Thus, the liberated slaves' well-documented name changes contained a repudiation of the slave identity itself. Activists and writers from Booker T. Washington to Toni Morrison have insisted upon the political significance of naming, while advancing their own mastery over the naming process. Literary critics such as Henry Louis Gates, Jr. and Mary Dearborn have investigated the power and importance of naming in African and Native American cultures. See also NATURALIZATION, SIGNIFYIN(G).

Benston, Kimberly W. "I Yam What I Am: The Topos of (Un)naming in Afro-American Literature." In Henry Louis Gates, Jr., ed., *Black Literature and Literary Theory*. New York: Methuen, 1984.
Dearborn, Mary V. *Pocahontas's Daughters: Gender and Ethnicity in American Culture*. New York: Oxford University Press, 1986.
Gates, Henry Louis, Jr. "The Signifying Monkey and the Language of Signifyin(g): Rhetorical Difference and the Orders of Meaning." In *The Signifying Monkey: A Theory of African-American Literary Criticism*. New York: Oxford Uniersity Press, 1988.

NARCISSISM. Coined by Havelock Ellis with reference to the ancient Greek myth of Narcissus—the youth who fell in love with his own image—*narcissism* (NARsisIZum) is the psychoanalytic term for love of oneself or, more precisely, love directed toward one's own EGO. Freudian psychoanalysts understand narcissism as a sexual orientation that precedes the finding of appropriate love objects in the world, and remains a permanent reservoir of libidinal energy, which is drawn on in relating to those objects. This original CATHEXIS of a body image is crucial to the establishment of the ego and has been described by Jacques Lacan in the concept of the MIRROR STAGE. According to this account, the ego comes into being through the establishment of a specular relationship with one's own body image. In Freud's later texts, however, this state is called "secondary" narcissism, in contrast to "primary" narcissism, which is seen as a very early, objectless condition, characterized by the absence of any sense of separation from the world and a lack of distinction between the ID and anything that can be called an ego (see POLYMORPHOUS PERVERSITY).

Freud, Sigmund. *The Ego and the Id.* Trans. Joan Riviere, ed. James Strachey. New York: Norton, 1960.

—. "On Narcissism: An Introduction." In *Standard Edition of the Complete Psychological Works of Sigmund Freud*, vol. 14. Trans. James Strachey. London: Hogarth Press and Institute of Psycho-Analysis, 1974.

Lacan, Jacques. "The Mirror Stage as Formative of the Function of the 'I' as Revealed in Psychoanalytic Experience." In *Ecrits: A Selection.* Trans. Alan Sheridan. New York: Norton, 1977.

NARRATIVE INSTANT. A term specific to NARRATOLOGY and narratological analysis, *narrative instant* refers to the fictional point in time of the composition or utterance of the narrative. This is often a topic of critical concern in narratological analysis of first-person narratives. For example, in Charlotte Brontë's novel *Villette*, the narrator, Lucy Snowe, is also the protagonist. The STORY or HISTOIRE is specifically concerned with events during her adolescence and young adulthood, yet at one point she declares that since these events, her hair has turned white and lies beneath her white cap "like snow beneath snow," indicating that the fictional telling of the story is far removed from the time of the events that comprise it.

NARRATOLOGY. *Narratology* refers to the study of narrative in general and traces its antecedents as far back as Aristotle's *Poetics*. However, the term itself came into prominence in the 1970s and adopted many of the analytical methods of STRUCTURALISM and RUSSIAN FORMALISM. Unlike traditional critics of narrative and narrative techniques, narratologists do not treat narratives as fictional representations of life or reality but as formal, systematic structures. Their primary focus is to investigate the ways that narratives function and to identify the CODES and TROPES by which all (or most) narratives are governed. Two important works that deserve specific mention are Gérard Genette's *Narrative Discourse* (1980) and *Figures of Literary Discourse* (1982), which contributed significantly to studies of the intricate relations between a story and the varieties of discourse through which a story is narrated. The impact of Genette's work has been virtually to supersede the traditional, and much less subtle concept of point-of-view.

The reach of narratological analysis is difficult to overemphasize. It has been extremely influential, even for those whose primary concern is not the structure of narratives per se. Historians such as Hayden White, Marxist critics like Fredric Jameson, and philosophers like Arthur Danto have drawn on narratology as a basis for works that have had far-ranging effects in a number of disciplines. See also SEMIOTICS.

Danto, Arthur. *Narration and Knowledge: Including the Integral Text of Analytical Philosophy in History.* New York: Columbia University Press, 1985.

Genette, Gérard. *Narrative Discourse: An Essay in Method.* Trans. Jane E. Lewin. Ithaca, N.Y.: Cornell University Press, 1980.

—. *Figures of Literary Discourse.* Trans. Alan Sheridan. New York: Columbia University Press, 1982.

Jameson, Fredric. *The Political Unconscious: Narrative as a Socially Symbolic Act.* Ithaca, N.Y.: Cornell University Press, 1981.

Todorov, Tzvetan. *The Poetics of Prose.* Trans. Richard Howard. Ithaca, N.Y.: Cornell University Press, 1977.

White, Hayden. *Metahistory: The Historical Imagination in Nineteenth-Century Europe.* Baltimore: Johns Hopkins University Press, 1973.

—. *The Content of the Form: Narrative Discourse and Historical Representation.* Baltimore: Johns Hopkins University Press, 1987.

NARRATOR. See AUTHOR.

NATIONALISM. Nationalism is the belief or feeling that identity is closely tied to one's nation or nationality, the implication being that individual inhabitants of a country of origin share common traits or beliefs. Often, nationalism means the belief that one's country is superior to other countries, and this meaning is roughly synonymous with that of *jingoism*. The effort to unite communities divided by religion, ethnicity, etc., in relation to geographic boundaries or a common language is a relatively modern concept that arose, over the past two hundred years, as a consequence of the unification of European principalities into "nations" and with the expansion and decline of European empires. This innovation is a highly contested one, for traditionally one's identity began with a smaller social unit (family or village, religion, or race or ethnicity). As a collective phenomenon, nationalism often arises at times of conflict between nations, or between colonizers and colonized, and perhaps most commonly, in postcolonial periods. As Seamus Deane has said, "Almost all nationalist movements have been derided as provisional, actually or potentially racist, given to exclusivist and doctrinaire positions and rhetoric." On the other hand, nationalism, such as that of the Irish nationalists who oppose British rule, is seen as a strong defense against COLONIALISM. See also POSTCOLONIALISM.

Anderson, Benedict. *Imagined Communities: Reflections on the Origin and Spread of Nationalism*. Rev. and extended ed. London: Verso, 1991.
Deane, Seamus. "Introduction." In Seamus Deane, ed., *Nationalism, Colonialism and Literature*. Minneapolis: University of Minnesota Press, 1990.

NATURALISM. See REALISM.

NATURALIZATION. According to the concept of naturalization, what is "natural" in any given society—what is accepted as self-evidently and transcendentally "true"—is actually historically constructed. "Natural" knowledge has been *naturalized*: that is, made to *seem* natural by means of IDEOLOGY. The process of naturalization is thus contingent upon sociopolitical systems and ideologies. Indeed, Louis Althusser argues that ideological knowledge naturalizes itself by definition: it is never aware of itself as ideological and thus seems to refer to external "reality." This process extends to literature and literary criticism: concepts such as the creative imagination, the autonomy of art, and critical DISINTERESTED-NESS have been historically determined but made to seem "natural" to any understanding of literature. Materialist and historicist critics attempt to expose the constructed nature of these understandings, to view their function in obscuring the ideological and material aspects of art and the political nature of criticism. A key idea in NEW HISTORICISM and CULTURAL MATERIALISM, the concept of naturalization arose in opposition to all forms of ESSENTIALISM. See also AESTHETIC IDEOLOGY, IDEOLOGY.

Althusser, Louis. "Ideology and Ideological State Apparatuses." In *Lenin and Philosophy and Other Essays*. Trans. Ben Brewster. New York: Monthly Review Press, 1971.

Dollimore, Jonathan, and Alan Sinfield, eds. *Political Shakespeare: New Essays in Cultural Materialism*. Manchester, U.K.: Manchester University Press, 1985.
Veeser, H. Aram, ed. *The New Historicism*. New York: Routledge, 1989.

NATURWISSENSCHAFT/KULTURWISSENSCHAFT. These terms are the poles in a dichotomy stemming from the nineteenth-century German debate that attempted to justify the division of knowledge into human sciences (*Kulturwissenschaft* [KUHLturVEESenshaft] or GEISTESWISSENSCHAFT) and natural sciences (*Naturwissenschaft* [NAHturVEESenshaft]). Because *Naturwissenschaft* held out the possibility of verifiable truth and legitimated positivism as its method, it threatened to encroach upon the autonomous character of knowledge in the humanities (*Kulturwissenschaften*). A debate ensued, led by Wilhelm Dilthey's attempts to develop a coherent theoretical foundation for the humanities and thus to ensure its distinctiveness. Distinctions were based not only on differences of subject matter in each discipline, but on the formal character of their different epistemological goals. *Naturwissenschaft* sought knowledge of general laws and causes, while *Kulturwissenschaft* sought specific historical facts. The aim of the natural sciences is explanation (*Erklären*), while the human sciences pursue understanding (*Verstehen*). For humanists, this particular formulation remains the prevailing conception, although Dilthey, and more recently E. D. Hirsch and others, have found it completely inadequate.

Dilthey, Wilhelm. *Introduction to the Human Sciences: An Attempt to Lay a Foundation for the Study of Society and History*. Trans. Ramon J. Betanzos. Detroit: Wayne State University Press, 1988.
Hirsch, E. D. *Validity in Interpretation*. New Haven: Yale University Press, 1967.
Leavis, F. R. *Two Cultures? The Significance of C. P. Snow*. London: Chatto and Windus, 1962.
Snow, C. P. *Recent Thoughts on the Two Cultures: An Oration Delivered at Birkbeck College, London, 12th December, 1961*. London: J. W. Ruddock, 1961.

NEED. See DESIRE.

NEGRITUDE. Negritude was a literary movement with strong cultural and political overtones, prominent between 1930 and 1950 among black, French-speaking African and Caribbean writers, and closely linked to the concerns of many of the writers of the HARLEM RENAISSANCE in the United States. Negritude's founders were Léopold Sédar Senghor of Senegal (who was elected that country's first president in 1960), Léon Damas from French Guiana, and Aimé Césaire of Martinique, who first used the term in his long poem *Cahier d'un retour au pays natal*. Reacting against doctrines of Western racial and cultural superiority and the assimilationist pressure of colonialism on native cultures, the negritude writers attempted to invoke a pan-national black African social and artistic identity. Making some use of surrealism artistically and Marxism politically, negritude criticized the West's materialism, individualism, violence, and rationality, contrasting them with African values of group and tribal solidarity, rhythm and symbol in art, poetry, and religion, peacefulness, and intimate connection to nature. See also POSTCOLONIALISM.

Kennedy, Ellen Conroy, ed. *The Negritude Poets: An Anthology of Translations from the French*. New York: Viking, 1975.

Kesteloot, Lilyan. *Black Writers in French: A Literary History of Negritude*. Trans. Ellen Conroy Kennedy. Philadelphia: Temple University Press, 1974.

NEO-ARISTOTELIANISM. Although the term can be applied to any revival or appropriation of the ideas of the ancient Greek philosopher Aristotle, *Neo-Aristotelianism* generally refers to the ideas and practices of a group of literary critics and scholars based at the University of Chicago from the 1930s through the 1950s. Sometimes referred to as the Chicago School (see CHICAGO CRITICS), these Neo-Aristotelians analyzed individual literary texts with regard to principles presented in Aristotle's *Poetics*. Their work bears many affinities with that of the New Critics (see NEW CRITICISM)—including a tendency to treat a text as a unified whole, an inclination to regard the relationship of form and content as closely intertwined, and a disinclination to consider literature in its social and historical contexts. Unlike the New Critics, the Neo-Aristotelians were deeply concerned with the question of genre. Prominent Neo-Aristotelians include R. S. Crane, W. R. Keast, Richard McKeon, Norman MacLean, Elder Olson, and Bernard Weinberg.

Crane, Ronald Salmon. *Critics and Criticism, Ancient and Modern*. Chicago: University of Chicago Press, 1952.

NEW BLACK AESTHETIC. *New black aesthetic* is a term used by Trey
Ellis to describe the proliferation of critically and commercially successful work by young black artists in the 1980s. According to Ellis, this new
wave of black artistic output is fueled by an aesthetic made possible by
the highly politicized BLACK ARTS MOVEMENT of the 1960s and early
1970s, but which does not require the same sort of political responsibility as the earlier movement. The new black aesthetic allows for the parody of blackness itself, claiming freedom from both white envy and self-
hate. Driven by middle-class social and financial security, Ellis argues,
young black artists now have the freedom to create outside the boundaries of the restrictive black arts ideology, thus enabling them to explore
subjects previously off limits. Ellis points to the work of such diverse
artists as Spike Lee, Robert Townsend, Public Enemy, and Terry McMil-
lan as examples of this new artistic freedom. See also BLACK AESTHETIC.

Ellis, Trey. "The New Black Aesthetic." *Callaloo* 12(1), 1989.
Hunter, Tera. " 'It's A Man's Man's Man's World': Specters of the Old Re-Newed in
    Afro-American Culture and Criticism." *Callaloo* 12(1), 1989.
Lott, Eric. "Response to Trey Ellis's "The New Black Aesthetic." *Callaloo* 12(1), 1989.

NEW CRITICISM. An American literary critical movement from the
1930s through the 1960s, New Criticism concerned itself with treating
works of literature "objectively," viewing them as self-contained,
autonomous, and existing for their own sake. It was, arguably, the most
influential literary theory of the twentieth century. Not only the vitality
it enjoyed during its long period as a significant feature on the critical
landscape, but its institutionalization in works like Cleanth Brooks and
Robert Penn Warren's *Understanding Poetry* (1938), helped to make it the
critical orthodoxy through the middle years of the century and thus to be
reproduced as the theoretical model by which literary critics were
trained. The name of the movement comes from John Crowe Ransom's
1941 book *The New Criticism*, in which he analyzes the theoretical work
developed in Britain by T. S. Eliot, William Empson, and I. A. Richards,
as well as the theories of Yvor Winters. Ransom calls for a more "objective" criticism that would emphasize the intrinsic qualities of a work over
the biographical and historical context. By the mid-1940s, New Criticism
included among its numbers Allen Tate, W. K. Wimsatt, and R. P. Black-
mur. Despite their differences, these critics shared the theoretical
assumptions that a poem should be treated, as T. S. Eliot said, "primarily

as poetry and not another thing." As such, a poem is a self-sufficient object, and the critic's task is to recognize that autonomy and to understand that the work exists for its own sake. "Extrinsic" factors such as authorial intent only divert a reader from the object itself.

One of the distinctive characteristics of the New Criticism was its use of explication, or close reading, in which the complex interrelations and ambiguities of the form *and* the content of the work are subtly analyzed. New Critics viewed literature as a special kind of language (a premise often attacked by the CHICAGO CRITICS), in direct contrast to scientific, practical, or logical discourse. To this end, the New Critics argued that the essential components of any work, whether drama, lyric, or narrative, exist at the level of language and its workings. Thus, they focused on words, images, and symbols rather than upon character or plot. A text's literary value is often said to be indicated by its use of tension, PARADOX, or irony to achieve a "reconciliation of diverse impulses" or "an equilibrium of opposed forces."

Two of the most important New Critical texts are Brooks's *The Well Wrought Urn* (1947) and W. K. Wimsatt's *The Verbal Icon* (1954). René Wellek and Austin Warren's *Theory of Literature* (1973), which quickly became a standard text for graduate study in the seventies, furthers the legacy of New Criticism by favoring New Critical practices and theories over others. In recent years, New Criticism has been repudiated as being ahistorical and formalistic. Regardless, its influence in replacing biographical source study with text-centered approaches to literary works is undeniable. See also FORMALISM.

Lentricchia, Frank. *After the New Criticism.* Chicago: University of Chicago Press, 1980.

Webster, Grant. *The Republic of Letters: A History of Postwar American Literary Opinion.* Baltimore: Johns Hopkins University Press, 1979.

Wellek, René. *A History of Modern Criticism*, vol. 6. New Haven: Yale University Press, 1986.

NEW HISTORICISM. Adopted in 1982 by Stephen Greenblatt in a special issue of *Genre* to describe a new kind of historically based criticism, especially in Renaissance studies, *new historicism* has since been used to describe critical approaches as theoretically diverse as FEMINISM, DISCOURSE theory, Marxism, and even some DECONSTRUCTION. However, not all critical activity that relies on historical information is new historicism, nor, despite assertions by many to the contrary, is new historicism predominantly informed by Marxism. Although many have incorporated certain Marxist and neo-Marxist theories into their projects, it is Michel Foucault's work, especially his *The Order of Things, Discipline and Punish*, and *The Archaeology of Knowledge*, that has been most important to those who are properly considered "new historicists."

New historicism differs from old or traditional historicism in several ways. Following Foucault, it argues that "man" is a construct of social and historical circumstances and not an autonomous agent of historical change. There is nothing essential about the actions of human beings; there is no such thing as "human nature." Instead, individuals undergo a process of subjectification, which on one hand shapes them as conscious initiators of action, but on the other hand places them in social networks and cultural codes that exceed their comprehension or control. Since each individual's way of thinking is shaped by this process, it follows that the historian is also a product of subjectification, which is always partly informed by the past. This last point is very important to new historicism, for it reforms our ideas of what history may be. Instead of a body of indisputable, retrievable facts, history becomes textualized; that is, it becomes a group of linguistic traces that can be recalled, but which are always mediated through the historian/interpreter. Objective history is therefore an impossibility; every account is just that—another text, and like any novel, play, or poem, it is open to the same kind of critical interpretive scrutiny.

Since historical accounts are texts and must be evaluated as such, and since, by extension, history itself is a large amorphous text consisting of various and often disparate accounts, the relation of history to literature changes radically in new historicism. No longer does history act as the background to literary texts, and no longer are historical accounts considered reliable and unproblematic representations of what really went on during a particular time. In this respect, new historicism has attempted to eradicate distinctions between literature and history, arguing that each partakes of the other and that both participate in social networks and deploy cultural codes that cannot be fully articulated. Thus, one characteristic of new historicist criticism has been its extensive use of historical or nonliterary texts in its discussion of more traditional literary works.

New historicism has also been concerned to portray itself as politicized criticism. Again borrowing from Foucault, new historicists argue that homogeneous depictions of an era or of its way of thinking incorrectly invalidate the truly disparate and often contentious activities taking place in that age. New historicists repudiate, or in their words, "refuse," the idea of an "Elizabethan worldview" or a "Victorian frame of mind," and have often tried to show instead how structures of POWER ultimately reabsorb opposition and dissent, thus giving the appearance of a homogeneous or totalized society (see TOTALITY). The purpose of their investigations, they argue, is not only to show how dominant ideas and power structures can subvert radicalization in bygone eras, but how such domination also impinges on our own political choices.

It is precisely at this point that many disassociate themselves from new historicism. Some, like Carolyn Porter, argue that by conceiving of power as a constant, though ill-defined, entity functioning in all eras, new historicists have really done nothing new. Rather, they have merely replaced one transhistorical term, such as "man," with another. And like traditional humanism, in which man may be malleable but possesses an essential nature, power, as the new historicists use it, accommodates the specifics of the period, but remains essentially unchanged throughout time. Others, like Fredric Jameson, have argued that such a notion of power does not provide an adequate explanation of change, since all opposition is ultimately absorbed into the dominant ideology. Indeed, many critics, like Walter Cohen and Marguerite Waller, argue that by positing power as an unchanging, essential entity in all human relations, new historicism is really not historicism at all, nor can it ultimately be political, but rather is a project that seeks to propagate traditional humanist values instead of moving toward a POSTMODERN, non-human-centered way of viewing the world. Perhaps the most pertinent evaluation of the movement has been voiced by Jean Howard, who argues that although new historicism relinquished much of its potency in becoming the new critical orthodoxy, it has nevertheless performed a valuable service in forcing critics to focus on the problems of historical representation and knowledge that are a part of any critical endeavor. See also ESSENTIALISM, HISTORICISM, HUMANISM, MARXIST CRITICISM, POWER, SUBJECT.

Cohen, Walter. "Political Criticism of Shakespeare." In Jean E. Howard and Marion F. O'Connor, eds., *Shakespeare Reproduced: The Text in History and Ideology.* New York: Methuen, 1987.

Foucault, Michel. *The Order of Things: An Archaeology of the Human Sciences.* New York: Vintage, 1970.

—. *The Archaeology of Knowledge.* Trans. A. M. Sheridan. New York: Pantheon, 1972.

—. *Discipline and Punish: The Birth of the Prison.* Trans. Alan Sheridan. New York: Vintage, 1979.

Greenblatt, Stephen. "Introduction to *The Forms of Power and the Power of Forms in the Renaissance." Genre* 15, 1982.

Horwitz, Howard. "I Can't Remember: Skepticism, Synthetic Histories, Critical Action." *South Atlantic Quarterly* 87(4), 1988.

Howard, Jean. "The New Historicism in Literary Studies." *English Literary Renaissance* 16, 1986.

Jameson, Fredric. *The Political Unconscious: Narrative as a Socially Symbolic Act.* Ithaca, N.Y.: Cornell University Press, 1981.

Pechter, Edward. "The New Historicism and its Discontents: Politicizing Renaissance Drama." *Publications of the Modern Language Association* 102, May 1987.

Porter, Carolyn. "Are We Being Historical Yet." *South Atlantic Quarterly* 87(4), 1988.

Veeser, H. Aram, ed. *The New Historicism.* New York: Routledge, 1989.

Waller, Marguerite. "Academic Tootsie: The Denial of Difference and the Difference it Makes." *Diacritics* 17, 1987.

NEW LITERARY HISTORY. The phrase *new literary history* comes from the title of a journal founded in 1969 by Ralph Cohen and intended as a forum for work intended to rethink the problems endemic to the discipline of literary history, which had fallen into disrepute during the height of the NEW CRITICISM in the forties, fifties, and early sixties. This project, itself temporarily sidetracked by the emergence of DECONSTRUCTION in the seventies, returned to prominence in American literary criticism during the eighties with the advent of various forms of NEW HISTORICISM. Although the phrase can potentially cover a wide variety of critical efforts, it applies generally to forms of historical study that focus on works of literature but reject the tendency of older works of literary history to treat literature as if it existed in a closed aesthetic sphere, cut off from other aspects of history and culture. Recently, Jonathan Arac has emphasized the project of a new literary history in his book *Critical Genealogies.*

Arac, Jonathan. *Critical Genealogies: Historical Situations For Postmodern Literary Studies.* New York: Columbia University Press, 1987.

THE NEW NEGRO. *The New Negro* is a 1925 collection of essays, fiction, poetry, drama, music, and art, which listed as contributors most of the names usually associated with the HARLEM RENAISSANCE. In the title essay of the volume, editor Alain Locke claimed that his subject was characterized by a new race consciousness, spiritual expansion, and artistic maturity. Locke outlined the factors that he believed made Negro Americans "the advance-guard of the African peoples": the shift of the Negro population to sophisticated urban centers, class differentiation, race-welding, and a scientific rather than sentimental interest in art. The further advancement of the New Negro was seen to rely on proof of "his artistic endowments and cultural contributions." The viewpoint expressed by Locke and echoed by other contributors was dismissed by Garveyites and black radicals as elitist and void of political and economic understanding. More politically grounded versions of the "new negro" were offered by A. Philip Randolph in *The Messenger* and Langston Hughes in his essay "The Negro Artist and the Racial Mountain," which Robert Bone has called the "literary manifesto" of the New Negro movement.

Bone, Robert. *The Negro Novel in America.* New Haven: Yale University Press, 1958.

Hughes, Langston. "The Negro Artist and the Racial Mountain." *The Nation* 72, 1926.

Locke, Alain, ed. *The New Negro.* Preface by Robert Hayden. New York: Atheneum, 1977.

NEW PRAGMATISM. See PRAGMATISM.

"NEW WAVE" CINEMA/FRENCH "NEW WAVE." *Nouvelle Vague*, or New Wave cinema included the work of several young French filmmakers of the late 1950s and early 1960s: Jean-Luc Godard, François Truffaut, Eric Rohmer, Claude Chabrol, and Jacques Rivette. All of them began as critics for the French film journal *Cahiers du Cinéma* in the 1950s and espoused AUTEUR THEORY, rehabilitating the films of some Hollywood directors they claimed were genuine auteurs or cinematic artists, able to express their personal style and worldview even in studio genre productions, and rejecting the "cinema of quality," adaptations of literary works that they felt too often reflected literary rather than cinematic aesthetic values. Anxious to act on their theories, they borrowed money from friends and began making their own films; in 1959 Godard's *Breathless* (*A Bout de souffle*), Truffaut's *The 400 Blows* (*Les Quatre Cent Coups*), Chabrol's *The Cousins* (*Les Cousins*), and Rivette's *Paris Belongs to Us* (*Paris nous appartient*) appeared; Truffaut's film won the Grand Prize at the Cannes Festival, which seemed to ratify the New Wave's ideas about cinema.

New Wave films shared several traits. Unlike "cinema of quality," New

Wave films were shot on location rather than on elaborate stage sets. Natural lighting was substituted for elegant studio lighting. Actors were encouraged to depart from the script and improvise—in general, causal links between events presented were loosened to a point where the narratives were fairly discontinuous and fragmented, and the endings ambiguous. These changes in mise-en-scène (or the staging of the action) were accompanied by changes in montage or editing, which was more discontinuous (Godard, for example, favored the JUMP CUT), and in cinematography, principally in the degree of camera mobility (in New Wave cinema, there were frequent panning or tracking shots). New Wave film also incorporated hand-held camera scenes and featured long takes and freeze frames. These cinematographic and editing techniques were consistent with the practice of some of the Italian neo-realists (especially Roberto Rossellini, Vittorio De Sica, and Luchino Visconti) as it had been theorized by the critic Andre Bazin, the co-founder of *Cahiers du Cinema* who greatly influenced his younger colleagues. However, the New Wave directors did not see cinema as a neutral form through which something else was transparently recorded, whether the cinema of quality's novels or Bazin's "real." Instead, they saw cinema as having its own conventions and aesthetic values, which the filmmaker could explore and which were necessarily part of what a film was about. The impact of the New Wave on the film industry was significant. Even though its cinema was at odds with the cinematic values championed by critics of the time and demanded more from its audience, it nevertheless became so popular that by the mid-1960s it had been absorbed into the film industry and was being imitated (and diffused).

Monaco, James. *The New Wave: Truffaut, Godard, Chabrol, Rohmer, Rivette.* New York: Oxford University Press, 1976.

OBJECT. See SUBJECT/OBJECT.

OBJECT RELATIONS. The term *object relations* refers to a largely English school of psychology, which derives from the work of Melanie Klein and is primarily concerned with the relations of PREOEDIPAL children to their "objects" of desire—the mother, parts of the body (see PART-OBJECT), and those intermediate objects, like blankets and stuffed animals, that the best-known member of the school, D. W. Winnicott, called TRANSITIONAL OBJECTS. Unlike mainstream Freudian or Lacanian psychoanalysis, the object relations school does not view the OEDIPUS COMPLEX as the central determining factor in the child's development. Rather, that triangular structure is seen as subordinate to the preexisting two-way relationship between mother and child, which cannot be understood merely in terms of the satisfaction of INSTINCTS. Instead, the mother/child dyad is a relationship between two selves that takes on a quasi-material reality (Winnicott emphasizes the importance of physical contact between mother and infant); and the process of separating out that which is not a part of the self—conducted as a form of play in an uncontested, imaginary middle zone between subject and object—is crucial to the development of the child.

Like many English thinkers, Winnicott and colleagues like W. R. D. Fairbairn and Masud Khan refrained from systematic theorizing, preferring to let their ideas emerge out of clinical experience. Nevertheless, their writings have had considerable influence on contemporary theory, especially among feminists like Nancy Chodorow, who have both drawn on Winnicott's accounts of the relationship between mother and child and critiqued what they consider to be his excessive willingness to describe the reproduction of conventional gender roles as natural and inevitable.

Chodorow, Nancy. *The Reproduction of Mothering.* Berkeley: University of California Press, 1978.

Klein, Melanie. *Contributions to Psycho-Analysis 1921–1945.* London: Hogarth Press, 1965.

Rudnytsky, Peter L., ed. *Transitional Objects and Potential Spaces: Literary Uses of D. W. Winnicott.* New York: Columbia University Press, 1993.

Winnicott, D. W. *Playing and Reality.* New York: Basic Books, 1971.

OBJECTIVE CRITICISM. Objective criticism emphasizes a work's relationship to itself, stressing its self-sufficiency and autonomy independent of its circumstances of composition, authorial intention, or the reality it represents. Intrinsic criteria such as formal, structural, symbolic, and imagistic accomplishment constitute the basis for judging the quality of a work. Objective criticism has flourished since its various beginnings with T. S. Eliot, the NEW CRITICS, and the RUSSIAN FORMALISTS. While objective criticism has in recent times suffered greatly in theoretical circles, it remains the most practiced criticism in academia, particularly by those who deny adherence to any theory. See also CHICAGO SCHOOL, EXPRESSIVE CRITICISM.

OBJET PETIT A. In the psychoanalytic theory of Jacques Lacan, the term *objet petit a* (obZHAY peTEET AH) is given no formal definition; and Lacan insisted that it should be left untranslated as well, so that it remains a kind of algebraic variable. Nevertheless, it is possible to say in a general way what he intended by the term and what the logic is behind his refusal to define it. The French word *objet* means "object," and the *petit a* is the "small a" in the word *autre* (other), which is distinguished from *autre* written with a capital *A*. This lesser other refers to the objects of desire or, more precisely, to representations of those primordial forms (see PART-OBJECT) that offer the subject an image inseparable from his or her desire. Thus, the *objet petit a* is not the object itself (such as the breast) but an image of that object detached from the whole form of the mother's body, which had fully occupied the infant's world in the earliest stages of life. After the MIRROR STAGE, however, these SIGNIFIERS are repressed (see REPRESSION) and become unconscious fantasies that seem to promise a return to that lost world of wholeness and union. Yet in analysis they turn out to refer only to other signifiers in an endless chain. Therefore, since the *objet petit a* is a signifier without a signified, Lacan claimed that it should be given no fixed definition. Instead, like any other signifier, it must be understood by its context, where it functions as an emblem of the absence that desire seeks perpetually to fill.

Lacan, Jacques. *Ecrits: A Selection*. Trans. Alan Sheridan. New York: Norton, 1977.

OEDIPUS COMPLEX. In Freudian psychoanalysis, the Oedipus complex is a group of feelings—both of desire and hostility—that the child experiences toward his or her parents, and that Freud described as conforming to the Greek legend of Oedipus Rex, as it is related in Sophocles' play of the same name. Thus, the child feels sexual desire for the parent of the opposite sex and desires the death of the parent of the same sex, while simultaneously experiencing the anxieties attendant on these wishes (see CASTRATION COMPLEX). It first appears between the ages of three and five years, and returns at puberty, at which point it is resolved to a greater or lesser extent through the choice of an appropriate object outside the family. For Freud and later adherents to Freudian doctrine, this triangular structure is fundamental in determining the formation of the personality and the trajectory of adult desire, as well as a point of reference for the most varied pathologies; moreover, it is to be found universally.

The absoluteness of the Freudian position has been disputed by a range of other theorists. Psychoanalysts like Melanie Klein and the OBJECT RELATIONS school argue that a greater importance should be attached to the PREOEDIPAL phase, when the child is engaged more exclusively in a relationship with the mother. Adherents of this school seek to trace many forms of pathological behavior back to this two-part structure, rather than to the Oedipal triangle. This position has had a major influence on feminist theorists like Nancy Chodorow, whose work on mothering has gained considerable influence. In this group, too, can be placed the adherents of "anti-psychiatry," notably Félix Guattari, who with the philosopher Gilles Deleuze celebrated the preoedipal world of the schizophrenic as an alternative to the dominance of the Oedipus complex, which they saw as allied to the repressive structures of capitalist society (see DETERRITORIALIZATION, RHIZOME, SCHIZOANALYSIS). Finally, anthropologists like Bronislaw Malinowski and, more recently, Marie Cécile and Edmond Ortigues have questioned the universality of the Oedipus complex and sought to describe the different structures that appear in societies in which the nuclear family is not dominant or the father does not perform a disciplinary or repressive function.

Chodorow, Nancy. *The Reproduction of Mothering: Psychoanalysis and the Sociology of Gender.* Berkeley: University of California Press, 1978.

Deleuze, Gilles, and Félix Guattari. *Anti-Oedipus: Capitalism and Schizophrenia.* Trans. Robert Hurley, Mark Seem, and Helen R. Lane. New York: Viking, 1977.

Freud, Sigmund. *Three Essays on the Theory of Sexuality.* Trans. and ed. James Strachey. London: Hogarth Press, 1962.

Freud, Sigmund. "The Dissolution of the Oedipus Complex." In *Standard Edition of the Complete Psychological Works of Sigmund Freud,* vol. 19. Trans. James Strachey. London: Hogarth Press and Institute of Psycho-Analysis, 1974.

Ortigues, Marie Cécile, and Edmond Ortigues. *Oedipe Africain.* Paris: Librairie Plon, 1966.

ONTOLOGY. Literally translated as "the science of being," ontology refers to that branch of METAPHYSICS that deals with the study of existence itself, rather than the nature of existence of any particular object. Ontology concerns itself with distinguishing between "real existence" and "appearance" (*noumena* and *phenomena*), and with the ways that entities within disparate logical categories—numbers, objects, abstractions, etc.—may be said and known to exist. In a more particular sense, ontology may refer to a specific theory of being; thus, one may speak of Kant's or Plato's, or Heidegger's ontology. See also EPISTEMOLOGY, METAPHYSICS, PHENOMENOLOGY.

ORGANICISM. Organicism is an IDEALIST theory of texts which holds that a work is like a living organism in that it is autonomous, self-contained, and complexly organized around interdependent parts, none of which is greater than the whole. The work grows from its conception in the artistic imagination, obeying intrinsic laws and deriving its form from its own nature. Samuel Coleridge distinguishes between organic and mechanical forms. While mechanical form derives from extrinsic, predetermined forces, organic form is innate: "It shapes, as it develops, itself from within, and the fullness of its development is one and the same with the perfection of its outward form." The preferred metaphor for such organic development is indicated by Cleanth Brooks, who relates parts of a poem to the parts of a growing plant. Herein lies a justification for the close reading techniques of New Criticism: every detail of a text becomes significant, if, like a living plant, a text functions as a result of the interaction of its constituent components.

The notion of organicism has its first reference in Plato's *Phaedrus* when Socrates compares speech to a living organism. Later the concept became particularly popular with the English and German romantics as well as with Henry James, Benedetto Croce, and the New Critics. See also NEW CRITICISM.

ORIENTALISM. Although the term *Orientalism* originally referred in neutral fashion to the study of Eastern cultures and the use of Eastern themes and effects in the arts, it has more recently acquired pejorative implications following the publication of Edward Said's *Orientalism* in 1978. For Said, Orientalism is a DISCOURSE about the East, constructed by the West, which has functioned as an instrument of power by supporting first the enterprise of COLONIALISM itself and later the paternalist privileges still often assumed by Western writers when writing about the East. Thus, the characteristic tactic of Orientalism is to divide the world into "Orient" and "Occident" in order to make essentialist statements about the former (see ESSENTIALISM). These include such familiar stereotypes as the "unchanging" or historyless quality of the Orient, the inevitable corruption or despotism of Eastern political regimes, the predatory sexuality of Arabs, and the "femininity" of Eastern exoticism. See also POSTCOLONIALISM, SUBALTERN.

Clifford, James. "On Orientalism." *The Predicament of Culture: Twentieth-Century Ethnography, Literature, and Art.* Cambridge, Mass.: Harvard University Press, 1988.
Said, Edward. *Orientalism.* New York: Pantheon, 1978.

OTHER. In Lacanian psychoanalytic theory, which argues that individuals (SUBJECTS) are constructed through the acquisition of the power to express desires and needs through language, the Other is the ultimate signifier of everyone the subject is not, as well as everything the subject does not have. For Lacan, the discovery of the Other parallels the acquisition of the abilities to speak and to distinguish between *I* and *you*, which are tantamount to the acquisition of social identity. In the earliest stages of human existence, before language is acquired, the infant has no awareness of the difference between itself and anyone or anything else; it is unaware of the "relations between objects." Eventually the infant learns that desired people and things have constancy; they are not gone (*fort*) but have gone somewhere else—they go "there" (*da*) and so can be regained by asking for them (see Freud's discussion of the *fort/da* game in *Beyond the Pleasure Principle*). To a greater degree than Freud, Lacan believed that drives are from the very earliest moments of life worked out through interaction with the Other. In a more general and older sense, the phrase *the Other* has long been used by philosophers and social scientists to refer to anyone who is not I—the Other actually *defines* me because it is the ultimate signifier of everything I am not. Because the PHALLOGOCENTRISM and EUROCENTRISM of Western philosophy and other cultural discourses are so entrenched, the Other has often been defined as "Woman" or African or Asian—and hence the Other is what is feared, what exists to be conquered. As Simone de Beauvoir puts it in *The Second Sex*, "She [woman] is defined and differentiated with reference to man, not he with reference to her; she is the incidental, the inessential as opposed to the essential. He is the Subject, he is the Absolute—she is the Other. The category of the Other is as primordial as consciousness itself."

(It should be noted that de Beauvoir herself was familiar with Lacan's early work in this area.) See also OBJECT RELATIONS.

de Beauvoir, Simone. *The Second Sex.* Trans. H. M. Parshley. New York: Knopf, 1952.

Freud, Sigmund. *Beyond the Pleasure Principle..* Rev. ed. Trans. and ed. James Strachey. New York: Liveright, 1961.

Lacan, Jacques. "The Subject and the Other: Alienation." In *Four Fundamental Concepts.* Trans. Alan Sheridan, ed. Jacques-Alain Miller. New York: Norton, 1978.

OVERDETERMINATION. Overdetermination is a concept of causality introduced by Sigmund Freud, who explained that a single symptom or dream can be the product of more than one determining factor (see CONDENSATION). In contemporary criticism, however, the psychoanalytic origins of the concept are overshadowed by its use in the social sciences, and especially in the Marxism of Louis Althusser. For Althusser, historical change is not the product of developments in the economic base reflected in mechanical fashion by the superstructure, as more traditional Marxists have often maintained. Rather, Althusser argued that, like a dream, a given historical moment is the site of a multiplicity of forces, of which the economic is only determining "in the last instance." While the economic sets limits within which the political and ideological are obliged to operate, all of these levels enjoy a relative autonomy, so that large-scale change occurs only through the overlapping actions of a multiplicity of historical forces. See also LITERARY MODE OF PRODUCTION, MODE OF PRODUCTION.

Althusser, Louis. "Contradiction and Overdetermination." In *For Marx.* Trans. Ben Brewster. New York: Pantheon, 1969.

Freud, Sigmund. *The Interpretation of Dreams.* Trans. and ed. James Strachey. London: Hogarth Press, 1953.

P

PAINTERLY. In the broadest sense, the term *painterly* is used to describe paintings where the application of the paint itself comes to the fore—

where the strokes of the brush or (later) the marks of the palette knife or drips of paint are visible in the finished work. More specifically, Heinrich Wölfflin used the terms *linear* and *painterly* to distinguish between various historical and regional styles that developed during the Renaissance and baroque periods. According to his distinction, works characterized as linear depend more on drawing, with color used primarily to separate one form from another, whereas in a painterly work, the forms are less precisely separated from one another and the effect of the work is inextricably linked to the way that the paint has been applied to the surface.

Podro, Michael. *The Critical Historians of Art.* New Haven: Yale University Press, 1982.
Wölfflin, Heinrich. *Principles of Art History: The Problem of the Development of Style in Later Art.* Trans. M. D. Hottinger. New York: Dover, 1950.

PALIMPSEST. A term used by Sandra Gilbert and Susan Gubar, *palimpsest* describes the two levels—one overt, the other obscured—which in their view distinguish nineteenth-century women's writing. A palimpsest is literally a parchment from which writing has been partially or completely erased to make room for another text. Anxious about their ability to enter a patrilineal literary tradition, angry about their exclusion from this tradition, and afraid to express their anxiety and anger openly, writers like Emily Dickinson and Charlotte Brontë buried these taboo feelings beneath ostensibly conventional "cover stories." The result is that "surface designs conceal or obscure deeper, less socially acceptable levels of meaning." The surface heterosexual romance of *Jane Eyre*, for example, is commented on and undercut by the deeper, more dangerous story of Bertha Mason's insane rage. Gilbert and Gubar's notion of textual duplicity as a mark of female writing is akin to Nancy Miller's suggestion that women both reproduce conventional narratives and, at the same time, add a defiant "emphasis" of their own. It is also consistent with Elaine Showalter's location of women within a double cultural zone, where women's culture and the dominant culture overlap. Though Gilbert and Gubar have been criticized for implying that the underlying, feminist narrative is the only "real" one, their attempt to expose concealed, subversive meanings in women's texts has proven an enormously fruitful method for Anglo-American feminist critics. See also ANXIETY OF AUTHORSHIP, DOUBLE-VOICED TEXT, WILD ZONE.

Gilbert, Sandra M., and Susan Gubar. *The Madwoman in the Attic: The Woman Writer and the Nineteenth-Century Literary Imagination.* New Haven: Yale University Press, 1979.

Miller, Nancy K. "Emphasis Added: Plots and Plausibilities in Women's Fiction." In Elaine Showalter, ed., *The New Feminist Criticism.* New York: Pantheon, 1985.

PARADIGM. *Paradigm* has accumulated a number of special uses in contemporary theory. Most generally, it refers to a pattern or model. Since T. S. Kuhn's *The Structure of Scientific Revolutions*, it has taken on a meaning analogous to Michel Foucault's use of the term DISCOURSE: a system of beliefs and practices that establish the conditions of possibility for thought, speech, and action. In STRUCTURALIST theory, however, *paradigm* has come to designate a set of linguistic or other units that can be substituted for each other in the same position within a sequence. For instance, all words with the same grammatical function may constitute a paradigm, since replacing one with another has no effect on the syntax of a particular utterance. In the sentence, "My dog is savage," the noun "dog" may be replaced by the noun "piano" without changing the sentence's syntax in the least. This "vertical axis" of language is one of the two relationships a SIGN has to other signs. Its paradigmatic relationship is to other signs of the same class, which are absent in a given utterance. The other relationship is the syntagmatic, or sequential relationship of signs to each other. The term SYNTAGM designates the combination of these signs (usually words) in a meaningful order. This sentence, for example, is a syntagm. The syntagmatic is the "horizontal" axis of language. The paradigmatic/syntagmatic distinction corresponds to the metonymy (horizontal)/metaphor (vertical) contrast in analyses of figurative language. See also METAPHOR, METONYMY, PROBLEMATIC.

PARADOX. A paradox is a statement that seems to be self-contradictory or absurd but that provokes us into seeing how in one sense it could be true. Good examples of paradox abound in the poetry of the seventeenth-century writer, John Donne, who fashioned much of his poetry around paradoxes. For instance, in his sonnet "Batter My Heart. . . ," he writes to God:

> *Take me to you, imprison me, for I*
> *Except you enthrall me, never shall be free,*
> *Nor ever chaste, except you ravish me.*

Paradox was at one time considered a figure of speech, but modern critics have elevated it to a mode of understanding employed by poetry to challenge our usual habits of thought. Paradox was an especially important concern for the NEW CRITICS, who were instrumental in arguing for its epistemological importance. In his book *The Well Wrought Urn*, Cleanth Brooks claims that "the language of poetry is the language of paradox." Recent POSTSTRUCTURALIST theories of language and literature such as DECONSTRUCTION have contributed to the centrality of paradox, arguing that all uses of language ultimately disseminate themselves into unresolvable paradoxes or APORIA.

PAROLE. See LANGUE/PAROLE.

PART-OBJECT. This term designates an object that becomes the focus of one of the most fundamental or "component" INSTINCTS (oral, anal, etc.). Although the part-object is usually a part of the body, such as the breast or penis, a person can be identified or identify him or herself with a part-object (see IDENTIFICATION), and part-object love is seen by some theorists as a stage of psychosexual development. Moreover, in the work of Melanie Klein and her followers, part-objects may take on human qualities, such as benevolence or malevolence. See also FETISH, FIXATION, INFANTILE SEXUALITY.

Freud, Sigmund. *Three Essays on the Theory of Sexuality*. Trans. and ed. James Strachey. London: Hogarth Press, 1962.
—. "Fetishism." In *Standard Edition of the Complete Psychological Works of Sigmund Freud*, vol. 21. Trans. James Strachey. London: Hogarth Press and Institute of Psycho-Analysis, 1974.
Klein, Melanie. *Contributions to Psycho-analysis 1921–1945*. London: Hogarth Press, 1950.

PASTICHE. The concept of pastiche refers to the imitation of various styles without the sense of comic discrepancy that one finds in parody. As such, pastiche is a peculiarly postmodern species of "blank parody." The term has attained wide currency in discussions of POSTMODERN culture, in large part through the influence of Fredric Jameson's essay "Postmodernism and Consumer Society." According to Jameson, pastiche is what becomes of parody in an age in which the idea of a self-generated style has become a thing of the past. The great practitioners of modernism were all in one way or another creators of distinctive personal styles, which could be imitated and thus implicitly made fun of. In the post-modern age, however, social life has become fragmented to the point where this previously AVANT-GARDE practice has become the condition of society as a whole; so with the absence of a stable point of reference or concept of the *normal,* there can be no parody. In its place is this new form of non-parody or pastiche.

Jameson, Fredric. "Postmodernism and Consumer Society." In Hal Foster, ed., *The Anti-Aesthetic: Essays on Postmodern Culture.* Port Townsend, Wash.: Bay Press, 1983.

PATHETIC FALLACY. The pathetic fallacy is a literary convention in which human emotional qualities are attributed to natural phenomena that have no capacity for human feeling. Thus, the sky may "cry" or rain clouds "glower in anger." The term was coined by John Ruskin in volume 3 of his influential work *Modern Painters* (1856). For Ruskin, the overuse of this convention by the romantics, especially Shelley and Wordsworth, tended toward "morbidity" and distinguished them from poets of the first rank, like Shakespeare, who used it much less frequently. Although employed evaluatively by Ruskin, later critics have abandoned its pejorative sense and use it descriptively.

Ruskin, John. *Modern Painters.* 5 vols. London: Smith, Elder, 1856–1860.

PATRIARCHY. *Patriarchy* describes the systematic domination of women by men, achieved and maintained through male control of cultural, social, and economic institutions. Under patriarchy, attributes associated with men are valued, while those termed "feminine" are denigrated, and this value system is usually defended as the "natural" consequence of human biology. Long used in the social sciences to describe societies organized by male privilege and descent, the term is central to contemporary feminist analyses, in which it has been used with varying degrees of specificity.

Friedrich Engels, in *The Origin of the Family, Private Property and the State* (1884), suggested that patriarchy began with the emergence of private property and subsequent treatment of women as such. Simone de Beauvoir's *The Second Sex* (1949) went beyond Engels to explain that, under patriarchy, women are regarded as the OTHER, while men represent the "human." But the term did not gain general currency until the late 1960s, when radical feminists identified patriarchy as the structural basis of women's oppression, separate from, though working in concert with, the structures of capitalism, racism, imperialism, etc. In 1970, for example, Kate Millett's *Sexual Politics* argued that patriarchy derives authority from its universality (making it appear inevitable) and that it enforces this authority through institutionalized violence against women. In one of the earliest pieces of feminist criticism, Millett went on to link these assertions to depictions of violence against women in novels by D. H. Lawrence, Henry Miller, and Norman Mailer. Before the 1970s were over, however, some feminists had already begun to object that the notion of patriarchy was insufficiently complex and lacking in historical and cultural specificity. Gayle Rubin suggested that patriarchy be seen as only one possible "sex/gender system," and this framework helped to prevent the assumption that patriarchy is unchanging, that it takes the same form everywhere, and that it precludes other systems of oppression. The result has been to encourage more careful and specific uses of a term that continues to retain much of its original force. See also ANDROCENTRIC, RADICAL FEMINISM.

de Beauvoir, Simone. *The Second Sex.* Trans. H. M. Parshley. New York: Knopf, 1952.

Engels, Friedrich. *The Origin of the Family, Private Property, and the State.* Trans. Ernest Unterman. Chicago: Charles Kerr, 1902.

Millett, Kate. *Sexual Politics.* New York: Avon, 1970.

Rubin, Gayle. "The Traffic in Women: Notes on the 'Political Economy' of Sex." In Rayna R. Reiter, ed., *Toward an Anthropology of Women.* New York: Monthly Review Press, 1975.

PENIS ENVY. See CASTRATION COMPLEX.

PERFORMATIVE UTTERANCE. J. L. Austin's SPEECH ACT THEORY distinguishes between CONSTATIVE UTTERANCES (those statements that describe a state of affairs and may be either true or false) and performative utterances, which perform the action they describe. The statement "I promise not to be late," for instance, is performative and by saying it the speaker actually makes a promise. Austin categorizes such statements as performative utterances because the promise is implied. Austin further argues that even statements like "The cat is on the mat"—traditionally considered constative—are in fact performative; the speaker accomplishes the act of affirming that statement. The constative is therefore one special case of the performative. Although Austin's theory of speech acts critiques the older LOGOCENTRIC view that only constative statements are meaningful, Derrida criticizes Austin for his own logocentrism. Austin's scheme, Derrida argues, is itself logocentric when it must exclude "nonserious" statements (such as jokes and poems) because they do not actually perform an act; eventually Austin would have to know the speaker's intention to distinguish between serious and nonserious statements. See also ILLOCUTIONARY ACT, PERLOCUTIONARY ACT.

Austin, J. L. *How to Do Things with Words.* Cambridge, Mass.: Harvard University Press, 1962.
Culler, Jonathan. *On Deconstruction: Theory and Criticism after Structuralism.* Ithaca, N.Y.: Cornell University Press, 1982.

PERLOCUTIONARY ACT. In J. L. Austin's SPEECH ACT THEORY, a perlocutionary act is one of the three possible types or forces of utterance. When, by the performance of a locutionary and illocutionary act, a speech act has an effect (such as persuading or convincing), Austin considers it to be perlocutionary. If one were to say, "I would like to thank you for your help" (in itself a locutionary act), the statement has both an illocutionary force (one performs the act of thanking) and a perlocutionary force (one may convince another of the genuineness of the gratitude). See also CONSTATIVE UTTERANCE, ILLOCUTIONARY ACT, PERFORMATIVE UTTERANCE.

Austin, J. L. *How to Do Things with Words.* Cambridge, Mass.: Harvard University Press, 1962.
Pratt, Mary Louise. *Toward a Speech Act Theory of Literary Discourse.* Bloomington: Indiana University Press, 1977.

PERSPECTIVISM. *Perspectivism* is a term employed by E. D. Hirsch to describe the theory that interpretation varies in relation to the vantage point of the interpreter. As a hermeneutical model, it claims that individuals view literary texts from their own peculiar angle of vision and are in fact prisoners of their perspective. The result, according to Hirsch, is a modern form of hermeneutical skepticism that rejects the possibility of correct interpretation. Because all interpretations are perspective-laden, conflicting interpretations are equally correct but also equally incorrect. All interpretation therefore becomes misinterpretation. Hirsch condemns perspectivism for sanctioning relativism (particularly cultural, historical, and methodological relativism) and for "proclaiming the irreproducibility of original meaning." See also HERMENEUTICS, HISTORICISM.

Hirsch, E. D. *The Aims of Interpretation.* Chicago: University of Chicago Press, 1976.

PETRIFICATION. Petrification is a process of history by which radical or innovative forces of language are vitrified by succumbing to the institutionalized conventions and norms that they originally attempted to remedy. Through time even the most disruptive meanings are ultimately contained and reduced to fixed sites of truth, thus assigning them to "their place in history." In *Writing Degree Zero*, Roland Barthes illustrates how history persistently neutralizes all the attempts of writing to be "free of any servitude to a marked order of language." Even an innovative writer like Camus will be reduced to a formula over time: "The writer, attaining the status of a classic, becomes the imitator of his early creation; society makes a mannerism of his writing and returns him a prisoner of his own formal myth."

For Barthes, petrification is avoided by suspending closure of meaning through such disruptive devices as irony, paradox, or the self-abandonment of critical hedonism (JOUISSANCE). In the case of signification, freedom from petrification involves a continual movement away from fixed denotation toward the unceasing play of connotation.

Barthes, Roland. *Writing Degree Zero.* Trans. Annette Lavers and Colin Smith. London: Cape, 1967.

PHALLOCENTRISM. Coined on analogy with ETHNOCENTRISM, phallocentrism (FALoSENTRIZUM) names the belief that the male is superior to the female or, more generally, the belief that what is male is a legitimate, universally applicable point of reference for all things human. Another sense is conveyed in the following quotation from the American feminist Ann Rosalind Jones, who summarizes the phallocentric position: " 'I am the unified, self-controlled center of the universe,' man (white, European and ruling class) has claimed. 'The rest of the world, which I define as the Other, has meaning only in relation to me, as man/father, possessor of the phallus.' " A classic example of phallocentrism is Freud's use of the term "phallic stage" to refer to that period in the development of infantile sexuality when the child's libido is focused on the genitals. Because girls do not have a penis, feminists have argued, their sexuality is not fairly generalized in relation to the phallus (the symbolic representation of the penis). There is some debate over who first used the term; most sources cite Jacques Derrida, and it is certainly the French feminists influenced by his work who first centralized its usage. It has been used very generally to describe, critically, any male/masculine bias. See also LOGOCENTRISM, PHALLOGOCENTRISM.

Jones, Ann Rosalind. "Writing the Body: Toward an Understanding of *l'écriture féminine*." In Judith Newton and Deborah Rosenfelt, eds., *Feminist Criticism and Social Change*. New York: Methuen, 1985.

PHALLOGOCENTRISM. *Phallogocentrism* (FALogoSENtrizum) is a portmanteau word combining PHALLOCENTRISM and LOGOCENTRISM, and was coined to describe how patriarchal assumptions are so deeply embedded in existing languages that women (those denied access to the symbolic and real power of the PHALLUS) have no independent existence that can be expressed in language. Phallogocentric language excludes women from the category of the universal, so that "man" is synonymous with "human" (see HUMANISM). Just as logocentrism emphasizes the extent to which metaphysical assumptions about the superiority of speech over writing are built into language itself, phallogocentrism implies that masculine biases are similarly inseparable from linguistic conventions, and that these biases are profoundly related to the structures of METAPHYSICS. Thus, in a much-quoted passage, Jonathan Culler has written that "phallogocentrism unites an interest in patriarchal authority, unity of meaning, and certainty of origin." The distinguishing characteristics of phallogocentric discourse are usually said to be linearity and ego orientation, and are sometimes contrasted to a "feminine" language, which is said to be community-oriented and less structured (see ÉCRITURE FEMININE). More narrowly, the term has often been used to describe conventionally "masculine" languages, such as those of the sciences, philosophy, and high art.

Culler, Jonathan. *On Deconstruction: Theory and Criticism after Structuralism.* Ithaca, N.Y.: Cornell University Press, 1982.

Kristeva, Julia. "La femme, ce n'est jamais ça." In Elaine Marks and Isabelle de Courtivron, eds., *New French Feminisms.* Amherst: University of Massachusetts Press, 1980.

PHALLUS. The word *phallus* (FALus) can simply mean "penis," but it is more commonly used as a term for the representation of the penis. The phallus is taken by some to be the most important symbol in Western, if not global, culture. Because it can represent just about anything, deconstructionists have called the phallus the "universal signifier." It has been associated with male sexuality, the authority and power of men (especially that which they wield over women), authority and power in general, individuality, any kind of unity, God, and life itself. A "phallic symbol" is something that looks like a representation of a penis (i.e., a tall building, a cigar), and so also carries connotations of (male) power. See also PHALLOCENTRISM, PHALLOGOCENTRISM.

PHARMAKON. *Pharmakon* (FARmuhKAHN) is a Greek term with multiple contradictory meanings such as drug, medicine, remedy, cure, poison, charm, potion. Associated with the works of Plato and with Derrida's "La Pharmacie de Platon," *pharmakon* belongs to a family of terms (PHARMAKOS, *pharmakeus*) whose contradictory force Derrida employs to reveal the phenomenon of DIFFÉRANCE. *Pharmakon* evinces the underlying logic of discourse in the same manner as Derrida's other pivotal terms such as SUPPLEMENT, *hymen*, or *dissemination*. Specifically, in Plato's *Phaedrus*, writing is referred to as pharmakon, that is, as a cure or remedy for forgetfulness, but as Socrates illustrates, it is also a dangerous drug. As a double-edged word, pharmakon provides the textual moment in Plato when binary logic is visibly subverted by the logic of both/and. Pharmakon as both remedy and poison resembles writing and speech as they evoke the condition and play of difference.

PHARMAKOS. *Pharmakos* (FARmuhKOS) is the Greek word for scapegoat. Traditionally, the term refers to a particular type of stock character, the arbitrarily chosen victim whose sacrifice has a purging effect upon a community. In Derrida's "La Pharmacie de Platon," it is associated with

Plato's term for writing, PHARMAKON, in order to illustrate the logic of signification and the condition of difference. In the same way that the scapegoat is expelled to purify the community, so, too, Plato would expel writing in order to purify speech. As a representative remedy for evil, the expelled pharmakos must be chosen from within the community, thus clarifying and insuring the difference between good and evil, between pure internal and corrupt external realms. But this distinction can only be maintained if the evil or corrupt is always already within the good and pure community. Similarly, the expulsion of writing is purifying only if writing is always already inscribed within speech. *Pharmakos* thus joins the ranks of such Derridean terms as DIFFÉRANCE, SUPPLEMENT, and TRACE. See also DECONSTRUCTION.

PHENOMENOLOGICAL CRITICISM. See PHENOMENOLOGY.

PHENOMENOLOGY. As a philosophical method, phenomenology (fuhNAHMuhNAHLuhjee) was developed and promulgated by the German philosopher Edmund Husserl (1859–1938). Husserl's primary investigative interest was in analyzing human consciousness as "lived experience," or LEBENSWELT, independent of any prior assumptions, whether commonsensical or philosophical. For Husserl, human consciousness was a unified act that is dependent upon an interrelation between the thinking, perceiving SUBJECT and an OBJECT that is perceived. Thus, for Husserl, human consciousness means to be conscious of *something*. In order to analyze this activity phenomenologically, it is necessary for the investigator to suspend any presumptions about the nature of perception and to postpone or "bracket" conclusions as to whether the object perceived exists external to the consciousness of the perceiving subject; that is, whether it exists in what is commonly called "reality" or in the consciousness of the subject. Unlike ONTOLOGY, which is primarily concerned with the nature of existence of all objects, subjects, and abstractions, phenomenology focuses on the ways in which these things are perceived and informed by human consciousness.

Phenomenology exerted considerable influence on a number of mid-twentieth-century continental philosophers, most notably Martin Heidegger and Maurice Merleau-Ponty. It has also had an important effect on the works of theorists like Hans Georg Gadamer and Roman Ingarden, and its precepts have become fundamental to READER-RESPONSE theorists such as Hans Robert Jauss and Wolfgang Iser. Ingarden's theories have been especially formative. For him, the literary work begins with the author's intentional acts of consciousness. Ingarden borrows the term *intentional* from Husserl, and by it he does not mean "willed." Rather, he is referring to the consciousness as it is aware of and open to some object or objects (see INTENTIONALITY). The author's record of these conscious acts is the TEXT, which allows a reader to re-experience the work in his or her own consciousness. The text, however, is only schematic, full of a number of "potential" rather than fully realized elements. These are "places of indeterminancy," which an active reading completes and thus "co-creates" with the author what Ingarden calls a "concretized" work.

The group of literary theorists with whom phenomenological criticism is most closely associated are known as the GENEVA SCHOOL, after the University of Geneva, where most of them were faculty members during the 1950s and 1960s. This group includes Jean Starobinski, Jean-Pierre Richard, Marcel Raymond, and Georges Poulet, the most renowned of the group. They were closely associated with a number of non-Geneva-based theorists and critics, notably Gaston Bachelard, Maurice Blanchot, and Jean-Paul Sartre. J. Hillis Miller, who later became a leading proponent of DECONSTRUCTION and one of the YALE SCHOOL, gained distinction in the early years of his career as the most famous American phenomenological critic. His 1959 *Charles Dickens: The World of His Novels* is an excellent example of the phenomenological method. The Geneva critics held that an author's consciousness is the informing element in the creation of the fictional world of a literary work of art. By putting aside, or "bracketing," all prior assumptions about the author, it is possible to become a pure, passive receiver of the text and thus eventually to identify—one might even say merge—with the author's consciousness. Because of this preoccupation with identifying with an individual author's consciousness—as opposed to Husserl's attempts to characterize the nature of human consciousness common to all—the members of the Geneva school were sometimes referred to as critics of consciousness. Although some remnants of phenomenological criticism remain in the HERMENEUTICS of Gadamer and much reader-response criticism and REZEPTIONSÄSTHETIK, many of these assumptions have been opposed by the POSTSTRUCTURAL-IST thought of Jacques Derrida, Roland Barthes, and Michel Foucault, among others. See also AUTHOR, AUTHOR FUNCTION.

Bachelard, Gaston. *The Poetics of Space*. Trans. Maria Jolas. New York: Orion Press, 1964.

Blanchot, Maurice. *The Space of Literature*. Trans. Ann Smock. Lincoln: University of Nebraska Press, 1982.

Derrida, Jacques. *Speech and Phenomena, and Other Essays on Husserl's Theory of Signs*. Trans. David B. Allison. Evanston, Ill.: Northwestern University Press, 1973.

Lawall, Sarah. *Critics of Consciousness: The Existential Structures of Literature*. Cambridge, Mass.: Harvard University Press, 1968.

Magliola, Robert R. *Phenomenology and Literature*. West Lafayette, Ind.: Purdue University Press, 1977.

Poulet, Georges. *The Interior Distance*. Trans. Elliott Coleman. Ann Arbor: University of Michigan Press, 1964.

—. *Proustian Space*. Trans. Elliott Coleman. Baltimore: Johns Hopkins University Press, 1977.

PICTORIALISM. Pictorialism is used most frequently to describe a certain type of painted expression—"artistic" landscapes, views, etc.—and its impact in other media. The prime example is pictorial photography, which was a style of photography prevalent in the late nineteenth century that attempted to duplicate the aesthetics of painting in the artistic photograph. In photography, pictorialism was increasingly rejected by twentieth-century photographers, who were interested in using the camera to achieve effects not possible in painting.

PLAY. The idea that play is a characteristic of life that precedes all rational, cultural, and, indeed, human structures has had considerable influence in contemporary thought, beginning with the Dutch philosopher Johan Huizinga's influential book *Homo Ludens* (1938). Noting that play is not exclusive to the human species, Huizinga analyzed it as fundamental to a wide range of cultural activities; and this "ludic" emphasis, which derives from the tradition of Kantian aesthetics, is apparent in the work of such later thinkers as the philosopher Kostas Axelos, the anthropologist Roger Caillois, and the psychologist Jean Piaget. More recently, various forms of POSTSTRUCTURALIST thought have celebrated the disruptive or anarchic aspects of play as an antidote to the repressive or coercive qualities of language and dominant cultural institutions. Versions of this position appear, for example, in Jacques Derrida's insistence that the "play" of language undermines any attempt to assign a determinate meaning to a text (see DECONSTRUCTION, DIFFÉRANCE), as well as in the concept of the CARNIVALESQUE, which is closely identified with the work of Mikhail Bakhtin and his contemporary followers. Moreover, some gay critics have adopted a version of the concept to describe the liberating effects of the play of gender identities within subcultural groups (see CAMP).

Huizinga, Johan. *Homo Ludens*. Boston: Beacon Press, 1950.

PLEASURE PRINCIPLE. According to Freud, the psychic apparatus is governed by two principles: the pleasure principle, which directs the individual toward pleasure and away from unpleasure, and the reality principle, which regulates the search for pleasure by compelling the individual to approach it in ways that are compatible with the conditions imposed by his or her environment. In the economic scheme that Freud used to explain mental functioning, unpleasure results from an increase of psychic tension, so that the pleasure principle seeks above all the reduction of tension—although Freud came to recognize considerable complications in this scheme. Some of these arise from the doubts he entertained on the question of whether the reality principle is driven by a separate group of self-preservative instincts, or whether, as he eventually came to feel, these latter are merely part of a larger group of LIFE INSTINCTS, which include the instincts of both pleasure and self-preservation and are opposed to the DEATH INSTINCTS. Yet even this does not answer all the questions, for if pleasure is defined as a reduction of tension, potentially even to the zero degree, then it appears to have something in common with the death instincts or "nirvana principle," which strive to return the organism to just such an inorganic state. With these considerations in mind, Freud pointed out that in fact some pleasurable tensions do exist; in this view, pleasure is more appropriately related to the perpetuation of a constant level of tension or "principle of constancy," a concept that is present in his work from very early on. The question remains open, however; and Freud does not discount the possibility that the pleasure principle ultimately serves the death instincts.

Freud, Sigmund. *Beyond the Pleasure Principle*. Rev. ed. Trans. and ed. James Strachey. New York: Liveright, 1961.
—. "Two Principles of Mental Functioning." In *Standard Edition of the Complete Psychological Works of Sigmund Freud*, vol. Trans. James Strachey. London: Hogarth Press and Institute of Psycho-Analysis, 1974.

PLOT. *Plot* refers to the ordered presentation, or pattern, of events in prose or verse drama and narrative. Although this definition is almost universally applicable, specific uses of the term often carry additional connotations. Much of the confusion over the precise meaning of plot derives from crucial but frequently ignored distinctions between *plot*, STORY, and *incident*, three related but distinct terms that are sometimes used interchangeably. We can distinguish between these terms by comparing narrative and drama to a string of beads: the constituent "incidents" are the individual beads; the story is the string; and the plot is the order and method by which the beads are strung. Examples of the way that the same incidents may be arranged in two different orders or manners to tell the same story pervade history and literature. One of the most widely used illustrations is the story of Christ's birth and life: Jewish, Christian, and atheist writers tell the same story with different sets of emphases and, therefore, meanings.

Since the time of the Greek tragedies (4th century B.C.) Aristotle's *Poetics* has served as the principal source for critical and popular thinking about plot, which has been commonly—but not always correctly—understood to be identical with Aristotle's term *mythos*. Explicit in Aristotle's definition are concepts of plot as the representation of actions (MIMESIS) that are 1) *whole* and 2) *unified* by patterns of causality. Every plot has a proper shape or form: its *wholeness* is constituted by a beginning, middle, and end; its *unity* by the revelation of causes that link the end to the middle and the middle to the beginning.

Later critics as diverse as Samuel Taylor Coleridge, Henri Beyle (Stendhal), Henry James, E. M. Forster, and Vladimir Propp adopt and emphasize different aspects of the Aristotelian definition. For James, the representation of life or mimesis is the essence of plot and the distinction between plot and story is superfluous: "I cannot see what is meant by talking as if there were a part of a novel which is the story and part of it which for mystical reasons is not." On the other hand, Forster emphasizes causality: "The plot, then, is the novel in its logical intellectual aspect." The novelist "plans his book beforehand: or anyhow he stands above it, his interest in cause and effect give him an air of predetermination." By contrast, Propp emphasizes story and argues that narratives and drama "possess a particular construction which is immediately felt and which determines their category, even though we may not be aware of it."

In recent critical writings, the meaning of the term *plot* has become more stable. Working within the traditions of RUSSIAN FORMALISM and FRENCH STRUCTURALISM, critics such as Tzvetan Todorov and Gérard

Genette now make fairly consistent distinctions between story (what happens in a narrative or a drama) and plot (the presentation of events). See also FABULA/SUJET, NARRATOLOGY.

Aristotle. *Poetics*. Trans. Leon Golden; commentary O. B. Hardison. Englewood Cliffs, N.J.: Prentice Hall, 1968.

Brooks, Peter. *Reading for the Plot*. New York: Knopf, 1985.

Forster, E. M. *Aspects of the Novel*. New York: Harcourt Brace and World, 1954.

James, Henry. *The Future of the Novel: Essays on the Art of Fiction*. New York: Oxford University Press, 1948.

Propp, Vladimir. *Morphology of the Folktale*. 2d ed. Trans. Laurence Scott, ed. Louis A. Wagner. Austin: University of Texas Press, 1968.

PLURALISM. Pluralism is best described as a cultural attitude or ideology, closely associated with liberal HUMANISM, that upholds the democratic principle of allowing all points of view to be heard in a discussion. In the humanities, pluralism is at least nominally the official policy of the secular university, which aims to provide a home for all worthy forms of learning. Yet pluralism is often a frequent target of attacks from both the right, which sees it as standing suspiciously close to relativism, and the left, which argues variously that pluralism assumes an equality among points of view that does not exist in practice, and that it excludes certain points of view beforehand by defining the terms of the discussion in such a way as to render them illegitimate.

POLITICAL UNCONSCIOUS. *The Political Unconscious* is the title of Fredric Jameson's most influential book of Marxist literary criticism and refers to his contention that even the most apparently apolitical modern works of literature possess a political content, which exists beneath the surface of the text like the Freudian UNCONSCIOUS. The psychoanalytic term is, however, somewhat misleading in this context; for Jameson's idea is derived primarily from the Hegelian notion that the TOTALITY exists in each of its individual parts.

Jameson, Fredric. *The Political Unconscious: Narrative as a Socially Symbolic Act*. Ithaca, N.Y.: Cornell University Press, 1981.

POLYMORPHOUS PERVERSITY. The concept of polymorphous perversity (PAHLeeMORfuhs perVERsitee) has its origins in the later writings of Sigmund Freud, who describes the earliest stages of psychic growth as characterized by a state of "primary narcissism" (see NARCISSISM). At this point in the infant's development, its sexual feelings are not focused on any particular organ, but rather infuse the whole of its world, which is not perceived as distinct in any way from its body or EGO—indeed, the state of primary narcissism precedes the emergence of any distinction between ego and ID, and any direction of desire toward an object (see PREOEDIPAL). This concept of a polymorphous sexuality became a focus of interest in the work of the German Marxist philosopher Herbert Marcuse, especially the highly influential *Eros and Civilization* (1955), which argues that in a nonrepressive society the human body would no longer be needed mainly as an instrument of labor. Freed from the capitalist demand always to increase production, it would also escape the yoke of genital dominance and be resexualized in its entirety, opening the way to an eroticization of work, which would become inseparable from individual need. In recent years, this argument has been strongly criticized for its romantic idealism (Schiller is one of Marcuse's regular points of reference), and more recent writers have tended to emphasize the impossibility of any such return to an earlier state that presupposes a utopian escape from existing cultural forms.

Freud, Sigmund. *The Ego and the Id.* Trans. Joan Riviere, ed. James Strachey. New York: Norton, 1960.
Marcuse, Herbert. *Eros and Civilization: A Philosophical Inquiry into Freud.* Boston: Beacon, 1966.

POLYSEMY. In linguistics, *polysemy* (**PAHL**ee**SEE**mee) refers to a word's ability to denote two or more distinct meanings. For example, *field* may mean to catch or handle (as in to field a ground ball or field a question), or it may refer to an expanse of land. In recent years, many theorists have posited that all SIGNS are polysemous (or polysemic) and that the term can also be applied to entire texts.

POSITIVISM. Positivism is a philosophy of knowledge concerned with verifiable empirical facts as opposed to metaphysical ideas. It eschews IDEALISM in favor of the methods and principles of the natural sciences, substituting description of observable phenomena for explanation, asking the question how rather than why. As a philosophical movement, it originated with Auguste Comte in the mid-nineteenth century. Positivist literary scholarship was characterized by its genetic approach, the study of texts in relation to their observable historical causes, such as the author's biography, sources, statements of intention, and cultural context. Hippolyte Taine, an early proponent of literary positivism, attempted a naive form of scientific history by arguing that the genesis of any literary text could be traced to "la race, le milieu et le moment." The net result of the positivist approach was to deemphasize the centrality of literature to literary studies, making it secondary to such "extrinsic" disciplines as history, philosophy, anthropology, psychology, and sociology. The New Critics successfully countered this development with their formulation of the INTENTIONAL FALLACY and with their emphasis on the intrinsic approach to texts (see NEW CRITICISM).

POSTCOLONIAL CRITICISM. See THIRD WORLD CRITICISM.

POSTCOLONIALISM. *Postcolonialism* refers to a historical phase undergone by many of the world's countries after the decline of the European empires by the mid-twentieth century (see COLONIALISM). Following the dismantling of the empires, the people of many Asian, African, and Caribbean states were left to restore their precolonial culture, assess the cultural, linguistic, legal, and economic effects of colonial rule, and create new governments and national identities. Postcolonial literature, like that of the Indian writer Salman Rushdie, the Trinidadian writer V. S. Naipaul, and the Kenyan writer Ngugi, centers on the conflicts and contradictions, as well as the advantages and sense of liberation, that accompany life as an individual in a postcolonial state.

POSTMODERNISM. A highly disputed term, *postmodernism* in its simplest usage refers to the period of twentieth-century Western culture that immediately followed high modernism. For many, the beginning of the postmodern era corresponds to the use of atomic weapons and the rapid development of technology that followed. In this sense it is seen as both an extreme continuation of the countertraditional experiments of modernist art and literature and as a break from many of the conventions that became commonplace during modernism. The ALIENATION and ABSUR-

DITY that figured so prominently in modernism are still evident in post-modern literature and art, but rather than follow the modernist attempt to fashion a unified, coherent worldview from the FRAGMENTATION that defines existence, the postmodernist accepts, whether indifferently or with celebration, the INDETERMINACY of meaning and the decentered-ness of existence (see DECENTERING). The result in postmodern fiction is a play with the CONVENTIONS of the novel—authors often chat with characters, plots do not unfold as expected, and viable alternative reali-ties exist within the pages of the text.

Postmodernity has also been discussed in terms of the culture of advanced capitalist societies since the 1960s. This culture, according to theorists like Jean Baudrillard, is composed of disparate fragmentary experiences and images that constantly bombard the individual in music, video, television, advertising and other forms of electronic media. The speed and ease of reproduction of these images mean that they exist only as images, devoid of depth, coherence, or originality. It is in argu-ments such as this one that postmodernism is seen as challenging tradi-tional cultural values. And it is in such challenges that postmodernism is most often confused with the theoretical and critical project of post-structuralism, which shares this characteristic.

It is important to remember that while one use of *postmodernism* is to denote a specific period in Western culture, not all cultural works since World War II can be characterized as "postmodern." Most postmodernist works attempt to subvert the distinction between "high" and "low" cul-ture. The result is often a blending or PASTICHE of techniques, genres, and even media. In literature the works of Jorge Luis Borges, Thomas Pynchon, Kurt Vonnegut, Robert Coover, and Roland Barthes are espe-cially good examples of the ways that this combining takes place to dis-courage easy categorization. With these works it is not always possible to tell if one is reading an autobiography, a history, a novel, or literary crit-icism. Part of the point of such works is to exploit these distinctions as artificial and to emphasize the fragmentary quality of all texts. This way of seeing and representing the world has had a significant impact on other art forms, particularly film and music. The works of directors like Jean-Luc Godard and Robert Altman and of composers like Philip Glass, John Cage, and David Byrne are often cited as products of a postmodern sensibility that no longer feels bound, or necessarily reassured, by con-cepts of TOTALITY, unity, or determinate meaning. See also FRAGMENTA-TION, NEW WAVE CINEMA, REALISM, SIMULACRUM.

Benjamin, Walter. "The Work of Art in the Age of Mechanical Reproduction." *Illuminations.* Trans. Harry Zohn, ed. Hannah Arendt. New York: Harcourt Brace and World, 1968.

Docherty, Thomas, ed. *Postmodernism: A Reader.* New York: Columbia University Press, 1993.

Foster, Hal, ed. *The Anti-Aesthetic: Essays on Postmodern Culture.* Port Townsend, Wash.: Bay Press, 1983.

Greenberg, Clement. "The Notion of Post-Modern." In Ingeborg Hosterey, ed., *Zeitgeist in Babel: The Postmodernist Controversy.* Bloomington: Indiana University Press, 1991.

Hassan, Ihab. *Paracriticisms: Seven Speculations of the Times.* Urbana: University of Illinois Press, 1975.

Hutcheon, Linda. *A Poetics of Postmodernism.* New York: Routledge, 1988.

Huyssen, Andreas. *After the Great Divide: Modernism, Mass Culture, Postmodernism.* Bloomington: Indiana University Press, 1986.

Jameson, Fredric. *Postmodernism, or the Cultural Logic of Late Capitalism.* Durham, N.C.: Duke University Press, 1991.

Lyotard, Jean-François. *The Postmodern Condition: A Report on Knowledge.* Trans. Geoff Bennington and Brian Massumi. Minneapolis: University of Minnesota Press, 1984.

McHale, Brian. *Postmodern Fiction.* New York: Methuen, 1987.

POSTSTRUCTURALISM. The first thing that should be noted about *poststructuralism* is that it is often incorrectly used interchangeably with POSTMODERNISM to signify contemporary assumptions about aesthetics and language. This is understandable since both terms are broad and somewhat vague; moreover, they are interconnected in a number of ways. But while *postmodernism* is the broader umbrella term, covering everything from music to fashion to politics, *poststructuralism* denotes a variety of critical practices and theoretical agendas that arose out of STRUCTURALISM as both a reaction to and modification of many of its tenets. Since the mid-1970s, poststructuralism in its many forms has asserted itself as the prominent radical critique of orthodox habits of mind, culture, and language.

One of the most important moments in the early formation of poststructuralist thought was Jacques Derrida's 1967 lecture at Johns Hopkins University, "Structure, Sign, and Play in the Discourse of the Human Sciences." In this lecture, Derrida announces the advent of DECONSTRUCTION as he critiques the concept of structure in the work of Claude Lévi-Strauss. Derrida argues that the concept of structure is founded on an untenable paradox, which is endemic to Western METAPHYSICS. He points out that a structure must have a "center" or a "base" that is the origin of the properties of the structure. Yet the base or center is *outside* the structure and is not bound by its properties. An example in Christian theology would be the system of ethics we accept from God. Yet God, the origin, the center of that structure of ethics is not bound by it: he may kill, deceive, covet, with impunity. Structuralism, argues Derrida, perpetuates this paradox, despite its claims about the construction of meaning. By always attempting to resolve the paradox of the structure and its center, structuralism continually tries to move toward origins and explanations in search of a primary structure. But, as Derrida's formulation makes clear, there is always an outside to the structure, something upon which it is based. The move toward origin is one that can never be completed. Instead of bemoaning the continual recession of meaning, however, Derrida celebrates it as "freeplay." Once we no longer are compelled to discover origin and are reconciled to "decenteredness," our methods of understanding and explication will change accordingly.

This shift is indeed what poststructuralism affected. Since the early 1970s, the work of Derrida in philosophy, of Julia Kristeva and Jacques Lacan in psychoanalysis, of Michel Foucault and Michel de Certeau in history, of Jean-François Lyotard and Gilles Deleuze in cultural-political critique, and of countless others in literary and aesthetic criticism has abandoned explanation of meaning based upon origin, order based upon binary opposition, and a conception of the individual as a unified SUBJECT. Emphasis has instead been placed on the competition of DISCOURSES, on the ruptures in history, on the freeplay of meaning, and on the subject as decentered (see DECENTERING).

Poststructuralist theories and practices in general share an oppositional stance toward traditional intellectual categories. This has been especially pronounced in the refiguring of the subject. No longer depicted as unified or possessed of control or initiative, the subject is now often seen as a product of linguistic or discursive practices, without "essence" or an irreducible nature (see DECENTERED SUBJECT). This position has often been described as anti-humanism (see HUMANISM), since it argues that the very concept of "man," in the sense of "humanity," is itself a linguistic construct, devoid of any meaning outside of the system of relationships in which it exists. This logic has been used by poststructuralists to attack and attempt to undermine any theoretical system that claims universal validity. Another characteristic that the different varieties of poststructuralism share is an emphasis on the role of language in all signifying practices. This emphasis is easily noted in such concepts as TEXT, READING, and DISCOURSE, in which language plays a primary role not only in the construction of the possibilities of meaning, but for some poststructuralists even of those things we experience as reality. See also COGITO, ESSENTIALISM, INDETERMINACY, PRAGMATISM, SUBJECT/OBJECT.

Barthes, Roland. *The Pleasure of the Text.* Trans. Richard Miller. New York: Hill and Wang, 1975.

Baudrillard, Jean. *Simulations.* Trans. Paul Foss, Paul Patton, and Philip Beitchman. New York: Semiotext(e), 1983.

De Certeau, Michel. *Heterologies: Discourse on the Other.* Trans. Brian Massumi. Minneapolis: University of Minnesota Press, 1986.

Deleuze, Gilles, and Félix Guattari. *A Thousand Plateaus: Capitalism and Schizophrenia.* Trans. Brian Massumi. London: Athlone Press, 1988.

De Man, Paul. *Allegories of Reading: Figural Language in Rousseau, Nietzsche, Rilke, and Proust.* New Haven: Yale University Press, 1979.

Derrida, Jacques. *Of Grammatology.* Trans. Gayatri Chakravorty Spivak. Baltimore: Johns Hopkins University Press, 1976.

—. "Structure, Sign, and Play in the Discourse of the Human Sciences." In *Writing and Difference.* Trans. Alan Bass. Chicago: University of Chicago Press, 1978.

Foucault, Michel. *Discipline and Punish: The Birth of the Prison.* Trans. Alan Sheridan. New York: Vintage, 1979.

Harari, Josué V., ed. *Textual Strategies: Perspective in Post-Structuralist Criticism.* Ithaca, N.Y.: Cornell University Press, 1979.

Kristeva, Julia. *Powers of Horror: An Essay on Abjection.* Trans. Leon S. Roudiez. New York: Columbia University Press, 1982.

Lacan, Jacques. *Ecrits: A Selection.* Trans. Alan Sheridan. New York: Norton, 1977.

Young, Robert, ed. *Untying the Text: A Post-Structuralist Reader.* Boston: Routledge and Kegan Paul, 1981.

POWER. Power is defined in a great number of ways, but usually in one of two senses: 1) as the ability or skill to do something ("Shakespeare had great poetic power"); or 2) as the possession of the capacity to dominate or control someone or something else. It is the second sense that has received the greatest amount of critical attention. The crudest and probably oldest view is that the powerful are those who possess the greatest brute force. But, as Max Weber has pointed out, political power is not usually possessed or exercised in this way—those who possess and exercise "power" usually do so, not on the basis of the threat of physical violence, but on the basis of tradition, legal systems, IDEOLOGY, consensus, etc. Classical Marxists believe that power is always in the hands of those who control the economic BASE, the MEANS OF PRODUCTION, and is exercised primarily in two ways: through the state's judicial and legislative functions (closely allied with the interests of the capitalist owners) and through the exploitation of the worker. Michel Foucault, in contrast, argues that "theories of government and the traditional analyses of their mechanisms certainly don't exhaust the field where power is exercised and where it functions."

Similarly, many feminists have observed that male power over women occurs in all economic classes, in most (if not all) cultures, and thus its tenacity cannot be explained solely with reference to the distribution of wealth or form of government. Such broad explanations do little to clarify power as a specific, definable entity. Many theorists have argued that a Foucauldian concept of power as all pervasive and without a specific locus renders the term and the concept all but meaningless. Others have pointed out that such explanations make resistance seem futile, since all attempts to defy or work against power are ultimately "always already" figured in the structure of power. Thus, power becomes much like the Althusserian concept of ideology: it apparently has no history and there is no functioning outside of it.

These interpretations of power ignore Foucault's own assertion that power should not been seen only as oppressive, that it also enables, especially when employed locally against dominant forms of oppression. Edward Said has also pointed out that by thinking of the Foucauldian idea of power in terms of HEGEMONY, it is possible to conceive of it as resistive, allowing for combinations that meet the needs of a larger group than the power formation that currently exists.

Foucault, Michel. *Language, Counter-Memory, Practice.* Trans. by Donald F. Bouchard and Sherry Simon. Ithaca, N.Y.: Cornell University Press, 1977.
—. *Discipline and Punish: The Birth of the Prison.* Trans. Alan Sheridan. New York: Vintage, 1979.
—. *Power/Knowledge: Selected Interviews and Other Writings, 1972–1977.* Trans. and ed. Colin Gordon. New York: Pantheon, 1980.
Said, Edward. *The World, the Text, and the Critic.* Cambridge, Mass.: Harvard University Press, 1983.
Weber, Max. *Politics as a Vocation.* Trans. H. H. Gert and C. Wright Mills. Philadelphia: Fortress Press, 1968.

PRAGMATIC CRITICISM. See PRAGMATISM.

PRAGMATISM. In its most reductive sense, *pragmatism* may be defined as the view that all objects and abstractions can be known based upon an experimental handling of them and a knowledge of the results of that experimentation. As a philosophical and theoretical position, pragmatism was first formulated by the nineteenth-century American philosopher Charles Sanders Peirce, who argued that the meaning of a concept is found in its conceivable effects. Peirce's younger colleague, William James, first drew significant attention to the term in his 1898 lecture on its meaning and later with the publication of his book *Pragmatism: A New Name for Some Old Ways of Thinking* (1907). For both Peirce and James, the pragmatic method was intended to lead toward "true opinion" and "knowledge." Further, James saw it as an avenue to validating belief, and it was the philosophical underpinning for his important collection of essays *The Will to Believe* (1897). For Peirce, truth was validated by an "experimental method" that substantiated a general, public perception of an object or abstraction by demonstrating its effects under repeatable, controlled conditions. For James, truth was much more individualistic and subjective. He argued that experience in life is the measure by which truth can be validated, and that these experiences necessarily differ from individual to individual. Thus, for James, pragmatism did not devolve into what he calls "solving names" such as "God" or the "absolute." Instead, pragmatism strives to bring out of each utterance what James calls its "its practical cash-value"; the method then sets that value to work within one's experience. To James, this meant that pragmatism was not a solution but "a program for more work, and more particularly as an indication of the ways in which existing realities may be *changed.*" Especially important to James were the moral implications of such a method, effects which were of considerably less interest to Peirce.

In recent years, pragmatism has enjoyed a new popularity among philosophers and literary critics. In his 1979 book *Philosophy and the Mirror of Nature*, Richard Rorty, an American philosopher, argued that the concept of knowledge as accurate representation needed to be discarded. Following James and John Dewey, as well as being considerably influenced by Wittgenstein and Heidegger, Rorty argues that truth has nothing to do with correspondent reality, but rather is that which "proves itself to be good in the way of belief, and good, too, for definite assignable reasons." For Rorty, the issue of reality is somewhat mute: a sentence is not true because it corresponds directly to something real that exists outside of language; therefore, we need not concern ourselves with what "makes" it true. Unlike Peircean pragmatism, which was interested in establishing a clear conception of a thing that could be held by all as the "real," Rorty's version of pragmatism is more closely linked to James's conception of the true existing independently of concrete reality. One of the difficulties of Rorty's position is its dependence on such vague concepts as "good," which in themselves are highly changeable and subjective. Similarly, in his later works such as *Irony, Contingency, Solidarity*, Rorty extends his conception of pragmatism to a discussion of liberalism, arguing that a liberal is one who perceives cruelty to be the worst thing one human being can perpetrate upon another. As with the concept of goodness in his earlier works, however, *cruelty* remains an ambiguous term that has different meanings for different people.

In some respects, this ambiguity is the point. Pragmatism, or more properly the New Pragmatism of Rorty, is also sometimes called anti-foundationalism or anti-essentialism. Like James's program for more questioning, Rorty's method insists on the inability of any investigation to come to a resolution of the questions one asks. For Rorty, striving for knowledge is never a search for truth but rather is its own end, what he calls "edification." He is always interested in finding "new, better, and more fruitful ways of speaking"—an ongoing process.

For literary theorists, pragmatic criticism for hundreds of years was linked to the precepts of Horace's first-century text, *Art of Poetry*. For these critics, literature was to be judged according to the effects it had on readers or listeners, and its value was judged according to its ability to achieve these effects. This older form of pragmatic criticism has today become a branch of rhetoric, while the new pragmatism has established itself as a literary theoretical doctrine through the works of critics like Stanley Fish, Steven Knapp, and Walter Benn Michaels. Fish initially argued that literary interpretations were always governed by the conventions of an interpretive community, and that it was impossible for a critic to step outside those conventions. He later expanded his argument to claim the impossibility of criticism's having consequences. According to Fish, any theory founded on assumptions of truth or correspondence to reality cannot proceed, and therefore is without consequences; and any theory that is anti-foundationalist can have no consequences, since in its explanations of how we came to believe as we do (and thus promote itself as a belief), it "leaves untouched" the beliefs or assumptions whose history it is explaining. See also DECONSTRUCTION, ESSENTIALISM.

Fish, Stanley. *Is There a Text in this Class? The Authority of Interpretive Communities.* Cambridge, Mass.: Harvard University Press, 1980.

James, William. *The Will to Believe, and Other Essays in Popular Philosophy.* New York: Longmans, Green, 1896.

—. *Pragmatism: A New Name for Some Old Ways of Thinking*. New York: Longmans, Green, 1914.

Mitchell, W. J. T., ed. *Against Theory: Literary Studies and the New Pragmatism*. Chicago: University of Chicago Press, 1985.

Pierce, Charles Sanders. *The Collected Papers of Charles Sanders Peirce*. Eds. Charles Hartshorne and Paul Weiss. Cambridge, Mass.: Harvard University Press, 1931–60.

Rorty, Richard. *Philosophy and the Mirror of Nature*. Princeton: Princeton University Press, 1979.

—. *Consequences of Pragmatism*. Minneapolis: University of Minnesota Press, 1982.

—. *Contingency, Irony, Solidarity*. Cambridge: Cambridge University Press, 1989.

West, Cornel. *The American Evasion of Philosophy: A Genealogy of Pragmatism*. Madison: University of Wisconsin Press, 1989.

PRAGUE CIRCLE. Also called the Prague school, the Prague Circle was founded in Czechoslovakia in the late 1920s and lasted until the outbreak of World War II. Its members included Roman Jakobson, and Nikolay Trubetskoy (both Russian émigrés), J. Mukarovsky, and F. Vodicka. The Prague Circle was the first important movement to apply principles of Saussurian linguistics to the study of poetic language, and they in turn were important predecessors of the structuralists (particularly Jakobson). In general, the Prague Circle is associated with a belief that language is a coherent structure, and that individual speech acts function in relation to the laws governing that larger structure. They identified different types of language, including that which communicates information and the emotional state of the speaker, and calls attention to the act of expression itself (poetic language). Like the NEW CRITICS and other FORMALIST movements, the Prague Circle believed that the parts of a literary work functioned collectively for the good of the work as a whole. But, like Marxist critics, they also considered the function of poetic language in its relation to the nonlinguistic historical world. See also RUSSIAN FORMALISM, STRUCTURALISM.

Garvin, Paul, ed. *A Prague School Reader on Esthetics, Literary Structure and Style*. Washington, D.C.: Washington Linguistic Club, 1955.

Vachek, J. *A Prague School Reader in Linguistics*. Bloomington: Indiana University Press, 1964.

PREOEDIPAL. In psychoanalytic theory, the preoedipal period is that which precedes the onset of the OEDIPUS COMPLEX between the ages of three and five years old and is dominated in both sexes by the relationship of child and mother. Freud himself came to consider the role of this period in human development only during the latter part of his career, when he emphasized the importance of the female child's complex relationship with her mother in the development of feminine sexuality; however, later theorists have devoted much attention to the preoedipal phase from a variety of perspectives. Notable among them are psychoanalysts like Melanie Klein and the OBJECT RELATIONS school, who have disputed the orthodox Freudian insistence on the dominance of the Oedipus complex in structuring human relations; exponents of "anti-psychiatry" like Félix Guattari, who in a series of books co-written with the philosopher Gilles Deleuze celebrated the preoedipal world of the schizophrenic as a model for survival under capitalism (see DETERRITORIALIZATION, RHIZOME, SCHIZOANALYSIS); and feminists like Nancy Chodorow, whose *The Reproduction of Mothering* has been a major influence on recent feminist thought on the question of motherhood. See also MOTHERHOOD.

Chodorow, Nancy. *The Reproduction of Mothering: Psychoanalysis and the Sociology of Gender*. Berkeley: University of California Press, 1978.

Deleuze, Gilles, and Félix Guattari. *Anti-Oedipus: Capitalism and Schizophrenia*. Trans. Robert Hurley, Mark Seem, and Helen R. Lane. New York: Viking, 1977.

—. *Kafka: Toward a Minor Literature*. Trans. Dana Polan. Minneapolis: University of Minnesota Press, 1986.

—. *A Thousand Plateaus: Capitalism and Schizophrenia*. Trans. Brian Massumi. London: Athlone Press, 1988.

Freud, Sigmund. "Female Sexuality." In *Standard Edition of the Complete Psychological Works of Sigmund Freud*, vol. 21. Trans. James Strachey. London: Hogarth Press and Institute of Psycho-Analysis, 1974.

Klein, Melanie. *Contributions to Psycho-Analysis 1921–1945*. London: Hogarth Press, 1965.

PRESENCE. See ABSENCE/PRESENCE.

PRIMARY/SECONDARY PROCESS. In Freudian psychoanalysis, the primary and secondary processes are the modes of mental functioning that correspond respectively to the UNCONSCIOUS and the preconscious-conscious systems. In the unconscious, psychic energy moves freely from idea to idea along the shortest available route to satisfaction, in accordance with the mechanisms of DISPLACEMENT and CONDENSATION; whereas in the preconscious and conscious mind, the movement of psychic energy is checked and controlled by the need to recognize external obstacles to immediate gratification. See also PLEASURE PRINCIPLE, REALITY PRINCIPLE.

PRIMITIVE ACCUMULATION. The phrase *primitive accumulation* (*ursprüngliche Akkumulation*) was used ironically by Marx and refers to the fanciful hypothesis that capitalism must have begun when some proto-capitalist once upon a time, through abstinent living, accumulated a sum of money independently of the labor of others and so was able to become a buyer of labor power. Marx's actual view is that the "so-called secret of primitive accumulation" is to be found in the disruption of traditional agricultural economies through the forceful possession of land and consequent transformation of the peasants who once worked that land into dispossessed laborers.

Marx, Karl. *Capital*, vol. 1. Moscow: Progress Publishers, 1965.

PRIMITIVISM. The term *primitivism* is generally used to describe the infatuation of people of European descent with the cultures and works of art of tribal societies. Aspects of primitivism were most prevalent from the end of the nineteenth century through World War II, and primitivism was preceded during the nineteenth century by other forms of exoticism, particularly ORIENTALISM. Primitivism can take a variety of forms, but it generally involves a search on the part of Western artists for forms of expression and attitudes toward creativity not available in Western industrial society. Primitivism is also often used as a term of derogation, since the attitudes it describes often entail an unequal relationship between the Western artists who have been influenced by tribal art and the sometimes anonymous tribal artists whose work provides the source of inspiration.

Clifford, James . "Histories of the Tribal and the Modern." In *The Predicament of Culture: Twentieth-Century Ethnography, Literature, and Art*. Cambridge, Mass.: Harvard University Press, 1988.

Hiller, Susan, ed. *The Myth of Primitivism: Perspectives on Art*. New York: Routledge, 1991.

Rubin, William, ed. *"Primitivism" in 20th Century Art*. New York: Museum of Modern Art, 1984.

Torgovnick, Marianna. *Gone Primitive: Savage Intellects, Modern Lives*. Chicago: University of Chicago Press, 1990.

PRINCIPLE OF CONSTANCY. See PLEASURE PRINCIPLE.

PROAIRESIS. Any choice faced by characters at each point of a story is the proairesis (proayrEESis). The characters' choices in a narrative are not, as one might expect, infinite. Barthes, who talks of a "proairetic code," suggests that a group of actions falls into a sequence that readers identify with a general title that embodies the sequence. Michael Riffaterre indicates that these sequences are limited by "the context, the *telos*, the expectations allowed by the genre, the nature of the character," and so on. Thus, when Othello listens to Iago and then not only acts on his advice but ultimately murders Desdemona, he has been functioning in the proairetic; that is, he has chosen among a number of different actions, yet he also has made these choices in concert with the conditions presented by the play and his own character.

Barthes, Roland. *S/Z*. Trans. Richard Miller. New York: Hill and Wang, 1974.
Riffaterre, Michael. *Fictional Truth*. Baltimore: Johns Hopkins University Press, 1990.

PROBLEMATIC. In the Marxist philosophy of Louis Althusser, a problematic is the set of determinate theoretical conditions in which a given problem can be posed. Like such non-Marxist French thinkers as Gaston Bachelard and Michel Foucault (or, in the United States, Thomas Kuhn), Althusser argues that scientific thought about specific problems is governed by the framework of larger theoretical structures or PARADIGMS, which provide concepts and principles, but also set limits on what is thinkable at a given time. These structural limits or "conditions of possibility" thus have a determining effect on how a problem is understood. Problematics are not timeless, however; and a crucial focus of Althusser's thought is on the "ruptures" or "breaks" that take place when, at certain especially propitious moments in history, an old problematic gives way to a new one. Althusser locates one such moment in the transition, in Marx's writing, from the Hegelian theoretical framework of his earlier work to the more properly "scientific" thought of *Das Kapital*.

Althusser, Louis, and Etienne Balibar. *Reading "Capital."* Trans. Ben Brewster. London: Verso, 1970.

PROJECTION. Although this term has a broad usage outside of psychoanalysis, its most familiar designation is the process whereby emotions or wishes that a person cannot acknowledge in him or herself are relocated or "projected" onto another person or thing. Like INTROJECTION, this psychic defense mechanism, which encompasses occurrences as familiar as superstition and as extreme as paranoia, has its origins in the so-called oral phase of development and its governing logic of ingestion and expulsion. See INFANTILE SEXUALITY, MIRROR STAGE, NARCISSISM.

PROLEPSIS. From the Greek "an anticipating," *prolepsis* (proLEPsis) has three distinct theoretical uses. In argumentation, it is the preemption of an opponent's objections by answering them before they can be made. In literary discussions it is a figure of speech in which a description or an epithet is used before it is strictly applicable. In *Romeo and Juliet*, when Mercutio, after being mortally wounded by Tybalt, puns that "they've made worms' meat of me," he is being proleptic since he obviously is not yet dead. The third sense in which it may be used is in conjunction with NARRATOLOGICAL analyses of the order of events and presentation of them in texts. In this sense, a prolepsis is a "flashforward" in which a future event is related as an interruption of the present time of the text. See also ANACHRONY, ANALEPSIS.

PSYCHOANALYTIC CRITICISM. Psychoanalytic criticism begins with Sigmund Freud, who wrote about literature and art in a variety of essays, such as "The Theme of the Three Caskets" and "The Moses of Michelangelo." In these and other works, Freud inaugurated the practice of interpreting culture in the light of psychoanalytic discoveries, a project that he was to continue in a much more ambitious way in *Civilization and Its Discontents* (1930). Freud's interest in works of art was essentially that of a student of the psyche, and most of his essays concentrate on how literature reveals certain psychological mechanisms at work, such as the disguised WISH-FULFILLMENT outlined in "Creative Writers and Day-Dreaming" or the COMPULSION TO REPEAT described in "The 'Uncanny' " (although, to be sure, the latter essay has proven to be a highly complex document in the hands of contemporary readers like Neil Hertz). As Freud pointed out in a famous remark, the poets had gotten there before him, and he returned repeatedly to what he perceived as the natural affinity between psychoanalysis and works of art.

Freud's example was the first great influence on the practice of psychoanalytic criticism, and much American work from the middle decades of the twentieth century imitated Freud in offering psychoanalytic explanations for literary phenomena, though usually without his inventiveness and subtlety. As a result, such criticism tends to be reductive, explaining away the ambiguities of works of literature by reference to established psychoanalytic doctrine; and very little of this work retains much influence today. During the same period, however, a somewhat different use of psychoanalysis was made by European writers like Jean-Paul Sartre and the members of the FRANKFURT SCHOOL, who sought to integrate Freudian ideas into a philosophy that aimed at a broader social and historical understanding. Thus, psychoanalytic interpretations were treated by these writers not as universally valid but as information that was itself a form of historical evidence and therefore in need of interpretation within broader philosophical schemes derived from Hegelian Marxism. While this approach too had its limitations, it represented a considerable advance over the one-dimensional application of Freudian ideas and reflects a combination of interest and suspicion that has characterized many leftist appropriations of psychoanalysis down to the neo-Marxism and feminism of our own day.

In America, however, the next major wave of criticism to be influenced by psychoanalysis was not Freudian but Jungian in orientation, influenced by the ideas of Freud's dissident follower Carl Gustav Jung, whose concept of a collective unconscious that functions as a repository of archetypal forms proved suggestive to literary critics in search of transindividual and transhistorical categories of literary experience. These practitioners of archetypal or MYTH CRITICISM, who included influential figures like Northrop Frye, argued that all literature simply repeats a certain number of basic motifs or ARCHETYPES, which express such fundamental human experiences as birth and death or the change of the seasons. Although myth criticism would be strongly criticized for its lack of attention to historical and cultural differences, it enjoyed a substantial vogue in the late 1950s and early 1960s.

Since the middle 1960s, psychoanalytic criticism in America has had a number of notable champions, such as Norman Holland, whose approach has affinities with READER-REPONSE CRITICISM; however, by far the most important development has been the influence both in Europe and in this country of the French psychoanalyst Jacques Lacan, whose rereading of Freud's work was informed by structural linguistics (see STRUCTURALISM) as well as a high degree of philosophical sophistication. While Lacan's own remarks on literature did not offer an easily imitable example, his gnomic writings have provided the stimulus for critical work from a variety of approaches. Thus, Lacan's concept of the MIRROR STAGE was a crucial component in the French Marxist philosopher Louis Althusser's understanding of IDEOLOGY, and Althusser's English followers have shown similar enthusiasm for Lacanian ideas. Moreover, in an influential essay on Lacan, the American Marxist critic Fredric Jameson took up the project of uniting Freudianism with a Hegelian Marxism derived from Sartre and the Frankfurt school by focusing on the Lacanian categories of IMAGINARY, SYMBOLIC, and REAL. Feminist critics have also found Lacanian psychoanalysis to be a fruitful source of ideas; and an important school of film criticism, centered around the journal *Screen* (see SCREEN GROUP), has made interesting use of Lacan's ideas in the study of that medium (see FILM THEORY, MALE GAZE, VISUAL PLEASURE).

Still, not all recent psychoanalytic criticism has been Lacanian in orientation. The American critic Harold Bloom has adopted the Freudian notion of the OEDIPUS COMPLEX to his study of the relationships of influence between poets (see ANXIETY OF INFLUENCE); and his work has also inspired a feminist variant in the work of Sandra Gilbert and Susan Gubar (see ANXIETY OF AUTHORSHIP). Thus, in spite of criticism from Marxists and other critics on the left (see SCHIZOANALYSIS), who find the individualist emphasis of psychoanalysis misleading and even complicit with forces of domination, as well as feminist and gay critics, who object to patriarchal and heterosexist biases in the work of Freud and his followers, psychoanalysis remains an important and multi-faceted presence in contemporary criticism.

PSYCHANALYSE ET POLITIQUE. A feminist organization whose name means "psychoanalysis and politics," *Psychanalyse et Politique* (**PSEE**kahnah**LEES** ay **PO**Lee**TEEK**) was formed in Paris in 1973 under the leadership of the psychoanalyst Antoinette Fouqué. The group's focus on psychoanalysis distinguished it from the women's movement in the United States, which tended to dismiss or denounce the theories of Freud and Lacan. In their explorations of women's oppression and of the structure of woman's UNCONSCIOUS, "Psych et Po" stressed the differences between men and women, masculine and feminine. Because of this emphasis, they have sometimes been criticized for defining femininity as innate, and for being too utopian and ahistorical. In 1977, Simone de Beauvoir founded a rival journal, *Questions féministes*, which worked to discredit the preoccupation with psychoanalysis and philosophy as the keys to women's liberation. The main spokeswoman for "Psych et Po" has been Hélène Cixous, who is also a prolific writer for the group's publishing house, Editions des Femmes. See also ÉCRITURE FEMININE.

Cixous, Hélène. "Rethinking Difference: An Interview." In George Stambolian and Elaine Marks, eds., *Homosexualities and French Literature: Cultural Contexts, Critical Texts.* Ithaca, N.Y.: Cornell University Press, 1979.

Marks, Elaine, and Isabelle de Courtivron, eds. *New French Feminisms.* Amherst: University of Massachusetts Press, 1980.

Q

QUEST FOR LITERACY. This term comes from Robert Stepto's study of African-American narrative, *From Behind the Veil*, and is taken further in the critical writing of Henry Louis Gates, Jr. Stepto believes that the African-American literary tradition is shaped by certain "pregeneric myths," primary of these being "the quest for freedom *and* literacy." Most studies of black history and literature note the quest for freedom as a shaping force, but Stepto stresses the importance of recognizing the bonds among study, language, and freedom in classic texts such as Frederick Douglass's autobiography and W. E. B. Du Bois's *The Souls of Black Folk.* This dual quest, Stepto argues, provided both a subject and a structure for most early African-American writing, and continues to influence later literary forms. Gates notes that in the eighteenth and nineteenth centuries, slavery was justified on the grounds that African Americans were not only of a different race than whites, but also a different and lesser kind of being. Freedom and literacy were fundamentally linked because literacy was considered "a principal sign of reason," and reason, in turn, was the quality that separated humans from animals. Abolitionist literature and slave narratives asserted that African Americans' capacity for reason, proved by writing, meant that they were indeed "fully human." Gates thus claims that writing, for slaves, was "a commodity which they were forced to trade for their humanity." Gates suggests that this paradigm is still in force when black critics are compelled to use white literary-critical models to legitimate their work within a white academic power structure. See also RACE/ETHNICITY, STRATEGIES OF AUTHENTICATION.

Gates, Henry Louis, Jr. "Writing 'Race' and the Difference It Makes." In *"Race," Writing, and Difference*. Chicago: University of Chicago Press, 1986.
Stepto, Robert. *From Behind the Veil: A Study of Afro-American Narrative*. Urbana: University of Illinois Press, 1979.

R

RACE/ETHNICITY. Eighteenth-century writers such as Hume and Jefferson thought of race as a natural and inevitable category, and rarely spoke of it, except when confronting the dilemma of a black writer's claim to literacy. Centuries later, however, the ferment of the civil rights movement inspired many groups to claim a racial or ethnic identity, while forcing others to confront the issue of race in an unprecedented manner. The influence of POSTSTRUCTURALIST critical thought, which explored the arbitrary and linguistic basis of supposedly "natural" categories, further intensified this discussion of the meaning of race, and caused some critics to question the usefulness of the concept as a separate category of thought.

Two well-known contemporary critics who question the concept of race are Henry Louis Gates, Jr. and Werner Sollors. In "Writing 'Race' and the Difference It Makes," Gates argues that race is a metaphor or arbitrary linguistic category rather than a thing, and that racism consists in making this arbitrary category seem natural and fixed. Gates thus puts the term *race* within quotation marks to indicate its purely conventional status. Sollors takes up this point to argue that the static concept of race as an "authentic" or "pure" identity hides the ways that various ethnic groups in America have traditionally influenced one another. For Sollors, ethnicity, of which race is a subset, is not a matter of who you are *descended* from, but what group you *consent* to join: "American ethnicity . . . is a matter not of content but of the importance that individuals ascribe to it." Ethnicity is not a fixed category, but is rather a result of cultural interactions, formed in contrast to what is considered "non-ethnic." These critics are building on the insights of such earlier writers as Albert Murray, who argued in *The Omni-Americans* that critics must move beyond a simplistic obsession with "the sterile category of race" to realize that "identity is best defined in terms of culture, and the culture of [this] nation . . . is not all-white by any measurement ever devised. *American culture . . . is patently and irrevocably composite*" (original emphasis). In other words, standard American culture is not "white" but "mulatto".

Critics can use this idea of a "decentralized" ethnicity to discuss in an expanded manner the various ways that being "different" has informed American culture. This difference may not be purely racial or ethnic as it has traditionally been defined. For instance, Mary Dearborn argues that women writers, whether or not they come from historically defined ethnic groups, should be discussed as "ethnic" writers, since they also considered themselves outside of the standard (patriarchal) culture, wrote about similar themes, and used similar strategies of authentication.

Critics of this idea counter that diluting the concept of race by putting it "under erasure" or making it a subset of ethnicity deemphasizes the special nature of slavery and of specific racial prejudice. Moreover, if all groups, including those of the majority culture, become "ethnic," it may be easier to ignore real political inequalities. In other words, critics argue that shifting the concept of race to one of "race" or ethnicity conceals the specific situation of African Americans, and thus hurts the African-American political project. The argument over race versus ethnic studies thus parallels the argument over feminist versus gender studies. See also GENDER STUDIES, MELTING POT, POSTSTRUCTURALISM.

Chametzky, Jules. "Our Decentralized Literature: The Significance of Regional, Ethnic, Racial, and Sexual Factors." In *Our Decentralized Literature: Cultural Mediations in Selected Jewish and Southern Writers.* Amherst: University of Massachusetts Press, 1986.

Dearborn, Mary V. *Pocohantas's Daughters: Gender and Ethnicity in American Culture.* New York: Oxford University Press, 1986.

Gates, Henry Louis, Jr. "Writing 'Race' and the Difference It Makes." In Henry Louis Gates, Jr., ed., *"Race," Writing, and Difference.* Ed. Henry Louis Gates. Chicago: University of Chicago Press, 1986.

Murray, Albert. *The Omni-Americans: Black Experience and American Culture (Some Alternatives to the Folklore of White Supremacy)*. New York: Outerbridge and Dienstfrey, 1970.

Sollors, Werner. *Beyond Ethnicity: Consent and Descent in American Culture*. New York: Oxford University Press, 1986.

RADICAL FEMINISM. Radical feminism is a movement that arose in the late 1960s (peaking between 1967 and 1971), motivated by the failure of civil rights and New Left activists to address the oppression of women as a class. Groups included The Feminists, New York Radical Women, New York Radical Feminists, Redstockings, and many more; Alice Echols, Anne Koedt, Shulamith Firestone, Ellen Willis, Ti-Grace Atkinson, and countless others were among the participants. Like other radicals, radical feminists are committed to revolution and to building a mass movement, but unlike other leftists, they see what Firestone called "the dialectic of sex," not class, as the prototype for all other oppressions. Moreover, while seeking change in the public sphere, radical feminists also popularized the expression "the personal is political," by which they meant that marriage, domestic labor, childrearing, heterosexuality, etc., were not private activities but patriarchal institutions and additional targets of political activism. Thus, their strategies ranged from public demonstrations (such as the famous protest at the 1968 Miss America contest) to "consciousness-raising groups," in which personal experiences were recognized as part of larger patterns of sexism. Legacies of radical (as well as liberal) feminism include the women's health care movement, day care centers, women's shelters, and legalized abortion. As the 1970s progressed, radical feminism gave way to what is often called "cultural feminism," which elaborated radical feminism's focus on women as a class into a celebration of women's culture and community. It is primarily in this form—as "women's studies"—that radical feminism has made itself felt in the academy. See also LIBERAL FEMINISM, SOCIALIST FEMINISM.

Echols, Alice. *Daring to Be Bad: Radical Feminism in America, 1967–1975*. Minneapolis: University of Minnesota Press, 1989.

Firestone, Shulamith. *The Dialectic of Sex: The Case for Feminist Revolution*. New York: Morrow, 1970.

Koedt, Anne, Ellen Levine, and Anita Rapone, eds. *Radical Feminism*. New York: Quadrangle, 1973.

REACTION-FORMATION. In psychoanalysis, the term *reaction-for-mation* refers to an attitude or action that reveals the existence of a repressed wish by manifesting its opposite (see REPRESSION). For example, a person who exhibits an exaggerated shyness, may be concealing repressed exhibitionistic impulses. The reaction-formation is thus a mechanism of defense against a wish that the individual cannot acknowledge, usually because it represents too great a threat to his or her self-image (see NARCISSISM).

Freud, Sigmund. *Inhibitions, Symptoms and Anxiety.* Trans. Alix Strachey. London: Hogarth, 1948.

—. *Three Essays on the Theory of Sexuality.* Trans. and ed. James Strachey. London: Hogarth, 1962.

READER. See AUDIENCE, READER-RESPONSE CRITICISM.

READER-RESPONSE CRITICISM. Rather than denoting a specific method or critical theory, reader-response criticism refers to a number of different approaches that are primarily concerned with understanding and theorizing the ways in which texts are received, either by individual readers or readers belonging to specific categories, such as class, gender, ethnicity, etc. Since the 1960s and the popularization of the concept of the "death of the AUTHOR," reader-response criticism, in its various forms, has gained a considerable foothold in American and European literary criticism. By privileging the reader and focusing on the process of reading as, at least partially, a construction of the text, reader-response criticism has significantly contributed to discussions of issues such as the indeterminacy of meaning. Whether employing STRUCTURALIST, PSYCHOANALYTIC, PHENOMENOLOGICAL, or HERMENEUTIC techniques, all reader-response criticism has shared in shifting critical attention from the inherent, objective characteristics of the text to the engagement of the reader with the text and the production of textual meaning by the reader. A number of theoretical and practical issues concern all reader-response critics, whatever their philosophical orientation. Among the most important of these are the extent to which a text circumscribes or directs a particular response, which aspects of a text may be considered inherent and objective, and which are reader-constructed and thus subjective.

Also important to reader-response critics is an identification and description of the fundamental elements that inform a reader's response to a text. Some of the most important reader-response theorists are Wolfgang Iser, Hans Robert Jauss, Stanley Fish, and David Bleich. Jane Tompkin's 1980 anthology *Reader-Response Criticism* serves as a good introduction to examples of several varieties of this type of criticism. See also REZEPTIONSÄSTHETIK.

Bleich, David. *Subjective Criticism*. Baltimore: Johns Hopkins University Press, 1978.

Fish, Stanley. *Self-Consuming Artifacts: The Experience of Seventeenth-Century Literature*. Berkeley: University of California Press, 1972.

—. *Is There a Text in this Class?: The Authority of Interpretive Communities*. Cambridge, Mass.: Harvard University Press, 1980.

Holland, Norman. *The Dynamics of Literary Response*. New York: Oxford University Press, 1968.

—. *5 Readers Reading*. New Haven: Yale University Press, 1975.

Iser, Wolfgang. *The Implied Reader*. Baltimore: Johns Hopkins University Press, 1974.

—. *The Act of Reading: A Theory of Aesthetic Response*. Baltimore: Johns Hopkins University Press, 1978.

—. *Prospecting: From Reader Response to Literary Anthropology*. Baltimore: Johns Hopkins University Press, 1989.

—. *The Fictive and the Imaginary: Charting Literary Anthropology*. Baltimore: Johns Hopkins University Press, 1993.

Jauss, Hans Robert. *Toward an Aesthetic of Reception*. Trans. Timothy Bahti. Minneapolis: University of Minnesota Press, 1982.

REAL. The Real is one of the three cognitive dimensions or "orders" (the other two being the IMAGINARY and the SYMBOLIC) in the psychoanalytic theory of Jacques Lacan. Of the three, the Real is the most elusive, and it possesses a philosophical sophistication that sets it apart from older psychoanalytic concepts that depend on transparent ideas of reality, such as Freud's REALITY PRINCIPLE. For Lacan, objective perception or description is impossible, since our access to the external world is always mediated by Imaginary investments and the symbol systems through which it is apprehended. The Real is thus a kind of residue, which must remain outside of speech and language. Yet the Real is also present in the unconscious and is felt in dreams, symptoms, and the hallucinations of psychotics. These, too, point to the limits of the Imaginary and the Symbolic, limits which in this case are marked by the individual's biological needs. In Lacan's usage, the Real is quite a different thing from "reality," which refers simply to subjective reality. At the same time, it is ultimately inseparable from the other two orders, forming the hidden underside of Imaginary and Symbolic formations.

Lacan, Jacques. *Ecrits: A Selection.* Trans. Alan Sheridan. New York: Norton, 1977.

REALISM. In its literary usage the term *realism* is often defined as a method or form in fiction that provides a "slice of life," an "accurate representation of reality." Such a seemingly straightforward definition, however, belies a number of complexities that inform the concept of realism. First, and perhaps foremost, is the extreme differences in style and form among the texts that are usually identified as realistic. The term, though applicable to contemporary works, is most often used in discussion of nineteenth-century novels. Among those considered realists are George Eliot, Anthony Trollope, and George Gissing in England, Honoré de Balzac, Gustave Flaubert, and Emile Zola in France, Ivan Turgenev and Leo Tolstoy in Russia, and W. D. Howells, Theodore Dreiser, and Henry James in the United States. For the most part, it might be said of these authors' works that they focus on ordinary characters and the day-to-day events of those characters' lives. The plots of these works encompass all social classes and tend away from excessive sentimentalizing. The characters' speech and actions are appropriate for their education and social standing. Often these authors are extremely interested in the small details of experience, describing at length scenery, events, and seemingly unimportant objects. The representations of life found in these novelists' works seem corroborated by nonfiction works that deal with the same subject matter. Yet at the same time that these works are categorized as realistic, one would be hard put to find common styles, techniques of plotting, or political agendas among them.

Another difficulty with the concept of realism has to do with the fact that it is applied to *representations* of the world. The concept of "realistic fiction" is rather oxymoronic, since ostensibly a text should be either "realistic" or a "fiction," but it does not seem possible that it could be both. This contradiction is usually overcome by the response that "realistic fiction" attempts a faithful representation of concrete reality. Yet this too is a problematic assumption, since it begs the questions of the extent to which language, and thus fiction, actually constitute our perception of "reality." This is not to say that realist authors were not aware of their own subjectivity or the ways in which experience is mediated through language, but they (and the critics who have unproblematically adopted "realism" as an analytical term) tend to assume that the nature of the material world is relatively stable and representable.

A term often associated with realism, and in the nineteenth century synonomous with it, is *naturalism*. More accurately described as a literary movement within realism, naturalism is an attempt at even greater "scientific" and "objective" depiction of characters and the events in their lives. Emile Zola, who considered his novels "scientific experiments," asserted that both the actions and the nature of humans were wholly determined by evolutionary and biological forces beyond our control. His works unflinchingly portray the results of these forces in a dispassionate and "objective" manner. Especially characteristic of naturalistic novels is their detailed elaboration and their frankness in regard to bodily functions. Stephen Crane, Frank Norris, and Theodore Dreiser are often categorized as practitioners of naturalism.

In the 1930s the term *socialist realism* gained common currency in literary discussions of realism. Drawing on the work of Marxist theorist Georg Lukács, socialist, and Soviet, realism strove to combine "truthfulness and historical concreteness in artistic portrayal" with "the ideological remoulding and education of the toiling people in the spirit of socialism." This became the official doctrine governing writings by authors in the then Soviet Union. It has often been attacked both for its simplification of Lukács's conception of representation and for its blatant political agenda.

Another term that has been used in conjunction with discussions of realism is *magic realism*. Applied to a group of writers that include Latin American authors Jorge Luis Borges and Gabriel Garcia Márquez, as well as German Günter Grass and Englishman John Fowles, magic realism describes the technique of combining realistic depictions of events and characters with elements of the FANTASTIC, often drawn from dreams, myth, and fairy tales.

In recent years realism has come under considerable attack by poststructuralists (see POSTSTRUCTURALISM). Theorists such as Roland Barthes and Colin MacCabe have argued that "classic," nineteenth-century realism, in its reliance on closure (or the resolution of the plot) and its effacement of its own fictionality, reinscribe both characters and readers as essential, autononomous SUBJECTS. The basis for this subjectivity, they argue, is a middle-class "norm" that is always presented as the obvious and true. Thus, for such critics, the realist novel is a tool of bourgeois ideology that always affirms that ideology and the place (and activities) of the subject within it. Another poststructuralist theorist, Jean Baudrillard, has argued that while once realism may have been at a premium, existence today operates on the level of SIMULACRA. Because we live in a world in which representation is so easily produced and disseminated, it is these simulations themselves, rather than any sort of "reality," that constitute our being and our world. For Baudrillard, we have become so enmeshed in simulacra that our references are only to other simulations. See also MARXIST CRITICISM.

Auerbach, Erich. *Mimesis: The Representation of Reality in Western Literature.* Trans. W. R. Trask. Princeton: Princeton University Press, 1953.

Barthes, Roland. *S/Z.* Trans. Richard Miller. New York: Hill and Wang, 1974.

Baudrillard, Jean. *Simulations.* Trans. Paul Foss, Paul Patton, and Philip Beitchman. New York: Semiotext(e), 1983.

Belsey, Catherine. *Critical Practice.* New York: Methuen, 1980.

Levin, Harry. *The Gates of Horn.* New York: Oxford University Press, 1963.

Levine, George. *The Realistic Imagination: English Fiction from Frankenstein to Lady Chatterly.* Chicago: Chicago University Press, 1981.

Lukács, Georg. *Essays on Realism.* Trans. D. Fernbach. Cambridge, Mass.: MIT Press, 1980.

MacCabe, Colin. "Realism and the Cinema: Notes on Some Brechtian Theses." *Screen* 17(3), 1967.

REALITY PRINCIPLE. See PLEASURE PRINCIPLE.

REAPPROPRIATION. See APPROPRIATION.

REZEPTIONSÄSTHETIK. Associated with the work of German theorist and critic Hans Robert Jauss, *Rezeptionsästhetik* (reZEPseeuhnzesteteek) is often referred to in English simply as reception theory. A particular type of READER-RESPONSE CRITICISM, *Rezeptionsästhetik* has its methodological foundations in the philosophical HERMENEUTICS of Hans Georg Gadamer and the theory of PHENOMENOLOGY of Martin Heidegger. In his 1970 article, "Literary History as a Challenge to Literary Theory," Jauss argued that a reader approaches any text with a historically informed "horizon of expectations," which consists of a reader's knowledge and assumptions about the text and literature in general. This horizon is challenged, affirmed, and changed by the interaction of the reader with the objective, describable features of a text. A "meaning" emerges from this interaction, but the reader's horizon, because it is historical, is subject to change. Thus, meanings also are subject to the pressures of history as well as to the record of responses by previous readers of the text. *Rezeptionsästhetik* is much less concerned with the response of a single reader than with changing responses of readers over time. For Jauss, the process of reading, like Gadamer's of interpretation, is characterized as a "dialogue" between text and reader—a constant asking, affirming, negating, and challenging of questions and presuppositions. See also HERMENEUTIC CIRCLE.

Holub, Robert C. *Reception Theory: A Critical Introduction.* London: Methuen, 1984.
Jauss, Hans Robert. "Literary History as a Challenge to Literary Theory." *New Literary History* 2, 1970.
—. *Aesthetic Experience and Literary Hermeneutics.* Trans. Michael Shaw. Minneapolis: University of Minnesota Press, 1982.
—. *Toward an Aesthetic of Reception.* Trans. Timothy Bahti. Minneapolis: University of Minnesota Press, 1982.

RECONSTRUCTION. *Reconstruction* refers, in Roman Ingarden's theory of reading, to the reconstitution of the "blueprint" or schematic arrangement of a literary work and the means by which a reader gains access to the work as an objective entity. During the initial aesthetic reading, the original work as work is covered up by the CONCRETIZATION—a distinct, subjective, and determinate form of the work. The reconstruction subverts this actualization of the work's schemata by recovering the work's indeterminacies. The recovery of indeterminacy is the result of a series of steps that include ascertaining the location of indeterminacies, gauging their relative importance, and evaluating their aesthetic functions. The result is, as much as possible, an objective, non-aesthetic manifestation of the work in its original schematized form.

REFERENT. A referent is the entity to which an expression refers or points. In C. S. Peirce's SEMIOTICS, the process of signification is triadic, consisting of "a sign, its object, and its interpretant." For Peirce, a SIGN always stands for something external to it (the object) and is always addressed to someone, whose reception of it is the creation in his or her mind of an equivalent sign (the interpretant), which is still functioning referentially, in connection to the object. For Ferdinand de Saussure, who argued that the connection between SIGNIFIER and SIGNIFIED is arbitrary and conventional, the referent as an empirical entity is unnecessary and is always absorbed in the conceptional notion of the signified.

Peirce, Charles Sanders. *The Collected Papers of Charles Sanders Peirce.* Eds. Charles Hartshorne and Paul Weiss. Cambridge, Mass.: Harvard University Press, 1931–60..

Saussure, Ferdinand de. *Course in General Linguistics.* Trans. Roy Harris, eds. Charles Balley and Albert Sechehaye. London: Duckworth, 1983.

REFUNCTIONING. Walter Benjamin, following Bertolt Brecht's coinage of the word *Umfunktionierung*, used this notion to designate the process of transforming the "productive apparatus," or elements of the cultural heritage, in the interests of promoting political change. Thus, to use Benjamin's own example, the photographer must not simply refine his or her technique in the interest of trying to capture the world as it is; rather, the task is to transform the photographic project in such a way as to encourage the viewer to change the world—for example, by affixing a caption to the photograph. Although the best-known explanation of refunctioning is to be found in Benjamin's essay "The Author as Producer," the influence of Brecht's theories of the theater is apparent. See also ALIENATION EFFECT.

Benjamin, Walter. "The Author as Producer." *Reflections: Essays, Aphorisms, Autobiographical Writing.* Trans. Edmund Jephcott. New York: Harcourt Brace Jovanovich, 1978.

Brecht, Bertolt. *Brecht on Theatre.* Trans. and ed. John Willett. New York: Hill and Wang, 1964.

REGRESSION. As it is generally used in psychoanalysis, the term *regression* designates a return to an earlier point in a process. In a late (1914) addition to *The Interpretation of Dreams*, Freud distinguishes three kinds of regression: topographical, temporal, and formal. The first of these refers to the model of the psychic apparatus, in which the movement is typically from perception to action; in dreams, however, ideas are blocked from translation into motor activity and regress to the condition of perception. Temporal regression, by contrast, is regression to a previous stage of psychic development (such as the oral or anal stage) or older identifications or objects, whereas formal regression is a regression to less complex modes of expression or representation. See also FIXATION, INFANTILE SEXUALITY.

Freud, Sigmund. *The Interpretation of Dreams.* Trans. and ed. James Strachey. London: Hogarth Press, 1953.

—. *Introductory Lectures on Psycho-Analysis.* Trans. James Strachey. New York: Norton, 1965.

RELATIONS OF PRODUCTION. According to MARXIST CRITICISM, relations of production involve the social classes constituted by their different and unequal relationship to the FORCES OF PRODUCTION and the products that result from production itself. One class has economic ownership of the products and/or the means of production, which entitles it to dispose of the products and/or to control the work of the class of people that has a more limited economic ownership (economic ownership is not the same as legal ownership, which is defined by law and so has as much to do with the superstructure, to which the legal system belongs, as with the mode of production). In capitalism, for example, the proletariat owns only its own labor power, which it is obliged to sell to the capitalist for a wage. The capitalist then has the right to direct the proletariat's work and to dispose of the product of that work. In feudalism, by contrast, the serf owned his means of production but was obliged to let the lord dispose of a certain portion of the products of his labor. Because the dominant class is able to determine the way that a surplus is produced and used, it is responsible for the oppression of the class that must ensure a surplus of products beyond what is necessary for its own survival. The ALIENATION and suffering resulting from the structural inequality of the relations of production breed class antagonism. See also BASE AND SUPERSTRUCTURE, MARXIST CRITICISM, MODE OF PRODUCTION.

REPRESENTATION. In its simplest sense *representation* refers to the act of standing for or taking the place of an entity that either is not present or is unable to stand for itself. The concept of representation is one of the oldest in Western thought, having been the subject of extensive reflection for both Plato, who viewed it with suspicion, and Aristotle, who was the first in a long line of philosophers to see it as the activity most characteristic of human beings. Along with its traditional centrality to issues of aesthetics and language, representation has also become a major concept in political theory since the ENLIGHTENMENT; and this relationship between aesthetics or language and politics is crucial to much contemporary work on the topic. Questions about the relationship between an image or a piece of writing and the reality it seeks to represent might seem to have only a slight resemblance to questions about the ability of a public servant to represent a population of citizens; however, just as politicians understand the importance of "image," many contemporary critics argue that all images have, either explicitly or implicitly, a political content. Thus, a considerable amount of recent criticism has focused on this important link between texts and power. In particular, representations of women, racial minorities, and other oppressed groups have become the subject of a critique that takes as its point of departure the poststructuralist thesis that representations are in no way natural or simply verifiable against some external reality but are always constructed out of existing cultural codes (see DIFFERENCE, POSTSTRUCTURALISM). Of course, it is by no means surprising that our era should give special attention to the ways that power is encoded in images and writing, since the ubiquity of representation in postmodern culture is itself so prevalent a theme in contemporary criticism (see POSTMODERNISM, SIMULACRUM).

Aristotle. *Poetics.* Trans. Leon Golden; commentary O. B. Hardison. Englewood Cliffs, N.J.: Prentice Hall, 1968.

Auerbach, Erich. *Mimesis: The Representation of Reality in Western Literature.* Trans. Willard Trask. Princeton: Princeton University Press, 1953.

Pitkin, Hanna. *The Concept of Representation.* Berkeley: University of California Press, 1967.

Plato. *The Republic.* Trans. Allan Bloom. New York: Basic Books, 1968.

Wallis, Brian, ed. *Art After Modernism: Rethinking Representation.* Boston: Godine, 1984.

REPRESSION.   The term *repression* is sometimes used in a political context to describe efforts, usually by a government, to suppress the activities of a people or otherwise remove their freedom; however, the most common use of this term is in psychoanalysis, where it describes the mechanism whereby an IDEATIONAL REPRESENTATIVE is kept from the conscious mind. When it is psychologically impossible to accept the consequences of satisfying an INSTINCT, its ideational representatives are confined by means of repression to the UNCONSCIOUS, from which they may return in distorted form (see RETURN OF THE REPRESSED). Along with the unconscious, repression is one of the key concepts that made possible the development of psychoanalysis.

Freud, Sigmund. "Repression." In *Standard Edition of the Complete Psychological Works of Sigmund Freud*, vol. 14. Trans. James Strachey. London: Hogarth Press and Institute of Psycho-Analysis, 1974.

—. "The Unconscious." In *Standard Edition of the Complete Psychological Works of Sigmund Freud*, vol. 14. Trans. James Strachey. London: Hogarth Press and Institute of Psycho-Analysis, 1974.

RESISTING READER. The title of a 1979 book by Judith Fetterley, the term *resisting reader* refers to one who reads "against the grain" of the text. That is, a resisting reader is not interested so much in actualizing the meaning of a text as in calling that meaning into question. A resisting reader then views his or her activity as inherently political, and resists the imposition of traditional interpretations, preferring instead to look for ways that a text may detour from or deflate its usual reception and understanding. Such readings can be seen in the later works of Roland Barthes, such as *S/Z* and *The Pleasure of the Text*. In these studies, Barthes directly challenges a number of received opinions about specific texts and the activity of reading itself, arguing for plurality, excess, and transgression rather than the codification of meaning. These strategies of reading have been usefully adopted both by feminist critics and, more recently, by those involved in gay studies.

Barthes, Roland. *S/Z*. Trans. Richard Miller. New York: Hill and Wang, 1974.

—. *The Pleasure of the Text*. Trans. Richard Miller. New York: Hill and Wang, 1975.

RETURN OF THE REPRESSED. The *return of the repressed* is the name given by Freud to the process whereby an INSTINCTUAL REPRESENTATIVE that has been repressed from the conscious mind returns from the UNCONSCIOUS in a distorted form, which is the result of a compromise between the forces of REPRESSION and what has been repressed. It is a fundamental postulate of Freudian psychoanalysis that materials that have been repressed are not eliminated from the psyche but have a tendency to reappear in the form of dreams, symptoms, and other manifestations of the unconscious; sometimes such manifestations are triggered by events that coincidentally evoke the repressed ideas, which may return in a startling and unexpected fashion.

Freud, Sigmund. "Repression." In *Standard Edition of the Complete Psychological Works of Sigmund Freud*, vol. 14. Trans. James Strachey. London: Hogarth Press and Institute of Psycho-Analysis, 1974.

REVERSE SHOT. *Reverse shot* is a cinematic term for the technique of editing conversations and other exchanges between two characters in a film by alternately showing each character from the other's point of view. It is sometimes also used, together with the closely related term *reverse angle*, to describe the general technique of switching between a character's point of view and a point outside the character, as when a character passes into a room and we first see the room from the character's perspective and then see the character coming through the door from a point within the room. Reverse shots are one of the most familiar features of the mainstream style of film editing identified with CLASSIC HOLLYWOOD CINEMA.

REVISIONISM. Revisionism is the process by which previously held interpretations or understandings are reconsidered. It is often used to describe histories that question the mythic or heroic attributes of individuals and actions, and it can refer to reassessments from both the left and the right. Examples of revisionism written from the perspective of the left can be found, for example, in recent reassessments of historical narratives that take the viewpoint of the colonizers when describing conflicts between explorers and settlers of European descent and African, Native American, and Third World peoples. Revisionist historians have reevaluated such widely disseminated myths as the heroism of the settlers of the West in relation to Native Americans or the valor of Christopher Columbus, and more generally questioned the way in which most history and interpretation has been written from the perspective of the traditionally dominant white male culture of the West. By contrast, the most extreme (and for most, implausible) example of right-wing revisionism is the recent attempt to downplay or deny the Holocaust.

RHIZOME. Although the botanic definition of *rhizome* (REIzom) is a prostrate stem growing along or just under the ground, the word has acquired a more idiosyncratic meaning in the collaborative writings of the French poststructuralist philosopher Gilles Deleuze and the French psychiatrist and exponent of "anti-psychiatry" Félix Guattari (notably *A Thousand Plateaus*). In their work, *rhizome* is a complex metaphor that contrasts with the "rootedness" of traditional metaphysical systems (see DECEN-TERING, ESSENTIALISM, METAPHYSICS). Much as they celebrate the "nomadic" qualities of the schizophrenic, Deleuze and Guattari see the rhizome as an alternative to the repressive notions of territoriality concealed in the metaphor of "roots." See also DETERRITORIALIZATION, SCHIZOANALYSIS.

Deleuze, Gilles, and Félix Guattari. *A Thousand Plateaus: Capitalism and Schizophrenia.* Trans. Brian Massumi. London: Athlone Press, 1988.

ROMANCE. The word *romance* is often used to refer to narratives of chivalric adventure that are set in a distant time or place and involve elements of the supernatural. In its original medieval usage, the term had an even broader application and referred to any long tale in verse; however, since the end of the Middle Ages, it has been most often used to designate stories on the order of *Perceval* or *Sir Gawain and the Green Knight*. Thus, romance heroes are usually of high birth, and the world of romance is a world in which magical transformations are always a possibility.

Apart from these remarks, it is difficult to generalize about a term so widely and variously used over so long a period of time, except to say that it has meant many things to many people. During the ENLIGHTENMENT, for example, the word was practically synonymous with the idea of extravagant fiction or even outright falsehood, whereas some recent writers like Northrop Frye have elevated the idea of romance into the source and model of *all* storytelling. In contemporary criticism, one issue in which the concept of romance has figured crucially is the debate over the origins of the novel, which is often said to have come into being as a realistic genre in contrast to the fantastic orientation of earlier large-scale prose narratives. See also ROMANCE PLOT.

Frye, Northrop. *The Secular Scripture.* Cambridge, Mass.: Harvard University Press, 1976.

ROMANCE PLOT. From medieval troubadour lyrics to contemporary Harlequin paperbacks, the plot of heterosexual romance has presented both the only socially sanctioned destiny for the female protagonist and the only paradigm in terms of which she may properly express sexual desire. Women writing within this tradition have employed various strategies to enlarge its possibilities. Nancy Miller has argued that in women's novels of the eighteenth and nineteenth centuries, the romance plot is often crossed by an adventure or quest plot. Even when the former appears to prevail over the latter, the incongruity of the two may produce a subversive tension in these texts. Rachel Blau DuPlessis suggests that twentieth-century women writers have developed new ways to counter the romance's socializing tendencies, often "writing beyond" the convention of marriage (if not death) as the female protagonist's end. Yet romance plots continue to flourish in today's popular culture—on TV, in movies, and in popular fiction. Feminist scholarship on the popular romance has attempted to explain the genre's continuing appeal for women readers in part by consulting those readers themselves. Janice Radway, in her interviews with regular romance readers, found that these books can do preliminary feminist work by making women aware of the inconsistencies between the tales' romantic ideal and their own lives. Tania Modleski sees Harlequins as somewhat more ambiguous, both reconciling women to passivity and, at the same time, allowing them to vent some anger about this. See also COMPULSORY HETEROSEXUALITY, ROMANCE.

DuPlessis, Rachel Blau. *Writing Beyond the Ending: Narrative Strategies of Twentieth-Century Women Writers*. Bloomington: Indiana University Press, 1985.

Miller, Nancy K. "Emphasis Added: Plots and Plausibilities in Women's Fiction." In Elaine Showalter, ed., *The New Feminist Criticism*. New York: Pantheon, 1985.

Modleski, Tania. *Loving With a Vengeance: Mass-Produced Fantasies for Women*. New York: Methuen, 1984.

Radway, Janice A. *Reading the Romance: Women, Patriarchy and Popular Literature*. Chapel Hill: University of North Carolina Press, 1984.

RUPTURE. *Rupture* describes any kind of abrupt break (sometimes called "discontinuity"), whether textual or historical, significant for POSTSTRUC-TURALIST and SYMPTOMATIC READINGS. Althusser describes the *coupure épistémologique*, or epistemological rupture, as a discontinuity in the history of human thought, and Foucault identifies and analyzes moments in human history when the way of thinking about the world seems suddenly to shift, although these moments cannot be explained by reference to any MASTER NARRATIVE. The examination of such discontinuities proves to be a useful tool for the kind of historical analysis important for Marxist and poststructuralist critique; Derrida describes the rupture of the deconstructive movement as a "redoubling," where the interest in structure itself—the attention to the "structurality of structure"—leads to a break with how the concept was previously conceived. See also DECONSTRUCTION, GENEALOGY, PARADIGM.

Althusser, Louis. *Lenin and Philosophy and other Essays*. Trans. Ben Brewster. New York: Monthly Review Press, 1971.

Derrida, Jacques. "Structure, Sign and Play in the Discourse of the Human Sciences." In *Writing and Difference*. Trans. Alan Bass. Chicago: University of Chicago Press, 1978.

RUSSIAN FORMALISTS. The Russian Formalists were a group of linguists and literary critics whose primary interest was the study of the literariness or the set of devices and conventions that distinguish literary language from everyday language. As a movement, Russian Formalism lasted from about 1914 to 1928. It is connected with two parallel but distinct groups—the Leningrad (St. Petersburg) group, Opojaz, and the Moscow group, which is known as the Moscow Linguistic Circle. The Leningrad group included Viktor Shklovsky, Boris Eichenbaum, Sergei Bernstein, and later Boris Tomashevsky and Juri Tynjanov. The Moscow circle counted Roman Jakobson, G. O. Vinokur, and Petry Bogatyrev among its members. Like their American counterparts, the NEW CRITICS (whose theories were developed independently), the Russian Formalists repudiated biographical and historical criticism for an emphasis on the autonomy of the text. They sought to develop literary criticism as an "objective" study. Unlike the New Critics, however, the Russian Formalists had no interest in concepts of organicism, and were equally at ease in the discussion of lyric, drama, or narrative. An important contribution of this school was Shklovsky's concept of *ostranenie,* or DEFAMILIARIZATION. According to Shklovsky, language tends to become smooth, unconscious, and transparent. Literary works lay bare this aspect of language by "making strange" the world and thus renew the reader's capacity for fresh sensation. The EPIC THEATER of Bertolt Brecht is partially influenced by this notion.

Because of its emphasis on form and the foregrounding of the linguistic aspects of a literary text over its content, Russian Formalism was at great odds with Stalinist literary doctrine, and after Stalin consolidated his power in 1929, the Russian Formalists were suppressed. Their work was carried on in the West, however, by Jakobsen, who emigrated to Prague and who, together with Jan Mukrarovsky and René Wellek, was associated with the Prague Linguistic Circle (see PRAGUE CIRCLE). Both Jakobson and Wellek ultimately continued their careers in America. Another important group that evolved from the original Russian Formalists is the Bakhtin School, which remained in Russia and included Mikhail Bakhtin, Valentin Voloshinov, and Pavel Medvedev. These theorists combined many of the key tenets of Formalism and Marxism in their concepts of the DIALOGIC and multi-accentuality. The work of the Russian Formalists was "rediscovered" in the 1960s and was important to the development of a number of STRUCTURALIST theories of literature.

Erhlich, Victor. *Russian Formalism: History, Doctrine.* New Haven: Yale University Press, 1981.

Lemon, Lee T., and Marion J. Reese, trans. *Russian Formalist Criticism: Four Essays.* Lincoln: University of Nebraska Press, 1965.

Thompson, E. M. *Russian Formalism and Anglo-American New Criticism.* The Hague: Mouton, 1971.

Wellek, René. *The Literary Theory and Aesthetics of the Prague School.* Ann Arbor: University of Michigan Press, 1969.

S

SADISM. Sadism is a form of sexual behavior in which pleasure is derived from causing others to suffer pain or humiliation. The practice is named after the Marquis de Sade, a late eighteenth-century French nobleman and libertine who, while imprisoned, authored a number of novels (*Justine, Juliette*), stories (*Les crimes de l'amour*), and tracts (*La philosophie dans le boudoir*) that detail his tastes in extravagant profusion. The works of de Sade have drawn considerable interest among mid-twentieth-century French intellectuals, such as Simone de Beauvoir, Georges Bataille, Maurice Blanchot, and Pierre Klossowski; their influence on contemporary theoretical debates has in turn given the subject of sadism a degree of currency in America. Among Freudian psychoanalysts, sadism is understood as a fundamental impulse, present within the psyche of every individual from his or her earliest months; moreover, it is viewed as the prior counterpart of MASOCHISM, although this pairing has been questioned. When he came to introduce the concept of the DEATH INSTINCTS in the latter part of his career, Freud described sadism as one of their clearest manifestations.

Bataille, Georges. *L'Erotism: Death & Sensuality.* Trans. Mary Dalwood. San Francisco: City Lights, 1986.

Freud, Sigmund. *Beyond the Pleasure Principle.* Rev. ed. Trans. and ed. James Strachey. New York: Liveright, 1961.

—. "Instincts and Their Vicissitudes." In *Standard Edition of the Complete Psychological Works of Sigmund Freud,* vol. 14. Trans. James Strachey. London: Hogarth Press and Institute of Psycho-Analysis, 1974.

Klossowski, Pierre. *Sade My Neighbor.* Trans. Alphonso Lingis. Evanston, Ill.: Northwestern University Press, 1991.

SCALE/SHOT SCALE. Having to do with the FRAMING of the film image, *scale* refers to the size of the elements in the image onscreen. It is determined by the distance of the camera from what has been filmed and by the type of lens used in the filming. Distances range from the extreme close-up, through the medium shot to the extreme long shot. Whatever the camera distance, however, a zoom lens may make something relatively distant look close (in its telephoto range) or something relatively close look more distant (in its wide-angle range).

SCHIZOANALYSIS. The term *schizoanalysis* (SKITzoanALuhsis) describes the philosophical critique developed in the collaborative work of the French poststructuralist philosopher Gilles Deleuze and the French psychoanalyst and exponent of "anti-psychiatry" Félix Guattari. The prefix *schizo-* refers both to schizophrenics themselves and, more generally, to the process of splitting, dividing, and cracking, which is characteristic of Deleuze and Guattari's dismantling of totalizing thought (see TOTALITY). Schizoanalysis is typified by its celebration of deliberately imprecise concepts like "flows" and "intensities." The study of such processes in congenial authors like Antonin Artaud and Franz Kafka was a primary concern of Deleuze and Guattari, as is the critique of psychoanalysis, which they viewed as a reductive mode of interpretation that channels desire into forms congenial to capitalism, such as the

OEDIPUS COMPLEX. Nevertheless, schizoanalysis is not a theory of revolution so much as a strategy for survival under capitalism, against which their celebration of the free-floating, fragmented subject was primarily directed.

Deleuze, Gilles, and Félix Guattari. *Anti-Oedipus: Capitalism and Schizophrenia.* Trans. Robert Hurley, Mark Seem, and Helen R. Lane. New York: Viking, 1983.

—. *Kafka: Toward a Minor Literature.* Trans. Dana Polan. Minneapolis: University of Minnesota Press, 1986.

—. *A Thousand Plateaus: Capitalism and Schizophrenia.* Trans. Brian Massumi. London: Athlone Press, 1987.

Massumi, Brian. *A User's Guide to Capitalism and Schizophrenia: Deviations from Deleuze and Guattari.* Cambridge, Mass.: MIT Press, 1992.

SCHOOL OF CONSTANCE. The School of Constance refers to those working in reception theory and criticism at the University of Constance, Germany. The most prominent of this group is Hans Robert Jauss, whose REZEPTIONSÄSTHETIK is largely derived from the philosophical HERMENEUTICS of Hans Georg Gadamer and the PHENOMENOLOGY of Martin Heidegger.

SCOPOPHILIA. Translated from the Latin, *scopophilia* (SKOPoFILeeuh) means "pleasure in looking." For Freud, it named a sexual drive that manifests itself in a detached, inquiring gaze. The gaze can provide satisfactions independent of physical, tactile pleasure. The pleasure in looking at the sexual object is, Freud argued, an intermediary stage along the path to sexual fulfillment; this desire becomes a perversion when the looking becomes an individual's only goal (as in the case of the "peeping Tom"). For film theorists, movie-watching activates the scopophilic drive. We find pleasure in "taking other people as objects, subjecting them to a controlling and curious gaze." This visual pleasure is enabled by the theater experience, which promotes the viewer's fantasy of secretly observing a private world. According to much film theory, however, the form of most mainstream film narratives organizes looking and objectification according to gender—men are active individuals who look; women are passive objects to be looked at. Such films thus play on scopophilic desire to endorse a certain representation of women, a representation that denies women AGENCY and complexity; in order to give male vision privilege and control, the female form is ideal-ized and/or fragmented. See also MALE GAZE, VISUAL PLEASURE, VOYEURISM.

Freud, Sigmund. *Three Essays on the Theory of Sexuality.* Trans. and ed. James Strachey. London: Hogarth Press, 1962.

Mulvey, Laura. "Visual Pleasure and Narrative Cinema." In Constance Penley, ed., *Feminism and Film Theory.* New York: Routledge, 1988.

Willemen, Paul. "Voyeurism, The Look, and Dwoskin." In Philip Rosen, ed., *Narrative, Apparatus, Ideology: A Film Theory Reader.* New York: Columbia University Press, 1986.

SCREEN GROUP. Published under the auspices of the Society for Education in Film and Television, *Screen* has been an influential British journal of film theory since 1969. It was intended as the theoretical complement to the pedagogically oriented *Screen Education,* a journal it incorporated in 1982. Distinguishing themselves from romantic auteurists and dry structuralists, the journal editors sought theories specific to the process of film viewing and narration in capitalist culture. For *Screen* theorists, film is not an autonomous art-object with an essential meaning; rather, it is a semiotic practice, a series of images that actively produces meaning and thus positions the viewer to receive those meanings in certain ways. Early issues printed essays by the Russian Formalists, Bertolt Brecht, Walter Benjamin, and Christian Metz. By the mid-seventies, writers for *Screen* were forging links among feminism, semiotics, Marxism, and Lacanian psychoanalysis, introducing concepts like IDENTIFICATION, VOYEURISM, and FETISHISM into the study of ideology. In the late seventies, the abstractions of "screen theory" led to contentious and fertile debate over the magazine's direction, particularly its use of Lacan and its distance from the classroom. *Screen* maintained this self-critique through the eighties, an era that saw the journal refine its critical vocabulary and widen the scope of its analysis of visual culture to include television, new media technologies, and representations of race. See also FILM THEORY.

Hall, Stuart. "Recent Developments in Theories of Language and Ideology." In Stuart Hall, ed., *Culture, Media, Language: Working Papers in Cultural Studies, 1972–79.* London: Hutchinson, 1980.

MacCabe, Colin. *Tracking the Signifier: Theoretical Essays on Film, Linguistics and Literature.* Minneapolis: University of Minnesota Press, 1985.

Screen, vols. 1– . London: Society for Education in Film and Television, 1959–.

SELF-PRESERVATIVE INSTINCTS. See LIFE INSTINCTS.

SEMANTICS. Semantics is the study of meaning in language. Although the term comes from linguistics, where it referred originally to the historical study of meaning, it has moved into more general usage since the advent of STRUCTURALISM and other linguistic models in the social sciences and humanities.

SEMIOLOGICAL OPPOSITION. The concept of opposition is one of the main underpinnings of any semiotic investigation. According to Saussure, since all sign-systems are arbitrarily constructed, the significance of any individual sign can be determined by its opposition to all other signs. The word *cat*, for example, has meaning not because of some essential connection between the word and the thing to which it refers, but because of its difference from words such as *bat*, *mat*, and *car*. Sign-systems or languages are thus self-defining. In Greimas's SEMIOTIC RECTANGLE, every term has an opposing term that—even though absent—serves to define the first term. For Jakobson, meaning in a poem or any other text presents itself to us through opposition (what he calls "polarities") and equivalencies; there is no need to refer to anything outside the text. Although the principle of opposition is still very important, Jakobson's view is generally taken to be outmoded. In order to be able to perceive opposition *as* opposition, readers need to consult (or have a knowledge of) other texts or spoken language. See also PRAGUE CIRCLE, SEMIOTICS.

Saussure, Ferdinand de. *Course in General Linguistics.* Trans. Roy Harris, eds. Charles Bally and Albert Sechehaye. London: Duckworth, 1983.

SEMIOTIC RECTANGLE. The semiotic rectangle or "elementary structure of signification" is an idea developed by A. J. Greimas and François Rastier to demonstrate how a single pair of contrary terms can give rise to an entire system of SIGNS. Thus, any given opposition inevitably implies another opposition made up of the simple negations of the original two terms. For example, a pair of contrary terms like x and y implies a second pair, $-x$ and $-y$, constituting a four-part apparatus that can be diagrammed as a rectangle. These four terms can also be combined in various ways to produce another four (since a term cannot be combined with its own negation, there are four possibilities: *x/y*, *x/-y*, *-x/-y*, and *-x/y*); and such combinations can be shown to constitute the logical structure of sign systems ranging from the types of sexual relations recognized by a given culture to the cast of characters in a novel. This latter possibility has been frequently exploited by Fredric Jameson, who has done much to popularize the semiotic rectangle in American literary criticism.

Greimas, A. J., and François Rastier. "The Interaction of Semiotic Constraints." *Yale French Studies* 41, 1968.

Jameson, Frederic. *The Political Unconscious: Narrative as a Socially Symbolic Act.* Ithaca, N.Y.: Cornell University Press, 1981.

SEMIOTICS/SEMIOLOGY. Semiotics is the study of SIGNS and the ways that they produce meaning. Of central concern to semiotics are the ways that signs function socially, how they are organized in systems such as languages and CODES, and how they are produced and disseminated. While the philosophical concept of the sign has received attention from thinkers for centuries, it is only over the last one hundred years that there has been a concerted effort to formulate a separate discipline for the study of signs. And it has only been in recent years, roughly since the advent of STRUCTURALISM in the 1960s, that semiotics has had a profound influence on literature, art, and social theorizing and criticism.

The term *semiotics* is taken from the work of the American philosopher Charles Sanders Peirce (1839–1914), who viewed the science of signs as a generalized system and a branch of logic. He distinguished three types of signs based upon the relation between the thing signifying and that which it signifies. The ICON's relationship is founded on similarity or shared features, such as that between a photograph and its subject. The INDEX bears a causal relationship to its signified, such as that between a barometer reading and atmospheric pressure. The SYMBOL's relationship to its signified is a conventional one, and thus arbitrary. For example, the use of a flag to represent a country is an act of symbolic signification.

Though these distinctions have been used by a number of contemporary semioticians, the work of the Swiss linguist Ferdinand de Saussure

(1857–1913) has been more influential in the development of semiotics in this century. Saussure, whose theory of the sign in language is based upon the arbitrary connection between SIGNIFIER and SIGNIFIED, suggested that since language is but one of innumerable systems of signs, it would be possible to formulate a science of sign systems, a *semiology*, based upon his theory of signification as a function of difference. He believed that this theory could extend to an understanding of the ways that such activities as writing, military signals, and conventions of politeness communicate meaning.

The ascendancy of structuralism in France in the 1960s helped bring about a new interest in Saussure and, as a result, semiology (or semiotics as it is now usually called) gained a number of influential adherents. Not only was it a useful approach to literary texts, allowing the critic to DECODE the systems of signification in a work, but culture critics such as Roland Barthes successfully applied its principles to social/cultural phenomena as diverse as the striptease, professional wrestling, women's fashions, and children's toys. Other thinkers, such as Michel Foucault in his history of the medical clinic, and Jacques Lacan in his formulation of the unconscious as a language, have used many of the principles of semiotic analysis to inform their work.

While POSTSTRUCTURALIST critiques of semiotics have arisen in the past decade, most of which abjure an attempt to uncover determinate meaning, semiotic techniques still persist in all aspects of the human sciences. FILM THEORY in particular has benefited from the insights of psychoanalytic and feminist uses of semiotics. CULTURAL STUDIES, especially that not explicitly linked to the fundamentally Marxist project of the BIRMINGHAM CENTER FOR CONTEMPORARY CULTURE STUDIES, has also found semiotics one of many useful methodologies.

Barthes, Roland. *Elements of Semiology*. 1964. Trans. Annette Lavers and Colin Smith. London: Cape, 1967.

Eco, Umberto. *Theory of Semiotics*. Bloomington: Indiana University Press, 1979.

Hawkes, Terence. *Structuralism and Semiotics*. Berkeley: University of California Press, 1977.

Kristeva, Julia. *Desire in Language: A Semiotic Approach to Literature and Art*. Trans. Alice Jardine et al., ed. Leon S. Roudiez. Oxford: Blackwell, 1980.

Peirce, Charles S. *Values in a Universe of Chance: Selected Writings of Charles S. Peirce*. Ed. Philip P. Weiner. Stanford, Calif.: Stanford University Press, 1958.

Saussure, Ferdinand de. *Course in General Linguistics*. Trans. Roy Harris, eds. Charles Bally and Albert Sechehaye. London: Duckworth, 1983.

Silverman, Kaja. *The Subject of Semiotics*. New York: Oxford University Press, 1983.

SERIALIZATION. Serialization, the strategy of fragmenting or differentiating a concept into its component parts, is employed by such theorists as Norman Holland, E. D. Hirsch, and Roman Ingarden in their accounts of meaning. In the attempt to comprehend the concept of meaning, the theorist separates meaning into individual, conceptually autonomous phases, levels, or categories, which are causally related and thus presumably more accessible to critical scrutiny.

SEX/GENDER SYSTEM. Gayle Rubin introduced the term *sex/gender system* in 1975 to describe the cultural arrangements that regulate both sexual desires ("sex") and male/female roles ("gender"). Feminists in many disciplines have found the term extremely useful because it treats these desires and these roles as cultural products (not biological inevitabilities), which are therefore subject to change. Insisting that "patriarchy" is only one particular kind of sex/gender system, Rubin leaves room for the possibility of other, less restrictive and less hierarchical systems. Yet while sex/gender systems vary according to culture and historical moment, Rubin (drawing on the work of Marx, Freud, Jacques Lacan, and Claude Lévi-Strauss) maintains that most have arisen out of kinship systems that exchange women between men in order to cement male social and political bonds—what she calls the "traffic in women." Patriarchal systems of this kind require males and females to repress their similarities and accentuate their differences, instituting at once an antithesis between active/male and passive/female, and a notion of heterosexuality based on this antithesis. Rubin has since modified her position to argue that the construction and regulation of sexuality and of gender, while interrelated in complex ways, cannot be accounted for in terms of a single system. See also PATRIARCHY.

Rubin, Gayle. "The Traffic in Women: Notes on the 'Political Economy' of Sex." In Rayna R. Reiter, ed., *Toward an Anthropology of Women*. New York: Monthly Review Press, 1975.
—. "Thinking Sex: Notes for a Radical Theory of the Politics of Sexuality." In Carol S. Vance, ed., *Pleasure and Danger: Exploring Female Sexuality*. Boston: Routledge, 1984.

SEXUAL DIFFERENCE. Feminism has generally accepted the distinction that one's "sex" is defined by the biological difference between men and women, while "gender" refers to the social experience of those differences. Yet feminists have been divided over how to incorporate the concept of sexual difference into their project. Early academic feminists (in the late 1960s and well into the 1970s) broke ground by demanding equal time for women in their writings and in the classroom. These feminists maintained an ambivalent attitude toward the concept of difference: difference represented the stigma of their discrimination while it also provided them with a set of "women's values" that served as the basis of solidarity and political action. Carol Gilligan, for example, noted a fundamental difference in the moral perspectives of males and females, a particularly "feminine voice" in which females' moral judgments are expressed. Women's morality, according to Gilligan, is predicated on the interdependence of the self and others and on emotional understanding, while masculine morality follows from an ideal of the autonomous self and from an abstract notion of hierarchical justice rather than compassion or empathy. Gilligan points out that masculine morality has been used to define traditional morality, while the female voice has been described as deviant and inferior.

French feminism has claimed sexual difference as the site of a different kind of feminine voice, variously described by Hélène Cixous as ÉCRITURE FEMININE, by Luce Irigaray as *parler femme* ("womanspeak"), and by Julia Kristeva as the semiotic. None of these women fully accepts the distinction between "man" and "woman"; indeed, they question the binary logic which supports the male/female duality. Yet because this binary logic resides in language, it can only be subverted by a different type of language. This different, revolutionary language is for each of these thinkers a female or woman-identified language: a language celebrating that which has been traditionally defined as feminine. Thus, as Toril Moi has emphasized, the concept of "femininity" and therefore of difference is central for each of these thinkers.

Recent Anglo-American cultural materialist feminists such as Mary Poovey, Hazel Carby, and Nancy Armstrong have also seen difference as the crucial premise in the cultural production of gender. These critics investigate the cultural logic of gender in order to expose the constructed nature of sexual difference and categories of definition such as "man" and "woman." Unlike their French counterparts, however, they do not valorize difference or femininity. Because gender definitions are never seamless and universal but rather contain contradictions along the lines of class and race (among others), feminist cultural materialists avoid so-called essentialist terms like "feminine voice" and "female writing." They look at how gender is experienced differently by different social groups, and enlisted by often conflicting cultural ideologies. Difference is consequently viewed as a concept that both maintains and threatens to subvert the stability of the cultural logic of gender. See also DIFFERENCE, GENDER STUDIES, SEX-GENDER SYSTEM.

Armstrong, Nancy. *Desire and Domestic Fiction: A Political History of the Novel.* New York: Oxford University Press, 1987.

Carby, Hazel V. *Reconstructing Womanhood: The Emergence of the Afro-American Woman Novelist.* New York: Oxford University Press, 1987.

Cixous, Hélène. "The Laugh of the Medusa." In Elaine Marks and Isabelle de Courtivron, eds., *New French Feminisms.* Trans. Keith Cohen and Paula Cohen. Amherst: University of Massachusetts Press, 1980.

Eisenstein, Hester, and Alice Jardine, eds. *The Future of Difference.* Boston: G. K. Hall, 1980.

Gilligan, Carol. *In a Different Voice: Psychological Theory and Women's Development.* Cambridge, Mass.: Harvard University Press, 1982.

Irigaray, Luce. *This Sex Which is Not One.* Trans. Catherine Porter. Ithaca, N.Y.: Cornell University Press, 1985.

Kristeva, Julia. "La Femme, Ce n'est Jamais Ça." In Elaine Marks and Isabelle de Courtivron, eds., *New French Feminisms.* Trans. Keith Cohen and Paula Cohen. Amherst: University of Massaachusetts Press, 1980.

Moi, Toril. *Sexual/Textual Politics: Feminist Literary Theory.* New York: Routledge, 1985.

Poovey, Mary. *Uneven Developments: The Ideological Work of Gender in Mid-Victorian England.* Chicago: University of Chicago Press, 1988.

SEXUAL POLITICS. Sexual politics refers to the political character of gender relations, which are based on the unequal distribution of power between men and women. The term comes from Kate Millett's *Sexual Politics* (1970), one of the first books to propose a broad theory of systematic male domination. Here Millett widened the definition of "politics" to include all "power-structured relationships," particularly those between women and men. She argued that politics in this sense structures the personal realm, everyday life at home, as well as public institutions—thus the famous slogan, "the personal is political." Making visible men's power over women—in bed, in the classroom, in the workplace, in novels by respected authors—was, her work suggested, the first step in challenging it. Millett's examination of misogynist sexual politics in several literary texts provided an important model for later feminist literary critics. More recently, Catherine MacKinnon's work has brought the concept of sexual politics to bear on areas traditionally considered "political," analyzing the law and political philosophy in order to formulate a theory of feminist jurisprudence. See also FEMINIST CRITIQUE, MISOGYNY, PATRIARCHY.

MacKinnon, Catherine. *Toward a Feminist Theory of the State*. Cambridge, Mass.: Harvard University Press, 1989.
Millett, Kate. *Sexual Politics*. New York: Avon, 1970.

SHOT (OR TAKE). A shot (or take) is an uninterrupted run of the camera in which one or more FRAMES of film are continuously exposed, which results in the uninterrupted presentation of an image from a single FRAMING, whether static or mobile. A film may be made up of only one or of many hundreds of shots.

SHOT SCALE. See SCALE.

SIGN. In contradistinction to the term *word*, *sign* refers to the arbitrary association of sound-images (SIGNIFIER) and concepts (SIGNIFIED), where sound-image means the sound of, say, *H-O-R-S-E* or the image of the letters when the sound is written, and where concept means the idea or material object with which a community of speakers associates the sound-image. The term was employed by the German PHENOMENOLOGIST Edmund Husserl at the end of the nineteenth century, but has been more widely circulated in the twentieth century by the followers of the Swiss linguist and founder of SEMIOLOGY Ferdinand de Saussure. Husserl writes: "Every sign is a sign for something, but not every sign has 'meaning.' . . . In many cases it is not even true that a sign 'stands for' that of which we may say it is a sign." Saussure gives the now celebrated example of the sound of the combined letters *T-R-E-E* and the marks or images on a page by which the sounds are indicated. He argues that the linguistic sound-image is only *arbitrarily* related to the concept of the tree that we find in nature. In other words, the sound-image is distinct from the concept to which it refers. Only dictionaries—or the record of rules by which a group of people using a common language agree to assign specific sound-images to specific concepts—join the two components of a sign.

The theory of the sign circulated by the American founder of SEMI-OTICS, C. S. Peirce, has enjoyed a smaller circulation than that of Saussure's, but its distinction between three types of sign—the iconic, indexical, and symbolic—is extremely useful. In essence, Pierce's theory accounts for the ways that signifiers themselves produce meaning. Thus, a signifier may come in the form of a picture of a fish in the key to a map of a recreational area (iconic), where the icon of a fish means an area in which fish may be caught. This is an association by resemblance. It may take on an indexical meaning when it is used to refer to a low calorie, low cholesterol, and high protein recipe in a cookbook—an association by cause. And it may take on a symbolic meaning when it is used to refer to the death and rebirth of man through Christ—an association by arbitrary social agreement (see ICON).

While earlier philosophies teach us that words refer to things (see IDEALISM), the phenomenological and linguistic theories of Husserl, Saussure, and Peirce lead to a radical revision in our understanding of the ways that language is made to refer to the material or the phenomenologically experienced world of individual human beings. See also STRUCTURALISM.

Culler, Jonathan. *Structuralist Poetics: Structuralism, Linguistics and the Study of Literature.* London: Routledge, 1975.

Jameson, Fredric. *The Prison-House of Language.* Princeton: Princeton University Press, 1972.

Saussure, Ferdinand de. *Course in General Linguistics.* Trans. Roy Harris, eds. Charles Bally and Albert Sechehaye. London: Duckworth, 1983.

SIGNIFIER/SIGNIFIED. The signifier and the signified are the two fundamental components of Ferdinand de Saussure's definition of the SIGN. The signifier is the perceivable, communicated, material portion of the sign. It may be a sound, a mark, or a collection of marks that make up a word. The signified, in contrast, is the conceptual portion of the sign that is formulated in the reader or listener. For Saussure, the relationship between signifier and signified does not depend on an external entity that is represented in the sign; rather, that relationship is arbitrary and conventional. For example, the collection of letters *D-O-G* does not depend on any specific dog for its meaning, nor is there any essential "dogness" in that collection of letters that demands its connection to the signified (in English) of a domesticated canine.

SIGNIFYIN(G). *Signifyin(g)* is a term introduced to literary criticism and theory by Henry Louis Gates, Jr. in his book *The Signifying Monkey*. Long the object of sociolinguistic analysis, signifyin(g) in Gates's formulation names an African-American "trope of tropes," a metafigure denoting all rhetorical strategies that subvert the dominant meaning of language practices through forms of linguistic free play. Functioning by means of indirection, implication, and metaphorical reasoning, signifyin(g) subsumes the many vernacular forms of African-American culture, including "marking, loud-talking, testifying, calling out (of one's name), sounding, rapping, [and] playing the dozens." Alternately self-deprecating and boastful, insulting and respectful, signifyin(g), like most performative modes, depends on the contingencies of context and audience in order to accomplish its many meanings. Signifyin(g) appears both *within* and *between* African-American literary texts, informing the language and structure of novels such as *Their Eyes Were Watching God* and mediating the intertextual connections between works such as *Invisible Man* and *Mumbo Jumbo*. See also FREE INDIRECT DISCOURSE, TOASTS.

Gates, Henry Louis, Jr. *The Signifyin(g) Monkey: A Theory of African-American Literary Criticism*. New York: Oxford University Press, 1988.

Kochman, Thomas, ed. *Rappin' and Stylin' Out: Communication in Urban Black America*. Urbana: University of Illinois Press, 1982.

SIMILE. See METAPHOR.

SIMULACRUM. In the philosophy of Plato, *simulacrum* (SIMyooLAKruhm) is the name given to the false copy, which stands in contrast to the essence or Idea; it is a debased reflection, understood as inferior to the pristine abstraction from which it is derived. Reacting against the Platonic tradition, along with the whole of Western METAPHYSICS, recent theorists have rejected the distinction between appearance and essence, and given new attention to the simulacrum as a key feature of contemporary life. Thus, the French philosopher Gilles Deleuze has expanded on Nietzsche's description of the philosophy of the future as the "overthrow of Platonism" by demonstrating how the simulacrum puts into question the very concept of a true copy. In much modern art, the simulacrum refers not to some objective truth against which it can be judged, but only to other simulacra. While this condition is necessarily disorienting, it is also liberating in that it renders obsolete the hierarchies assumed by the Platonic tradition. Recognizing the special applicability of this line of thought to the culture of our era, Jean Baudrillard has made the concept of the simulacrum central to his analysis of postmodern consumer society, with its endless networks of media and advertising images that, according to Baudrillard, precede any reality to which they might be said to refer (see POSTMODERNISM).

Baudrillard, Jean. "The Precession of Simulacra." In Brian Wallis, ed., *Art After Modernism: Rethinking Representation.* Boston: Godine, 1984.

Deleuze, Gilles. *The Logic of Sense.* Trans. Mark Lester. New York: Columbia University Press, 1990.

SIMULATION. Simulation is a process whereby a representation of something real comes to replace the thing being represented. The term was first used with this special sense by the French linguist Michel Pêcheux to describe the way language makes it possible to transform something specific and concrete into something universal and abstract. Jean Baudrillard cites, as a classic example of simulation, the story by Jorge Luis Borges in which "the cartographers of the Empire draw up a map so detailed that it ends up exactly covering the territory" to the point that the real territory beneath the map is eradicated, or visible only at the "tattered" margins of the map. For Baudrillard, the simulation is not a fake, a mere copy of something real, for it has a power and meaning that in many ways exceeds that of the real. When we value the representation of something more than the thing itself—as we might enjoy a film about downhill skiing more than actually skiing, which involves greater expense, much travel and waiting, and the fear of injury—we are participating in what Baudrillard calls the "orders" of simulation. Baudrillard sees history as a series of new orders of simulation, all leading to the disappearance or death of all meaning. See also SIMULACRUM.

Baudrillard, Jean. *Simulations.* Trans. Paul Foss, Paul Patton, and Philip Beitchman. New York: Semiotext(e), 1983.

SITUATIONIST INTERNATIONAL. The Situationist International (SI) was a small, AVANT-GARDE Marxist group that, in the decade or so prior to 1968, articulated a cogent critique of commodity fetishism and of the passivity encouraged by a spectacular society. The SI was formed in 1957 through the amalgamation of several other avant-garde groups, including the Lettrist International and the International Movement for an Imagist Bauhaus. Like the lettrists—and unlike more traditional Marxists, with their focus on production—the situationists emphasized the importance of everyday life as a sphere for critique and intervention. They used the term SPECTACLE to describe a society in which existence is continually mediated by images designed to encourage consumption.

The situationists initially promoted aesthetic productions that would use such strategies as REAPPROPRIATION to break down the distinction between art and life. But in 1962 the SI declared art production "antisituationist" because it tended to take place in a separate sphere from revolutionary activity. Instead, SI members were required to respond to all aspects of life with situationist strategies. Rather than seeking converts, the SI enforced critical engagement through frequent expulsions and, in 1972, the SI dissolved itself as a group, at least in part as a response to problems created by their success and popularity in 1968.

Debord, Guy. *Society of the Spectacle.* Detroit: Black and Red, 1977.

Knabb, Ken, ed. and trans. *Situationist International Anthology.* Berkeley, Calif.: Bureau of Public Secrets, 1981.

Sussman, Elisabeth, ed. *On the Passage of a Few People Through a Rather Brief Moment in Time: The Situationist International 1957–1972.* Cambridge, Mass.: MIT Press, 1989.

SOCIALISM. Generally speaking, socialism is the belief that the state should control (but not necessarily own) the means of production so as to ensure the fairest distributions of power, goods, and services to its members. In classical Marxism, socialism is a stage between capitalism and communism. Ownership of the resources and means of production has passed from private hands to society as a whole; the state still exists, but only as a means of regulating ownership. The good of society is considered a responsibility of the state, but the state serves as an administrator and a distributor, not a disseminator of doctrine or ideology. In the later stage of true communism, the state will "wither away" because it will no longer be necessary. Today, *socialism* is often used to describe something that is, in practice, deemed compatible with capitalism. That is, many Western European countries that protect private ownership are nonetheless considered socialist to the extent that they provide free health care, education, and other services. As a result, today's socialists

tend to occupy a middle ground between support for complete government regulation of industry and free enterprise. Historically, the vague-
ness of the term has allowed it to be used by parties ranging from the far
left to the far right: the National Socialist Party of Germany in the 1930s
(the Nazis), the Socialist Party of France, Christian Socialism, and the
socialism of Britain's Labour Party have little in common beyond their
use of the term. Although the concept is an ancient one, the term *socialist* was first used widely to describe early nineteenth-century conceptions
of utopian communities, such as those of Charles Fourier and Henri de
Saint-Simon in France and Robert Owen in Britain.

Cole, G. D. H. *A History of Socialist Thought.* New York: St. Martin's, 1964–67.
Lichtheim, George. *The Origins of Socialism.* New York: Praeger, 1969.
Marx, Karl. *Early Writings.* Trans and ed. T. B. Bottomore. New York: McGraw-Hill, 1964.

SOCIALIST FEMINISM. Also known as Marxist feminism, socialist
feminism arose alongside radical and LIBERAL FEMINISM in the 1970s.
More than simply combining Marxist analyses of class relations with
radical feminist analyses of gender relations, it seeks to redefine both by
putting them into dialogue, addressing the inadequacies of each. Target-
ing male supremacy as well as capitalism, issues of reproduction as well
as production, women as mothers as well as wage laborers, socialist feminists have elaborated the concept of women's "invisible labor" (unpaid
work such as cooking, cleaning, and childcare) as an illustration of the
interrelated exploitations of capitalism and patriarchy. Although academic feminism in the United States has, since the mid-1980s, begun to
address issues of class and race along with those of gender, socialist feminism has its strongest roots in England. Notable socialist feminists nevertheless include the Americans Zillah Eisenstein and Heidi Hartmann as
well as British scholars Sheila Rowbotham and Michele Barrett. See also
RADICAL FEMINISM.

Barrett, Michele. *Women's Oppression Today: Problems in Marxist Feminist Analysis.*
　　London: New Left Books, 1980.
Eisenstein, Zillah R., ed. *Capitalist Patriarchy and the Case for Socialist Feminism.* New
　　York: Monthly Review Press, 1979.
Rowbotham, Sheila. *Women, Resistance, and Revolution.* New York: Pantheon, 1972.

SOCIALIST REALISM. See REALISM.

SOUS RATURE. See ERASURE.

SPECTACLE. Although there have been public spectacles since well before the twentieth century, the term was used by members of the French movement centered around the journal *Internationale Situationniste* and known as the Situationists to describe the particular cultural condition in which people's self-conceptions are screened by forms of mass culture such as music, film, and (particularly) television. Since the publication of Situationist Guy Debord's *La Société du spectacle* in 1967, the concept of the spectacle has gained increasing prominence as a way of describing mass-media-based culture. According to Debord, in the society of the spectacle, lived experience is replaced by representations, and these images mediate or intervene in all levels of social interaction. See also SIMULATION, SITUATIONIST INTERNATIONAL.

Debord, Guy. *The Society of the Spectacle*. Detroit: Black and Red, 1977.

SPEECH ACT THEORY. Speech act theory is a school of linguistics that focuses on what language does rather than what language is. The theory was originated in the 1960s by a group of English linguists, of whom J. L. Austin and John R. Searle are the best known. They distinguished between two types of statement: those which make (true or false) reference to a present reality and those which, in a sense, bring a new sense of reality about. The latter statements (promises, warnings, greetings, etc.) do something particular to the receiver of their message. An individual speech act can be as short as a one-word sentence (e.g., "Stop!") and reach any length. A literary work can be classified as a speech act, for its primary purpose is to produce an effect upon the reader. As Terry Eagleton points out, eventually Austin came to see all speech as acting, for it can do such things as inform or deceive. See also CONSTATIVE UTTERANCE, PERFORMATIVE UTTERANCE, PERLOCUTIONARY ACT.

Austin, J. L. *How to Do Things with Words*. Cambridge, Mass.: Harvard University Press, 1962.

Pratt, Mary Louise. *Toward a Speech Act Theory of Literary Discourse*. Bloomington: Indiana University Press, 1977.

Searle, John R. *Speech Acts: An Essay in the Philosophy of Language*. London: Cambridge University Press, 1969.

STATEMENT. A statement is a declaration (usually linguistic) of a fact or opinion. It is, however, a specialized term for historians and philosophers of DISCOURSE—most notably Michel Foucault. For Foucault, a statement is any isolated manifestation of a larger discourse of power, a relationship between language and practice that is so close that they are practically the same thing. In *The Archaeology of Knowledge*, he explains a methodology that involves collecting all of the individual statements made within a specific field—e.g., "medicine, grammar, or political economy"—and then attempting to understand the discourse they comprise by describing the relations among them, grouping and regrouping statements around the "permanent and coherent concepts" they all share, seeking the "identity and persistence of themes." The end of this project is not to rebuild a basis for the traditional historian's claim that all the phenomena of a given era can be explained in relation to one dominant theme that looms over everything and determines language and practice. Rather, it posits history as generated by the constant combining and recombining of statements themselves—for Foucault, a historical era is characterized less by its theme or zeitgeist than the major trope through which it tends to make or combine its statements.

Foucault, Michel. *The Archaeology of Knowledge.* Trans. A. M. Sheridan Smith. New York: Pantheon, 1972.

STORY. A story is a chronological sequence of propositions consisting of actions and attributions that are invoked by a text. The story constitutes the raw material, the chronological series of events, manipulated by an author into a PLOT. Existing in a spatiotemporal plane beyond the text, the story may be viewed as the particular series of events that occurred in real time preceding the author's narration. As the basis of plot, story may be completely rearranged and organized to accommodate plot and narrative meaning. The distinction between story and plot has been of particular significance to RUSSIAN FORMALISM and STRUCTURALISM. The view that story is separable from its narration is partly based on Emile Benveniste's observation that languages such as French and Greek have a special verb tense that distinguishes between a narration and the actual events narrated. In SEMIOTICS, story may also be associated with DIEGESIS. In this case, the story is the product that results from the reader's construal of a text. See also FABULA/SUJET, NARRATOLOGY.

Benveniste, Emile. *Problems in General Linguistics*. 1966. Trans. Mary Elizabeth Meek. Coral Gables, Fla.: University of Miami Press, 1971.

STRATEGIES OF AUTHENTICATION. *Strategies of authentication* is a term introduced by Robert Stepto in his book on African-American narrative, *From Behind the Veil*. The term refers to the literary situation of mid-nineteenth-century America, when the authors of slave narratives had to prove to their primarily white audiences that they had truly been slaves, and that their accounts of slavery were not fictions. This problem was solved by framing the slave narratives with documents (usually written by white authors) testifying to the experiences, ability, and character of the ex-slave. In the more sophisticated slave narratives, the authors integrate these documents and voices within their texts, thus gaining greater autonomy and control. The lack of control by African-American authors over the meaning of their texts paralleled the slaves' earlier lack of control over their bodies and the meaning of their lives. It also meant that early African-American literature was double-voiced, in that it fought a usually hidden battle for the control of meaning with surrounding white authorities. In a less literal sense, then, we can extend the term to refer to the various strategies, whether of plot, style, or genre, by which a minority text adjusts to the demands of the standard marketplace. The phrase is important for African-American criticism because it pinpoints the terms on which minority voices are admitted to the larger culture, as well as pointing to how African-American authors have historically subverted such limitations to regain control and assert their voice. See also DOUBLE-VOICED TEXT.

Stepto, Robert B. *From Behind the Veil: A Study of Afro-American Narrative*. Urbana: University of Illinois Press, 1979.

STRATEGY OF CONTAINMENT. The contemporary Marxist critic Fredric Jameson has coined the phrase *strategy of containment* to describe the ways that the various methods of interpretation create the illusion that their readings of works of literature are complete and self-sufficient. Patterned after Marx's description of the ways that the classical schools of political economy avoided the consequences of their own best insights, Jameson's concept is thus a tool with which to analyze the workings of ideology and is premised on the Hegelian idea that no interpretation can be complete unless it understands the literary work in relation to the whole of the social TOTALITY.

Jameson, Fredric. *The Political Unconscious: Narrative as a Socially Symbolic Act.* Ithaca, N.Y.: Cornell University Press, 1981.

STRUCTURAL ANTHROPOLOGY. See STRUCTURALISM.

STRUCTURALISM. Structuralism is a complex intellectual movement that first established its importance in France in the 1950s and 1960s. By the late 1960s and early 1970s the work of thinkers like Claude Lévi-Strauss, A. J. Greimas, and Roland Barthes began to exert considerable influence in the United States and England, especially among linguists and literary critics.

The foundations of structuralism are diverse. Formulated in large part on the Swiss linguist Ferdinand de Saussure's (1857–1913) theory of language as based on a system of differences rather than resemblances or similarities, it is also informed by the work of the RUSSIAN FORMALISTS and the narratological work of Vladimir Propp, especially his 1928 work *Morphology of the Folktale* (see NARRATOLOGY). One of the most important contributions of structuralism to contemporary thought is its fundamental assumption that all human activity is constructed, not natural or "essential" (see ESSENTIALISM). When the anthropologist Lévi-Strauss applied this principle to cultural analysis, he emphasized the importance of the systems of conventions—of how and what a culture eats, the ways that a culturally important story is sequenced and told, or the ways that kinship relationships are formulated—over the specific content such orderings govern. For structuralists, it is the systems of organization themselves that are significant, since they are selected against a number of other possible orderings. These structures are homologous to Saussure's concept of langue. They signify a system of differences that govern the possibilities of their contents, which are homologous to the concept of parole (see LANGUE/PAROLE), or the specific utterance within such a system. Thus, any activity, from the actions in a narrative to not eating one's peas with a knife, takes place within a system of differences and has meaning only in its relations to other possible activities within that system, not to some meaning that emanates from nature or the divine.

In literary studies the concepts of structuralism have found their most influential articulations in SEMIOTICS and SEMIOLOGY. The impact of structuralism has perhaps been most important in its critique of MIMETIC THEORIES of literature, which until the advent of structuralism and POSTSTRUCTURALISM had dominated literary studies. Unlike mimetic criticism, structuralist analyses of literary texts do not argue for meaning as an expression of the AUTHOR or a reflection of "reality." Instead of focusing on meaning per se, structuralist critiques are more interested in *how* a text means. For structuralists, a text is an objective entity which enables CODES and CONVENTIONS that are not reliant upon AUTHOR, AUDIENCE (reader), or, for that matter, reality. The aim of such a critique is to demonstrate the ways that these codes and conventions function to limit the possibilities of meaning in a text. Although there have been some notable attempts to apply structuralist theories to the analysis of poetry, such as Michael Riffaterre's *Semiotics of Poetry*, the difficulty with such works has been the reproduction of those aspects of FORMALISM which have been most stridently attacked: the conception of the text as autonomous and impersonal, standing outside the social practices of language, and an emphasis on obscure patterns and structures that are unavailable to all but the most sophisticated—and in some accounts "creative"—critic.

Structural analyses of narrative have been considerably better received. Roland Barthes' groundbreaking *S/Z*, which identifies the various codes at work in a short story by Balzac, became a model of such critiques. Others, like Gérard Genette in his *Figures of Discourse* and Tzvetan Todorov in *The Poetics of Prose*, also provided early examples of the ways that structuralism might be used as a method of narrative analysis. The impact of structuralism has been felt in disciplines outside of literature and anthropology. In CULTURAL STUDIES, Roland Barthes's *Mythologies* offers insightful and witty structuralist-informed analyses of fashion, wrestling, and other cultural phenomena. The historical analyses of Michel Foucault in works like *The Birth of the Clinic* and especially *The Order of Things* have often been labeled "structuralist," though Foucault repeatedly denied the appellation. The work of the French Marxist philosopher Louis Althusser is commonly described as structural Marxism, while the psychoanalyst Jacques Lacan's theory that the unconscious is organized like a language also has affinities with structuralist thought. In recent years, poststructuralism has repudiated the claims of scientific or objective analysis that accompanied much early structuralist work. This is not to say that poststructuralism has abandoned its antecedents

entirely. While addressing issues like author, IDEOLOGY, and reader—
issues usually disregarded by structuralism—it has continued to insist on
the conventional, constructed character of meaning and on the importance of difference in that construction, even as it has used them to critique structuralism itself. See also ACTANTIAL MODEL, PARADIGM.

Barthes, Roland. *S/Z*. Trans. Richard Miller. New York: Hill and Wang, 1974.
—. *Mythologies*. Trans. Annette Lavers. New York: Hill and Wang, 1972.
—. "Introduction to the Structural Analysis of Narratives." In *Image, Music, Text*.
     Trans. Stephen Heath. New York: Hill and Wang, 1977.
Culler, Jonathan. *Structuralist Poetics: Structuralism, Linguistics and the Study of Litera-
     ture*. London: Routledge, 1975.
Foucault, Michel. *The Order of Things: An Archaeology of the Human Sciences*. New
     York: Vintage, 1970.
—. *The Birth of The Clinic*. Trans. A. M. Sheridan Smith. New York: Vintage, 1975.
Genette, Gérard. *Figures of Literary Discourse*. Trans. Alan Sheridan. New York: Colum-
     bia University Press, 1982.
Hawkes, Terence. *Structuralism and Semiotics*. Berkeley: University of California Press,
     1977.
Lévi-Strauss, Claude. *Structural Anthropology*. Trans. Claire Jacobson and Brook
     Grundfest Schoepf. New York: Basic Books, 1963.
Macksey, Richard, and Eugenio Donato, eds. *The Structuralist Controversy*. Baltimore:
     Johns Hopkins University Preess, 1972.
Piaget, Jean. *Structuralism*. Trans. and ed. Chaninah Maschler. New York: Basic Books,
     1970.
Riffaterre, Michael. *The Semiotics of Poetry*. Bloomington: Indiana University Press,
     1978.
Scholes, Robert. *Structuralism in Literature: An Introduction*. New Haven: Yale Univer-
     sity Press, 1974.
Todorov, Tzvetan. *The Poetics of Prose*. Trans. Richard Howard. Ithaca, N.Y.: Cornell
     University Press, 1977.

STRUCTURE OF FEELING. *Structure of feeling* is a term associated
with the cultural analysis of Raymond Williams, who first used it in his
Preface to Film and developed it as a methodological concept in *The Long
Revolution.* According to Williams, we are most aware of our "particular
sense of life, our particular community" when we notice the ways that we
are different from each other, even as we participate in a common culture. It is this difference even in our commonality that Williams defines
as a "structure of feeling." His examples from *The Long Revolution* use
generational differences to illustrate his point. He argues that a new generation, which has been taught the culture of the period, will nonetheless

formulate its own shared response to the world. Many aspects of that response will be traceable to the culture it inherited from the previous generation, but some aspects of it, says Williams, will "not appear to have come 'from' anywhere." In the *New Left Review*'s series of interviews with Williams, this concept comes under considerable attack, especially for what often appears to be its reliance on experience as a necessary prerequisite for knowledge of a culture.

Williams, Raymond. *The Long Revolution.* New York: Columbia University Press, 1961.
—. *Marxism and Literature.* Oxford: Oxford University Press, 1977.
—. *Politics and Letters: Interviews with the"New Left Review."* New York: Schocken, 1979.
— with Michael Orrom. *Preface to Film.* London: Film Drama, 1954.

STYLISTICS. Stylistics is the study of the formal characteristics or "surface" structures of texts, typically with attention to the distinctiveness of individual authors' or various epochs' styles. As such, stylistics is very often author-, rather than reader-centered. Roland Barthes identifies two different conceptions of style: that which opposes FORM to content, where style is seen as an ornament to content (as in the classical concept of *elocutio*); and that which distinguishes between code and message, where style is regarded as the message's DEVIATION from a coded norm. In the latter case, style may be analyzed with the concepts of deviation, addition, and choice between alternative messages. In each case, however, it is extremely difficult to determine what the norm might be and to imagine what writing without style (a degree-zero of writing) would look like. See also CODE.

Barthes, Roland. "Style and Its Image." In Seymour Chatman, ed. and trans., *Literary Style: A Symposium.* New York: Oxford University Press, 1971.

SUBALTERN. *Subaltern* is an adjective meaning "of lower rank"; it is still used in the British military to describe the ranks below captain. In recent political and cultural theory, especially that associated with the SUBALTERN STUDIES group and with Gayatri Chakravorty Spivak, *subaltern* is used as a catchall designation for members of subordinated populations—the colonized, women, blacks, the working class—although it is most often used to describe those oppressed by British colonialism and by the political and economic upheavals of the POSTCOLONIAL period.

The advantage of the term, however, is that it does not privilege any one category over the others; that is, it involves no commitment to the precedence of, say, economic oppression over racial oppression. At the same time, it does imply insurgency: the subaltern is a participant in a movement to overthrow the cultural and political forces that ensure his or her subordinate status.

Spivak, Gayatri Chakravorty. *In Other Worlds.* New York: Methuen, 1987.

SUBALTERN STUDIES. *Subaltern Studies* is the name of a circle of intellectuals and the journal they publish, based in New Delhi, India. The term is also used more generally and can also refer to the academic study of the lives and writings of SUBALTERNS. Deeply influenced by Marxist, semiotic, feminist, and deconstructionist ideas, the *Subaltern Studies* group aims, according to Gayatri Spivak, at "politicization for the colonized." In many ways, this group works for change by striving to seize control of and alter the overriding narratives that determine the subjectivity, identity, and speech of the subaltern. Although deeply political, the members of the *Subaltern Studies* group view political change as happening through alterations in consciousness and culture, changes led by an enlightened, disinterested intellectual class. This view reflects the influence of the Italian Marxist Antonio Gramsci, who used the term *subaltern* to refer to Italy's rural peasant classes. The work of the *Subaltern Studies* group has been instrumental in pushing issues of POSTCOLONIALISM to the fore of critical and theoretical endeavors in the West.

Spivak, Gayatri Chakravorty. *In Other Worlds.* New York: Methuen, 1987.
Subaltern Studies: Writings on South Asian History and Society. Ed. Ranajit Guha. Vols. 1–, 1982–.

SUBCULTURE. Generally speaking, the term *subculture* refers to a distinctive clique within a larger social group. Much work on the subject by members of the BIRMINGHAM CENTER FOR CONTEMPORARY CULTURAL STUDIES and other practitioners of CULTURAL STUDIES has stressed the ways that subcultures offer forms of symbolic resistance to the pressures of a discriminatory capitalist society. Unlike traditional leftist politics, subcultural activity does not aim to overthrow the dominant culture in the name of some more humane vision, but seeks only a measure of autonomy expressed in symbolic gestures, such as the distinctive forms of clothing, speech, and music that characterize groups like punks or skinheads. As Dick Hebdige argues in *Subculture: The Meaning of Style*, this is a "struggle within signification," which, ironically, feeds back into the dominant culture by providing it with the innovations it requires to sustain sales of new products. Moreover, subcultures often directly reflect some of the least appealing aspects of the dominant culture, such as racism and misogyny, leading critics to caution against treating them as independent entities or idealizing the forms of resistance that they offer.

Hall, Stuart. *Resistance Through Rituals: Youth Subcultures in Post War Britain.* London: Hutchinson, 1976.
Hebdige, Dick. *Subculture: The Meaning of Style.* London: Methuen, 1979.

SUBJECT/OBJECT. The subject/object division is a problem that has beleaguered thinkers since humans first recognized themselves as distinct from their surroundings and as able to have an effect on those surroundings. Reductively put, the subject may be seen as that which acts and the object as that which is acted upon. The importance of this simple distinction is that in the concept of the subject, human activity and AGENCY are present. Thus, when in describing certain critical perspectives the terms take on their adjectival forms, "subjective" and "objective," the implication is that subjective criticism is based upon particular human desires, needs, or interests (usually of the AUTHOR), while objective criticism is devoid of these impulses. When used in this sense, "subjective" almost always has pejorative connotations, since in its indulgence of the personal it cannot claim the same universality that "objective" criticism can.

Traditionally, science and other disciplines based upon EMPIRICISM have claimed a greater degree of objectivity inasmuch as they work inductively, deriving principles from observation. In the fields of literary and art criticism, FORMALISM often aligns itself with such claims, arguing that the literary text or work of art is an autonomous object and as such can be perceived and understood from a relatively objective point of view. In recent years, however, claims to objective knowledge have come under considerable attack. Arguing that even the act of perceiving is an essentially subjective activity, opponents of objective criticism have pointed out that it is impossible to evaluate or critique any work outside the domain of IDEOLOGY and that in fact objectivity of any sort is an impossibility. All we have is consensus regarding facts or truth—CONVENTIONS that we act upon and reaffirm, but which may be upset at any moment.

This emphasis on the constructedness of reality significantly informs another use of the term *subject* by many poststructuralist critics and theorists. In this sense, *subject* refers to the thinking, acting person. But in contrast to the term *individual*, which connotes a certain amount of autonomy and unity, *subject* indicates a being who is constituted in and by language or ideology, who is not determined merely by consciousness, unconsciousness, or identification with a particular race, class, gender, or sexuality (see DECENTERED SUBJECT). For the psychoanalyst Jacques Lacan, the subject forms an "imaginary self" in a moment of "misrecognition." An infant looking into a mirror suddenly "misrecognizes" itself as more unified than it actually is. No distinction between itself as observer (subject) and its reflection (object) is made. This misrecognition of the reflection as the image of the self becomes the basis for all the child's conceptions of itself, conceptions that are fundamentally based on a fiction.

The Marxist theorist Louis Althusser adapts Lacan's theory of the MIRROR STAGE in his discussion of the subject and ideology. According to Althusser, an "individual" always already exists in ideology and therefore is also "always already a subject." By this he means that all cognizant beings live what he calls an "imagined relation" to the real. For Althusser, there is no access to reality per se, only to the way that one structures an imaginary relation to it. The subject can exist only in ideology, and he is "hailed" or "interpellated" by it. That is, ideology seems to pick the subject out as necessary and central to its functioning; it reinforces a sense of self as the center of existence. In his important essay, "Ideology and Ideological State Apparatuses," Althusser uses the example of a police officer shouting "Hey, you there." The individual turns around, feeling that it was "*really*" her that was hailed. This act of answering, of course, is an act of identification—the person, by answering the call of the officer (ideology), singles herself out as the one whom the police officer is seeking.

The theorist Michel Pêcheux follows closely upon Althusser's insights. He argues that the subject ultimately "forgets" that she is an ideological formation and comes to see herself as the author of her own discourse. He also comments on the act of identification upon which "hailing" depends. He argues that the subject must identify herself in terms of the DISCOURSE that predominates her existence; "the interpellation of the individual as subject of his discourse is achieved by the identification (of the subject) with the discursive formation that dominates him (i.e., by which he is constituted as subject)." Althusser and Pêcheux's use of ideology and discourse as the phenomena that form the subject and determine his or her actions turns on a double meaning and thus complicates their conception of the subject and "subjectivity." For Pêcheux and Althusser, the subject is the actor inasmuch as he or she functions within ideology, but is also acted upon by discourse or ideology, is *subjected* to the conditions of possibility within a particular ideology. And, since without human beings there could be no ideology, we find that within their schema the "hailed" or interpellated individual exists both as the subject and object of ideology in the sense that subject and object were discussed at the beginning of this entry—the former as actor, agent, the latter as that which is acted upon.

The theorist Michel Foucault also took up the issue of subjectivity. In his early work such as *The Order of Things*, his conclusions seem close to Althusser's, though he does not adopt a Marxian perspective and repudiates the use of the DIALECTIC as an analytical tool. Later, however, Foucault became increasingly interested in ethical issues and their relation to subjectivity, and in his last works such as *The Care of the Self*, he appeared to be moving toward a concept of "self-creation" outside of universal ethical principles. For Foucault, the formation of the subject becomes almost an issue of aesthetics: the subject is responsible for inventing his own "art" of living and must produce himself as subject. This conception of the subject has led many to accuse Foucault of reversing his earlier anti-humanist position and of embracing, in only a half-disguised way, the concept of individualism so important to HUMANISM's constructions of the self.

Althusser, Louis. "Ideology and Ideological State Apparatuses." In *Lenin and Philosophy and Other Essays*. Trans. Ben Brewster. New York: Monthly Review Press, 1971.

Cadava, Eduardo, Peter Connor, and Jean-Luc Nancy, eds. *Who Comes after the Subject?* New York: Routledge, 1991.

Lacan, Jacques. *Ecrits: A Selection*. Trans. Alan Sheridan. New York: Norton, 1977.

—. "The Subject and the Other: Alienation." In *Four Fundamental Concepts of Psychoanalysis*. Trans. Alan Sheridan, ed. Jacques-Alain Miller. New York: Norton, 1978.

Lonergan, Bernard J. F. *The Subject*. Milwaukee: Marquette University Press, 1968.

Pêcheux, Michel. *Language, Semantics, and Ideology: Stating the Obvious*. Trans. Harbans Nagpal. London: Macmillan, 1982.

Strozier, Robert M. *Saussure, Derrida, and the Metaphysics of Subjectivity*. New York: Mouton de Gruyter, 1988.

SUBJECTIVITY. See AGENT, SUBJECT/OBJECT.

SUBLIMATION. In Freudian psychoanalysis, *sublimation* is the name given to the process by which activities such as artistic creation and intellectual inquiry, which have no overt connection with sexuality, come to be driven by sexual energy. In sublimation, sexual instinct is diverted into a nonsexual, socially esteemed channel. Freud's use of the term draws on both the meaning that the word has in chemistry—the process by which a solid passes into a gaseous state—and the use of the term SUBLIME in the fine arts to mean elevated or uplifting.

SUBLIME. Although in contemporary discussion the term *sublime* usually refers to the awe one feels in the presence of greatness, the concept is actually quite ancient, dating back to the Greek treatise called *Peri Hupsous*, which was probably written in the first century A.D. and has been attributed (probably falsely) to Longinus. In this work, the word *hupsous* does not mean quite the same thing as its traditional English equivalent, "sublimity," but a more generalized sense of excellence or distinction in writing that has won immortal fame. The *Peri Hupsous* is thus primarily a rhetorician's manual, although certain passages do point toward the complexities with which the concept of the sublime has been associated in later criticism. This later history begins in the last quarter of the seventeenth century, when the attentions of major critics like Nicolas Boileau-Despreaux and John Dryden brought the concept into fashion. The sublime proved a popular topic for aesthetic reflection throughout the eighteenth century and was elaborated by writers as various as John Dennis, Joseph Addison, Edmund Burke, David Hume, and Immanuel Kant. Although there are marked differences between their accounts, certain features remain constant. All agree that the sublime involves a sense of wonder or awe (colored by fear, according to English theorists), which is created by the experience of grandness or "vastness"; and in some cases writing on the sublime comes close to being nothing more than a list of objects said to produce the effect in question: mountains, oceans, Milton, an angry deity, etc. At its most sophisticated, however, eighteenth-century reflection on the sublime shows a new interest in aesthetic psychology, with attention shifting away from the sublime object and onto the response of the reading or perceiving subject. This interest in dramatically uncontained or overwhelming phenomena and the psychological effects that they produce constitutes a notable exception to the dominant aesthetic values of the neo-classical age (roughly 1660–1789), with its emphasis on order, symmetry, and—to use the term with which the sublime is most frequently contrasted—the "beautiful." In this respect, it is an important precursor of the romantic era, when the experience of the sublime is assimilated to that period's characteristic interest in forms of transcendence.

In our own era, the sublime has enjoyed much attention from critics writing in the wake of DECONSTRUCTION, who have promoted a Longinian aesthetic of the sublime as an antidote to what is generally understood as the Aristotelian bias of the NEW CRITICS (see also CHICAGO SCHOOL). Even more influentially, the French philosopher Jean-François Lyotard has celebrated the explosive qualities of the sublime moment as a means to unsettle repressive totalities.

Burke, Edmund. *A Philosophical Enquiry into the Origin of Our Ideas of the Sublime and Beautiful.* Ed. James T. Boulton. Notre Dame, Ind.: University of Notre Dame Press, 1968.

Dennis, John. *The Grounds of Criticism in Poetry. The Critical Works of John Dennis,* vol. 1. New York: Garland, 1971.

Fry, Paul. "Longinus at Colonus: The Grounding of Sublimity." In *The Reach of Criticism: Method and Perception in Literary Theory.* New Haven: Yale University Press, 1983.

Kant, Immanuel. *Critique of Judgement.* Trans. J. H. Bernard. New York: Hafner Press, 1951.

Longinus. *On the Sublime. Classical Literary Criticism.* Trans. James A. Arieti and John M. Crossett. New York: E. Mellen Press, 1985.

Lyotard, Jean-François. "Answering the Question: What is Postmodernism?" In *The Postmodern Condition: A Report on Knowledge.* Trans. Geoff Bennington and Brian Massumi. Minneapolis: University of Minnesota Press, 1984.

Monk, Samuel H. *The Sublime: A Study of Critical Theories in XVIII-Century England.* Ann Arbor: University of Michigan Press, 1960.

Weiskel, Thomas. *The Romantic Sublime: Studies in the Psychology of Transcendence.* Baltimore: Johns Hopkins University Press, 1976.

SUPEREGO. In Freud's "second topography" (the first divided the psyche into preconscious-conscious and UNCONSCIOUS systems), the superego performs the role of censor and controls such functions as the sense of conscience and discipline. As such, it conflicts with the other parts of the psychical apparatus, the EGO and the ID, and comes into being with the

INTERNALIZATION of parental injunctions following the OEDIPUS COM-PLEX (although some theorists, such as Melanie Klein, have argued that it is in fact constituted much earlier).

Freud, Sigmund. *The Ego and the Id*. Trans. Joan Riviere, ed. James Strachey. New York: Norton, 1960.

SUPPLEMENT. In the deconstructive philosophy of Jacques Derrida, the logic of the supplement is what undoes the metaphysical oppositions around which Western thought is organized (see DECONSTRUCTION, METAPHYSICS). Derrida argues that all metaphysical systems, no matter what term they offer as embodying presence, have need of a supplementary term, which compensates for the absence of this source (see ABSENCE/PRESENCE): for example, speech needs WRITING to stand in for it when the face-to-face immediacy of the speech situation is lacking. As Derrida has shown, however, in each case the supplement actually can be seen to undermine this hierarchical relationship. Thus, in Derrida's own example from his reading of Rousseau, masturbation serves as a supplement to intercourse, just as writing serves as a supplement to the "intercourse" of conversation. When the latter becomes unavailable, its supplement entices Rousseau with the mental illusion of a present partner. And yet at the same time that he condemns masturbation as a way of "cheating Nature," Rousseau is compelled to admit that it has its advantages over "natural" relations, which are never so perfectly realized as the imaginary ones. In the same way, he observes that even though he has classified writing as a mere imitation of speech, it nevertheless allows him to express himself more perfectly than actual speech situations, which tend to make him nervous. In spite of their apparent artificiality, then, writing and masturbation both offer a reminder of the sense of presence that is lacking in their supposedly more "natural" counterparts. Derrida's point is that even in those activities which are traditionally accorded priority, the loss of presence has already taken place, and that heterosexuality and speech are themselves nothing more than attempts to compensate for this sense of a fundamental absence. It is his contention that a similar "supplementary logic" can be located in all such metaphysical oppositions.

Derrida, Jacques. *Of Grammatology*. Trans. Gayatri Chakravorty Spivak. Baltimore: Johns Hopkins University Press, 1976.

SURPLUS VALUE. Surplus value refers to the difference between the value of a COMMODITY realized in exchange and the value of the capital involved in the production of the commodity. In a capitalist society it usually takes the form of profit. For Marx, the capitalist's desire and need to extract surplus value is the way in which exploitation takes place in capitalism. The capitalist owns the commodity: he has exchanged wages for the worker's labor, which produced the commodity. The capitalist then exchanges the commodity for more than he paid the worker in wages and the material expended in its production. The initial value of the commodity is equal to the value of the labor, which is expressed in wages and the value of the material (capital) used in producing it. When the capitalist exchanges the commodity in the marketplace and receives more for it than he expended in wages, he appropriates the results of surplus unpaid labor.

SURREALISM. Although forms of surrealism are still practiced around the world today, the heyday of this twentieth-century AVANT-GARDE movement was between the world wars in Paris, where it quickly came under the charismatic leadership of the poet André Breton, whose 1924 "Manifesto of Surrealism" declared the movement's adherence to the imagination, dreams, the fantastic, and the irrational. Surrealism emerged out of the earlier dadaist movement and counted among its adherents artists and writers working in a variety of media, including such figures as Tristan Tzara, who had been an instigator of Zurich DADA. Although interested in chance, like their dadaist predecessors, the surrealists were less concerned with developing techniques like collage than with exploring free association, automatism, and other manifestations of the UNCONSCIOUS, which was viewed as a realm of freedom and untapped energy. If there is such a thing as a signature surrealist style, it features violent juxtapositions of normally unrelated images in an attempt to jog the mind out of rational habits of thought, as in the phrase from the nineteenth-century French poet Lautréamont, offered by Breton as a precursor of surrealism: "The chance meeting of a sewing machine and an umbrella on a dissecting table." Although less specifically political than other twentieth- century avant-garde movements (CONSTRUCTIVISM, for example), the surrealists also dabbled in revolutionary politics, forged various ties with the Communist Party, and sought ways to develop their concept of freedom in the political sphere.

Under Breton's leadership, surrealism was very self-consciously a movement, and those who disagreed with him were publicly excommunicated in statements published in the various surrealist journals. These outcasts form an important group in their own right and include such major figures as the writer and philosopher Georges Bataille, whose journal *Documents* became an important forum for dissident surrealist ideas.

Ades, Dawn. *Dada and Surrealism Reviewed.* London: Arts Council of Great Britain, 1978.

Breton, André. *What is Surrealism? Selected Writings.* Ed. Franklin Rosemont. New York: Monad, 1978.

Gershman, Herbert. *The Surrealist Revolution in France.* Ann Arbor: University of Michigan Press, 1974.

Kraus, Rosalind, and Jane Livingston. *L'Amour Fou: Photography and Surrealism.* New York: Abbeville, 1985.

Nadeau, Maurice. *The History of Surrealism.* Trans. Richard Howard. New York: Macmillan, 1965.

SUTURE. Originally a medical term for the juncture of two adjoining tissues, bones, or organs, *suture* was used by the Lacanian psychoanalyst J. A. Miller to describe how a speaker's identity is formed in relation to his or her acquisition and use of language to make statements about the self. When I use the pronoun "I" to refer to myself, I am entering into a conscious, communally shared system of signification—I am joining, or suturing, a part of myself to something outside of me. That "I," however, is a mere substitute for myself; using it represents a fundamental alienation from the UNCONSCIOUS drives and desires that can never be articulated within language. In FILM STUDIES, where the term has received its widest use, suture is the system through which a viewer's subjectivity or identity is constructed in the act of watching a film. Different films perform suture differently. In CLASSIC HOLLYWOOD CINEMA, the suture system is fairly fixed. The viewer's desires to possess what he or she sees and to know what is going on are manipulated by the position of the camera, which encourages us to identify (usually) with the film's protagonist (see IDENTIFICATION). In psychoanalysis and film studies, the term is mainly used to describe how that desire to identify, to desire and know fully, is always frustrated—the film teases us by continually promising that there is more to behold (beyond the edge of the frame, outside the line of vision of the camera). Something of the viewer, or the user of language, is lost as it is absorbed by the system of signification, whether common speech or film language.

Heath, Stephen. "Notes on Suture." *Screen* 19(2), 1977/78.
Miller, Jacques-Alain. "Suture (Elements of the Logic of the Signifier)." *Screen* 18(4), 1977/78.
Silverman, Kaja. *The Subject of Semiotics.* New York: Oxford University Press, 1983.

SYLLEPSIS. Syllepsis (siLEPsis) is a rhetorical construction, either grammatical or ungrammatical, in which one word is applied to two other words or phrases (usually) in two different senses. Usually the word applied is a preposition—he left in anger and a cab—or a verb, as in Pope's line from "The Rape of the Lock": "Or stain her honor or her new brocade." Some rhetoricians argue that *zeugma* (ZOOGmuh), rather than syllepsis, is the proper term for the ungrammatical application of a word to yoke together two others, as in the example, "The book *was* read, but the instructions unheeded." Here "was" does not agree in number with "instructions." This distinction between syllepsis and zeugma is rarely made, however, and the two are often used interchangeably.

SYMBOLIC. This term, used as a substantive, names one of the three cognitive dimensions or "orders" (the other two being the IMAGINARY and the REAL) in the psychoanalytic theory of Jacques Lacan. In the mature human being, all three orders function together to constitute consciousness; however, this is not the case from birth, and the entry into the Symbolic parallels the formation of the OEDIPUS COMPLEX (see also NAME-OF-THE-FATHER, MIRROR STAGE). Lacan's use of the concept draws on STRUCTURALISM in general and the work of Claude Lévi-Strauss in particular: it refers quite simply to language itself and the entire realm of culture, conceived as a symbol system structured on the model of language. Lacan's crucial contribution here is the argument that the UNCONSCIOUS, which Freud had already conceived as the repository of IDEATIONAL REPRESENTATIVES, is in fact structured like a language and functions by mechanisms analogous to figures of speech (see CONDENSATION, DISPLACEMENT, METAPHOR, METONYMY). Moreover, the idea of a preestablished order conveys the further sense that the development of human beings involves their insertion into a structure that is also a law for them.

Lacan, Jacques. *Ecrits: A Selection.* Trans. Alan Sheridan. New York: Norton, 1977.

SYMPTOMATIC READING. A symptomatic reading applies the psychoanalytic model of interpretation to texts other than the discourse of an analysand. In such a reading, the rifts, discontinuities, and marginalia in an apparently unified text are seen as symptoms that may be explained by uncovering a repressed content. The idea is prominent in the work of Marxist thinkers like Louis Althusser, who analyzed Marx's own writings in this fashion, as well as Fredric Jameson, whose concept of a POLITICAL UNCONSCIOUS attempts to unite the psychoanalytic model with Hegelian Marxism. Thus, Jameson argues that "interpretation proper . . . always presupposes, if not a conception of the unconscious itself, then at least some mechanism of mystification or repression in terms of which it would make sense to seek a latent meaning behind a manifest."

Althusser, Louis. *For Marx*. Trans. Ben Brewster. New York: Pantheon, 1969.
Jameson, Fredric. *The Political Unconscious: Narrative as a Socially Symbolic Act*. Ithaca, N.Y.: Cornell University Press, 1981.

SYNCHRONY. Synchrony (SINkronee), which refers to the study of language on the basis of its relations to alternative, simultaneous rather than historical elements, is one of a pair of terms (the other being DIACHRONY) associated with SEMIOLOGY, the science of signs founded by the Swiss linguist Ferdinand de Saussure. Rejecting the assumptions underlying historical analysis, which had dominated nineteenth-century linguistics, Saussure argued that language systems should be studied as they are constituted at a given moment, in the belief that the relations between simultaneous elements have priority in the communication of meaning over the historical derivation of those elements. Thus, Saussure claimed that the meaning of a word is determined synchronically, by its relation to adjacent words in the structure, rather than diachronically, by its etymology. The word *mutton*, for example, acquires a meaning from adjacent English words such as *sheep* or *lamb*, not from the French word from which it derives (*mouton*). Indeed, *mouton* does not mean exactly the same thing as *mutton*, since the French language does not have separate words for the animal and the meat. The point is that meaning is not inherent in individual words but is created by relationships of similarity and difference within a system. Although this position has been criticized for the difficulties it creates in trying to give an adequate account of historical change, it is fundamental to all varieties of STRUCTURALISM and remains a central assumption of much current thought about language and culture. See also LANGUE/PAROLE, PARADIGMATIC, SYNTAGMATIC.

Saussure, Ferdinand de. *Course in General Linguistics.* Trans. Roy Harris, eds. Charles Bally and Albert Sechehaye. London: Duckworth, 1983.

SYNECDOCHE. See METONYMY.

SYNTAGM. See PARADIGM.

T

TAKE. See SHOT.

TARTU SEMIOTICIANS. Also known as the Moscow-Tartu semioticians, this group of scholars of the former Soviet Union associated with Tartu State University in Estonia in the 1960s and 1970s, set out to investigate what they called "secondary modeling systems" or human cultural activities (literature, religion, folklore, table manners, etc.) involved in shaping a society's view of the world. These cultural activities are composed of sign-systems with rules or grammars that can be analyzed as "languages." Unlike the RUSSIAN FORMALISTS of the 1920s, the Tartu semioticians believe that it is necessary to formulate a scientific theory of culture as a whole. Literature or linguistic practices, therefore, cannot be seen in isolation from other cultural activities. One of the leading figures in the movement, Juri Lotman, argues that although poems must be understood semiotically as sets of relations of similarities and oppositions, the meaning of those relations depends on other, wider systems of meaning, including the reader's own set of expectations. Lotman and others of the group also contribute to the study of cybernetics (see CYBORG) and GENERATIVE POETICS. See also SEMIOTICS.

Lotman, Juri. *The Structure of the Artistic Text.* Trans. Ronald Vroon. Ann Arbor: University of Michigan Press, 1977.

Shukman, Ann. *Literature and Semiotics.* New York: North-Holland Publishing, 1977.

TELOS. *Telos* is the Greek word for "end" or "goal," and a teleology or teleological argument assigns meaning to events by viewing them as progressing toward a goal. Although many of the most influential philosophies of history in Western thought have been teleological (as is, for example, Christian theology or the philosophy of Hegel), POSTMODERN critics have rejected teleology as a form of METAPHYSICS, in which events are accorded significance depending on the extent to which they reveal the imagined goal towards which they are said to be moving. See also ARCHE.

TEL QUEL GROUP. The *Tel Quel* (TEL KEL) group were a number of French intellectuals associated with the AVANT-GARDE literary journal *Tel Quel*, which was founded in 1960 and in the following decade was instrumental in the dissemination of POSTSTRUCTURALIST thought. Initially supportive of the ideas of the PCF, the French communist party, the journal later espoused Maoism and Chinese communism, but by the mid- to late 1970s had become anti-communist, to a point where it even celebrated U.S. PLURALISM. The shift away from Mao began about the same time as the failure of the worker and student activist struggles in France in May 1968.

The thinkers most closely associated with *Tel Quel* include Roland Barthes, Jacques Derrida, Julia Kristeva, and Philippe Sollers. They participated in the elaboration of a crucial poststructuralist concept, ÉCRITURE, which they argued was a revolutionary writing practice because it broke with REALISM and interrogated the CODES of representation that helped sustain bourgeois dominance. *Écriture* was not about the death of meaning, as the detractors of poststructuralism argued, but about the birth of POLYSEMY or the multiplication of meanings, which put into question the notion of absolute truths and undermined conventional theories of reading (whether didactic, mimetic, or expressive) and of history, thereby helping to denaturalize and destabilize the timeless verities that the *Tel Quel* group saw as legitimating the bourgeois interpretation—and experience—of reality.

Barthes, Roland. "Writers, Intellectuals, Teachers." *Tel Quel*, 1971.
Ka, Shushi. "Paradise Lost? An Interview with Philippe Sollers." *Sub-Stance* 30, 1981.
Roudiez, Leon. "Twelve Points from *Tel Quel*." *L'Esprit creatur* 14(4), 1974.

TESTIFYIN(G). According to the linguist Geneva Smitherman (who spells the term *testifyin'*), testifying is a form of speech used by black Americans at public occasions such as church meetings or services. The testifyin(g) speaker tells a story conveying some feeling or moral or religious lesson with which all present are assumed to identify. Although the stories told are usually autobiographical and particular to the speaker, Smitherman observes that their tellings are highly "ritualized" and communicate "some experience in which all blacks have shared." To testify, Smitherman writes, "is to tell the truth through 'story.' "

Smitherman, Geneva. *Talkin' and Testifyin'*. Boston: Houghton Mifflin, 1977.

TEXT. In its most usual sense, *text* refers to any written or printed document, whether literary or not. Roland Barthes, in his essay "From Work to Text," argues that a text is a structure of language for which usual notions of closure, meaning, and authorial intention do not apply. For Barthes a text continually produces meaning independent of its association with an author. It interacts with a reader, is produced by the reader, and is a source of joy or JOUISSANCE. In contrast, a "work" fills a recognizable role; its meanings are interpretable and finite; it does not exist independently of its author; and rather than being produced by the reader it is consumed by her, providing, at most, only pleasure. Following Barthes, the term *text* has been adopted by poststructuralists to refer to any DISCOURSE that produces meaning through its infinite play of SIGNS. Some critics and theorists have gone as far as to refer to any system of signs as a text. Because for many existence and knowledge are only available within systems of signification, it has become a commonplace to hear the world itself referred to as a text. See also INTERTEXTUALITY, SEMIOTICS.

Barthes, Roland. *The Pleasure of the Text*. Trans. R. Miller. New York: Hill and Wang, 1975.

—. "From Work to Text." In *Image, Music, Text*. Trans. Stephen Heath. New York: Hill and Wang, 1977.

Kristeva, Julia. *The Kristeva Reader*. Ed. Toril Moi. New York: Columbia University Press, 1986.

TEXTUALITY. To refer to any object's textuality is to imply that the object has coherence and a degree of autonomy and stability, such that it may be "read." According to Stanley Fish, textuality is not an inherent property of certain objects, but a property assigned to objects by those producing or analyzing them. Whether or not Fish is right in his view that textuality is a purely social construct, it is true that literary critics have at different moments favored certain terms for such cultural artifacts: books, works, texts, literary productions, etc. Each term suggests a slightly different way of looking at the object in question. When a critic calls something a text, he or she usually presupposes a coherent whole that is abstracted from such idiosyncrasies as the typeface or margins that happen to appear in a particular edition. Some analysts have regarded self-sufficiency or autonomy as characteristic of textuality, but for poststructuralists texts are woven out of other texts; thus, textuality implies INTERTEXTUALITY.

Fish, Stanley. *Is There a Text in This Class?: The Authority of Interpretive Communities*. Cambridge, Mass.: Harvard University Press, 1980.

THEATRICALITY. *Theatricality* is a term used by Michael Fried in contrast to the term ABSORPTION to describe differences in the way the spectator interacts with a work of art. Unlike absorption, which describes an interaction in which the viewer's experience of a work is not dependent on an awareness of his or her own position in time and space, theatricality is linked to a heightened awareness of just those qualities. In "Art and Objecthood," Fried identifies theatricality with minimalist sculpture, which can only be experienced through the process of moving around it, thereby causing the viewer's experience of the work to unfold in conjunction with his or her experience of time and space.

Although Fried is critical of theatricality in the visual arts, other critics, such as Rosalind Krauss, have placed great importance on these very qualities. In *Passages in Modern Sculpture*, Krauss used a phenomenological approach to discuss the way that many works of modern sculpture make the viewer aware of his or her existence in the same space as the work.

Fried, Michael. "Art and Objecthood." *Artforum* (June), 1967.
—. *Absorption and Theatricality: Painting and Beholder in the Age of Diderot.* Berkeley: University of California Press, 1980.
Krauss, Rosalind. *Passages in Modern Sculpture.* Cambridge, Mass.: MIT Press, 1981.

THIRD WORLD/THIRD-WORLD CRITICISM. *Third-world criticism* refers to criticism of the cultural output of a third-world country, criticism written by residents of that country, or to criticism of third-world cultures in general. The modifier *third-world* (adapted from the French phrase *tiers monde*) has been applied to nations that share one or several of the following traits: 1) an economy "undeveloped" in comparison with that of capitalist or socialist countries; 2) recent emergence from colonial rule; 3) relatively small natural resources or low agricultural production; 4) relatively low levels of industrialization; 5) turbulent political instability; and 6) a refusal to form alliances with the powers of the first and second worlds. Although many have rejected the term because it implies inferiority and obscures the differences among the societies thus labeled, it has also been used as part of a critique of first-world imperialism. In the latter sense, the term *third-world criticism* has often been used interchangeably with POSTCOLONIAL CRITICISM.

TOASTS. Toasts are narrative folk poems from the African-American oral tradition that date at least to the late nineteenth century. They are recited in communal settings, mostly among black men, in male spaces (the pool hall, the street corner). As folk culture, the poems draw on received myths and legends, on stories already known to the listeners: Stagolee's fight with Billy Lyons; Shine's escape from the *Titanic*; the Signifying Monkey's deception of the unwitting Lion. For these reasons of context and content, the value of toasts—or, better, a toast-telling session—lies in how the toasts are performed, how a storyteller can individualize the legends' constants through rhetorical flourishes, and how audience members can be engaged to offer their own revision of the tale on the spot. These excessively lewd poems usually follow a four-stress line pattern, the lines arranged in rhymed couplets. The narrative drama itself is usually a struggle between two persons or between two or three animals, the actions presented consecutively, with dialogue between the principal characters interspersed throughout. Toasts—variants of which are heard in the work of rap artists and reggae deejays—are a reservoir for the practices of SIGNIFYIN(G), the verbal artistry that, according to Henry Louis Gates, Jr., informs African-American literary and vernacular culture.

Abrahams, Roger D. *Deep Down in the Jungle . . . : Negro Narrative Folklore from the Streets of Philadelphia.* Rev. ed. Chicago: Aldine, 1970.

Gates, Henry Louis, Jr. *The Signifying Monkey: A Theory of African-American Literary Criticism.* New York: Oxford University Press, 1988.

Jackson, Bruce, comp. *"Get Your Ass in the Water and Swim Like Me": Narrative Poetry from Black Oral Tradition.* Cambridge, Mass.: Harvard University Press, 1974.

TOTALITY. See MARXIST CRITICISM.

TRACE. See ERASURE.

TRADITION. The concept of tradition involves the recognition that customs, beliefs, values, styles, and other forms of culture are passed down from one generation to the next, as well as the feeling—sometimes encouraged, sometimes resented—that this inheritance should be respected for the beneficent influence that it exerts on the present. Although tradition is occasionally rejected entirely as repressive or deadening (as was the case with certain modernist artistic movements like FUTURISM and DADA), a more common course among twentieth-century writers has been to allow for the value of tradition even while arguing that new works of art must differ to some extent from their predecessors. Thus, in his influential essay "Tradition and the Individual Talent," T. S. Eliot observed that "the most individual parts of [a poet's] work may be those in which the dead poets, his ancestors, assert their immortality most vigorously," in the course of explaining that each new work fundamentally alters the tradition that it joins. The importance of this view lies in its understanding of tradition as a living and changeable force, something that is at least partially chosen and constructed in the present rather than received as an inert lump from the past. In such a view, tradition is also something to be fought over, as is the case with Eliot's espousal of the English metaphysical poets or F. R. Leavis's *The Great Tra-*

dition, which aggressively asserts the superiority of a group of nine-teenth-century English novelists in the belief that the concerns of their works remain central to contemporary life and therefore offer the most valuable precedent for contemporary writers to build upon. These crit-ics assume a view of tradition as bound to a particular culture or nation-ality; but more recently, with the rise of women's studies, ethnic studies, and gay studies, critics have sought traditions in the work of writers who share backgrounds defined by such qualities as gender, ethnicity, or sex-ual preference. See also CULTURAL LITERACY.

Eliot, T. S. "Tradition and the Individual Talent." In *Selected Prose of T. S. Eliot*. Ed. Frank Kermode. London: Faber and Faber, 1975.

Leavis, F. R. *The Great Tradition*. Garden City, N.Y.: Doubleday, 1954.

TRANSFERENCE. *Transference* is a psychoanalytic term used to describe the process by which UNCONSCIOUS wishes are manifested in the context of a given relationship, such as the analytic situation; the term is most frequently used with the assumption that the relationship between patient and analyst is implied. In the analytic situation, infantile fantasies are deliberately allowed to reemerge and work themselves out; and it is this process, along with its interpretation and resolution, that constitutes psychoanalytic treatment. See also COUNTERTRANSFERENCE.

Freud, Sigmund. "The Dynamics of Transference." In *Standard Edition of the Complete Psychological Works of Sigmund Freud*, vol. 12. Trans. James Strachey. London: Hog-arth Press and Institute of Psycho-Analysis, 1974.

TRANSITIONAL OBJECT. The term *transitional object* is associated with D. W. Winnicott and OBJECT RELATIONS psychoanalysis. It describes those objects of the PRE-OEDIPAL child's oral desire between the ages of four months and one year that are so much a part of the self that they are almost inseparable from it, like the blanket a child sucks as he or she falls asleep. Winnicott calls the transitional object a paradox because it is so close to the subject that it is almost an extension of the self and therefore not quite a distinct object (hence "transitional"). In fact, the child uses it and other "transitional phenomena" (gestures and oral activities like babbling and laughing) to sort the self from what is other or external to that self and to test out what parts of experience he or she can control. The transitional object signifies first of all the breast, which the child can manipulate or master by symbolizing it, affording both fear and relief and so functioning as a defense against the anxiety of separation from the mother. As the child plays with transitional phenomena he/she marks out the boundaries of the self and its objects, dividing up reality and moving toward true object (or other-oriented versus self-oriented) relations.

Because the transitional object is not a fixed delusion or security prop, it is not a fetish (see FETISHISM). Indeed, object relations theorists have suggested that the play of illusion it enables develops into creative artistic play rather than fetishism. Some psychoanalysts influenced by the object relations school and the aesthetic theory based on it have expanded on the notion of transitional phenomena to discuss how they enable the subject not only to constitute itself (and the bounds of the self) but to reconstitute itself and in the process shift the possibly narrow bounds within which the self coheres. Thus, Julia Kristeva has suggested that what is revolutionary about art is just this ability to remake the self through an encounter with the ABJECT, the liminal or transitional not-quite not-other, which can include not only colors and almost meaningless sounds but also urine, blood, feces, and other taboo excreted bits of the self that are potentially "contaminating." For these critics, Winnicott sometimes errs by assuming that objects and subjects are clearly demarcated before their encounter, whereas what they would stress is the importance of fantasy and its role in constituting both objects and subjects, whose boundaries are therefore flexible, in accord with desire, rather than fixed by some presumed "objective reality."

Kristeva, Julia. *Desire in Language: A Semiotic Approach to Literature and Art.* Trans. Alice Jardine et al., ed. Leon S. Roudiez. Oxford: Blackwell, 1980.
—. *The Powers of Horror: An Essay on Abjection.* Trans. Leon S. Roudiez. New York: Columbia University Press, 1982.
Winnicott, D.W. "Transitional Objects and Transitional Phenomena." *International Journal of Psycho-Analysis* 34, 1953.
Wright, Elizabeth. *Psychoanalytic Criticism: Theory in Practice.* New York: Methuen, 1984.

TRICKSTER. African-American critics have traced the history of the trickster to Yoruba mythology and the God of the Crossroads, Eshu Elegbara. Eshu wears a cap that is black on one side and white on the other to remind those making a decision to consider a situation from all sides. Henry Louis Gates, Jr. sees Eshu as the figure for interpretation—the need to see all possible meanings inherent in a text at a "verbal cross-roads." According to Gates, Eshu has been conflated in African tales with the figure of a monkey, and is thought to have been translated into the Signifying Monkey (the African-American trickster figure) during the passage of the slaves from Africa to America. Gates distinguishes between Eshu and the Signifying Monkey, saying that Eshu "serves as a figure for the nature and function of interpretation and double-voiced utterance, while the Signifying Monkey serves as the figure of figures, as the trope within which are several other peculiarly black tropes." Critics of African-American literature often find texts "double-voiced" because they transform oral narrative into written text, and because the African-American vernacular functions as a subtext within the literary form of the dominant culture. See also DOUBLE-VOICED TEXT, VERNACULAR.

Baker, Houston A., Jr. *Blues, Ideology, and Afro-American Literature: A Vernacular Theory.* Chicago: University of Chicago Press, 1984.

Gates, Henry Louis, Jr. *The Signifying Monkey: A Theory of African-American Literary Criticism.* New York: Oxford University Press, 1988.

Thompson, Robert Farris. *Flash of the Spirit: African and Afro-American Art and Philosophy.* New York: Random House, 1983.

TROPE. A trope is a figure of speech, such as a METAPHOR or a METONYMY, or a usage that diverges from the norm. The study of tropes is an important part of traditional rhetoric, which has received new emphasis in contemporary criticism with the close attention given to language by critical schools like DECONSTRUCTION. A related use of the term was to refer to a phrase or verse added to expand upon the text of a choral prayer in medieval Catholic liturgy, a practice that was discontinued by Pius V in 1570.

TROPOLOGICAL CRITICISM. Tropological criticism is the study of tropes, usually with a focus on their history. A TROPE is a figure of speech, but, as it is used by tropological critics, it can also describe a mode of thought. Tropological criticism has two goals: 1) to define the dominant tropes of an epoch; and 2) to find those tropes in literary and non-literary works. Tropological criticism is by and large an interdisciplinary practice; it attempts to identify the tropes that the literary and non-literary texts of a given period have in common. Michel Foucault, an important exemplar for modern tropological critics, identified analogy as the dominant trope of the Renaissance, synecdoche as the dominant trope of the nineteenth century, and so on. According to the historiographer Hayden White, "troping is the soul of discourse," and so the identification of tropes is the key to writing the history of discourse, language, and ideas and their use.

Foucault, Michel. *The Order of Things: An Archaeology of the Human Sciences.* New York: Vintage, 1970.
White, Hayden. *Tropics of Discourse: Essays in Cultural Criticism.* Baltimore: Johns Hopkins University Press, 1978.

TRUTH VALUE. Logical-positivist philosophers judge statements on the criterion of truth value—that is, whether a statement may be deemed true. According to Barbara Herrnstein Smith, " 'truth-value' is seen as a measure of the extent to which such a message, when properly unwrapped, accurately and adequately reflects, represents, or corresponds with some independently determinate fact, reality, or state of affairs." But, Smith argues, there is in fact no such thing as a permanent and unchanging truth value, only contingent value, one that is not based on any "objective" property of the statement. Paradoxically, literary and artistic productions—productions that rely precisely on fiction and artifice—are valued by critics of many different persuasions for their truth. Michael Riffaterre, in contradistinction to Smith, holds that the truth value of fiction is maintained even when readers' particular truths differ, whether through the passage of time or a change in culture. Riffaterre disagrees with humanist critics who argue that great and "universal" authors, such as George Eliot, in her metanarrative or diegetic comments, provide us with insights into the "human condition." Instead, he claims that fiction seems true only because it tautologically accomplishes the expectations it sets up. Characters' behavior and choices in a realistic novel, for example, appear true only because the characters have already been defined in such a way as to anticipate their behavior and choices.

Riffaterre, Michael. *Fictional Truth.* Baltimore: Johns Hopkins University Press, 1990.
Smith, Barbara Herrnstein. *Contingencies of Value.* Cambridge, Mass.: Harvard University Press, 1988.

TYPIFICATION. Typification is an idea associated with the Marxist philosopher Georg Lukács, who used it as a means of distinguishing the kind of characterization found in the nineteenth-century historical novels that he championed. Instead of creating exceptional heroes, whose lives are presented as isolated individual destinies, the historical novelist (Sir Walter Scott above all) invents a protagonist who typifies an entire class of people, thus demonstrating that the potential for heroism is widespread among the masses and only requires an opportunity for expression. That opportunity is provided by history, and it is through the representation of such "types" that the historical novelist brings history to life. See also COLLECTIVE SUBJECT.

Lukács, Georg. *The Historical Novel.* Trans. Hannah Mitchell and Stanley Mitchell. New York: Humanities Press, 1965.

TYPOLOGY. In Christian theology, typology is a branch of HERMENEUTICS that establishes relationships between persons, places, things, and events of the Old and New Testaments. Intellectual historians engage in typological analyses in order to trace the movement from a dominant Judaic to a dominant Christian culture. Literary critics have found typological interpretation invaluable in understanding the meanings of Christian poetry and polemic, as well as the symbolic modes and governing rules or laws of literature in the Christian European tradition.

In rabbinical commentary and Jewish liturgy, early Christians found a forward-looking orientation that prophesied a new messiah, a new Exodus, a new Jerusalem. The authors of the New Testament wrote about Christ as a fulfillment of such anticipations: Christ said, "Think not that I have come to abolish the law and the prophets; I have come not to abolish them but to fulfill them" (Matthew 5:17). The Pauline epistles (the fourteen Books of the New Testament, beginning with Romans and ending with Hebrews, of which First and Second Corinthians are perhaps the most frequently cited examples) supply other texts claiming the fulfillment of Old Testament events, persons, and promises. These letters also provide the formulaic paradigms for typological interpretation: "The law has but a shadow of the good things to come instead of the true form of these realities" (Hebrews 10:1). Based on many passages such as these, early interpreters of the Bible (exegetes) formalized techniques to explain a whole network of relationships. In typological interpretations, "figures" or "types" in the Old Testament are understood to prefigure or shadow forth "anti-types" in the New Testament: thus, Moses descending from Mount Sinai with the Ten Commandments is the type of which Christ delivering the Sermon on the Mount and pronouncing the Beatitudes is the anti-type.

Typology is similar to, but profoundly different from, allegorical interpretations of Scripture (see ALLEGORY). In allegorical interpretations, such as those by the Jewish scholar Philo of Alexandria and the Church Father Origen, the literal sense and structure of the text is downplayed for the sake of a moral or ethical meaning. Typological interpretations have various emphases. In the twentieth century, Eric Auerbach has written on the historiographical implications of typological interpretation in *Scenes from the Drama of European Literature*. Auerbach notes that when the figural interpretation "changed the Old Testament from a book of laws and history of the people of Israel into a series of figures of Christ and the Redemption," it obtained an "immense persuasive power": "The Celtic and Germanic peoples . . . could accept the Old Testament" now figurally drained of "Jewish history and national character." In this way, figural interpretations were a technique of what was, according to Jean Danielou, anti-Jewish Christian propaganda.

Auerbach, Eric. *Scenes from the Drama of European Literature: Six Essays.* New York: Meridian, 1959.

Bercovitch, Sacvan. *Typology and Early American Literature.* Amherst: University of Massachusetts Press, 1972.

Lewalski, Barbara K. *Protestant Poetics and the Seventeenth-Century Religious Lyric.* Princeton: Princeton University Press, 1979.

U

UNCONSCIOUS. Designating one of the basic concepts of psychoanalysis, this term is used both as a noun and as an adjective. In the latter usage, its meaning is most general and refers to all psychological materials that are not available to the conscious mind; usually, no distinction is made in this usage between the unconscious proper and the "preconscious," which is a system whose materials are not present to consciousness but are nevertheless available in the form of memories. In its more specific usage as a noun, the term *unconscious* designates one of the systems that constitute the topography of the psyche as Freud originally conceived it. The unconscious contains materials that are repressed from the preconscious and conscious mind and can only reenter that system in other forms (so-called compromise formations, such as the contents of dreams). In the unconscious itself, these materials take the form of INSTINCTUAL REPRESENTATIVES and are governed by the mechanisms of DISPLACEMENT and CONDENSATION; moreover, they can often be seen to reflect the continuing influence of childhood wishes.

Although the basic tenets of Freudian thought on this subject have remained constant, the concept of the unconscious underwent changes over the course of Freud's career and after. Freud himself adapted it to what has become known as his "second topography" of the mind (see ID, EGO, and SUPEREGO); and later thinkers like Jacques Lacan have added their own refinements. Thus, under the influence of linguistics, Lacan argued that the unconscious is "structured like a language" and correlated the mechanisms of condensation and displacement with the rhetorical figures of METAPHOR and METONYMY.

UNDECIDABILITY. The concept of undecidability, the inability to choose between competing or contradictory meanings, has been the focus of the debate between structuralist and deconstructionist critics. Jacques Derrida, citing the case of the word *hymen* in Mallarmé, tries to show that language always conveys contradictory meanings: hymen as the figure for marriage represents the union of desire and its accomplishment, but the hymen is also the membrane that keeps them separate. For Derrida, it is impossible to select either one of the readings as the "correct" one. Structuralists, however, while admitting that all words have multiple meanings, have argued that context determines and limits those meanings. In Derrida's use of *hymen*, as in Jonathan Culler's example of the injunction "Don't obey me all the time," it is very easy to decide on a meaning: in the context of their arguments, both stand for examples of undecidability itself. Undecidability, structuralists argue, is just one special and limited use of meaning. Even so, deconstructionists resist choosing only those meanings that accord with the context. Culler points out that "our inclination to use notions of unity and thematic coherence to exclude possibilities that are manifestly awakened by the language and that pose a problem" is precisely what is called into question by DECON-STRUCTION. See also APORIA, STRUCTURALISM.

Culler, Jonathan. *On Deconstruction: Theory and Criticism after Structuralism*. Ithaca, N.Y.: Cornell University Press, 1982.

USE VALUE. *Use value* refers to one of the fundamental aspects of the Marxist concept COMMODITY, the other being EXCHANGE VALUE. A commodity is a product that enters into exchange, but that can only do so if it is perceived to be of use to someone. However, it is important to remember that use value is not quantitatively related to exchange value. Rather, exchange value is contingent upon the conditions of the commodities' production. For Marx, use value is of far less importance than exchange value, since it is exchange that defines the relations between individuals in a capitalist society, and thus should be the focus of political economy.

Marx, Karl. *Capital*, vol. 1. Moscow: Progress Publishers, 1965.

V

VALIDITY. E. D. Hirsch argues that since genuine certainty about an author's intended meaning is impossible, critics must try to find a valid interpretation of what the author *probably* meant. For Hirsch, there are a number of different valid interpretations, but to be so they must move within a "system of typical expectations and probabilities" which an author's meaning permits. Many of Hirsch's critics argue against the notion that the meaning of a text is located in the author's intention, and some object to calling one interpretation more valid than another. Still, even the most pluralistic critic would find certain readings unacceptable. In fairness to Hirsch, he has openly defined criteria for determining which readings are unacceptable, and by distinguishing "significance" (a property assigned by the reader) from meaning (the author's), he has allowed for a degree of plurality of readings. See also PLURALISM, TRUTH VALUE.

Hirsch, E. D. *Validity in Interpretation.* New Haven: Yale University Press, 1967.

VERISIMILITUDE. From the Latin phrase *veri similis* (meaning "like the truth"), verisimilitude (VERisiMILitood) is lifelikeness, the degree to which a text convinces its reader that its action, characters, language, and other elements are credible and probable. The term is sometimes used synonymously with "realism," but more often it refers to how well a text remains true to the reality it establishes or which exists within its genre, not a reality external to itself. That is, a tale containing supernatural or fantastic elements may also have a high degree of verisimilitude, as long as it conforms to its own established reality. French critics distinguish between ordinary and extraordinary verisimilitude; the former refers to how well characters and events remain recognizable, predictable and consistent, while the latter refers to surprise, supernaturalism, or the use of deus ex machina. See also REALISM, VRAISEMBLANCE.

VERNACULAR. *Vernacular* is an old term that derives from a Latin word with a variety of applications to indigenous things, the most important of which is the native language of a country or people; sometimes it is extended to include native customs or productions as well. In the African-American tradition, however, the literal meaning of the term is "a slave born on his master's estate." Critics of African-American literature use *vernacular* to designate the expression of the "black experience" within a text that has been created in the language of the dominant culture. Thus, Houston Baker, Jr. points out that when African slaves mastered English in order to create texts, the English language also "mastered" them because they were forced to express their experience of domination in the language of the master himself. African-American texts are therefore always double-voiced, for authors must translate their culture into the forms and language of the Western tradition. According to Henry Louis Gates, Jr., this results in "specific uses of literary language that are shared, repeated, critiqued, and revised" by African-American artists. See also DOUBLE-VOICED TEXT, TRICKSTER.

Baker, Houston A., Jr. *Blues, Ideology, and Afro-American Literature: A Vernacular Theory*. Chicago: University of Chicago Press, 1984.

—. *Modernism and the Harlem Renaissance*. Chicago: University of Chicago Press, 1987.

Gates, Henry Louis, Jr. *The Signifying Monkey: A Theory of African-American Literary Criticism*. New York: Oxford University Press, 1988.

VISUAL PLEASURE. Visual pleasure is a concept associated with the work of Laura Mulvey, whose essay "Visual Pleasure and Narrative Cinema" provided a key statement of the relationship between Lacanian psychoanalysis and feminist film theory. Relying on the psychoanalytic theory of FETISHISM, Mulvey argued that what is primarily fetishized in CLASSIC HOLLYWOOD CINEMA is the female body, which is itself transformed into an image of mysterious perfection that denies the threat of castration represented by women, as in the films of von Sternberg with Marlene Dietrich (the alternate possibility, that of VOYEURISM, is represented by Hitchcock). In order to participate in this visual or "scopophilic" pleasure (see SCOPOPHILIA), women are forced to take the position of a male viewer in relation to the female body; and this dominance of the MALE GAZE is viewed as an instrument in the cinema's ideological subjugation of women. Although Mulvey's argument has had considerable influence on feminist thought about film and the visual arts, it has also been criticized as excessively prohibitive in its rejection of all traditional forms of visual pleasure—notably by Mulvey herself when the article was reprinted in her book *Visual and Other Pleasures*.

Mulvey, Laura. *Visual and Other Pleasures*. Bloomington: Indiana University Press, 1989.

VOLUNTARISM. *Voluntarism* refers to belief in the priority of will in human affairs over such larger determining forces as, in the theological context, God or, in the political context, economic and social conditions. In recent years, the latter application has become the most familiar, and *voluntarism* is generally used as a term of derogation by Marxists and other proponents of a more systematic or "scientific" study of the historical conditions necessary to support political change.

VOYEURISM. Voyeurs take pleasure in looking without themselves being seen. This behavior can satisfy a basic sexual desire (SCOPOPHILIA), while also providing the distanced observer with stories of scandal and intrigue. Contemporary film theorists have argued that voyeuristic impulses explain much of our pleasure and interest in moviegoing. The theater experience encourages an illusion of privacy: able to see only the projected light before us, we vicariously enjoy the moral dramas of other lives without ourselves being observed by those persons. But theorists have also conceived of voyeurism in terms of the male spectatorship structuring much of mainstream narrative cinema. The role of woman as object, icon, and spectacle in the visual organization of these films disrupts the linear action and narrative flow of the story; while the active MALE GAZE (of characters and spectators) can often possess these figures, representations of women fleetingly pose a threat to this orderly process. In psychoanalytic terms, their position, which marks sexual difference for the viewer, invokes the threat of castration for the male UNCONSCIOUS. Male voyeurism contains this threat by construing it as a scandal in need of prosecution, and the woman as a guilty party for evoking this anxiety. Pleasure for the voyeur, as Laura Mulvey argues, is associated with SADISM: it "lies in ascertaining guilt, . . . asserting control, and subjecting the guilty person through punishment or forgiveness." Hitchcock's *Vertigo* presents something of an allegory of this process. See also VISUAL PLEASURE.

Metz, Christian. *The Imaginary Signifier: Psychoanalysis and the Cinema.* Trans. Celia Britton, Annwyl Williams, Ben Brewster, and Alfred Guzzetti. Bloomington: Indiana University Press, 1982.

Mulvey, Laura. "Visual Pleasure and Narrative Cinema." In *Visual and Other Pleasures.* Bloomington: Indiana University Press, 1989.

Willemen, Paul. "Voyeurism, the Look, and Dwoskin." In Philip Rosen, ed., *Narrative, Apparatus, Ideology: A Film Theory Reader.* New York: Columbia University Press, 1986.

VRAISEMBLANCE. The French word for VERISIMILITUDE or credibility, *vraisemblance* (VRAYsahm**BLAHNS**) refers to the cultural models into which a text is placed so that its meaning can be recuperated, made available for understanding. It is the discursive matrix into which the strange and deviant are brought in order to be made coherent or "natural."

Tzvetan Todorov states that "one can speak of the *vraisemblance* of a work in so far as it attempts to make believe that it conforms to reality and not to its own laws." Underlying *vraisemblance* is "a principle of integration between a discourse and another or several others," thus making it the basis of INTERTEXTUALITY, the structuralist notion of the interrelationship shared by all texts. In *Structuralist Poetics* Jonathan Culler offers five levels of *vraisemblance* or five ways "in which a text may be brought into contact with and defined in relation to another text which makes it intelligible": 1) the socially given text defined by language as the "real" world; 2) the general cultural text—the generic types and commonplaces specific to a particular culture and time; 3) the literary or artificial text which subscribes to the conventions of genre; 4) the text explicitly exposed as literary, artificial, or conventional; and 5) the complex texts and intertextuality of irony and parody.

Culler, Jonathan. *Structuralist Poetics: Structuralism, Linguistics and the Study of Literature.* London: Routledge, 1975.

Todorov, Tzvetan. *The Poetics of Prose.* Trans. Richard Howard. Ithaca, N.Y.: Cornell University Press, 1977.

Vattimo, Gianni. *The Transparent Society.* Trans. David Webb. Baltimore: Johns Hopkins University Press, 1992.

—. *The Adventure of Difference: Philosophy after Nietzsche and Heidegger.* Trans. Cyprian Blamires. Baltimore: Johns Hopkins University Press, 1993.

VULGAR FREUDIANISM. Vulgar Freudianism is a reductive form of interpretation, which typically exhibits a predilection for crude symbol-hunting. Moreover, it inevitably assumes that Freudian theory possesses an authority lacking in other systems of thought, so that the work of interpretation is considered to be done when the text at hand has been translated into common psychoanalytic terms—hence the pompously diagnostic quality of many vulgar Freudian interpretations.

VULGAR MARXISM. Vulgar Marxism is a form of interpretation that understands the economic BASE as directly determining all aspects of social life in unmediated fashion (see also DETERMINISM). Sometimes called *economism*, vulgar Marxism was attacked under this rubric by Lenin, who concentrated on the undervaluing of the political in favor of the economic in the writings of Eduard Bernstein; and such significant later figures as Georg Lukács and Antonio Gramsci also offered analyses of this tendency, both concentrating on the error of believing that history can be analyzed in the manner of the natural sciences, as if it were an unchanging object governed by natural laws.

Gramsci, Antonio. "Some Theoretical and Practical Aspects of Economism." In *Selections From the Prison Notebooks*, pt. 2. Trans. Quintin Hoare and Geoffrey Nowell Smith. New York: International Publishers, 1971.

Lenin, Vladimir. *What Is to Be Done?* Trans. Joe Fineberg and George Hanna; introduction by Robert Service. London: Penguin, 1988.

Lukács, Georg. "What Is Orthodox Marxism?" In *History and Class Consciousness*. Trans. Rodney Livingstone. Cambridge, Mass.: MIT Press, 1971.

WEAK THOUGHT. *Weak thought* (*il pensiero debole*) is a slogan associated with the work of a group of contemporary Italian philosophers, notably Gianni Vattimo and Aldo Gargani. Reacting against the long Italian tradition of creating all-encompassing, "strong" systems of thought, the exponents of weak thought mount a critique of metaphysics that owes much to Heidegger but refuses his attempt to create a new ONTOLOGY. Rather, like many French poststructuralists, weak thinkers recognize the impossibility of dispensing with metaphysical discourse (see METAPHYSICS), instead preferring to underline the metaphorical status of ontological language and the limits of universal reason. Like much POSTSTRUCTURALISM, therefore, weak thought insists on a self-consciousness about the metaphorical status of language and a recognition of the heterogeneity of experience.

Borradori, Giovanna, ed. *Recoding Metaphysics: The New Italian Philosophy*. Evanston, Ill.: Northwestern University Press, 1988.

Gargani, Aldo, ed. *Crisi della ragione: Nuovi modelli nel rapporto tra sapere e attivita umane*. Torino: Einaudi, 1979.

Vattimo, Gianni. *The Transparent Society*. Trans. David Webb. Baltimore: Johns Hopkins University Press, 1992.

WILD ZONE. *Wild zone* is a term introduced by Elaine Showalter in her 1981 essay "Feminist Criticism in the Wilderness" to designate a specifically female area of culture. Showalter adapts an anthropological model developed by Edwin and Shirley Ardener, in which a dominant cultural group, such as men in a patriarchy, establishes structures that exclude or "mute" other groups, such as women. The Ardeners diagram the relation between these two groups as two intersecting circles, an arc of each circle lying outside the border of the other. Women have access to the arc outside their direct experience through men's representations of it, which constitute the official culture. The outer zone of women's culture is less accessible, however, and in some sense beyond the parameters of what counts as culture altogether—therefore "wild." Showalter concedes that "there can be no writing or criticism totally outside the dominant culture," so that the notion of a female wild zone is "a playful abstraction"; yet the idea of a "herland" has been nonetheless attractive to feminist utopian writers like Charlotte Perkins Gilman, to some cultural feminists who romantically view women as closer to nature than men, and to French feminists for whom such a wild zone is the source of a revolutionary women's writing. Showalter's own reading of the Ardener figure concludes that women are not outside male culture, but simultaneously inside both male culture *and* a muted women's culture, and this is reflected in writing that is characteristically DOUBLE-VOICED. See also CULTURAL FEMINISM, ÉCRITURE FEMININE, GYNOCRITICS, PALIMPSEST.

Ardener, Shirley, ed. *Perceiving Women.* New York: Wiley, 1975.
Showalter, Elaine. "Feminist Criticism in the Wilderness." In Elaine Showalter, ed., *The New Feminist Criticism.* New York: Pantheon, 1985.

WISH-FULFILLMENT. In psychoanalytic theory, a wish-fulfillment is a psychological manifestation in which a desire is satisfied in imaginary form. Fantasies ("daydreams"), dreams, and symptoms are all wish-fulfillments, in which the original desire can be discovered through interpretation. This concept is a key element of the psychoanalytic theory of dreams, which takes as its central assumption the thesis that dreams are the fulfillments of wishes. Although Freud would eventually qualify this assertion, it remains a fundamental postulate, which allowed him to recognize the same structure in symptoms that emerge in analysis.

The concept of the wish-fulfillment has proven to be an especially fruitful one for theorists of narrative, who have the example of Freud's own ideas on the subject to work from. According to this theory, imaginative literature is an extension of the childhood habit of forming wish-fulfilling fantasies, which are altered through the literary techniques of the poet to remove their repellently personal character. Thus, lured in by the "forepleasure" offered by the purely formal attractions of the work, the reader comes to participate in the far more powerful disguised fantasy at its core (see PSYCHOANALYTIC CRITICISM). This concept of narrative as a fulfillment of wishes that usually cannot be satisfied in reality later becomes an important part of many structuralist theories of narrative, such as the anthropologist Claude Lévi-Strauss's claim that mythical narratives offer an imaginary resolution of real contradictions in the cultural beliefs of a people.

WOMANIST. *Womanist* is a term introduced and defined by Alice Walker in her 1983 collection of essays *In Search of Our Mothers' Gardens* as a "black feminist or feminist of color. From the black folk expression of mothers to female children, 'You acting womanish,' i.e., like a woman." Walker uses the term as an alternative to "feminist," which she criticizes as having a narrow application to white women of the middle and upper classes. A womanist "appreciates and prefers women's culture," but need not be a lesbian. She is "committed to survival and wholeness of an entire people, male and female." Although many women of color have joined Walker in criticizing the racism and classism of the mainstream feminist movement, several have argued for retaining the designation "feminist." bell hooks, for example, defines feminism as "a movement to end sexism and sexist oppression" and contends that women of color must reclaim feminism for their struggle against oppression based upon race, class, and sexual orientation as well as gender. See also BLACK FEMINIST CRITICISM.

hooks, bell. *Feminist Theory From Margin to Center*. Boston: South End Press, 1984.
Hull, Gloria, Patricia Bell Scott, and Barbara Smith, eds. *All the Women Are White, All the Blacks Are Men, but Some of Us Are Brave*. Westbury, N.Y.: Feminist Press, 1982.
Walker, Alice. *In Search of Our Mothers' Gardens*. San Diego: Harcourt Brace Jovanovich, 1983.

WOMEN'S STUDIES. Women's studies is a broad area of interdisciplinary inquiry occurring both inside and outside the academy, emerging out of the late twentieth-century women's movement. The first women's studies courses were offered in the late 1960s in the United States and England, and the first full-fledged women's studies program was established at San Diego State University in 1970. Since that time, more than 400 women's studies programs have been developed in the United States alone.

Women's studies has (at least) four interrelated tasks. First, it seeks to reclaim and preserve the history, arts, literature, and culture of women buried beneath or treated as peripheral by male-centered historical and cultural accounts. Examples of this project include reviving the works of black women intellectuals active at the turn of the century, adding them to a tradition long dominated by Booker T. Washington and W. E. B. Du Bois; reprinting nineteenth-century "sentimental" novels by women, best-sellers in their day but out of print and condescended to until recently; mounting museum exhibits of women Renaissance painters, some of whose works were wrongly attributed to their male relatives.

Second, on the basis of the archeological work described above, women's studies is concerned with developing a theoretical understanding of female social identity and culture, an understanding that ideally takes into account the ways that race, class, sexual identity, and other variables influence the meaning of "femininity." Literary critics, for instance, have attempted to identify the characteristics that distinguish women's writing, while ethicists have sought to define the principles underlying women's moral judgments.

The third task of women's studies grows out of the first two: elaborating the implications of its findings about women's culture, it would radically revise entire areas of knowledge. Identifying a masculine bias across the disciplines, women's studies calls into question the supposed "objectivity" of traditional scholarship, including the hard sciences. Its contributions have forced literary scholars to rethink their criteria for literary value; historians to rethink their characterizations of historical periods; anthropologists to rethink their conceptions of social status; psychologists to rethink their definitions of "maturity," and so forth.

The final (and in some sense "first") task of women's studies is, as the intellectual arm of the women's movement, to foster progressive social and political change for women and other oppressed groups, outside as well as within the university. The difficulty of continuing to relate sometimes abstruse scholarship to the needs of women in the world has been one of women's studies' key challenges. See also CULTURAL FEMINISM, GENDER STUDIES.

Bowles, Gloria, and Renate Duelli Klien, eds. *Theories of Women's Studies*. London: Routledge, 1983.

Hull, Gloria, Patricia Bell Scott, and Barbara Smith, eds. *All the Women are White, all the Blacks are Men, but Some of Us are Brave: Black Woman's Studies*. Old Westbury, N.Y.: Feminist Press, 1982.

Rich, Adrienne. "Toward a Woman-Centered University." In *On Lies, Secrets, and Silence: Selected Prose, 1966–1978*. New York: Norton, 1979.

WRITING. See AUTHOR, ÉCRITURE, SUPPLEMENT.

YALE MANIFESTO. See YALE SCHOOL.

YALE SCHOOL. During the 1970s a small group of literary critics, all teaching at Yale University and all at least loosely connected with the French philosopher Jacques Derrida, came to be linked with the advent of DECONSTRUCTION in U.S. literary theory and criticism. These critics—Harold Bloom, Geoffrey Hartman, J. Hillis Miller, and Paul de Man—varied widely in their approaches to literary texts, but because of the highly theoretical character of their criticism, their proximity to each other in the Yale English and comparative literature departments, as well as their joint publication, with Derrida, of a collection of essays entitled *Deconstruction and Criticism* (1979), they seemed to affirm themselves as a "school." But in the preface to that collection, which is also sometimes referred to as the "Yale Manifesto," Geoffrey Hartman writes, "Derrida, de Man, and Miller are cerftainly boa-deconstructors, merciless and consequent, though each enjoys his own style of disclosing again and again the 'abysm' of words. But Bloom and Hartman are barely deconstructionists. They even write against it on occasion." Later analysts of the Yale critics have concurred and the school itself, insofar as it ever existed, has all but disbanded. De Man died in 1984; Bloom's and Hartman's work has continued to diverge from the main currents of deconstruction;

Miller is now a professor at the University of California, Irvine, which has also become Derrida's primary U.S. academic affiliation. Nonetheless, the Yale School was responsible for publicizing what Hartman called a "revival of philosophic criticism" and for directly and indirectly training an entire generation of theoreticcally informed literary critics and scholars.

Bloom Harold, et al. *Deconstruction and Criticism.* New York: Seabury Press, 1979.

Z

ZEUGMA. See SYLLEPSIS.

BIBLIOGRAPHY

Abrahams, Roger D. *Deep Down in the Jungle . . . : Negro Narrative Folklore from the Streets of Philadelphia*. Rev. ed. Chicago: Aldine, 1970.

Abrams, Meyer Howard. *The Mirror and the Lamp: Romantic Theory and the Critical Tradition*. New York: Oxford University Press, 1953.

Adams, Hazard. *Philosophy of the Literary Symbolic*. Tallahassee: Florida State University Press, 1983.

Ades, Dawn. *Photomontage*. London: Thames and Hudson, 1976.

—. *Dada and Surrealism Reviewed*. London: Arts Council of Great Britain, 1978.

Adorno, Theodor W. *Noten zur Literatur*. 4 vols. Berlin: Surhkamp Verlag, 1958–74.

—. *Prisms*. Trans. Samuel Weber and Shierry Weber. London: Spearman, 1967.

—. *Negative Dialectics*. Trans. E. B. Ashton. New York: Seabury Press, 1973.

— and Max Horkheimer. *Dialectic of Enlightenment*. Trans. John Cummings. New York: Seabury Press, 1972.

— et al. *The Authoritarian Personality*. New York: Harper, 1950.

Alcoff, Linda. "Cultural Feminism versus Post-Structuralism: The Identity Crisis in Feminist Theory." *Signs* 13(3), 1988.

Althusser, Louis. "Contradiction and Overdetermination." In *For Marx*. Trans. Ben Brewster. New York: Pantheon, 1969.

—. "Marxism and Humanism." In *For Marx*.

—. "Ideology and Ideological State Apparatuses." In *Lenin and Philosophy and Other Essays*. Trans. Ben Brewster. New York: Monthly Review Press, 1971.

— and Balibar, Etienne. *Reading "Capital."* Trans. Ben Brewster. New York: Schocken, 1970.

Altieri, Charles. "An Idea and Ideal of a Literary Canon." *Critical Inquiry* 10, 1983.

Altman, Dennis. *The Homosexualization of America, the Americanization of the Homosexual.* New York: St. Martin's, 1982.

Anderson, Benedict. *Imagined Communities: Reflections on the Origin and Spread of Nationalism.* Rev. ed. London: Verso, 1991.

Anderson, Jervis. *This Was Harlem: A Cultural Portrait, 1900–1950.* New York: Farrar, Straus, and Giroux, 1982.

Appollonio, Umbro, ed. *Futurist Manifestos.* London: Thames and Hudson, 1973.

Arac, Jonathan. *Critical Genealogies: Historical Situations For Postmodern Literary Studies.* New York: Columbia University Press, 1987.

Ardener, Shirley, ed. *Perceiving Women.* New York: Wiley, 1975.

Aristotle. *Nicomachean Ethics.* Trans. H. Rackham. New York: G. P. Putnam's Sons, 1926.

—. *Topics.* Trans. E. S. Forster. Cambridge, Mass.: Harvard University Press, 1926.

—. *Poetics.* Trans. Leon Golden; commentary O. B. Hardison. Englewood Cliffs, N.J.: Prentice-Hall, 1968.

Armstrong, Nancy. *Desire and Domestic Fiction: A Political History of the Novel.* New York: Oxford University Press, 1987.

Arnold, Matthew. *Culture and Anarchy: An Essay in Political and Social Criticism.* London: Smith, Elder, 1869.

—. "The Study of Poetry." In *The Complete Works of Matthew Arnold*, vol. 9. Ed. R. H. Super. Ann Arbor: University of Michigan Press, 1960–77.

—. "The Function of Criticism at the Present Time." In *Poetry and Criticism of Matthew Arnold.* Ed. A. Dwight Culler. Boston: Houghton Mifflin, 1961.

Auerbach, Erich. *Mimesis: The Representation of Reality in Western Literature.* Trans. Willard. R. Trask. Princeton: Princeton University Press, 1953.

—. *Scenes from the Drama of European Literature: Six Essays.* New York: Meridian, 1959.

Aune, Bruce. *Rationalism, Empiricism, and Pragmatism: An Introduction.* New York: Random House, 1970.

Austin, John Langshaw. *How To Do Things With Words.* Cambridge, Mass.: Harvard University Press, 1962.

Bachelard, Gaston. *The Poetics of Space.* Trans. Maria Jolas. New York: Orion Press, 1964.

Baker, Houston A., Jr. *The Journey Back: Issues in Black Literature and Criticism.* Chicago: University of Chicago Press, 1980.

—. *Blues, Ideology, and Afro-American Literature: A Vernacular Theory.* Chicago: University of Chicago Press, 1984.

—. *Modernism and the Harlem Renaissance.* Chicago: University of Chicago Press, 1987.

—. "An Editor from Chicago: Reflections on the Work of Hoyt Fuller." In *Afro-American Poetics: Revisions of Harlem and the Black Aesthetic.* Madison: University of Wisconsin Press, 1988.

Bakhtin, Mikhail. *Rabelais and His World.* Trans. Helene Iswolsky. Cambridge, Mass.: MIT Press, 1968.

—. "Discourse Typology in Prose." In Ladislav Matejka and Krystyna Pomorska, eds., *Readings in Russian Poetics: Formalist and Structuralist Views.* Cambridge, Mass.: MIT Press, 1971.

—. *The Dialogic Imagination.: Four Essays.* Trans. Caryl Emerson and Michael Holquist, ed. Michael Holquist. Austin: University of Texas Press, 1981.

—. *Problems of Dostoevsky's Poetics*. Ed. and trans. Caryl Emerson. Minneapolis: University of Minnesota Press, 1984.

Balsamo, Anne. "Reading Cyborgs Writing Feminism." *Communication* 10 (3/4), 1988.

Baraka, Imamu Amiri. "Black is a Country." In *Home, Social Essays*. New York: William Morrow, 1966.

—. "The Myth of Negro Literature." In *Home, Social Essays*.

—. *Black Music*. New York: William Morrow, 1967.

Barratt-Brown, Michael. *The Economics of Imperialism*. Harmondsworth: Penguin, 1974.

Barrett, Michele. *Women's Oppression Today: Problems in Marxist Feminist Analysis*. London: New Left Books, 1980.

Barrett, William. *Irrational Man: A Study in Existential Philosophy*. New York: Doubleday, 1958.

Barron, Stephanie, and Maurice Tuchman, eds. *The Avant-Garde in Russia, 1910–1930: New Perspectives*. Cambridge, Mass.: MIT Press, 1980.

Barthes, Roland. *Elements of Semiology*. Trans. Annette Lavers and Colin Smith. London: Cape, 1967.

—. *Writing Degree Zero*. Trans. Annette Lavers and Colin Smith. London: Cape, 1967.

—. "Style and Its Image." In Seymour Chatman, ed. and trans., *Literary Style: A Symposium*. New York: Oxford University Press, 1971.

—. "Writers, Intellectuals, Teachers." *Tel Quel*, 1971.

—. "Authors and Writers." In *Critical Essays*. Trans. R. Howard. Evanston, Ill.: Northwestern University Press, 1972.

—. *Mythologies*. Trans. Annette Lavers. New York: Hill and Wang, 1972.

—. *S/Z*. Trans. Richard Miller. New York: Hill and Wang, 1974.

—. *The Pleasure of the Text*. Trans. Richard Miller. New York: Hill and Wang, 1975.

—. "From Work to Text." In *Image, Music, Text*. Trans. Stephen Heath. New York: Hill and Wang, 1977.

—. "Introduction to the Structural Analysis of Narratives." In *Image, Music, Text*.

—. "The Death of the Author." In *Image, Music, Text*.

Bataille, Georges. *L'Erotism: Death & Sensuality*. Trans. Mary Dalwood. San Francisco: City Lights, 1986.

Baudrillard, Jean. *Simulations*. Trans. by Paul Foss, Paul Patton, and Philip Beitchman. New York: Semiotext(e), 1983.

—. "The Precession of Simulacra." In Wallis, ed., *Art After Modernism: Rethinking Representation*.

Bazin, André. *What is Cinema? Essays*. 2 vols. Trans. Hugh Gray. Berkeley: University of California Press, 1967–72.

Beardsley, Monroe C. *Aesthetics: Problems in the Philosophy of Criticism*. New York: Harcourt Brace Jovanovich, 1958.

Belsey, Catherine. *Critical Practice*. New York: Methuen, 1980.

Benedikt, Michael, ed. *Cyberspace: First Steps*. Cambridge, Mass.: MIT Press, 1991.

Benjamin, Walter. "What is Epic Theater?" In *Illuminations*. Trans. Harry Zohn, ed. Hannah Arendt. New York: Harcourt Brace and World, 1968.

—. "The Work of Art in the Age of Mechanical Reproduction." In *Illuminations*. Trans. Harry Zohn, ed. Hannah Arendt. New York: Harcourt Brace and World, 1968.

—. *The Origin of German Tragic Drama*. Trans. John Osborne. London: New Left Books, 1977.

—. "The Author as Producer." In *Reflections: Essays, Aphorisms, Autobiographical Writing.* Trans. Edmund Jephcott. New York: Harcourt Brace Jovanovich, 1978.

Bennett, Jonathan Francis. *Kant's Dialectic.* London: Cambridge University Press, 1974.

Bennett, Tony. *Formalism and Marxism.* London: Methuen, 1979.

Benston, Kimberly W. "I Yam What I Am: The Topos of (Un)naming in Afro-American Literature." In Henry Louis Gates, Jr., ed., *Black Literature and Literary Theory.* New York: Methuen, 1984.

Benveniste, Emile. *Problems in General Linguistics.* Trans. Mary Elizabeth Meek. Coral Gables, Fla.: University of Miami Press, 1971.

Bercovitch, Sacvan. *Typology and Early American Literature.* Amherst: University of Massachusetts Press, 1972.

—. *The American Jeremiad.* Madison: University of Wisconsin Press, 1978.

Berger, John. *Ways of Seeing.* Harmondsworth: Penguin, 1972.

Berkeley, George. *Three Dialogues Between Hylas and Philonous.* Ed. Colin M. Turbayne. New York: Liberal Arts Press, 1954.

—. *A Treatise Concerning the Principles of Human Knowledge.* Menston, U.K.: Scolar Press, 1971.

Berman, Art. *From the New Criticism to Deconstruction: the Reception of Structuralism and Poststructuralism.* Urbana: University of Illinois Press, 1988.

Blanchot, Maurice. *The Space of Literature.* Trans. Ann Smock. Lincoln: University of Nebraska Press, 1982.

Bleich, David. *Subjective Criticism.* Baltimore: Johns Hopkins University Press, 1978.

Bloom, Allan. *The Closing of the American Mind.* New York: Simon and Schuster, 1987.

Bloom, Harold. *The Anxiety of Influence: A Theory of Poetry.* New York: Oxford University Press, 1973.

—. *Kabbalah and Criticism.* New York: Seabury Press, 1975.

—. *A Map of Misreading.* New York: Oxford University Press, 1975.

—. *Poetry and Repression: Revisionism from Blake to Stevens.* New Haven: Yale University Press, 1976.

—. *Agon: Toward a Theory of Revisionism.* Oxford: Oxford University Press, 1982.

— et al. *Deconstruction & Criticism.* New York: Seabury Press, 1979.

Bone, Robert. *The Negro Novel in America.* New Haven: Yale University Press, 1958.

Boone, Joseph A., and Michael Cadden, eds. *Engendering Men: The Question of Male Feminist Criticism.* New York: Routledge, 1990.

Bordwell, David, and Kristen Thompson. *Film Art: An Introduction.* Reading, Mass.: Addison-Wesley, 1979.

Borradori, Giovanna, ed. *Recoding Metaphysics: The New Italian Philosophy.* Evanston, Ill.: Northwestern University Press, 1988.

Bowen, Barbara. "Untroubled Voice: Call and Response in *Cane.*" In Henry Louis Gates, Jr., ed., *Black Literature and Literary Theory.* New York: Methuen, 1984.

Bowles, Gloria, and Renate Duelli Klien, eds. *Theories of Women's Studies.* London: Routledge, 1983.

Brantlinger, Patrick. *Crusoe's Footprints: Cultural Studies in Britain and America.* New York: Routledge, 1990.

Brecht, Bertolt. *Brecht on Theatre.* Ed. and Trans. John Willett. New York: Hill and Wang, 1964.

Brentano, Franz. *Psychology from an Empirical Standpoint.* Trans. Antos C. Rancurello, D. B. Terrell, and Linda L. McAlister, ed. Linda L. McAlister. New York: Humanities Press, 1973.

Breton, André. *What is Surrealism? Selected Writings.* Ed. Franklin Rosemont. New York: Monad, 1978.

Brod, Harry, ed. *The Making of Masculinities: The New Men's Studies.* Boston: Allen and Unwin, 1987.

Brod, R. I., and P. P. Franklin, eds. *Profession 82.* New York: Modern Language Association, 1982.

Bromwich, David. "The Genealogy of Disinterestedness." In *A Choice of Inheritance: Self and Community From Edmund Burke to Robert Frost.* Cambridge, Mass.: Harvard University Press, 1989.

Brooks, Peter. *Reading for the Plot.* New York: Knopf, 1984.

Bryson, Norman. *Vision and Painting: The Logic of the Gaze.* New Haven: Yale University Press, 1983.

Buber, Martin. *I and Thou.* Trans. Walter Kaufmann. New York: Scribner, 1970.

Bürger, Peter. *Theory of the Avant-Garde.* Trans. Michael Shaw. Minneapolis: University of Minnesota Press, 1984.

Burke, Edmund. *A Philosophical Enquiry into the Origin of Our Ideas of the Sublime and Beautiful.* Ed. James T. Boulton. Notre Dame Ind.: University of Notre Dame Press, 1968.

Butler, Judith. *Gender Trouble: Feminism and the Subversion of Identity.* New York: Routledge, 1990.

Butters, Ronald R., John M. Clum, and Michael Moon, eds. *Displacing Homophobia: Gay Male Perspectives in Literature and Culture.* Durham, N.C.: Duke University Press, 1989.

Cadava, Eduardo, Peter Connor, Jean-Luc Nancy, eds. *Who Comes after the Subject?* New York: Routledge, 1991.

Camus, Albert. *The Myth of Sysiphus.* Trans. Justin O'Brien. London: H. Hamilton, 1955.

Carby, Hazel. "White Women Listen . . ." In *The Empire Strikes Back: Race and Racism in 70's Britain.* London: Hutchinson and University of Birmingham, 1982.

—. *Reconstructing Womanhood: The Emergence of the Afro-American Woman Novelist.* New York: Oxford University Press, 1987.

Case, Sue-Ellen. "Toward a Butch-Femme Aesthetic." *Discourse* 11(1), 1989.

Cassirer, Ernst. *An Essay on Man: An Introduction to a Philosophy of Human Culture.* New Haven: Yale University Press, 1945.

—. *A Philosophy of Symbolic Forms.* Trans. Ralph Manheim. New Haven: Yale University Press, 1953–57.

—. *The Individual and the Cosmos in Renaissance Philosophy.* Trans. Mario Domandi. New York: Harper and Row, 1963.

Cha, Theresa Hak Kyung, ed. *Apparatus.* New York: Tanam Press, 1980.

Chai, Leon. *Aestheticism: The Religion of Art in Post-Romantic Literature.* New York: Columbia University Press, 1990.

Chambers, Iain. *Popular Culture: The Metropolitan Experience.* London and New York: Methuen, 1986.

Chametzky, Jules. "Our Decentralized Literature: The Significance of Regional, Ethnic, Racial, and Sexual Factors." In *Our Decentralized Literature: Cultural Mediations in Selected Jewish and Southern Writers.* Amherst: University of Massachusetts Press, 1986.

Chase, Richard Voleny. *Quest for Myth.* New York: Greenwood Press, 1969.

Chatman, Seymour. *Story and Discourse.* Ithaca, N.Y.: Cornell University Press, 1978.

Chesnutt, Charles. *The Conjure Woman.* Ann Arbor: University of Michigan Press, 1969.

Chodorow, Nancy. *The Reproduction of Mothering: Psychoanalysis and the Sociology of Gender.* Berkeley: University of California Press, 1978.

Chomsky, Noam. *Syntactic Structures.* New York: Mouton, 1957.

—. "Three Models for the Description of Language." In R. Duncan Luce, Robert R. Bush, Eugene Galanter, eds., *Readings in Mathematical Psychology.* New York: Wiley, 1963–65.

—. *Aspects of the Theory of Syntax.* Cambridge Mass.: MIT Press, 1965.

Christian, Barbara. *Black Women Novelists: The Development of a Tradition: 1892–1976.* Westport, Conn.: Greenwood Press, 1980.

Cixous, Hélène. "Rethinking Difference: An Interview." In George Stambolian and Elaine Marks, eds., *Homosexualities and French Literature: Cultural Contexts, Critical Texts.* Ithaca N.Y.: Cornell University Press, 1979.

—. "The Laugh of the Medusa." In Marks and de Courtivron, eds., *New French Feminisms.*

— and Catherine Clément. *The Newly Born Woman.* Trans. Betsy Wing. Minneapolis: University of Minnesota Press, 1986.

Clifford, James. "Histories of the Tribal and the Modern." In *The Predicament of Culture: Twentieth-Century Ethnography, Literature, and Art.* Cambridge, Mass.: Harvard University Press, 1988.

—. "On Orientalism." In *The Predicament of Culture: Twentieth-Century Ethnography, Literature, and Art.*

Cohen, Walter. "Political Criticism of Shakespeare." In Jean E. Howard and Marion F. O'Connor, eds., *Shakespeare Reproduced: The Text in History and Ideology.* New York: Methuen, 1987.

Cole, G. D. H. *A History of Socialist Thought.* New York: St. Martin's Press, 1964–67.

Coleridge, Samuel Taylor. *The Statesman's Manual* In *Lay Sermons,* ed. R. J. White, vol. 6 of *Collected Works.* Ed. K. Coburn. London: Routledge and Kegan Paul, 1969–1984.

Colletti, Lucio. *Marxism and Hegel.* Trans. Lawrence Garner. London: New Left Books, 1973.

Collingwood, R. G. *An Essay on Metaphysics.* Oxford: Oxford University Press, 1940.

—. *The Idea of History.* Oxford: Clarendon Press, 1951.

Combahee River Collective. "A Black Feminist Statement." In Cherrrie Moraga and Gloria Anzaldúa, eds., *This Bridge Called My Back: Writings by Radical Women of Color.* Watertown, Mass.: Kitchen Table Press, 1981.

Cowley, Fraser. *A Critique of British Empiricism.* London: Macmillan, 1968.

Crane, Ronald Salmon, ed. *Critics and Criticism, Ancient and Modern.* Chicago: University of Chicago Press, 1952.

Croce, Benedetto. *Philosophy, Poetry, History: An Anthology of Essays.* Trans. Cecil Sprigge. London: Oxford University Press, 1966.

—. *The Essence of the Aesthetic.* Trans. Douglas Ainslie. Folcraft, Pa.: Folcraft Library Editions, 1974.

Cruse, Harold. *The Crisis of the Negro Intellectual.* New York: William Morrow, 1967.

Crusius, Timothy. *Discourse: A Critique and Synthesis of Major Theories.* New York: Modern Language Association, 1989.

Culler, Jonathan. *Structuralist Poetics: Structuralism, Linguistics and the Study of Literature.* London: Routledge, 1975.

—. *On Deconstruction: Theory and Criticism after Structuralism.* Ithaca N.Y.: Cornell University Press, 1982.

Daly, Mary. *Gyn/Ecology: The Metaethics of Radical Feminism.* Boston: Beacon Press, 1978.

Daniel, Walter C. *Black Journals of the United States.* Westport, Conn.: Greenwood Press, 1982.

Danto, Arthur. *Narration and Knowledge: Including the Integral Text of Analytical Philosophy of History.* New York: Columbia University Press, 1985.

Davidson, Cathy, and Esther Broner, eds. *The Lost Tradition.* New York: Frederick Ungar, 1980.

Deane, Seamus. "Introduction." In Seamus Deane, ed., *Nationalism, Colonialism and Literature.* Minneapolis: University of Minnesota Press, 1990.

Dearborn, Mary V. *Pocahontas's Daughters: Gender and Ethnicity in American Culture.* New York: Oxford University Press, 1986.

de Beauvoir, Simone. *The Second Sex.* Trans. H. M. Parshley. New York: Knopf, 1952.

Debord, Guy. *The Society of the Spectacle.* Detroit: Black and Red, 1977.

De Certeau, Michel. *Heterologies: Discourse on the Other.* Trans. Brian Massumi. Minneapolis: University of Minnesota Press, 1986.

Deleuze, Gilles. *Masochism: An Interpretation of Coldness and Cruelty.* Trans. Jean McNeil. New York: G. Braziller, 1971.

—. *The Logic of Sense.* Trans. Mark Lester. New York: Columbia University Press, 1990.

—. *Nietzsche and Philosophy.* Trans. Hugh Tomlinson. London: Athlone Press, 1983.

—. *Empiricism and Subjectivity: An Essay on Hume's Theory of Human Nature.* Trans. Constantin V. Boundas. New York: Columbia University Press, 1991.

— and Félix Guattari. *Anti-Oedipus: Capitalism and Schizophrenia.* Trans. Robert Hurley, Mark Seem, and Helen R. Lane. New York: Viking, 1977.

—. *Kafka: Toward a Minor Literature.* Trans. Dana Polan. Minneapolis: University of Minnesota Press, 1986.

—. *A Thousand Plateaus: Capitalism and Schizophrenia.* Trans. Brian Massumi. London: Athlone Press, 1988.

De Man, Paul. *Allegories of Reading: Figural Language in Rousseau, Nietzsche, Rilke, and Proust.* New Haven: Yale University Press, 1979.

—. *Blindness and Insight: Essays in the Rhetoric of Contemporary Criticism.* 2d rev. ed. Minneapolis: University of Minnesota Press, 1983.

—. "The Rhetoric of Temporality." In *Blindness and Insight.*

Dennis, John. *The Grounds of Criticism in Poetry. The Critical Works of John Dennis.* New York: Garland, 1971.

Derrida, Jacques. *Speech and Phenomena, and Other Essays on Husserl's Theory of Signs.* Trans. David B. Allison. Evanston, Ill.: Northwestern University Press, 1973.

—. *Of Grammatology.* Trans. Gayatri Chakravorty Spivak. Baltimore: Johns Hopkins University Press, 1976.

—. "Structure, Sign, and Play in the Discourse of the Human Sciences." In *Writing and Difference.* Trans. Alan Bass. Chicago: University of Chicago Press, 1978.

—. *Positions.* Trans. Alan Bass. Chicago: University of Chicago Press, 1981.

—. *Margins of Philosophy.* Trans. Alan Bass. Chicago: University of Chicago Press, 1982.

Descartes, René. *A Discourse on Method.* Trans. John Veitch. New York: E. P. Dutton, 1949.

—. *Meditations on First Philosophy.* Trans. and ed. George Heffernan. Notre Dame, Ind.: University of Notre Dame Press, 1990.

Dewey, John. *Individualism, Old and New.* New York: Minton, Balch, 1930.

Dews, Peter. "Power and Subjectivity in Foucault." *New Left Review* 4, 1984.

—. *Logics of Disintegration: Post-Structuralist Thought and the Claims of Critical Theory.* London: Verso, 1987.

Dilthey, Wilhelm. *Meaning in History.* Ed. H. P. Rickman. London: Allen and Unwin, 1961.

—. *Introduction to the Human Sciences: An Attempt to Lay a Foundation for the Study of Society and History.* Trans. Ramon J. Betanzos. Detroit: Wayne State University Press, 1988.

Docherty, Thomas, ed. *Postmodernism: A Reader.* New York: Columbia University Press, 1993.

Dollimore, Jonathan, and Alan Sinfield, eds. *Political Shakespeare: New Essays in Cultural Materialism.* Manchester, U.K.: Manchester University Press, 1985.

Dreyfus, Hubert L., and Paul Rabinow. *Michel Foucault: Beyond Structuralism and Hermeteutics.* 2d ed. Chicago: University of Chicago Press, 1983.

D'Souza, Dinesh. *Illiberal Education: The Politics of Race and Sex on Campus.* New York: Free Press, 1991.

Duberman, Martin, Martha Vicinus, and George Chauncey, Jr. *Hidden from History: Reclaiming the Gay and Lesbian Past.* New York: New American Library, 1989.

Du Bois, W. E. B. "Of Our Spiritual Strivings." In *The Souls of Black Folk.* New York: Blue Heron Press, 1953.

DuPlessis, Rachel Blau. *Writing Beyond the Edge: Narrative Strategies of Twentieth-Century Women Writers.* Bloomington: Indiana University Press, 1985.

Eagleton, Terry. *Criticism and Ideology: A Study in Marxist Literary Theory.* London: Verso, 1976.

—. *Marxism and Literary Criticism.* Berkeley: University of California Press, 1976.

—. *Literary Theory: An Introduction.* Minneapolis: University of Minnesota Press, 1983.

—. *Against the Grain: Essays 1975–1985.* London: Verso, 1986.

—. *The Ideology of the Aesthetic.* Cambridge: Blackwell, 1990.

—. *Ideology: An Introduction.* London: Verso, 1991.

Easthope, Antony. "The Question of Literary Value." *Textual Practice* 4(3), 1990.

Echols, Alice. *Daring to be Bad: Radical Feminism in America, 1967–1975.* Minneapolis: University of Minnesota Press, 1989.

Eco, Umberto. *A Theory of Semiotics.* Bloomington: Indiana University Press, 1979.

—. *Semiotics and the Philosophy of Language.* Bloomington: Indiana University Press, 1984.

—. *Travels in Hyperreality.* Trans. William Weaver. San Diego: Harcourt Brace Jovanovich, 1986.

Eisenstein, Hester, and Alice Jardine, eds. *The Future of Difference.* Boston: G. K. Hall, 1980.

Eisenstein, Zillah R. *The Radical Future of Liberal Feminism.* New York: Longman, 1981.

—, ed. *Capitalist Patriarchy and the Case for Socialist Feminism.* New York: Monthly Review Press, 1979.

Eliot, T. S. "The Function of Criticism." In *Selected Essays.* London: Faber and Faber, 1975.

—. "Tradition and the Individual Talent." In *Selected Prose of T. S. Eliot.* Ed. Frank Kermode. London: Faber and Faber, 1975.

Ellis, Trey. "The New Black Aesthetic." *Callaloo* 12(1), Winter 1989.

Else, G. F. *Aristotle's "Poetics": The Argument.* Cambridge, Mass.: Harvard University Press, 1957.

Empson, William. *Seven Types of Ambiguity.* London: Chatto and Windus, 1930.

Engels, Friedrich. *The Origin of the Family, Private Property, and the State.* Trans. Ernest Unterman. Chicago: Charles Kerr, 1902.

—. *Dialectics of Nature.* Moscow : Foreign Languages Publishing House, 1954.

Erhlich, Victor. *Russian Formalism: History, Doctrine.* New Haven: Yale University Press, 1981.

Esslin, Martin. *The Theatre of the Absurd.* Garden City N.Y.: Anchor, 1969.

Evans, J. D. G. *Aristotle's Concept of Dialectic.* New York: Cambridge University Press, 1977.

Faderman, Lillian. *Surpassing the Love of Men: Romantic Friendship and Love Between Women from the Renaissance to the Present.* New York: Morrow, 1981.

Fanon, Frantz. *The Wretched of the Earth.* Trans. Constance Farrington. New York: Grove, 1968.

Felman, Shoshona. *The Literary Speech Act: Don Juan with J. L. Austin, or Seduction in Two Languages.* Trans. Catherine Porter. Ithaca, N.Y.: Cornell University Press, 1983.

Feltes, N. N. *Modes of Production of Victorian Novels.* Chicago: University of Chicago Press, 1986.

Ferenczi, Sandor. "Introjection and Transference." In *Selected Papers.* New York: Basic Books, 1950–55.

Feyerabend, Paul K. *Problems of Empiricism.* Cambridge: Cambridge University Press, 1981.

Firestone, Shulamith. *The Dialectic of Sex: The Case for Feminist Revolution.* New York: Morrow, 1970.

Fish, Stanley. *Self -Consuming Artifacts: The Experience of Seventeenth-Century Literature.* Berkeley: University of California Press, 1972.

—. *Is There a Text in This Class? The Authority of Interpretive Communities.* Cambridge, Mass.: Harvard University Press, 1980.

Fiske, John, and John Hartley. *Reading Television.* London: Methuen, 1978.

Fleischam, Avrom. *The English Historical Novel: Walter Scott to Virginia Woolf.* Baltimore: Johns Hopkins University Press, 1971.

Forster, E. M. *Aspects of the Novel.* New York: Harcourt Brace and World, 1954.

Foster, Hal, ed. *The Anti-Aesthetic: Essays on Postmodern Culture.* Port Towsend, Wash.: Bay Press, 1983.

Foucault, Michel. *Madness and Civilization.* Trans. Richard Howard. New York: Pantheon, 1965.

—. *The Order of Things: An Archaeology of the Human Sciences.* New York: Vintage, 1970.

—. *The Archaeology of Knowledge.* Trans. A. M. Sheridan Smith. New York: Pantheon, 1972.

—. *The Birth of the Clinic.* Trans. A. M. Sheridan Smith. New York: Vintage, 1975.

—. *Language, Counter-Memory, Practice: Selected Essays and Interviews.* Trans. Donald F. Bouchard and Sherry Simon. Ithaca, N.Y.: Cornell University Press, 1977.

—. "Nietzsche, Genealogy, History." In *Language, Counter-Memory, Practice.*

—. "What is an Author?" In *Language, Counter- Memory, Practice.*

—. *The History of Sexuality.* Trans. Robert Hurley. New York: Pantheon, 1978.

—. *Discipline and Punish: The Birth of the Prison.* Trans. Alan Sheridan. New York: Vintage, 1979.

—. *Power/Knowledge: Selected Interviews and Other Writings, 1972–1977.* Trans. and ed. Colin Gordon. New York: Pantheon, 1980.

—. "The Subject and Power." *Critical Inquiry* 8, 1982.

—. "Nietzsche, Freud, Marx." Trans. Jon Anderson and Gary Hentzi. *Critical Texts 3.2,* 1986.

Frazer, J. G. *The Golden Bough.* New York: Macmillan, 1922.

Freud, Sigmund. *Group Psychology and the Analysis of the Ego.* Trans. James Strachey. London: International Psycho-Analytical Press, 1922.

—. *Inhibitions, Symptoms, and Anxiety.* Trans. Alix Strachey. London: Hogarth Press, 1948.

—. *The Interpretation of Dreams*. Trans. and ed. James Strachey. London: Hogarth Press, 1953.

—. *The Ego and the Id*. Trans. Joan Riviere, ed. James Strachey. New York: Norton, 1960.

—. *Beyond the Pleasure Principle*. Rev. ed. Trans. and ed. James Strachey. New York: Liveright, 1961.

—. *Totem and Taboo*. Trans. James Strachey. London: Routledge, 1961.

—. *Civilization and Its Discontents*. Trans. and ed. James Strachey. New York: Norton, 1962.

—. *Three Essays on the Theory of Sexuality*. Trans. and ed. James Strachey. London: Hogarth Press, 1962.

—. *Introductory Lectures on Psychoanalysis*. Trans. James Strachey. New York: Norton, 1965.

—. *New Introductory Lectures on Psychoanalysis.*Trans. and ed. James Strachey. New York: Norton, 1965.

—. *The Standard Edition of the Complete Psychological Works of Sigmund Freud*. 24 vols. Trans. James Strachey. London: Hogarth Press and Institute of Psycho-Analysis, 1974.

—. "A Child is Being Beaten." In *The Standard Edition of the Complete Psychological Works of Sigmund Freud*, vol. 17.

—. "Creative Writers and Day-Dreaming." In *The Standard Edition of the Complete Psychological Works of Sigmund Freud*, vol. 9.

—. "The Dissolution of the Oedipus Complex." In *The Standard Edition of the Complete Psychological Works of Sigmund Freud*, vol. 19.

—. "The Dynamics of Transference." In *The Standard Edition of the Complete Psychological Works of Sigmund Freud*, vol. 12.

—. "The Economic Problem of Masochism." In *The Standard Edition of the Complete Psychological Works of Sigmund Freud*, vol. 19.

—. "Female Sexuality." In *The Standard Edition of the Complete Psychological Works of Sigmund Freud*, vol. 21.

—. "Fetishism." In *The Standard Edition of the Complete Psychological Works of Sigmund Freud*, vol. 21.

—. "From the History of an Infantile Neurosis." In *The Standard Edition of the Complete Psychological Works of Sigmund Freud*, vol. 17.

—. "Instincts and Their Vicissitudes." In *The Standard Edition of the Complete Psychological Works of Sigmund Freud*, vol. 14.

—. "Mourning and Melancholia." In *The Standard Edition of the Complete Psychological Works of Sigmund Freud*, vol. 14.

—. "Negation." In *The Standard Edition of the Complete Psychological Works of Sigmund Freud*, vol. 19.

—. "Neurosis and Psychosis." In *The Standard Edition of the Complete Psychological Works of Sigmund Freud*, vol. 19.

—. "On Narcissism: An Introduction." In *The Standard Edition of the Complete Psychological Works of Sigmund Freud*, vol. 14.

—. "On the Psychical Mechanism of Hysterical Phenomena." In *The Standard Edition of the Complete Psychological Works of Sigmund Freud*, vol. 2.

—. "Repression." In *The Standard Edition of the Complete Psychological Works of Sigmund Freud*, vol. 14.

—. "Two Principles of Mental Functioning." In *The Standard Edition of the Complete Psychological Works of Sigmund Freud*, vol.

—. "The Uncanny." In *The Standard Edition of the Complete Psychological Works of Sigmund Freud*, vol. 17.

—. "The Unconscious." In *The Standard Edition of the Complete Psychological Works of Sigmund Freud*, vol. 14.

— and Joseph Breuer. *Studies in Hysteria*. Trans. A. A. Brill. Boston: Beacon Press, 1961.

Fried, Michael. "Art and Objecthood." *Artforum*, June 1967.

—. *Absorption and Theatricality: Painting and Beholder in the Age of Diderot*. Berkeley: University of California Press, 1980.

Fromm, Erich. *Marx's Concept of Man*. New York: F. Ungar, 1961.

Fry, Paul H. "Longinus at Colonus: The Grounding of Sublimity." In *The Reach of Criticism: Method and Perception in Literary Theory*. New Haven: Yale University Press, 1983.

Frye, Northrop. *Anatomy of Criticism*. Princeton: Princeton University Press, 1957.

—. *The Secular Scripture*. Cambridge, Mass.: Harvard University Press, 1976.

Fuss, Diana. *Essentially Speaking*. New York: Routledge, 1990.

—, ed. *Inside/Out: Lesbian Theories, Gay Theories*. New York: Routledge, 1991.

Gadamer, Hans-Georg. *Truth and Method*. Ed. Garrett Barden and John Cummung. New York: Continuum Press, 1975.

—. *Hegel's Dialectic : Five Hermeneutical Studies*. Trans. P. Christopher Smith. New Haven: Yale University Press, 1976.

Gargani, Aldo, ed. *Crisi della ragione: Nuovi modelli nel rapporto tra sapere e attivita umane*. Torino: Einaudi, 1979.

Garin, Eugenio. *Italian Humanism*. Trans. Peter Munz. New York: Harper and Row, 1965.

Garvin, Paul, ed. *A Prague School Reader on Esthetics, Literary Structure and Style*. Washington, D.C.: Washington Linguistic Club, 1955.

Gates, Henry Louis, Jr. "Writing 'Race' and the Difference It Makes." In Henry Louis Gates, Jr., ed., *"Race," Writing, and Difference*. Chicago: University of Chicago Press, 1986.

—. *The Signifying Monkey: A Theory of African-American Literary Criticism*. New York: Oxford University Press, 1988.

—. "The Signifying Monkey and the Language of Signifyin(g): Rhetorical Difference and the Orders of Meaning." In *The Signifying Monkey: A Theory of African-American Literary Criticism*.

Gayle, Addison, Jr., ed. *The Black Aesthetic*. New York: Doubleday, 1971.

Genette, Gérard. *Narrative Discourse: An Essay in Method*. Trans. Jane E. Lewin. Ithaca, N.Y.: Cornell University Press, 1980.

—. *Figures of Literary Discourse*. Trans. Alan Sheridan. New York: Columbia University Press, 1982.

—. *Nouveau Discours du Récit*. Paris: Editions du Seuil, 1983.

Gershman, Herbert. *The Surrealist Revolution in France*. Ann Arbor: University of Michigan Press, 1974.

Geuss, Raymond. *The Idea of a Critical Theory*. Cambridge: Cambridge University Press, 1981.

Gibson, William. *Neuromancer*. New York: Ace Books, 1984.

Giddens, Anthony. *Central Problems in Social Theory*. Berkeley: University of California Press, 1979.

Giddings, Paula. *When and Where I Enter:The Impact of Black Women on Race and Sex in America*. New York: William Morrow, 1984.

Gilbert, Sandra J., and Susan Gubar. *The Madwoman in the Attic: The Woman Writer and the Nineteenth-Century Literary Imagination*. New Haven: Yale University Press, 1979.

Gilligan, Carol. *In a Different Voice: Psychological Theory and Women's Development*. Cambridge, Mass.: Harvard University Press, 1982.

Gilman, Charlotte Perkins. *The Man-made World; or, Our Androcentric Culture*. New York: Source Book Press, 1970.

Godzich, Wlad. "Afterword." In Samuel Weber, *Institution and Interpretation*. Minneapolis: University of Minnesota Press, 1987.

Goldmann, Lucien. *The Hidden God: A Study of Tragic Vision in the Pensées of Pascal and the Tragedies of Racine*. Trans. P. Thody. New York: Humanities Press, 1964.

Goodman, Nelson. *Ways of Worldmaking*. Indianapolis: Hackett, 1978.

Graff, Gerald. "Co-optation." In Veeser, ed., *The New Historicism*..

Gramsci, Antonio. "Notes on Italian History." In *Selections from the Prison Notebooks*. Trans. and ed. Quintin Hoare and Geoffrey Nowell Smith. New York: International Publishers, 1971.

—. *Selections from Political Writings, 1921–1926*. Trans. and ed. Quintin Hoare. New York: International Publications, 1978.

—. *Prison Notebooks*, vol. 1. New York: Columbia University Press, 1992.

Graves, Robert. *The White Goddess*. New York: Creative Age Press, 1948.

Greenberg, Clement. "Avant-Garde and Kitsch." In *Art and Culture*. Boston: Beacon Press, 1961.

—. "The Notion of Post-modern." In Ingeborg Hosterey, ed., *Zeitgeist in Babel: The Postmodernist Controversy*. Bloomington: Indiana University Press, 1991.

Greenblatt, Stephen. "Introduction to *The Forms of Power and the Power of Forms in the Renaissance*." *Genre* 15, 1982.

—. *Shakespearean Negotiations: The Circulation of Social Energy in Renaissance England*. Berkeley: University of California Press, 1988.

Greimas, A. J. *Du Sens*. Paris: Editions du Seuil, 1970.

—. "Narrative Grammar: Units and Levels." *Modern Language Notes* 86, 1971.

—. "Elements of a Narrative Grammar." *Diacritics* 7, 1977.

—. *Structural Semantics:An Attempt at a Method*. Trans. Daniele McDowell et al. Lincoln: University of Nebraska Press, 1983.

— and Francois Rastier. "The Interaction of Semiotic Constraints." *Yale French Studies* 41, 1968.

Grossberg, Lawrence. *It's a Sin: Essays on Postmodernity, Politics and Culture*. Sidney, Australia: Power Publications, 1988.

—, C. Nelson, and Paula Treichler. *Cultural Studies* New York: Routledge, 1992.

Group Mu. *General Rhetoric*. Trans. Paul B. Burrell and Edgar M. Slotkin. Baltimore: Johns Hopkins University Press, 1981.

Guggenheim Museum, Solomon R. *Expressionism: A German Institution, 1905–1920*. New York: Solomon R. Guggenheim Foundation, 1980.

Gutman, Herbert G. *The Black Family in Slavery and Freedom 1750–1925*. New York: Vintage, 1976.

Habermas, Jürgen. *Legitimation Crisis*. Trans. Thomas McCarthy. Boston: Beacon Press, 1975.

Hall, Radclyffe. *The Well of Loneliness*. London: Virago, 1982.

Hall, Stuart. "Rethinking the "Base and Superstructure' Metaphor." In Jan Bloomfield, ed.,

Papers on Class, Hegemony, and Party: the Communist University of London. London: Lawrence and Wishart, 1977.

—. "Recent Developments in Theories of Language and Ideology." In Stuart Hall, ed., *Culture, Media, Language: Working Papers in Cultural Studies, 1972–79.* London: Hutchinson, 1980.

— and Tony Jefferson, eds. *Resistance Through Rituals: Youth Subculture in Post War Britain.* London: Hutchinson, 1976.

Hampshire, Stuart. *Freedom of the Individual.* London: Chatto and Windus, 1975.

Harari, Josué V., ed. *Textual Strategies: Perspectives in Post-Structuralist Criticism.* Ithaca, N.Y.: Cornell University Press, 1979.

Haraway, Donna. "A Manifesto for Cyborgs: Science, Technology, and Socialist Feminism in the 1980s." *Socialist Review* 80, 1985.

Hartman, Geoffrey. "Structuralism: The Anglo-American Adventure." In Jacques Ehrmann, ed., *Structuralism.* New York: Anchor, 1970.

Hassan, Ihab. *Paracriticisms: Seven Speculations of the Times.* Urbana: University of Illinois Press, 1975.

Hawkes, Terence. *Metaphor.* London: Methuen, 1972.

—. *Structuralism and Semiotics.* Berkeley: University of California Press, 1977.

Hayek, F. A. von. *The Counter-Revolution of Science: Studies in the Abuse of Reason.* Glencoe, Ill.: Free Press, 1952.

Heath, Stephen. *The Nouveau Roman: A Study in the Practice of Writing.* London: Elek, 1972.

—. "Notes on Suture." *Screen* 19(2), 1977–78.

Hebdige, Dick. *Subculture: The Meaning of Style.* London: Methuen, 1979.

Hegel, Georg Wilhelm Friedrich. *Lectures on the Philosophy of History.* Trans. J. Sibree. London: G. Bell and Sons, 1894.

—. *Encyclopedia of Philosophy.* Trans. Gustav Emil Mueller. New York: Philosophical Library, 1959.

—. *Science of Logic.* Trans. A. V. Miller. London: Allen and Unwin, 1969.

—. *The Phenomenology of the Mind.* Trans. Lawrence S. Stepelevich. New York: Macmillan, 1990.

Heidegger, Martin. *Existence and Being.* London: Vision Press, 1949.

—. *Being and Time.* Trans. John Macquarrie and E. S. Robinson. New York: Harper, 1962.

—. *Basic Writings.* Ed. David Farrell Krell. New York: Harper and Row, 1977.

Heilbrun, Carolyn G. *Toward a Recognition of Androgyny.* New York: Norton, 1982.

— and Catherine R. Stimpson. "Theories of Feminist Criticism: A Dialogue." In Josephine Donovan, ed., *Feminist Literary Criticism.* Lexington: University Press of Kentucky, 1975.

Held, David. *Introduction to Critical Theory: Horkheimer to Habermas.* Berkeley: University of California Press, 1980.

Henderson, Stephen. *Understanding the New Black Poetry.* New York: William Morrow, 1973.

Henry Art Gallery. *Art into Life: Russian Constructivism, 1914–32.* New York: Rizzoli, 1990.

Herbert, Robert L. *Impressionism: Art, Leisure, and Parisian Society.* New Haven: Yale University Press, 1988.

Herder, J.G. "Ideen zur Philosophie der Geschicte der Menchheit." *Sämtliche Werke,* vol. 13. Berlin, 1877–1913.

Herskovits, Melville J. *The Myth of the Negro Past.* Boston: Beacon Press, 1990.

Hiller, Susan, ed. *The Myth of Primitivism: Perspectives on Art*. New York: Routledge, 1991.

Hirsch, E.D. *Validity in Interpetation*. New Haven: Yale University Press, 1967.

——. *The Aims of Interpretation*. Chicago: University of Chicago Press, 1976.

——. *Cultural Literacy*. Boston: Houghton Mifflin, 1987.

Hirsch, Foster. *The Dark Side of the Screen: Film Noir*. New York: Da Capo Press, 1983.

Hirsch, Marianne. *The Mother/Daughter Plot: Narrative, Psychoanalysis, Feminism*. Bloomington: Indiana University Press, 1989.

Hoggart, Richard. *The Uses of Literacy*. London: Chatto and Windus, 1957.

Holderness, Graham, ed. *The Shakespeare Myth*. Manchester, U.K.: Manchester University Press, 1988.

Holland, Norman. *The Dynamics of Literary Response*. New York: Oxford University Press, 1968.

——. *5 Readers Reading*. New Haven: Yale University Press, 1975.

Hollibaugh, Amber, and Cherrie Moraga. "What We're Rollin' Around in Bed With: Sexual Silences in Feminism." In Ann Snitow, Christine Stansell, and Sharon Thompson, eds., *Powers of Desire: The Politics of Sexuality*. New York: Monthly Review Press, 1983.

Holub, Robert C. *Reception Theory: A Critical Introduction*. London: Methuen, 1984.

hooks, bell. *Ain't I a Woman*. Boston: South End Press, 1981.

——. *Feminist Theory From Margin to Center*. Boston: South End Press, 1984.

——. *Yearning: Race, Gender, and Cultural Politics*. Boston: South End Press, 1990.

—— and Cornel West. *Breakin' Bread: Insurgent Black Intellectual Life*. Boston: South End Press, 1991.

Horkheimer, Max. *Critical Theory*. Trans. Matthew J. O'Connell et al. New York: Herder and Herder, 1972.

Horwitz, Howard. "I Can't Remember: Skepticism, Synthetic Histories, Critical Action." *South Atlantic Quarterly* 87(4), 1988.

House, John, and MaryAnne Stevens, eds. *Post-Impressionism: Cross-Currents in European Painting*. New York: Harper and Row, 1979.

Howard, Jean. "The New Historicism in Literary Studies." *English Literary Renaissance* 16, 1986.

Hoy, David Couzens. *The Critical Circle*. Berkeley: University of California Press, 1978.

Huggins, Nathan Irvin. *Harlem Renaissance*. New York: Oxford University Press, 1971.

Hughes, Langston. "The Negro Artist and the Racial Mountain." *The Nation* 72, 1926.

Huizinga, Johan. *Homo Ludens*. Boston: Beacon Press, 1950.

Hull, Gloria T. *Color, Sex, & Poetry: Three Women Writers of the Harlem Renaissance*. Bloomington: Indiana University Press, 1987.

——, Patricia Bell Scott, and Barbara Smith, eds. *All the Women Are White, All the Blacks Are Men, But Some of Us Are Brave*. Old Westbury, N.Y.: Feminist Press, 1982.

Hume, David. *A Treatise of Human Nature*. Oxford: Clarendon Press, 1965.

Hunter, Tera. " 'It's A Man's Man's Man's World': Specters of the Old Re-Newed in Afro-American Culture and Criticism." *Callaloo* 12(1), Winter 1989.

Hurston, Zora Neale. *Mules and Men*. Bloomington: Indiana University Press, 1935.

Husserl, Edmund. *Ideas: General Introduction to Pure Phenomonology*. Trans. W. R. Boyce-Gibson. New York: Humanities Press, 1967.

——. *Logical Investigations*. Trans. J. N. Findlay. New York: Humanities Press, 1970.

—. *The Paris Lectures.* Trans. Peter Kostenbaum. The Hague: Martinus Nijhoff, 1975.

Hutcheon, Linda. *A Poetics of Postmodernism.* New York: Routledge, 1988.

Huyssen, Andreas. *After the Great Divide: Modernism, Mass Culture, Postmodernism.* Bloomington: Indiana University Press, 1986.

Ingarden, Roman. *The Cognition of the Literary Work of Art.* Trans. Ruth Ann Crowley and Kenneth R. Olson. Evanston, Ill.: Northwestern University Press, 1973.

Inglis, Fred. *Media Theory: An Introduction.* Oxford: Blackwell, 1990.

Ionesco, Eugene. *Rhinoceros.* Trans. Derek Prouse. London: Calder and Boyars, 1960.

Irigaray, Luce. *This Sex Which is Not One.* Trans. Catherine Porter. Ithaca, N.Y.: Cornell University Press, 1985.

Iser, Wolfgang. *The Implied Reader.* Baltimore: Johns Hopkins University Press, 1974.

—. *The Act of Reading: A Theory of Aesthetic Response.* Baltimore: Johns Hopkins University Press, 1978.

—. *Prospecting: From Reader Response to Literary Anthropology.* Baltimore: Johns Hopkins University Press, 1989.

—. *The Fictive and the Imaginary: Charting Literary Anthropology.* Baltimore: Johns Hopkins University Press, 1993.

Jackson, Bruce, comp. *"Get Your Ass in the Water and Swim Like Me": Narrative Poetry from Black Oral Tradition.* Cambridge, Mass.: Harvard University Press, 1974.

Jacobus, Mary, ed. *Women Writing and Writing About Women.* New York: Barnes and Noble, 1979.

Jakobson, Roman. "Closing Statement." In *Linguistics and Poetics.*

—. *Selected Writings.* The Hague: Mouton, 1971.

—. *Language in Literature.* Eds. Krystyna Pomorska and Stephen Rudy. Cambridge, Mass.: Belknap Press, 1987.

James, Henry. *The Future of the Novel: Essays on the Art of Fiction.* New York: Oxford University Press, 1948.

James, William. *The Will to Believe, and Other Essays in Popular Philosophy.* New York: Longmans, Green, 1896.

—. *Pragmatism: A New Name for Some Old Ways of Thinking.* New York: Longmans, Green, 1914.

Jameson, Fredric. *Marxism and Form: Twentieth Century Dialectical Theories of Literature.* Princeton: Princeton University Press, 1971.

—. *The Prison-House of Language.* Princeton: Princeton University Press, 1972.

—. *The Political Unconscious: Narrative as a Socially Symbolic Act.* Ithaca, N.Y.: Cornell University Press, 1981.

—. "Postmodernism and Consumer Society." In Hal Foster, ed., *The Anti-Aesthetic: Essays on Postmodern Culture.*

—. *Postmodernism, or the Cultural Logic of Late Capitalism.* Durham, N.C.: Duke University Press, 1991.

Jardine, Alice A. *Gynesis: Configurations of Women and Modernity.* Ithaca, N.Y.: Cornell University Press, 1985.

Jaspers, Karl. *The Perennial Scope of Philosophy.* Trans. Ralph Manheim. New York: Philosophical Library, 1949.

Jauss, Hans Robert. "Literary History as a Challenge to Literary Theory." *New Literary History* 2, 1970.

—. *Aesthetic Experience and Literary Hermeneutics.* Trans. Michael Shaw. Minneapolis: University of Minnesota Press, 1982.

—. *Toward an Aesthetic of Reception.* Trans. Timothy Bahti. Minneapolis: University of Minnesota Press, 1982.

Jay, Karla, and Joanne Glasgow, ed. *Lesbian Texts and Contexts: Radical Revisions.* New York: New York University Press, 1990.

Jay, Martin. *The Dialectical Imagination: A History of the Frankfurt School.* Boston: Little, Brown, 1973.

Jones, Ann Rosalind. "Writing the Body: Toward an Understanding of *l'écriture feminine.*" In Judith Newton and Deborah Rosenfelt, eds., *Feminist Criticism and Social Change.* New York: Methuen, 1985.

Jones, Ernest. "Early Development of Female Sexuality." In *Papers on Psychoanalysis.* 5th ed. Boston: Beacon, 1961.

Jordan, Z. A. *The Evolution of Dialectical Materialism.* New York: St. Martin's Press, 1967.

Joyner, Charles. *Down by the Riverside: A South Carolina Slave Community.* Urbana: University of Illinois Press, 1984.

Jung, Carl Gustav. "On the Relation of Analytical Psychology to Poetic Art." In *Contributions to Analytical Psychology.* Trans. H. G. Baynes and Cary F. Baynes. New York: Harcourt Brace Jovanovich, 1928.

—. *The Archetypes and the Collective Unconscious. Collected Works,* vol. 9. Trans. R. F. C. Hull. New York: Pantheon, 1959.

—. *Psychology of the Unconscious.* Trans. Beatrice M. Hinkle. Princeton: Princeton University Press, 1991.

Ka, Shushi. "Paradise Lost? An Interview with Phillippe Sollers." *Sub-Stance* 30, 1981.

Kael, Pauline. *I Lost it at the Movies.* Boston: Little, Brown, 1965.

Kamuf, Peggy, ed. *A Derrida Reader: Between the Blinds.* New York: Columbia University Press, 1991.

Kant, Immanuel. *Critique of Judgement.* Trans. J. H. Bernard. New York: Hafner Press, 1951.

—. *Critique of Pure Reason.* Trans. Norman Kemp Smith. New York: St. Martin's Press, 1965.

—. "What is Enlightenment?" In *Philosophical Writings.* Trans. Lewis White Beck, ed. Ernst Behler. New York: Continuum, 1986.

Kaplan, E. Ann, ed. *Women in Film Noir.* Rev. ed. London: British Film Institute, 1980.

—. "Is the Gaze Male?" In E. Ann Kaplan, ed., *Women and Film: Both Sides of the Camera.* New York: Methuen, 1983.

Kellner, Bruce, ed. *The Harlem Renaissance: A Historical Dictionary of the Era.* New York: Methuen, 1987.

Kennedy, Ellen Conroy, ed. *The Negritude Poets: An Anthology of Translations from the French.* New York: Viking, 1975.

Kermode, Frank. *The Classic: Literary Images of Permanence and Change.* New York: Viking, 1975.

—. "Institutional Control of Interpretation." *Salmagundi* 43, 1979.

Kesteloot, Lilyan. *Black Writers in French: A Literary History of Negritude.* Trans. Ellen Conroy Kennedy. Philadelphia: Temple University Press, 1974.

Kierkegaard, Søren. *The Concept of Irony, With Constant Reference to Socrates.* Trans. Lee M. Capel. New York: Harper, 1965.

—. *Fear and Trembling.* Trans. and ed. Howard V. Hong and Edna H. Hong. Princeton: Princeton University Press, 1983.

Kimmel, Michael S., ed. *Changing Men: New Directions in Research on Men and Masculinity.* Newbury Park, Calif.: Sage, 1987.

Klein, Melanie. *Contributions to Psycho-analysis 1921–1945.* London: Hogarth Press, 1965.

Klossowski, Pierre. *Sade My Neighbor.* Trans. Alphonso Lingis. Evanston, Ill.: Northwestern University Press, 1991.

Knabb, Ken, ed. and trans. *Situationist International Anthology.* Berkeley, Calif.: Bureau of Public Secrets, 1981.

Kochman, Thomas, ed. *Rappin' and Stylin' Out: Communication in Urban Black America.* Urbana: University of Illinois Press, 1972.

Koedt, Anne, Ellen Levine, and Anita Rapone, eds. *Radical Feminism.* New York: Quadrangle, 1973.

Krafft-Ebing, Richard von. *Psychopathia Sexualis..* Trans. Franklin S. Klaf. New York: Bell, 1965.

Krauss, Rosalind E. *Passages in Modern Sculpture.* Cambridge, Mass.: MIT Press, 1981.

—. "Grids." In *The Originality of the Avant-Garde and Other Modernist Myths.* Cambridge, Mass.: MIT Press, 1985.

— and Jane Livingston. *L'Amour Fou: Photography and Surrealism.* New York: Abbeville, 1985.

Kristeva, Julia. *Desire in Language: A Semiotic Approach to Literature and Art.* Trans. Alice Jardine et al., ed. Leon S. Roudiez. Oxford: Blackwell, 1980.

—. "La Femme, ce n'est Jamais Ca." In Elaine Marks and Isabelle de Courtivron, eds., *New French Feminisms.*

—. *Powers of Horror: An Essay on Abjection.* Trans. Leon S. Roudiez. New York: Columbia University Press, 1982.

—. *The Kristeva Reader.* Ed. Toril Moi. New York: Columbia University Press, 1986.

Kuhn, Thomas, S. *The Structure of Scientific Revolutions.* Chicago: University of Chicago Press, 1962.

Lacan, Jacques. *Ecrits: A Selection.* Trans. Alan Sheridan. New York: Norton, 1977.

—. "On a Question Preliminary to Any Possible Treatment of Psychosis." In *Ecrits.*

—. "The Agency of the Letter in the Unconscious or Reason Since Freud." In *Ecrits.*

—. "The Mirror Stage as Formative of the Function of the 'I' as Revealed in Psychoanalytic Experience." In *Ecrits.*

—. "The Subject and the Other: Alienation." In *Four Fundamental Concepts of Psycho-analysis.* Trans. Alan Sheridan, ed. Jacques-Alain Miller. New York: Norton, 1978.

LaCapra, Dominick. *Rethinking Intellectual History.* Ithaca, N.Y.: Cornell University Press, 1983.

—. *History and Criticism.* Ithaca, N.Y.: Cornell University Press, 1985.

Laclau, Ernesto, and Chantal Mouffe. *Hegemony and Socialist Strategy: Towards a Radical Democratic Politics.* Trans. Winston Moore and Paul Cammack. London: Verso, 1985.

Landow, George P. *Hypertext: The Convergence of Contemporary Critical Theory and Technology.* Baltimore: Johns Hopkins University Press, 1992.

Larrain, Jorge. *Marxism and Ideology.* London: Macmillan, 1983.

Lauter, Paul. "Race and Gender in the Shaping of the American Literary Canon." *Feminist Studies* 9, 1983.

Lawall, Sarah. *Critics of Consciousness: The Existential Structures of Literature*. Cambridge, Mass.: Harvard University Press, 1968.

Leavis, F. R. *The Great Tradition*. Garden City, N.Y.: Doubleday, 1954.

——. *Two Cultures? The Significance of C. P. Snow*. London: Chatto and Windus, 1962.

——. *Revaluation: Tradition and Development in English Poetry*. London: Chatto and Windus, 1963.

—— and Denys Thompson. *Culture and Environment*. London: Chatto and Windus, 1933.

Leibniz, Gottfried Wilhelm. *Discourse on Metaphysics*. Trans. Peter Lucas and Leslie Grant. Manchester, U.K.: Manchester University Press, 1953.

——. *Monadology, and Other Philosophical Writings*. Trans. Paul Schrecker and Anne Martin Schrecker. Indianapolis: Bobbs-Merrill, 1965.

Lemon, Lee T., and Marion J. Reis, trans. *Russian Formalist Criticism: Four Essays*. Lincoln: University of Nebraska Press, 1965.

Lenin, Vladimir. *Imperialism: The Highest Stage of Capitalism*. Rev. trans. London: Lawrence and Wishart, 1948.

——. *What Is to Be Done?* Trans. Joe Fineberg and George Hanna; introduction by Robert Service. London: Penguin, 1988.

Lentricchia, Frank. *After the New Criticism*. Chicago: University of Chicago Press, 1980.

Levin, Harry. *The Gates of Horn*. New York: Oxford University Press, 1963.

Levine, George. *The Realistic Imagination: English Fiction from Frankenstein to Lady Chatterly*. Chicago: University of Chicago Press, 1981.

Levinson, Daniel J. "The Study of Ethnocentric Ideology." In T. W. Adorno et al., eds., *The Authoritarian Personality*. New York: Norton, 1982.

Lévi-Strauss, Claude. *Structural Anthropology*. Trans. Claire Jacobson and Brook Grundfest Schoepf. New York: Basic Books, 1963.

——. *The Savage Mind*. Trans. George Weidenfeld and Nicolson Ltd., eds. Julian Pitt-Rivers and Ernest Gellner. Chicago: University of Chicago Press, 1966.

——. *The Elementary Structures of Kinship*. 1949. Trans. James Harle Bell and John Richard von Sturmer. Boston: Beacon Press, 1969.

Protestant Poetics and the Seventeenth-Century Religious Lyric. Princeton: Princeton University Press, 1979.

Lewis, David Levering. *When Harlem Was in Vogue*. New York: Knopf, 1981.

Lichtheim, George. *The Concept of Ideology and Other Essays*. New York: Vintage, 1967.

——. *The Origins of Socialism*. New York: Praeger, 1969.

Locke, Alain, ed. *The New Negro*. Preface by Robert Hayden. New York: Atheneum, 1969.

Locke, John. *An Essay Concerning Human Understanding*. Menston, U.K.: Scolar Press, 1970.

Lodder, Christina. *Russian Constructivism*. New Haven: Yale University Press, 1983.

Lonergan, Bernard J. F. *The Subject*. Milwaukee: Marquette University Press, 1968.

Longinus. *On the Sublime. Classical Literary Criticism*. Trans. James A. Arieti and John M. Crossett. New York: E. Mellen Press, 1985.

Lorau, Rene. *L'Analyse institutionnelle*. Paris: Editions de Minuit, 1970.

Lotman, Juri. *The Structure of the Artistic Text*. Trans. Ronald Vroon. Ann Arbor: University of Michigan Press, 1977.

Lott, Eric. "Response to Trey Ellis's 'The New Black Aesthetic.'" *Callaloo* 12, 1989.

Lovell, Terry. "Sociology of Aesthetic Structures and Contextualism." In Denis McQuail, ed., *Sociology of Mass Communications*. Harmondsworth: Penguin, 1978.

Lukács, Georg. *Studies in European Realism, 1935–39*. Trans. Edith Bone. London: Hillway, 1950.

—. *The Historical Novel*. Trans. Hannah Mitchell and Stanley Mitchell. New York: Humanities Press, 1965.

—. *History and Class Consciousness*. Trans. Rodney Livingstone. Cambridge Mass.: MIT Press, 1971.

—. *Essays on Realism*. Trans. D. Fernbach. Cambridge Mass.: MIT Press, 1980.

Lyotard, Jean-François. *The Postmodern Condition: A Report On Knowledge*. Trans. Geoff Bennington and Brian Massumi. Minneapolis: University of Minnesota Press, 1984.

—. *The Differend: Phrases in Dispute*. Trans. Georges Van Den Abbeck. Minneapolis: University of Minnesota Press, 1988.

— and Jean-Loup Thébaud. *Just Gaming*. Trans. Wlad Godzich and Brian Massumi. Minneapolis: University of Minnesota Press, 1985.

MacCabe, Colin. "Realism and the Cinema: Notes on Some Brechtian Theses." *Screen* 17(3), 1967.

—. *Tracking the Signifier: Theoretical Essays on Film, Linguistics and Literature*. Minneapolis: University of Minnesota Press, 1985.

Macdonell, Diane. *Theories of Discourse: An Introduction*. Oxford: Blackwell, 1986.

McDowell, Deborah E. "New Directions for Black Feminist Criticism." In Elaine Showalter, ed., *The New Feminist Criticism*.

—. "The Changing Same: Generational Connections and Black Women Novelists." *New Literary History* 18, 1987.

McGann, Jerome J. *The Romantic Ideology: A Critical Investigation*. Chicago: University of Chicago Press, 1983.

McHale, Brian. "Free Indirect Discourse: A Survey of Recent Accounts." *Poetics and Theory of Literature* 3.

—. *Postmodernist Fiction*. New York: Methuen, 1987.

Macherey, Pierre. *A Theory of Literary Production*. Trans. Geoffrey Wall. Boston: Routledge and Kegan Paul, 1978.

MacKinnon, Catherine. *Toward a Feminist Theory of the State*. Cambridge, Mass.: Harvard University Press, 1989.

Macksey, Richard, and Eugenio Donato, eds. *The Structuralist Controversy*. Baltimore: Johns Hopkins University Press, 1972.

Magliola, Robert R. *Phenomenology and Literature*. West Lafayette, Ind.: Purdue University Press, 1977.

Mandelbaum, Maurice. *History, Man, and Reason: A Study in Nineteenth-Century Thought*. Baltimore: Johns Hopkins University Press, 1971.

Mao Tse-tung. *The Chinese Revolution and the Chinese Communist Party*. Peking: Foreign Languages Press, 1954.

Marcuse, Herbert. *Reason and Revolution*. Boston: Beacon Press, 1960.

—. *One Dimensional Man*. Boston: Beacon Press, 1964.

—. *Eros and Civilization: A Philosophical Inquiry into Freud*. Boston: Beacon Press, 1966.

Marks, Elaine, and Isabelle de Courtivron, eds. *New French Feminisms*. Trans. Keith Cohen and Paula Cohen. Amherst: University of Massachusetts Press, 1980.

Marx, Karl. *Early Writings*. Trans. and ed. T. B. Bottomore. New York: McGraw-Hill, 1964.

—. *Capital*. Vols. 1 and 3. Moscow: Progress Publishers, 1965.

—. "Preface." In *Foundations of the Critique of Political Economy*. Trans. S. W. Ryazanskaya, ed. Maurice Dobb. New York: International Publications, 1970.

—. *Grundrisse*. Trans. Martin Nicolaus. New York: Vintage, 1973.

— and Friedrich Engels. *German Ideology*. Trans. S. Ryazanskaya. Moscow: Progress Publishers, 1968.

Massumi, Brian. *A User's Guide to Capitalism and Schizophrenia: Deviations from Deleuze and Guattari*. Cambridge, Mass.: MIT Press, 1992.

Meinecke, Friedrich. *Die Enstehun des Historismus*. 2 vols. Munich: Oldenbourg, 1936.

Meszaros, Istvan. *Lukàcs' Concept of Dialectic*. London: Merlin Press, 1972.

Metz, Christian. *The Imaginary Signifier: Psychoanalysis and the Cinema*. Trans. Celia Britton, Annwyl Williams, Ben Brewster, and Alfred Guzzetti. Bloomington: Indiana University Press, 1982.

Mill, John Stuart. *A System of Logic*. 10th ed. London: Longmans, Green, and Co., 1879.

—. *The Subjection of Women*. Ed. Sue Mansfield. Arlington Heights, Ill.: AHM Publishing, 1980.

—. *On Liberty*. Ed. John Gray. Oxford: Oxford University Press, 1991.

Miller, J. Hillis, "The Geneva Critics." *Modern French Criticism: From Proust and Valery to Structuralism*. Chicago: University of Chicago Press, 1972.

—. *The Ethics of Reading*. New York: Columbia University Press, 1987.

Miller, Jacques-Alain. "Suture (Elements of the Logic of the Signifier)." *Screen* 18(4), 1977–78.

Miller, Nancy K. "Emphasis Added: Plots and Plausibilities in Women's Fiction." In Elaine Showalter, ed., *The New Feminist Criticism*.

—. "Changing the Subject: Authorship, Writing, and the Reader." In Teresa de Lauretis, ed., *Feminist Studies/Critical Studies*. Bloomington: Indiana Univeristy Press, 1986.

Miller, Perry. *Errand into the Wilderness*. Cambridge, Mass.: Harvard University Press, 1956.

Millett, Kate.*Sexual Politics*. New York: Avon, 1970.

—. "Toward a Feminist Poetics." In Elaine Showalter, ed., *The New Feminist Criticism*.

Mitchell, W.J.T., ed. *Against Theory: Literary Studies and the New Pragmatism*. Chicago: University of Chicago Press, 1985.

—. *Iconology: Image, Text, Ideology*. Chicago: University of Chicago Press, 1986.

Modleski, Tania. *Loving with a Vengeance: Mass-Produced Fantasies for Women*. New York: Methuen, 1984.

Moffett, Charles S., ed. *The New Painting: Impressionism 1874–1886*. San Francisco: Fine Arts Museums of San Francisco, 1986.

Moi, Toril. *Sexual/ Textual Politics: Feminist Literary Theory*. New York: Routledge, 1985.

Monaco, James. *The New Wave: Truffaut, Godard, Chabrol, Rohmer, Rivette*. New York: Oxford University Press, 1976.

—. *How to Read a Film: the Art, Technology, Language, History, and Theory of Film and Media*. New York: Oxford University Press, 1977.

Monk, Samuel H. *The Sublime: A Study of Critical Theories in XVIII-Century England*. Ann Arbor: University of Michigan Press, 1960.

Montrose, Louis. "The Poetics and Politics of Culture." In Aram Veeser, ed., *The New Historicism*.

Motherwell, Robert, ed. *The Dada Painters and Poets: An Anthology*. Boston: G. K. Hall, 1981.

Mulvey, Laura. "Visual Pleasure and Narrative Cinema." In Constance Penley, ed., *Feminism and Film Theory*. New York: Routledge, 1988.

—. *Visual and Other Pleasures.* Bloomington: Indiana University Press, 1989.

Murray, Albert. *The Omni-Americans: Black Experience and American Culture (Some Alternatives to the Folklore of White Supremacy).* New York: Outerbridge and Dienstfrey, 1970.

Nadeau, Maurice. *The History of Surrealism.* Trans. Richard Howard. New York: Macmillan, 1965.

Neal, Larry. "The Black Arts Movement." In Addison Gayle, Jr., ed., *The Black Aesthetic.*

Nestle, Joan. "The Fem Question." In Carol S. Vance, ed., *Pleasure and Danger: Exploring Female Sexuality.* Boston: Routledge, 1984.

Newton, Esther. "The Mythic Mannish Lesbian: Radclyffe Hall and the New Woman." In Martin Bauml Duberman, Martha Vicinus, and George Chauncey, Jr., eds., *Hidden from History: Reclaiming the Gay and Lesbian Past.* New York: New American Library, 1989.

Nietzsche, Friedrich. "On Truth and Lie in an Extra-Moral Sense." In *The Portable Nietzsche.* Trans. and ed. Walter Kauffman. New York: Viking, 1954.

—. *The Birth of Tragedy.* Trans. Francis Golffing. Garden City, N.Y.: Doubleday, 1956.

—. *The Genealogy of Morals.* Trans. Francis Golffing. New York: Doubleday, 1956.

Noddings, Nel. *Caring: A Feminine Approach to Ethics and Moral Education.* Berkeley: University of California Press, 1984.

Norris, Christopher. *Deconstruction: Theory and Practice.* London: Methuen, 1982.

Ogden, C. K., and I. A. Richards. *The Meaning of Meaning.* New York: Harcourt, Brace, 1923.

Ollmann, Bertell. *Alienation: Marx's Conception of Man in Capitalist Society.* Cambridge: Cambridge University Press, 1971.

Olsen, Stein. *The End of Literary Theory.* Cambridge: Cambridge University Press, 1987.

Ortony, Andrew, ed. *Metaphor and Thought.* New York: Cambridge University Press, 1979.

Ortigues, Marie-Cécile, and Edmond Ortigues. *Oedipe Africain.* Paris: Librairie Plon, 1966.

Palmer, Richard. *Hermeneutics: Interpretation Theory in Schleiermacher, Dilthey, Heidegger, and Gadamer.* Evanston, Ill.: Northwestern University Press, 1969.

Panofsky, Erwin. *Studies in Iconology.* New York: Oxford University Press, 1939.

—. "The History of Art as a Humanistic Discipline." In *Meaning in the Visual Arts.* Garden City, N.Y.: Doubleday, 1955.

—. *Perspective as Symbolic Form.* Trans. Christopher S. Wood. Cambridge, Mass.: MIT Press, 1991.

Passeron, Jean-Claude, and Pierre Bourdieu. *Reproduction in Education, Society and Culture.* Trans. Richard Nice. London: Sage, 1977.

Pater, Walter. *The Renaissance.* Ed. Donald L. Hill. Berkeley: University of California Press, 1980.

Pêcheux, Michel. *Language, Semantics, and Ideology: Stating the Obvious.* Trans. Harbans Nagpal. London: Macmillan, 1982.

Pechter, Edward. "The New Historicism and its Discontents: Politicizing Renaissance Drama." *Publications of the Modern Language Association* 102, May 1987.

Peirce, Charles Sanders. *The Collected Papers of Charles Sanders Peirce.* Eds. Charles Hartshorne and Paul Weiss. Cambridge, Mass.: Harvard University Press, 1931–60.

—. *Values in a Universe of Chance: Selected Writings of Charles S. Peirce.* Ed. Philip P. Weiner. Stanford: Stanford University Press, 1958.

Perloff, Marjorie. *The Futurist Moment: Avant-Garde, Avant Guere, and the Language of Rupture.* Chicago: University of Chicago Press, 1986.

Piaget, Jean. *Structuralism.* Trans. and ed. Chaninah Maschler. New York: Basic Books, 1970.

Pierce, John R. *Symbols, Signals, and Noise.* New York: Harper, 1961.

Pinkard, Terry P. *Hegel's Dialectic : The Explanation of Possibility.* Philadelphia: Temple University Press, 1988.

Pitkin, Hanna. *The Concept of Representation.* Berkeley: University of California Press, 1967.

Plato. *The Republic.* Trans. Allan Bloom. New York: Basic Books, 1968.

Podro, Michael. *The Critical Historians of Art.* New Haven: Yale University Press, 1982.

Poggioli, Renato. *The Theory of the Avant-Garde.* Trans. Gerald Fitzgerald. Cambridge, Mass.: Harvard University Press, 1968.

Poovey, Mary. *Uneven Developments: The Ideological Work of Gender in Mid-Victorian England.* Chicago: University of Chicago Press, 1988.

Popper, Karl. *The Poverty of Historicism.* New York: Basic Books, 1960.

Porter, Carolyn. "Are We Being Historical Yet." *South Atlantic Quarterly* 87(4), 1988.

Poulet, Georges. *The Interior Distance.* Trans. Elliott Coleman. Ann Arbor: University of Michigan Press, 1964.

—. *Proustian Space.* Trans. Elliott Coleman. Baltimore: Johns Hopkins University Press, 1977.

Pratt, Mary Louise. *Toward a Speech Act Theory of Literary Discourse.* Bloomington: Indiana University Press, 1977.

Propp, Vladimir. *Morphology of the Folktale.* Trans. Lawrence Scott, ed. Louis A. Wagner. Austin: University of Texas Press, 1968.

Pryse, Marjorie, and Hortense J. Spillers, eds. *Conjuring: Black Women, Fiction, and Literary Tradition.* Bloomington: Indiana University Press, 1985.

Raabe, Paul, ed. *The Era of German Expressionism.* Trans. J. M. Ritchie. Woodstock, N.Y.: Overlook Press, 1974.

Radway, Janice A. *Reading the Romance: Women, Patriarchy and Popular Literature.* Chapel Hill: University of North Carolina Press, 1984.

Rewald, John. *The History of Impressionism.* New York: Museum of Modern Art, 1973.

—. *Post-Impressionism: From Van Gogh to Gauguin.* New York: Museum of Modern Art, 1978.

Rich, Adrienne. *Of Woman Born: Motherhood as Experience and Institution.* New York: Norton, 1976.

—. *On Lies, Secrets, and Silence: Selected Prose, 1966–1978.* New York: Norton, 1979.

—. "Toward a Woman-Centered University." In *On Lies, Secrets, and Silence: Selected Prose, 1966–1978.*

—. "Compulsory Heterosexuality and Lesbian Existence." In *Blood, Bread and Poetry: Selected Prose 1979–1985.* New York: Norton, 1986.

—. "Split at the Root: An Essay on Jewish Identity." In *Blood, Bread, and Poetry: Selected Prose 1979–1985.*

Richter, Hans. *Dada: Art and Anti-Art.* Trans. David Britt New York: H. N. Abrams, 1965.

Ricoeur, Paul. *The Conflict of Interpretations: Essays in Hermeneutics.* Evanston, Ill.: Northwestern University Press, 1974.

—. *The Rule of Metaphor: Multi-Disciplinary Studies of the Creation of Meaning in Language.* Trans. Robert Czerny et al. Toronto: Toronto University Press, 1977.

Riffaterre, Michael. *The Semiotics of Poetry.* Bloomington: Indiana University Press, 1978.

—. *Text Production.* Trans. Terese Lyons. New York: Columbia University Press, 1983.

—. *Fictional Truth.* Baltimore: Johns Hopkins University Press, 1990.

Rimmon, Shlomith. "A Comprehensive Theory of Narrative: Genette's *Figures III* and the Structuralist Study of Fiction." *Poetics and Theory of Literature* 1, 1976.

Rorty, Richard. *Philosophy and the Mirror of Nature.* Princeton: Princeton University Press, 1979.

—. *Consequences of Pragmatism.* Minneapolis: University of Minnesota Press, 1982.

—. "Habermas and Lyotard on Postmodernity." In Richard J. Bernstein, ed., *Habermas and Modernity.* Cambridge, Mass.: Polity, 1985.

—. *Contingency, Irony, and Solidarity.* Cambridge: Cambridge University Press, 1989.

Rosen, Philip, ed. *Narrative, Apparatus, Ideology: A Film Theory Reader.* New York: Columbia University Press, 1986.

Ross, Andrew. "Uses of Camp." In *No Respect: Intellectuals and Popular Culture.* New York: Routledge, 1989.

—. *Strange Weather: Culture, Science, and Technology in the Age of Limits.* London: Verso, 1991.

Ross, Marlon B. *The Contours of Masculine Desire: Romanticism and the Rise of Women's Poetry.* New York: Oxford University Press, 1989.

Roudiez, Leon. "Twelve Points from *Tel Quel.*" *L'Esprit Créateur* 14(4), 1974.

Rowbotham, Sheila. *Women, Resistance, and Revolution.* New York: Pantheon, 1972.

Rubin, Gayle. "The Traffic in Women: Notes on the 'Political Economy' of Sex." In Rayna R. Reiter, ed., *Toward an Anthropology of Women.* New York: Monthly Review Press, 1975.

—. "Thinking Sex: Notes for a Radical Theory of the Politics of Sexuality." In Carol S. Vance, ed., *Pleasure and Danger: Exploring Female Sexuality.* Boston: Routledge, 1984.

Rubin, Isaak. *Essays on Marx's Theory of Value.* Trans. Milos Samardzija and Fredy Perlman. Detroit: Black and Red, 1972.

Rubin, William Stanley. *Dada, Surrealism, and their Heritage.* New York: Museum of Modern Art, 1968.

—, ed. *"Primitivism" in 20th Century Art.* New York: Museum of Modern Art, 1984.

Ruddick, Sara. *Maternal Thinking: Toward a Politics of Peace.* New York: Ballantine, 1989.

Rudnytsky, Peter L., ed. *Transitional Objects and Potential Spaces: Literary Uses of D. W. Winnicott.* New York: Columbia University Press, 1993.

Ruskin, John. *Modern Painters.* 5 vols. London: Smith, Elder, 1856–1860.

Ruthven, K. K. *Myth.* London: Methuen, 1976.

Said, Edward. *Orientalism.* New York: Pantheon, 1978.

—. *The World, the Text, and the Critic.* Cambridge, Mass.: Harvard University Press, 1983.

Sartre. Jean-Paul.. *Existentialism and Humanism.*Trans. Philip Mairet. London: Methuen, 1948.

—. *What is Literature?.* Trans. Bernard Frechtman. London: Methuen, 1950.

—. *Being and Nothingness.* Trans. Hazel E. Barnes. New York: Washington Square Press, 1956.

—. *Critique of Dialectical Reason, Theory of Practical Ensembles.* Trans. Alan Sheridan-Smith, ed. Jonathan Ree. London: New Left Books, 1976.

Sassoon, Anne Showstack. *Gramsci's Politics.* New York: St. Martin's, 1980.

Saussure, Ferdinand de. *Course in General Linguistics.* Trans. Roy Harris, ed. Charles Bally and Albert Sechehaye. London: Duckworth, 1983.

Schlegel, Friedrich von. *Philosophical Fragments.* Trans. Peter Firchow. Minneapolis: University of Minnesota Press, 1991.

Scholes, Robert E. . New Haven: Yale University Press, 1974.

—. *Fabulation and Metafiction.* Urbana: University of Illinois Press, 1979.

—. *Textual Power: Literary Theory and the Teaching of English.* New Haven: Yale University Press, 1985.

Schulz, Max F. *The Muses of John Barth: Tradition and Metafiction from "Lost in the Funhouse" to "The Tidewater Tales."* Baltimore: Johns Hopkins University Press, 1990.

Screen. Vols. 1–. London: Society for Education in Film and Television, 1959–.

Searle, John R. *Speech Acts: An Essay in the Philosophy of Language.* London: Cambridge University Press, 1969.

Sedgwick, Eve Kosofsky. *Between Men: English Literature and Male Homosocial Desire.* New York: Columbia University Press, 1985.

—. *Epistemology of the Closet.* Berkeley: University of California Press, 1990.

Segal, Lynne. *Slow Motion: Changing Masculinities, Changing Men.* London: Virago, 1990.

Seidler, Victor. *The Achilles Heel Reader: Men, Sexual Politics and Socialism.* New York: Routledge, 1991.

—. *Recreating Sexual Politics: Men, Feminism and Politics.* New York: Routledge, 1991.

Short, Robert. *Dada and Surrealism.* Secaucus, N.J.: Chartwell, 1980.

Showalter, Elaine. *A Literature of Their Own: British Women Novelists from Bronte to Lessing.* Princeton: Princeton University Press, 1977.

—, ed. *The New Feminist Criticism.* New York: Pantheon, 1985.

—. "Feminist Criticism in the Wilderness." In Elaine Showalter, ed., *The New Feminist Criticism.*

—. "Toward a Feminist Poetics." In Elaine Showalter, ed., *The New Feminist Criticism.*

—. "Critical Cross-Dressing: Male Feminists and the Woman of the Year." In Alice Jardine and Paul Smith, eds., *Men in Feminism.* New York: Methuen, 1987.

—, ed. *Speaking of Gender.* New York: Routledge, 1989.

Shukman, Ann. *Literature and Semiotics.* New York: North-Holland Publishing, 1977.

Silverman, Kaja. *The Subject of Semiotics.* New York: Oxford University Press, 1983.

Simon, John K., ed. *Modern French Criticism: From Proust and Valery to Structuralism.* Chicago: University of Chicago Press, 1972.

Smith, Barbara. "Toward a Black Feminist Criticism." In Elaine Showalter, ed., *The New Feminist Criticism.*

Smith, Barbara Herrnstein. *On the Margins of Discourse.* Chicago: University of Chicago Press, 1978.

—. *Contingencies of Value.* Cambridge, Mass.: Harvard University Press, 1988.

Smith, David Lionel. "The Black Arts Movement and Its Critics." *American Literary History* 3, 1991.

Smith, Paul. *Discerning the Subject.* Minneapolis: University of Minnesota Press, 1988.

Smith-Rosenberg, Caroll. "The Female World of Love and Ritual: Relations Between Women in Nineteenth-Century America." In *Disorderly Conduct: Visions of Gender in Victorian America.* New York: Knopf, 1985.

Smitherman, Geneva. *Talkin' and Testifyin'.* Boston: Houghton Mifflin, 1977.

Snow, C. P. *Recent Thoughts on the Two Cultures: An Oration Delivered at Birkbeck College, London, 12th December, 1961.* London: J. W. Ruddock, 1961.

Sollers, Philippe. *Théorie des Exceptions.* Paris: Gallimard, 1986.

Sollors, Werner. "Ethnic Modernism and Double Audience." In *Beyond Ethnicity: Consent and Descent in American Culture.* New York: Oxford University Press, 1986.

—. "Melting Pots." In *Beyond Ethnicity: Consent and Descent in American Culture.*

Sontag, Susan. "Notes on 'Camp.' " In *Against Interpretation.* New York: Dell, 1966.

Spector, Judith, ed. *Gender Studies: New Directions in Feminist Criticism.* Bowling Green, Ohio: Bowling Green State University Popular Press, 1986.

Spitzer, Leo. *Linguistics and Literary History: Essays in Stylistics.* Princeton: Princeton University Press, 1948.

—. *A Method of Interpreting Literature.* Northampton Mass.: Smith College, 1949.

Spivak, Gayatri Chakravorty. *In Other Worlds.* New York: Methuen, 1987.

—. "Can the Subaltern Speak?" In Cary Nelson and Lawrence Grossberg, eds., *Marxism and the Interpretation of Culture.* Urbana: University of Illinois Press, 1988.

Stallybrass, Peter, and Allon White. *The Politics and Poetics of Transgression.* London: Methuen, 1986.

Stepto, Robert. *From Behind the Veil: A Study of Afro-American Narrative.* Urbana: University of Illinois Press, 1979.

Stimpson, Catherine. "Zero Degree Deviancy: The Lesbian Novel in English." *Critical Inquiry* 8, 1981.

Strozier, Robert M. *Saussure, Derrida, and the Metaphysics of Subjectivity.* New York: Mouton de Gruyter, 1988.

Subaltern Studies: Writings on South Asian History and Society. Vols. 1–. Ed. Ranajit Guha. Delhi: Oxford University Press, 1982–.

Sussman, Elisabeth, ed. *On the Passage of a Few People Through a Rather Brief Moment in Time: The Situationist International 1957–1972.* Cambridge, Mass.: MIT Press, 1989.

Szwed, John F. "Race and the Embodiment of Culture." *Ethnicity* 2, 1975.

Taylor, Ronald, ed. *Aesthetics and Politics: Ernst Bloch, Georg Lukács, Bertolt Brecht, Walter Benjamin, Theodor Adorno.* London: New Left Books, 1977.

Thompson, E. M. *Russian Formalism and Anglo-American New Criticism.* The Hague: Mouton, 1971.

Thompson, Robert Farris. *Flash of the Spirit: African and Afro-American Art and Philosophy.* New York: Random House, 1983.

Timms, Edward, and Peter Collier, eds. *Visions and Blueprints: Avant-Garde Culture and Radical Politics in Early Twentieth-Century Europe.* Manchester, U.K.: Manchester University Press, 1988.

Todorov, Tzvetan, "The Two Principles of Narrative," trans. by Philip E. Lewis, Diacritics 1, Fall 1971.

Todorov, Tzvetan. *The Fantastic: A Structural Approach to a Literary Genre.* Trans. Richard Howard. Cleveland: Press of Case Western Reserve University, 1973.

—. "The Structural Analysis of Literature: The Tales of Henry James." In David Robey, ed., *Structuralism, an Introduction.* Oxford: Clarendon Press, 1973.

—. *The Poetics of Prose.* Trans. Richard Howard. Ithaca, N.Y.: Cornell University Press, 1977.

— et al. *Qu'est-ce que le structuralisme?* Paris: Editions du Seuil, 1968.

Torgovnick, Marianna. *Gone Primitive: Savage Intellects, Modern Lives.* Chicago: University of Chicago Press, 1990.

Trilling, Lionel. *Beyond Culture.* New York: Viking, 1965.

Troeltsch, Ernst. *Der Historismus und Seine Probleme.* Tübingen: Mohr, 1922.

Turner, Graeme. *Film as Social Practice.* London and New York: Routledge, 1988.

—. *British Cultural Studies: An Introduction.* Boston: Unwin Hyman, 1990.

Vachek, J. *A Prague School Reader in Linguistics.* Bloomington: Indiana University Press, 1964.

Vattimo, Gianni. *The Transparent Society.* Trans. David Webb. Baltimore: Johns Hopkins University Press, 1992.

—. *The Adventure of Difference: Philosophy After Nietzsche and Heidegger.* Trans. Cyprian Blamires. Baltimore: Johns Hopkins University Press, 1993.

Veeser, H. Aram, ed. *The New Historicism.* New York: Routledge, 1989.

Wagner, Richard. *Oper und Drama.* In *Gesammelte Schriften.* 14 vols. Ed. Julius Kapp. Leipzig: Hesse and Becker, 1914.

Walker, Alice. *In Search of Our Mothers' Gardens.* San Diego: Harcourt Brace Jovanovich, 1983.

Wallace, Mitchell. *Invisibility Blues: From Pop to Theory.* London: Verso, 1990.

Waller, Marguerite. "Academic Tootsie: The Denial of Difference and the Difference it Makes." *Diacritics* 17, 1987.

Wallis, Brian, ed. *Art After Modernism: Rethinking Representation.* Boston: Godine, 1984.

Warren, B. *Imperialism: Pioneer of Capitalism.* Ed. John Sender. London: New Left Books, 1980.

Waugh, Patricia. *Metafiction : The Theory and Practice of Self-Conscious Fiction.* London: Methuen, 1984.

Weber, Max. *Politics as a Vocation.* Trans. H. H. Gert and C. Wright Mills. Philadelphia: Fortress Press, 1968.

Webster, Grant. *The Republic of Letters: A History of Postwar American Literary Opinion.* Baltimore: Johns Hopkins University Press, 1979.

Weiskel, Thomas. *The Romantic Sublime: Studies in the Psychology of Transcendence.* Baltimore: Johns Hopkins University Press, 1976.

Wellek, René. *The Literary Theory and Aesthetics of the Prague School.* Ann Arbor: University of Michigan, 1969.

—. *A History of Modern Criticism*, vol. 6. New Haven: Yale University Press, 1986.

— and Austin Warren. *Theory of Literature.* London: J. Cape, 1955.

Wescher, Herta. *Collage.* Trans. Robert E. Wolf. New York: Abrams, 1971.

West, Cornel. *The American Evasion of Philosophy: A Genealogy of Pragmatism.* Madison: University of Wisconsin Press, 1989.

Wheelwright, Philip. *The Burning Fountain.* Bloomington: Indiana University Press, 1954.

White, Hayden. *Metahistory: The Historical Imagination in Nineteenth-Century Europe.* Baltimore: Johns Hopkins University Press, 1973.

—. *Tropics of Discourse: Essays in Cultural Criticism.* Baltimore: Johns Hopkins University Press, 1978.

—. *The Content of the Form: Narrative Discourse and Historical Representation.* Baltimore: Johns Hokpins University Press, 1987.

Wilde, Oscar. *The Decay of Lying.* New York: Sunflower, 1902.

Willemen, Paul. "Voyeurism, the Look, and Dwoskin." In Philip Rosen, ed., *Narrative, Apparatus, Ideology: A Film Theory Reader.*

Willett, John. *Expressionism.* New York: McGraw-Hill, 1970.

Williams, Raymond. *The Long Revolution.* New York: Columbia University Press, 1961.

—. *Modern Tragedy.* Stanford: Stanford University Press, 1966.

—. *The Country and the City.* New York: Oxford University Press, 1973.

—. *Television: Technology and Cultural Form.* New York: Schocken Books, 1975.

—. *Marxism and Literature.* Oxford: Oxford University Press, 1977.

—. *Politics and Letters: Interviews with the New Left Review.* New York: Schocken, 1979.

—. *Problems in Materialism and Culture.* London: Verso, 1980.

—. *Culture and Society 1780–1950.* New York: Columbia University Press, 1983.

— and Michael Orrom. *Preface to Film.* London: Film Drama, 1954.

Williams, Sherley A. "The Blues Roots of Contemporary Afro-American Poetry." In Michael S. Harper and Robert B. Stepto, eds., *Chant of Saints: A Gathering of Afro-American Literature, Art, and Scholarship.* Chicago: University of Illinois Press, 1979.

Willis, Paul. *Learning to Labour.* Farnborough, Eng.: Saxon House, 1977.

Wimsatt, W. K., and Monroe Beardsley. *The Verbal Icon.* Lexington: University Press of Kentucky, 1954.

Winnicott, D. W. "Transitional Objects and Transitional Phenomena." *International Journal of Psycho-Analysis* 34, 1953.

—. *Playing and Reality.* New York: Basic Books, 1971.

Wittgenstein, Ludwig. *Philosophical Investigations.* Trans. G. E. M. Anscombe. Oxford: Blackwell, 1968.

Wolff, Janet. *The Social Production of Art.* New York: St. Martin's, 1981.

Wölfflin, Heinrich. *Principles of Art History: The Problem of the Development of Style in Later Art.* Trans. M. D. Hottinger. New York: Dover, 1950.

Wollstonecraft, Mary. *A Vindication of the Rights of Woman.* Ed. Carol H. Poston. New York: Norton, 1975.

Wolseley, Roland E. *The Black Press, U.S.A.* 2d ed. Ames: Iowa State University Press, 1990.

Woolf, Virginia. *A Room of One's Own.* New York: Harcourt, Brace, Jovanovich, 1957.

Wright, Elizabeth. *Psychoanalytic Criticism: Theory in Practice.* New York: Methuen, 1984.

Young, Robert, ed. *Untying the Text: A Post-Structuralist Reader.* Boston: Routledge and Kegan Paul, 1981.

Zimmerman, Bonnie. "What Has Never Been: An Overview of Lesbian Feminist Criticism." In Showalter, ed., *The New Feminist Criticism.*

INDEX OF NAMES